Murder and Madness

Topics in Kentucky History
James C. Klotter, Series Editor

Murder & Madness

The Myth of the Kentucky Tragedy

Matthew G. Schoenbachler

The University Press of Kentucky

Paperback edition 2011

Scholarly publisher for the Commonwealth,
serving Bellarmine University, Berea College, Centre College of Kentucky, Eastern Kentucky University, The Filson Historical Society, Georgetown College, Kentucky Historical Society, Kentucky State University, Morehead State University, Murray State University, Northern Kentucky University, Transylvania University, University of Kentucky, University of Louisville, and Western Kentucky University.

Editorial and Sales Offices: The University Press of Kentucky
663 South Limestone Street, Lexington, Kentucky 40508-4008
www.kentuckypress.com

15 14 13 12 11 5 4 3 2 1

The Library of Congress has cataloged the hardcover edition as follows:

Schoenbachler, Matthew G., 1967–
Murder and madness : the myth of the Kentucky tragedy / Matthew G. Schoenbachler.
p. cm. — (Topics in Kentucky history)
Includes bibliographical references and index.
ISBN 978-0-8131-2566-4 (hbk. : alk. paper)
1. Murder—Kentucky—Case studies. 2. Sharp, Solomon P., 1780–1825.
3. Beauchamp, Jereboam O., 1802–1826. 4. Beauchamp, Ann, 1786–1826.
5. Kentucky—Civilization—19th century. I. Title.
HV6533.K4S36 2009
364.152'3092—dc22 2009031487
ISBN 978-0-8131-3387-4 (pbk. : alk. paper)

This book is printed on acid-free paper meeting the requirements of the American National Standard for Permanence in Paper for Printed Library Materials.

Manufactured in the United States of America.

Member of the Association of
American University Presses

For Dana, Adam, Benjamin, and Sarah

. . . He knew
How to make madness beautiful, and cast
O'er erring deeds and thoughts, a heavenly hue
Of words, like sunbeams, dazzling as they past
The eyes, which o'er them shed tears feelingly and fast.

—Byron, *Childe Harold's Pilgrimage,*
canto 3, stanza 77

Contents

Acknowledgments

Years ago I told Nancy Flachskam, the director of interlibrary loans at Kentucky Wesleyan College, that she would be the first I would thank when my book was published. It isn't much, but it's the least I can do for someone who hunted down hundreds of books, articles, reels of microfilm, sheets of microfiche, and other assorted and obsolete microprints. Her counterpart at the University of North Alabama, Sue Nazworth, has likewise been of invaluable assistance. My research assistants, Estill Frodge, Erica Hines, and Beth Keister, dutifully if not always cheerfully read bleached-out microfilm, tracked down citations, tabulated information from tax lists, and performed other assorted and mundane tasks. I honestly appreciate their diligence and pray they now are not completely disenchanted with historical research. The assistance of Ken Williams of the Kentucky Historical Society was above the call of duty. Nancy Baird and Jonathan D. Jeffrey at Western Kentucky University were immensely helpful and immensely gracious as well, as were Gayla Coates and Dorothy Steers at the Simpson County Archives. Jane Minder and Jim Prichard at the Kentucky Department of Libraries and Archives, both of whom I befriended years ago as an intern there, likewise considerably facilitated my research. The staffs at the Kentucky Historical Society, the Filson Historical Society, and the Library of Congress—especially Bruce Kirby—were as patient as they were helpful. I especially appreciate the help and friendship of B. J. Gooch of Transylvania University's Special Collections. I am grateful to Kentucky Wesleyan College, which provided research assistance despite its own limited resources, and to the University of North Alabama for a number of research grants at timely junctures.

As well, I thank those who have unselfishly shared their expertise with a complete stranger: Peter X. Accardo, Catherine Claire Geoghegan, Rodney Hessinger, Sylvia D. Hoffert, and James O. Horton. The people at the University Press of Kentucky—Anne Dean Watkins, Jim Klotter, and Stephen Wrinn—have been a joy to work with, while Anna Laura Bennett's meticulous reading improved the manuscript immensely. Thanks also to those who aided my fruitless search to track down the Matthew Jouett portraits of Solomon and Leander Sharp: Julie Thies of the Speed Art Museum in Louisville; former educators at the Holland Hall Preparatory School in Tulsa, Oklahoma, Bettye Jewell, Mary Yeakey, Eleanor Carmack, and Nelda Lane, all of whom must have made the establishment a special place to learn; and, finally, Sharp family descendants Mary Grace Harvey, Eliza Dennis, and Sean Arnold.

Over the years Craig Thompson Friend—through his friendship, his scholarship, and his unselfish advice and patience—has taught me more than he realizes. Lorri Glover, without whose companionship and spirit I don't think I would have ever made it through graduate school, is a continuing inspiration. This book would not have existed without Larry Nelson, who opened my eyes to the wonders of the past, and Theda Perdue, who expended a tremendous amount of energy trying to turn me into a decent historian. The late Lance Banning introduced me to the landscape of early America and, by his intellectual rigor and integrity, provided an unparalleled example of a conscientious scholar.

"Whiles I spend almost all the day abroad amongst others, and the residue at home among mine own," Thomas More wrote in his *Utopia,* "I leave to myself, I mean to my book, no time. For when I come home, I must common with my wife, chat with my children, and talk with my servants. All the which things I reckon and account among business, for as much as they must of necessity be done, and done must they needs be unless a man will be stranger in his own house." Alas, I have no servants, nor have I ever thought of time spent with my family as a "necessity" or as "business," but I do catch More's drift. My desire not to become a stranger in my own house has postponed the publication of this work considerably, and I am proud of that. To Dana, Sarah, Benjamin, and Adam, I dedicate this book.

Introduction

> This is not an ordinary case, when its history shall be known. And have not all its features marked it extraordinary, as the deed was horrid and unparalleled?
>
> —Jereboam O. Beauchamp to Governor Joseph Desha, June 5, 1826

> The Governor heard the whole of it without uttering a word; and after it was closed, merely observed, that he wished he could know the whole truth in relation to the murder and its cause.
>
> —*Frankfort (KY) Argus of Western America,* July 12, 1826

November 6, 1825, outside Frankfort, Kentucky. It had been weeks since the last rain, and the woods burned along the road to Frankfort. In the still air of the late afternoon, the smoke hung thick, and it stung the young man's eyes and made his head throb. To ease the pain, he tied around his forehead a dampened handkerchief, worn so low he had to raise his head to see in front of him. Perhaps he thought it would hide his features; perhaps in his youthful conceit he imagined it made him resemble the intrepid French mariners of whom he had read. His name was Jereboam Orville Beauchamp, and he was on his way to see Solomon Porcius Sharp, the former congressman and state attorney general. Sharp, the heir apparent to the leadership of his party, had just been elected to his sixth term as a Kentucky representative, and it was widely assumed he would be chosen speaker of the house the next morning.[1]

But Sharp did not live so long, for Jereboam Beauchamp called him from his bed that night and stabbed him to death. Although the young man escaped the scene, he was soon apprehended and his trial scheduled six months from then. In the meantime, a political firestorm broke out, as Sharp's allies claimed the murder was in fact a political assassination and that Beauchamp had not acted alone. During the two-week trial held in May

1826, Beauchamp's lawyers maintained his innocence and may well have even won acquittal had their client not foolishly attempted to suborn a witness. Found guilty, the twenty-three-year-old Beauchamp was sentenced to hang six weeks later. While he was awaiting execution, his wife and coconspirator, Anna Cooke Beauchamp, joined him in his dungeon where they composed a confession, which not only admitted that Jereboam had killed Solomon Sharp but claimed he had done so because Sharp had seduced and abandoned Anna years earlier. Shortly before Jereboam's execution, he and Anna stabbed themselves. Her suicide attempt succeeded; his did not, and the dying man lived long enough to be taken to the gallows and hanged. Jereboam and Anna were buried together in a single coffin, over which a tombstone inscription tells a sentimental story of seduction, honor, and revenge.

This is what was almost instantly labeled the "Kentucky Tragedy"—the phrase was first used within weeks of the deaths of the Beauchamps—and the bizarre, sordid, and titillating episode would inspire generations of novels and plays and a handful of short histories. Yet of all of the writing prompted by the incident—fiction and nonfiction alike—no one has improved on Robert Penn Warren's characterization nearly sixty years ago: It was "so confused and comic and pretentious and sad, and it seems very strange to us." Warren mused,

> After the pride, passion, agony, and bemused aspiration, what is left is in our hands. Here are the scraps of newspaper, more than a century old, splotched and yellowed and huddled together in a library, like November leaves abandoned by the wind, damp and leached out, back of the stables or in a fence corner of a vacant lot. Here are the diaries, the documents, and the letters, yellow too, bound in neat bundles with tape so stiffened and tired that it parts almost unresisting at your touch. Here are the records of what happened in that courtroom, all the words taken down. Here is the manuscript he himself wrote, day after day, as he waited in his cell, telling his story. . . . We have what is left, the lies and half-lies and the truths and half-truths. We do not know that we have the Truth. But we must have it. Puzzling over what is left, we are like the scientist fumbling with a tooth and thigh bone to reconstruct for a museum some great, stupid beast extinct with the ice age.[2]

So what, after all, is left? Certainly a compelling narrative. As plotlines go, the story has it all: violence, death, sex—even drugs. And so the first and most elemental aim of this study is a plausible reconstruction of what happened, an aspiration that seemed far easier at the outset of the project than it ever did again. Basic questions of when and where and who did what (to say nothing of why) often became maddeningly difficult to answer. And although some very good work has been done on the Kentucky Tragedy, one is struck by the sheer amount of imprecision and outright falsehood that has stubbornly clung to the episode; Warren, like most others who have engaged the story, was struck by the hurricane of "lies and half-lies and the truths and half-truths." The primary source material is hopelessly contradictory, for the murder and the trial became utterly politicized in the hothouse of Kentucky's so-called relief war of the early and mid-1820s. Like the viewer of Akira Kurosawa's *Rashomon,* we are forced, finally, to recognize that a definitive account is doomed to failure. As certainty recedes, the temptation is to declare that the truth is that there is no truth. But whether due to a lack of postmodern sophistication or a lack of patience with such an intellectual cop-out, we must try to get as close as possible to plausible reconstruction. As Warren understood, "We do not know that we have the Truth. But we must have it." No matter how refined our theoretical assumptions, no matter how loathe we may be to admit it, the impulse, the instinct, remains, What happened?[3]

Most of what we do know about the Kentucky Tragedy comes from three remarkable documents: the published proceedings of Beauchamp's murder trial, Beauchamp's confession, and a vindication of Solomon Sharp written by his devoted brother, Dr. Leander Sharp. The transcripts of the trial—one version printed in Amos Kendall's *Argus of Western America,* the other published in pamphlet form shortly after the verdict was returned—substantially agree with one another and provide exceptional and credible information on the crime and its aftermath. But the other two sources—*The Confession of Jereboam O. Beauchamp* and *Vindication of the Character of the Late Col. Solomon P. Sharp*—are far more problematic. The *Confession,* a story written in a Frankfort dungeon as Beauchamp awaited execution, is easily the more famous of the two and was republished as recently as 1966. It is the wellspring of the myth of the Kentucky Tragedy, primarily because it hews so closely to the dominant literary trends of the romantic era and continues to appeal to our desire for the sensational. The *Vindication,* conversely, presents a painstaking defense of Sharp's life and character that contests almost every assertion the Beauchamps made. The pamphlet, although published by Amos Kendall in 1827, was never distributed, and knowledge of its very existence was long lost when, in 1877, twenty-five copies fell out of a partition during the remodeling of the Sharp mansion, long after the *Confession* had dictated the memory of the episode.[4]

Commentators and scholars have often regarded the *Vindication* and the *Confession* as equally valid—or perhaps equally flawed—sources. Far too many, trying to reconcile the two discrepant accounts, have fallen back on a "he said; she said" explanation; as one historian opines, "Obviously, neither the *Confession* nor the *Vindication* can be taken at face value." Yet this truism of all historical research—that no document is completely reliable—does not suggest that all sources are equally dependable. And in the case of the Kentucky Tragedy, we have one document that is essentially a gambit to avoid death written by two people possessed of a near pathological habit of deception, and another document that, although certainly not impartial and written in a red haze of contempt and grief, amasses hundreds of depositions and sworn statements, many of which were, as the incident's first serious historian pointed out, attested to by "prominent citizens and reliable witnesses, who would not and, indeed, could not afford to perjure themselves by making false statements." Yet contemporaries and later scholars alike have given precedence to the *Confession;* the best collection of documents relating to the events—Loren Kallsen's *Kentucky Tragedy,* published in 1963—reprints the *Confession* in full while excising more than half of the *Vindication* and including *The Letters of Ann Cook,* a self-evident forgery that perpetuates the Beauchamps' mythology. For almost two centuries, the *Confession* and *The Letters of Ann Cook* have been accepted as genuine, while the more reliable *Vindication* has been overlooked, downplayed, or bowdlerized.[5]

To construct a plausible account of this story—intrinsically fascinating as it may be—is not enough, for the question remains: So what? Richard Wightman Fox, in analyzing another sordid, dramatic, and complex episode—the Henry Ward Beecher sex scandal of the 1870s—came to the insight that the narratives constructed "were not simply raw material from which the facts were to be extracted; they were the facts." People at or near the center of this postbellum uproar created a multitude of stories, all of which, Fox saw, told something about "their lives, their relationships, their culture." The insight is well taken; narratives attempt to assign meaning to a swirling and kaleidoscopic reality whose significance is not as self-evident as we sometimes assume. And yet it is precisely those stories that are of so much use to the historian, for they will always bear the unmistakable imprint of their times and provide insight into their eras.[6]

Americans had essentially two accounts of the Beauchamp-Sharp episode from which to choose: one by the Beauchamps and the other by the family, friends, and political allies of Sharp. The former was embodied in the *Confession*—which, although attributed to Jereboam Beauchamp, was almost certainly the work of both him and Anna—and in the inscription they composed to adorn their tombstone. Jereboam and Anna's tale was almost instantly dubbed the "Kentucky Tragedy," and it is essentially the story that has come down to us today: The Mephistophelian Solomon Sharp seduced and abandoned the virtuous Anna Cooke; after the child they conceived was born dead, Anna withdrew from society. Such is how Jereboam Beauchamp finds her. Told of her humiliation, our young hero pledges to avenge Anna's dishonor and eventually kills the cowardly reprobate. Convicted on the basis of perjured testimony and political machination, Jereboam is sentenced to die. Awaiting execution, he proudly admits to the murder and proclaims that his death will "teach a certain class of heroes, who make their glory to consist in triumphs over the virtue and the happiness of worthy unfortunate females, to pause sometimes in their mad career."[7]

Sharp's defenders immediately contested this maudlin tale. Although the fullest expression of the counternarrative—the *Vindication*—was not made public for half a century, the basic account was readily available via reports in the region's newspapers and periodicals, which were then reprinted throughout the nation. This was a story of political assassination, of how Sharp's enemies had goaded a naive yet hot-blooded and reckless young man into murdering a good and eminent statesman. As Dr. Sharp summarized, Beauchamp's "private feelings were excited by the falsehoods of political partizans, invented and communicated to him for the purpose of producing the ruin or the death of my brother."[8]

Of these two stories, it was precisely the far less plausible version—the one that contained numerous and demonstrable falsehoods, the one bereft of corroborating testimony and known (at least locally) to be a transparent attempt to escape execution—that was seized on by commentators across the nation immediately after the events, by later moralists with a penchant for sensationalism, and especially by novelists and playwrights who, for the balance of the antebellum era, churned out fictionalizations they claimed—and let it be said, believed—to be true. To understand why this unlikely story had such power, we must come to terms with a conceptual category that historians have been remarkably disinclined to engage: romanticism.

The very term "romanticism" invites ambiguity; generations ago, Arthur

O. Lovejoy declared it a "linguistically extraordinary word" devoid of any commonly understood meaning and therefore "useless as a verbal symbol." Ever since, historians seem to have tacitly agreed; outside discussions of the transcendentalist movement and the Hudson River school of painters, the concept does not commonly appear among the work of early Americanists. It is a significant omission, for as Lovejoy appended, "there emphatically *was* something which—for lack of any other brief name—may still be called a Romantic period." And, as Jacques Barzun has added, we cannot ignore or expunge the concept of romanticism, for the term "is there, embedded in history and in a billion books and minds."[9]

Certainly the romantic movement mattered in early America. As Henry F. May has noted, "Romanticism dominated America more completely than it did any European country except perhaps Germany." Henry Clay observed in 1826, "We live in an age of romance." Yet two recent and magisterial overviews of early America by Sean Wilentz and Daniel Walker Howe—both of which summarize and build on the scholarship of a generation—barely mention the romantic movement. If we contrast the importance of the Enlightenment to our understanding of eighteenth-century America with our chronic disregard for the romantic movement's influence on the nineteenth century, the oversight is even more peculiar and egregious. In fact, romanticism—the "counter-Enlightenment"—actually may have been more important in its time than the Enlightenment was in the eighteenth century: "Because Romanticism pervaded every aspect of American culture, from low to high, from politics and religion to literature," May continues, "it achieved a dominance that the Enlightenment, for all its great figures and lofty doctrines, had never attained."[10]

But what was romanticism? Although often reduced to the triumph of emotion over reason, romanticism, in the broadest sense, can more accurately been seen as the triumph of will over rationality, the emergence of a zeitgeist that emphasized individual resolve at the expense of Enlightenment ideals of order, stability, and tradition. At the heart of the movement lay a conviction that true freedom is undermined by externally imposed goals and values; only when the individual has the ability to choose between good and evil—and not when that choice is co-opted by church or state or society—can one create an authentic value system. Morality, in other words, is "moulded by the will"—not discovered but actually created. This desire to formulate self-generated moral codes logically if not inevitably transformed into a secularized antinomianism—the idea that "genius creates its own rules."[11]

To fully chart romanticism's influence on early America is clearly beyond the limits of this study—and very likely beyond the bounds of any single study—for the romantic movement was remarkably multifaceted. And yet another insight of Lovejoy's—that "one may perhaps speak of not a, but several Romantic movements"—is crucial in making the concept more manageable, more comprehensible, for the romanticism of intellectuals in New England was certainly not like the romanticism of slavery's defenders in the Cotton South, and neither was like the romanticism of a very peculiar pair in Kentucky in the 1820s.[12]

If the complex and plural romantic movement is broken down into smaller components, clearly two variants were determinative in the Kentucky Tragedy—variations that might best be labeled the "pathetic" and the "demonic," both of which were inextricably bound with particular forms of romantic literature that encouraged an effacement of the boundary between fact and fiction. The former variation, the pathetic, was a feminine-encoded segment of romanticism that idealized young women as unruly yet virtuous—independent yet vulnerable to the villainous schemes of black-hearted seducers. This cultural script permeated American society, thanks largely to the ubiquitous and phenomenally popular novels of the era—most famously Susanna Rowson's *Charlotte Temple* and Hannah Webster Foster's *The Coquette,* but there were many, many such tales in circulation—all of which claimed to be founded on actual events. The latter variation, the demonic, was at the extreme of the romantic movement and posited an equally influential, albeit male, cultural stereotype—a headstrong, passionate, willful, and death-obsessed protagonist whose origin was so closely associated with one literary star that he was known as the Byronic hero. Made famous in Byron's epic poems *Childe Harold's Pilgrimage* (1812–1818) and *Don Juan* (1819–1824), as well as his shorter works like *The Giaour* (1813), *The Corsair* (1814), *Lara* (1814), and *Manfred* (1817), this archetype personified demonic romanticism and set free the radical yet latent moral antinomianism imbedded within the movement. Made fashionable and alluring by verse, demonic romanticism expressed the growing alienation of young Americans in the rapidly changing world of the early nineteenth century.[13]

As we will see, these literary creations existed within a dialectical relationship with the social forces of the early-nineteenth-century transatlantic world. Fictional icons were neither fashioned nor received in a cultural vacuum—they were a means by which creators and audiences alike attempted to make sense of rapid transformations of their day. In turn, these heroes and heroines proved enormously attractive to young Americans, and for at least some readers whose emotional investment in these tales was considerable, they seem to have served not only as models of behavior but as agents of socialization.

By all accounts, Anna and Jereboam Beauchamp—immersed as they were in the Byronic verse epics that were just then reaching their height of popularity and the increasingly shopworn sentimental novels—were among this group peculiarly influenced by the pathetic and demonic ideals of their day. Although they claimed, when it suited their purposes, to be exemplars of southern honor and decency, a closer look at their actual behavior suggests that they identified far more with romantic antiheroes than with the dominant social prescriptions of the South. Jereboam, for his part, reveled in adopting the persona of a brooding young man who believed himself superior to the common run of humanity, a consummate rebel who had generated his own moral code. Anna, meanwhile, like the beautiful, doomed heroines of countless seduction tales, had little use for the "appropriate" considerations of her gender—in particular, marriage and piety. Far from the betrayed, youthful ingenue depicted in the *Confession* and elsewhere, she was, in fact, an "unruly woman" on the precipice of middle age who had spent her adult life defying the conventions of her day. (However, for all the couple's rebelliousness, there was, as we will see, one social barrier—race—that they could not bring themselves to transgress.)

Alternately, the couple's intimate familiarity with this literature gave them the tools to craft a tale they hoped would save Jereboam from the hangman. Understanding that the public wanted a melodramatic story of feminine virtue assailed, masculine honor inflamed, and the daring revenge of a young rebel, they concocted a story designed to save Jereboam from execution. It is a testament to the Beauchamps' ingenuity that two such cultural insurgents could cast themselves as the hero and heroine of a morality tale of innocence betrayed and righteous justice exacted. The skill with which Anna and Jereboam tapped into and manipulated the moral touchstones of the culture—and the very fact that they did so—is astounding. Yet, having fully internalized the unrestrained extremes of romanticism, they believed it possible to create their own truth. And because they had so well judged the temper of their times, they were, to some extent, correct. America embraced the Beauchamps' story and all but ignored the protests of those near the events who knew better. In time, their story was repeated until it became accepted as fact. Thereafter, the Kentucky Tragedy moved seamlessly into a second life in the young nation's fiction, as a generation of playwrights and novelists rehashed the tale for thirty-five years. Gleefully taking the Beauchamps at their word, these authors transformed the episode into the era's most popular melodrama and engraved the Beauchamps' narrative on the nation's collective memory. And so a generation of dramatists—including Edgar Allan Poe and William Gilmore Simms, along with a host of lesser lights—recycled an episode shaped by literary cliché into further literary cliché.[14]

What is so remarkable about this story is that the Beauchamps were able, at least partially, to distance themselves from their culture—to see it as outsiders might. Like intuitive anthropologists, they understood that many of the beliefs and expectations of their world were socially constructed and thus capable of manipulation or subversion. This process is most clearly seen in the *Confession* itself, in which the pair recreated themselves as the literary archetypes of seduction victim and Byronic hero. A similar but distinct process was their putative embrace of honor—their attempt to justify the murder itself as an honorable defense of wronged womanhood. Here Anna and Jereboam's self-conscious, even cynical, manipulation of their image is most apparent. Jereboam, in particular, had no use for any social imperative that gave primacy to the community at the expense of the individual. As contemporaries were quick to point out, no man of honor kills an unarmed opponent in his own house in the dead of night and then embarks on a campaign of deception, denying all the while that he committed the murder or even had any animosity toward his victim. And precisely at the moment he was claiming to be avenging the seduction of a pure, "injured female," Jereboam himself had a warrant for bastardy hanging over his head. Jereboam was less "dishonorable," at least as his contemporaries would have defined the term, than "a-honorable," for the demonic species of romanticism was manifestly incompatible with the welter of values subsumed under the term "honor," most clearly the injunction that an honorable person exhibit an overweening concern with the public's evaluation of himself or herself. The Beauchamps, despite so much that has been written about them, did not exemplify the dominant tendencies in southern society—they defied them.[15]

In more particular instances, the Beauchamps betrayed an audacious certainty that they could mold perceptions and beliefs to suit their purposes. Jereboam, while in jail awaiting trial, authored an extensive script with which a key witness named John F. Lowe—a law officer—was to perjure himself. Anna was then to direct Lowe, coaching him until the false testimony appeared to be his own. The entire effort, once detected, went far toward securing Jereboam's conviction, but here the relevant point is his and Anna's attempt to script reality, to make the word incarnate.

Jereboam Beauchamp displayed this penchant for manipulation until the day he died. His suicide attempt the morning of his execution was a means of depriving the audience of a drama he did not author. Yet, unable to avoid his star turn, he scripted his own part. As the death caravan passed through the streets of Frankfort to the gallows, Beauchamp waved to the young women who leaned out of their windows and wept for a man they believed to be unjustly dying for defending his wife's honor. Arriving at the execution grounds, Beauchamp refused to submit to well-understood protocol—he ignored the preachers, he never expressed remorse, he refused to address the crowd, and, finally, he requested a lively tune be played just before he was hanged. Disorderly, self-assertive, and completely aware of what he was doing, Jereboam Beauchamp subverted his own execution.

Although care needs to be taken when drawing generalizations from the actions of these two peculiar individuals, Anna and Jereboam's belief that they could transcend and manipulate basic components of their culture implies that we may overestimate the power of social structure to dictate behavior. And thus the episode is suggestive in another, still broader sense.

Joyce Appleby has written of the mid-twentieth century's "discovery of structure," the way in which historians of the past sixty years have been explicitly or implicitly guided by such concepts as structure, process, pattern, system, and organization. The sources of such structuralism are extensive: the histories of the Braudel-era Annales School and the Cambridge Group for the History of Population and Social Structure, the analyses of language systems by Quentin Skinner and J. G. A. Pocock, the sociology of Talcott Parsons, and the cultural anthropology of Clifford Geertz. The abstractions developed by such scholars suggest not only "permanence, uniformity, and continuity" through time but limitation, constraint, and checks on individual volition. In the postwar era, such concepts revolutionized scholarly discourse, and ever since, they have served to connect scholars as disparate as mid-twentieth-century historians of ideas, the "new social historians" of the 1970s and 1980s, and the students of early American republicanism. And despite the postmodern, poststructuralist patina of more recent years, these assumptions still undergird a great deal of the history being produced.

Yet historians' adoption of both the models and language of social science does raise problems, one being that structuralism can inhibit the ability to explain individual or aberrant behavior. At its crudest, structuralism so ensnares and immobilizes past peoples in webs of social relations that there is little room for individual volition or contingency, even while it overstates the power of societal prescriptions, boundaries, and dictates.[16]

Microhistory—the study of small-scale events, "faintly exotic but somehow emblematic"—has clearly begun to demonstrate that large-scale models can obscure as much as they reveal.[17] Moreover, just as the recent vogue of the counterfactual What if? question has emphasized temporal contingency—that events did not have to unfold the way they did—perhaps it is time to explore *behavioral* contingency in a more systematic fashion.[18] The structural categories that guide us through the past—southern honor, western violence, American acquisitiveness, evangelical discipline, to name but a few—are indispensable, yet too rigid an adherence to such frameworks does not prepare us to understand the individuality and unpredictability of past humanity—the singularity of those who can no longer protest our labeling them as prototypes of this or that social tendency. Microhistory forces on us conclusions that macrohistorical, structuralist models would not have predicted but that may bring us toward a fuller understanding of the past.

To conceive of the past as a dialectic of structure and behavior, of imperative and independence, advances our understanding considerably. As Gordon Wood has advocated, a central responsibility of the scholar is to examine the ways in which "people make their social and intellectual history but are at the same time bound by what they have made." Such histories better illuminate the relationship between individual volition and social demand. Structures—whether demographic or social or political or linguistic—although powerful, were not invincible, and resistance and even rebellion were always distinct possibilities.[19]

Microhistories can help us fruitfully examine this dialectic by "exploring and connecting a wide range of data sources," in the words of Richard D. Brown, "so as to produce a contextual, three-dimensional, analytic narrative in which actual people as well as abstract forces shape events." And thus I have attempted to construct an analytical narrative that seeks to make sustained connections between the particular story at hand and general currents of early America mapped by other historians: western expansion, early American reading practices and the rise of the novel, crime and punishment, honor, and transformations in family norms, sexuality, gender roles, and politics. In addition to these, I underscore another explanatory scheme, romanticism, which helps us understand not only the Beauchamps' bizarre behavior but the alacrity with which America embraced their tale. Such an approach, by allowing a fine-grained examination of the intersection of social imperatives and individual autonomy, can help answer many of the trenchant criticisms of the microhistorical turn—that it inclines "toward the blatantly antiquarian in its relish for the small particulars of the past"; that it makes the past look "more inscrutable than ever"; that it runs the risk of being "dismissed as selective and unrepresentative"; that the entire genre, as Wood puts it, amounts to no more than "little trees in search of a forest."[20]

Although social structures certainly did exist in the antebellum era and were not so weak as to be casually defied, the Beauchamps' behavior suggests that such social dictates were not as impervious or imperious as we have assumed. Culture directs and inhibits, as does language, but it does not follow that everyone—then or now—was equally directed and inhibited by social structure. It is here, at the intersection of singularity and typicality, that a clearer conception of the early nineteenth century might be found. And thus this history tries to highlight the ideas that people, then as now, did not necessarily feel bound by social prescriptions and felt capable of crossing what seemed to them to be arbitrary boundaries.

In many ways, the so-called Kentucky Tragedy was supremely atypical, and the Beauchamps were as aberrant, deviant, and bizarre individuals as early America ever produced. The mythology they created bore little resemblance to actual events: Anna was never seduced, and Jereboam was no defender of honor or female purity. But they had a better story than the truth and they knew what the people wanted to hear, and that is how the Beauchamps, although they both paid with their lives, got away with murder in the end. They won a postmortem victory by successfully fashioning events according to the dominant cultural scripts of the early republic for which they themselves had no use. By successfully negotiating structure and aberration, they confected a story that overwhelmed reality. And yet back there among the ruins of time lay a reality that the Beauchamps' fantasies could not efface, remains that may yet tell us a great deal about early America.[21]

CHAPTER 1

The Architect of His Own Fortunes

Solomon Porcius Sharp

We wither from our youth, we gasp away—
Sick—sick; unfound the boon, unslaked the thirst,
Though to the last, in verge of our decay,
Some phantom lures, such as we sought at first—
But all too late,—so are we doubly curst.
Love, fame, ambition, avarice—'tis the same—
Each idle, and all ill, and none the worst—
For all are meteors with a different name,
And death the sable smoke where vanishes the flame.

—Byron, *Childe Harold's Pilgrimage,*
canto 4, stanza 124

Across almost two centuries, to look on the level, self-assured visage of Solomon Porcius Sharp, captured by Matthew Jouett sometime in the early 1820s, is to know that he took great pride in his accomplishments. Sharp's short life was, among other things, an object lesson in the opportunities of young America, a self-willed demonstration of the ability of ambitious white men through discipline or luck or both to rise from abject poverty to prominence and stature. As one early Kentucky historian wrote, "It was the fortune of this able man to illustrate, by his own career, the noble tendency of our republican institutions, and to teach to his youthful countrymen the important lesson that each may, and must be, the architect of his own fortunes, and there is no station to which the humblest may not aspire."[1]

For the day and age, Solomon Sharp's means of ascent were not unusual—a combination of vivid personality, legal acumen, and enough military experience to justify a title in the state militia. More remarkable was the rapidity of Sharp's rise: at twenty-two, he was already serving the first of five terms in the Kentucky General Assembly; a few weeks shy of his twenty-fifth birthday, he was elected a U.S. congressman; at thirty-four, he became Kentucky's attorney general. He married into one of the state's leading families and all the while built a highly respected law practice that made him a very wealthy man. Even allowing for the standard hyperbole of nineteenth-century biographies, Solomon Sharp had indeed "compressed into his brief life of thirty-eight years more . . . activity and . . . accomplished work than ordinarily is compassed by the 'three-score and ten' allotment of man."[2]

If the arc of Sharp's career comports well with the myths of American mobility, it is difficult to recover the personality of the man himself. No collection of his papers exists, little of his private correspondence survives, and we have only a handful of his public pronouncements. Moreover, most descriptions of Sharp were written by partisans after his murder had politicized his memory. This is what we do know.

He was born on August 22, 1787, in Washington County, Virginia, the fifth child of Thomas Sharp, a "plain, unpretending old Revolutionary soldier" who had seen action at King's Mountain, and Jean Maxwell Sharp, a native of Scotland who had married Thomas in 1775. Although reputedly descended from John Sharp, Lord Archbishop of the diocese of York under the later Stuart dynasty, the line of the family that had made its way to the Kentucky frontier was of infinitely more modest means, and Thomas, like many other westerners of his day, struggled merely to secure clear title to enough land to support his growing family.[3]

It was this desire for a freehold that pulled the Sharps over the mountains and led them through homes in four states in nine years. What Jean Sharp thought of the family's rootlessness we do not know. If she was like the thousands of other ordinary women of the day and age who were given little say in the matter, she may well have resented Thomas's wanderlust. Certainly more than one traveler to the West remarked on women's discontent; as one put it, "Amongst the poorer class throughout this country, the women appear to be less satisfied than the men." Not the least of their objections was being ripped from their networks of family and community back east. One emigrant recalled of his decision to leave Virginia in 1784,

> As I was walking one evening among my little corn on a poor spot, having nine children, I made up my mind to move to [Kentucky], as I had an idea for years. I knew it would be a killing stroke to my wife when she heard of my determination, for she was so attached to the church and neighbors that she could not give them up. . . . When I returned to the house I met her between the two houses after sunset; I told her what I had concluded on, when she burst into tears and begged me to decline, but it was in vain.

In mid-1795, the year the Sharp family finally found purchase in Logan County, Kentucky, Jean Maxwell Sharp died. Solomon was eight years old.[4]

Logan County was in the heart of western Kentucky's Green River area—a region sometimes referred to as the Southside. It was not a land to make one rich, but it was, as one resident put it, well suited for "a man who has but a small property and a large family who he wishes to procure lands for." Thomas Sharp was one of thousands who, fitting this description, poured into the region in the waning years of the eighteenth century, causing people in older regions of the state to marvel at the "prodigious spirit for removing to Green River." It was made possible by a 1795 state law that opened for general settlement almost 6 million acres of land at thirty cents an acre previously reserved for Virginia veterans. Southside delegates to the General Assembly—known as the Green River Band and led by Felix Grundy and the erstwhile Yankee Matthew Lyon—soon pushed the gates open wider still by allowing settlers to purchase Green River lands on credit, make payments in installments, and postpone repayment for up to twelve years.[5]

But early Kentucky, despite persistent myths to the contrary, was no land of rugged equality. In central Kentucky's Bluegrass region—the first settled and most densely populated portion of the state—wealthy planters and merchants lived beside the farming and laboring majority, most of whom rented the land they lived on. In the Green River area, landholdings were more equitably distributed. There, in the West's west, two-hundred-acre farms were the norm, and Logan County boasted the state's highest rate of landholding. Still, only five in nine Logan County households owned land.[6]

The Sharps, for the first two years of the family's residence in western

Kentucky, were among the 40-odd percent of Green River households that were landless. Very likely, their restless search for competency had paradoxically and cruelly exhausted their resources. Such was not uncommon; upon arriving in Kentucky, one settler remembered that when his family reached their Henry County farm in May 1797, "our money was gone. Our only chance to raise bread was to clear the forest in the wilderness." Another recalled that "the first residence of our family was in a covered pen or shed, built for sheep adjoining the cabin of its owner." Yet even if they were penniless, hope remained for the early settlers of western Kentucky, for not only was land available, but so was the prospect of assistance. In particular, the initial necessity of providing shelter and the annual ritual of the harvest demanded community effort, as very often did sickness, childbirth, disability, and old age. Harry Toulmin, an English immigrant to early Kentucky, was struck by the process of community building on the frontier. After cutting the timber, a settler "gives notice to his neighbors, who assemble and raise the building for him. He provides meat and bread for them, and sometimes a little whiskey. . . . He must have assistance in rolling his logs, but he repays it by helping those who help him." It was a hard world and, by no choice or fault of its own, an insular world. Chilton Allan remembered, "All other colonies were within reach of succour & supplies. Kentucky was in the midst of an interminable wilderness. 5,000 Indians between the Ohio and the Lakes, regarded it as their hunting ground. They could get no aid from Virginia. . . . Kentucky actually took its root in its inherent resources, before it received any essential supply from abroad. Its first meat was killed in its forests. Its first grain was raised from its soil. Its first wealth was in its own lands. And its first commerce, the exportation of its own produce."[7]

Assuaging the isolation and the indignity of landlessness was the fact that many tenants realistically expected to soon secure title to a small farm. And within a few years, Thomas Sharp bought 200 acres on the Muddy River a few miles northeast of the young town of Russellville, the county seat of Logan County. There he built a log house. By 1797 he claimed 100 acres of what Kentucky tax assessors deemed "second rate" land, and he was able to purchase a slave and six horses. By the turn of the century, his landholdings had increased by another 345 acres, enough to situate the family about midway up the socioeconomic scale of the county.[8]

Kentucky was born in war and did not know peace for twenty years. Not since the initial European colonization of North America in the early seventeenth century had a people moved so far into a hostile country and severed ties so completely with the world they had known. As late as 1795, the Reverend David Barrow remarked that Kentucky "does evidently abound without any connection with any other part of the universe." For the first generation of Kentuckians, the struggle to defend themselves against the ever-present threat of Indian attack overshadowed all other concerns. Barricaded in frontier "stations," the trans-Appalachian emigrants managed, just barely, to hold their ground against the onslaughts of outraged natives. As one immigrant's guide later put it, "If any part of the inhabited earth could be said to have been peopled in 'tears and blood,' that was, emphatically, Kentucky." Not until "Mad" Anthony Wayne's 1794 invasion of the Northwest Territory, his victory at the Battle of Fallen Timbers, and the subsequent Treaty of Greenville did the bloody Indian wars subside in Kentucky. Only then, as Kentuckians always maintained, did the Revolutionary War end in Kentucky. Well after, the memory of the struggle was kept alive; as late as 1835, according to Michel Chevalier, "the story of this long struggle between the whites and the Red man is still repeated in the barrooms of the West."[9]

Habits born in the crucible of early Kentucky died hard. The decades of warfare—to say nothing of the traditional belligerence associated with the "highlander" culture of the English isles from which so many of the pioneers were descended—had inured the Kentuckians to brutality, and the state's well-earned reputation for violence would persist for generations to come. Although the Green River area was settled at the tail end of the Indian wars, many Southside residents, including Sharp's father, were veterans of such conflicts and intimately acquainted with the horrific interracial violence of the late eighteenth century.[10]

The Methodist itinerant preacher Peter Cartwright—whose family had migrated to the area at almost the same time as Sharp's—painted a bleak portrait of this turbulent society in his memoirs: "Logan County, when my father moved to it [in 1793], was called 'Rogues' Harbor,'" a place where "murderers, horse thieves, highway robbers, and counterfeiters fled until they combined and actually formed a majority." Random violence plagued the area, as gunfights broke out in the streets of Russellville, and murder was commonplace: "The honest and civil part of the citizens would prosecute these wretched banditti, but they would swear each other clear; and they really put all law at defiance, and carried on such desperate violence and outrage that the honest part of the citizens seemed to be driven to the necessity of uniting and combining together, and taking the law into their own hands, under the name of Regulators. This was a desperate state of things." Although, as Cartwright attested, "horse-thieves and murderers were driven away, and civilization advanced considerably," the chronic violence continued, and it went well beyond the rough-and-tumble disorder common to backwoods settlements—fights in which drunken men maimed one another.[11] Western Kentucky was the scene of a number of atrocities that did not spare white, black, or Indian, young or old, male or female. In 1803 in Eddyville, a town in western Kentucky settled by the aging Jeffersonian stalwart Matthew Lyon, a couple of local thugs with no apparent motive or provocation beat to death a Chickasaw named Jimmy after he passed out in a tavern.[12] One of the more notorious and grisly murders in the early republic took place in Livingston County, about seventy-five miles northwest of Logan County. There, Lilburne Lewis, nephew of Thomas Jefferson, tortured and decapitated a slave for the heinous crime of breaking a water pitcher. More harrowing still were the murderous rampages of the brothers Harpe: Micaja and Wiley. These two psychopaths, known respectively as Big Harpe and Little Harpe, cut a swath through western Kentucky in the late 1790s, murdering "every defenceless being who fell in their way without distinction of age, sex, or colour." Big Harpe himself claimed to have murdered his own infant child whose crying he found bothersome. Finally apprehended, the madman was decapitated by the husband of one of his victims, and his head was placed in the fork of a tree at a junction known to this day as Harpe's Head crossing.[13]

At times bordering on social anarchy, the Southside appalled observers farther east. In 1796, John Breckinridge, a rising lawyer in central Kentucky who would soon become Jefferson's attorney general, denounced the region as "filled with nothing but hunters, horse thieves, and savages," a place where "wretchedness, poverty and sickness will always reign." In 1810, Virginian Thomas Joynes hurled what Kentuckians surely deemed to be one of the more cutting assessments of the region's inhabitants: "In their manners and ways of living," the Southside residents "approximate nearer to the aborigines of the country than any I have ever seen."[14]

Yet such a bleak picture, as the Reverend Cartwright took care to point out, was "but a partial view of frontier life." In particular, it underestimated the settlers' determination to bring order to the social chaos, to find some balm to sooth the violence and isolation of early Kentucky. The primary means of doing so was religion, in particular an evangelical strain of Christianity in which tens of thousands of Kentuckians found solace. In fact, the origins of the Great Revival—if not of the Second Great Awakening itself—

can be traced to the Logan County of Sharp's adolescence. It was an unlikely setting, if later accounts of Kentucky's earliest evangelists are to be believed. In 1796 the Reverend John Rankin described Logan County as a place where no one "seemed to have any light or knowledge of living religion, or any desire for it." Yet in the midsummer of 1800, it was among these "nothingarians" and "anythingarians" that John and William McGee ignited a revival in the Red River Presbyterian church of James McGready. The enthusiasm quickly spread to McGready's two other congregations, one of which was situated in the Sharps' neighborhood along the Muddy River. There, in August 1800, people converged from "distant parts of the two states." One celebrant remembered,

> The meeting house, it was found, hours before preaching time, could not seat the third part of those already gathered. And still they came, by dozens, fifties, and hundreds. A temporary pulpit, therefore was quickly erected under the foliage of a contiguous grove of thick and broad-spreading trees, seats were made of large timber felled, and laid upon the ground. Here the thousands seated themselves and the worship commenced. Soon the presence of the all-pervading power of the Most High was felt by all. Some crying for mercy, some in ecstasies of joy and praise, strewed the ground.

The excitement was all-consuming and the uproar unprecedented, and it surely drew thirteen-year-old Solomon Sharp to see what all the commotion was about. Coming of age at the turn of the century, Sharp was of a generation that one observer described as "virtually unchurched." Yet the revivals converted a great number of young people, and indeed, their involvement goes some way toward explaining the Great Revival's more bizarre behavior. McGready himself testified that "it was truly affecting to see little boys and girls, of nine, ten, and twelve years of age, and some younger, lying prostrate on the ground, weeping, praying, and crying out for mercy."[15]

We have no direct evidence to tell us what Solomon thought of these religious festivals. But in marked contrast to Cartwright and dozens of other evangelical ministers who later chronicled their conversions on the Kentucky frontier, young Sharp does not seem to have been influenced in any significant way by the Great Revival. Moreover, there is no evidence that any member of the Sharp household was particularly pious or even attended church. Sharp himself had a lifelong reluctance to publicly discuss matters of religion, and even after his marriage to a devout young woman, he did not regularly attend services and had to deflect charges of deism. Sharp's later voting record as a legislator reveals a pronounced secularism: he supported the renewal of a lottery (which then-governor Gabriel Slaughter, a devout Baptist, vetoed on the grounds that it might "relax the morality and honest industry of the country") and voted against a bill that would have permitted "ministers of the Gospel" to be exempt from toll charges on any turnpike in the state. Sharp's lack of piety may be partly explained by the absence of Jean Sharp, for the evangelical upsurge received disproportionate support from women, who predominated at Kentucky's early camp meetings. Whatever the reasons, the "ecstasies" of the awakening seem to have left little impression on young Solomon.[16]

He would not have been alone. Despite the furor it generated, the Great Revival was by no means uncontroversial in early Kentucky. Traditionalists—latter-day "Old Lights"—were repulsed by the outlandish behavior of the "fallen"—those who cried out, collapsed in ecstasy, and, at their most extreme, indulged in jerking and barking exercises. Others were appalled by the illiteracy of the ministers—"without-method Methodists" who spouted "happy compounds of illiterateness and fanaticism."[17]

Yet the criticism of the revivals was not solely doctrinal squabbling. In fact, by some estimates, a majority of southerners thought the evangelical style bizarre well into the nineteenth century. Most of these people who looked askance at the revivals were simply a part of the unchurched majority unwilling to heed the evangelicals' call to renounce the fleeting pleasures of this world. But, somewhat surprising on the rough and untutored Kentucky frontier, there also existed a number of people whose rejection of the revival's emotionalism signaled an allegiance to a rationalistic cosmology—in particular, deism. Around the turn of the century, Kentucky newspapers often published articles recommending skepticism, most of them titled "Natural Reason" or "A Friend to Reason," echoing Thomas Paine's *Age of Reason*—which, to the profound horror of the backcountry preachers, had been serialized in Kentucky's leading newspaper, Lexington's *Kentucky Gazette.*[18]

Not surprisingly, deism was associated with the well educated of the West, the "honorable and intelligent men" who had been exposed to the skepticism of the Enlightenment. It was they who were "generally immune to the appeal of the revival," while the common folk were much more likely to participate in the revivals and indulge in the "exercises." In 1802, Frenchman F. A. Michaux wrote that, in Lexington, "the better-informed people differ from the opinion of the multitude with respect to this species of extacy." In 1805, Pennsylvanian Josiah Espy discerned a gulf between "the great body of the well-informed and wealthy" Kentuckians who "were immersed in infidelity and dissipation," and the "more illiterate" who "were downright fanatics and zealots in religion." The Reverend James Gallaher, looking back years after the evangelical style had become ascendant, remembered, "Ah! It was reputable, it was literary, it was scientific, to scowl at the gospel, and pour forth 'great swelling words' against all that was sacred." Somewhat more surprising was that deism appealed to some younger residents of the West. The Reverend Robert Stuart recalled that in early Kentucky "the writings of Infidels . . . [were] extensively circulated," their deist principles "imbibed by the youth particularly," who "became scoffers at religion and blasphemers against God."[19]

The Sharps were certainly not of Kentucky's elite, but it is fairly clear that Thomas Sharp wanted his children to be. Without the means to give his sons and daughters material support of any significance, Thomas apparently instilled in them an uncommon ambition to rise above their origins. Such is suggested not only by Thomas's wanderlust but more clearly in the subsequent careers of his children. All five sons became professionals, and all achieved distinction in their chosen fields: two became accomplished physicians, two more renowned lawyers, and another a prosperous merchant. Three—Solomon, Leander, and Fidelio—were elected to the Kentucky General Assembly. Of the three daughters, moreover, at least two married "much respected citizens" and presided over affluent and refined households.[20]

In this respect, Solomon Sharp's father was very similar to the parent of another remarkable man who rose from the social and geographical periphery of early Kentucky to achieve eminence. Daniel Drake, a prominent physician and educator whose fame would in time spread throughout the West, was born two years before Solomon and was raised outside the town of May's Lick, in northern Kentucky. In his memoirs—an exceptional account of growing up on the late-eighteenth-century frontier—Drake related the ambitions of his father, Isaac: "His poverty he regretted; his ignorance he deplored. His natural instincts were to knowledge, refinement, and honorable influence in the affairs of the world. . . . He had formed a conception of something *more* elevated."[21]

By dreaming of something "more elevated," by pushing their children to excel, Thomas Sharp and Isaac Drake culturally distanced themselves from their neighbors. Travelers to the Green River district routinely, almost inevitably, described Southsiders as lazy degenerates who rarely worked after securing enough to eat. Virginian Thomas Joynes insisted that "the inhabitants in this part of the country generally live in miserable log huts, and are extremely poor. This poverty arises principally from their indolence, which is extreme. From the fertility of the land, very little labor is required to raise an abundant supply of corn, and hogs require very little attention, so that the men are not generally employed in labor more than one-fourth their time; the balance they employ in hunting and drinking whiskey." Soon after moving to western Kentucky from Virginia, Colonel Charles Lewis, Thomas Jefferson's brother-in-law, was not impressed with his new neighbors: "The males of every discription here don't work more than one fourth of their time." Another traveler to the state reported, "Too many, instead of resting on one day in seven, work only on one day in six." This love of ease was later both celebrated and immortalized in the phenomenally popular "Hunters of Kentucky," an account of the American victory at the Battle of New Orleans:

A bank was rais'd to hide our breast
Not that we thought of dying
But that we always like to rest
Unless the game is flying.[22]

And therefore it was precisely because young Solomon "ate no idle bread, spent no leisure hours," that he and his brothers were unusual. Yet, as Drake explained, there was a price for such ambition in an agrarian, insular world; it was not exactly frowned on, but it did raise eyebrows. In Drake's case, once it became known that he would leave the neighborhood to study medicine, the novelty of the young man's course "excited a considerable sensation. It was decided that I was to be a gentleman, and lead a life of ease and gentility. . . . Some of them cautioned me against getting proud." Intellectual refinement of any degree was simply not a priority among many early westerners. As Abraham Lincoln would remember of the society directly across the Ohio River in Indiana, a region settled largely by western Kentuckians, "There was absolutely nothing to excite ambition for education."[23]

But Thomas Sharp thought otherwise, and he provided as best as he could for his children's schooling. Unfortunately, that was not much. The deficiencies of Solomon's education—acquired during his intermittent attendance at one of Logan County's fledgling academies—would later be painfully evident, even by the relaxed standards of the trans-Appalachian West. One of his eulogists later wrote, "He always felt the want of literary acquisitions and was for a time jeered by envious rivals for his provincial pronunciation and grammatical inaccuracies." One of Solomon's few surviving letters—an 1813 missive to Henry Clay concerning military affairs during the War of 1812—clearly betrays his truncated education: "Great hopes are entertained that the increas of our gallent Navy, and the liberal encouragement of the recruiting Servise by increas of Wages and bounty." (Sharp went on to relate the "conciderable intrust" that Kentuckians had shown in the appointment of cabinet officials.) Years later, when Sharp was Kentucky's attorney general, his enemies taunted him for being unable to "employ the English language with sufficient accuracy" and "too ignorant to understand the constitution."[24]

Yet, if never exactly erudite, Sharp did acquire the rudiments of an education and soon gravitated toward the profession of choice for ambitious young men: law. We do not know with whom he read law—or indeed if he did study law with a practicing attorney. He may very well have followed the path of his older brother, Fidelio, a respected lawyer in Christian County, Kentucky, who never served an apprenticeship with a licensed attorney, instead acquiring his legal knowledge through "his books, which were obtained singly as necessity required, and read, often by the light of the midnight fire." Yet any preparation at all would have separated Sharp from most of his peers; Micah Taul, with whom Sharp later served in Congress, was admitted to the Kentucky bar despite that he "had never *read a Law Book.*" Any man in the state, wrote Roland Trevor, "with a single year's study, would be an overmatch for half who practice."[25]

With such lax standards, Kentucky in the early nineteenth century was crawling with lawyers—self-taught and conventionally trained alike. The first full-time attorney, John Brown, entered Kentucky in 1783; not ten years later, one community of fewer than one hundred white families reported thirty-nine practicing lawyers. The glut was caused primarily by the extraordinary, almost absurd, confusion over land titles. Haphazard surveys and massive, disorderly immigration had given rise to a "shingling" effect, whereby innumerable land claims overlapped. By the early 1780s, the state, as one historian aptly summarized, was the scene of "an appalling legal circus," a tangle of land suits that would not be sorted out until the middle of the next century. One immigrant's directory warned that a newcomer, when "purchasing a farm of a farmer, is nearly certain of having included in the bargain three of four actions at law, to determine whose property it really is."[26]

Even with this bounty of litigation, competition among the lawyers was fierce, and from the crucible emerged an extraordinarily talented group, among them Henry Clay, John Pope, George Bibb, Jesse Bledsoe, John Rowan, and Felix Grundy. One young and ambitious lawyer, James Buchanan, learned firsthand just how competitive the frontier bar was. In 1812, the future president—then a twenty-one-year-old with dreams of making a name for himself in the West—left Pennsylvania for Kentucky. He settled in Elizabethtown with high hopes, but in less than a year, he was back in his home state. As he later told Kentucky congressman Ben Hardin, "I went to Kentucky . . . expecting to be a great man there, but every lawyer I met at the bar was my equal, and more than half of them my superiors, so I gave it up."[27]

Sharp ran headlong into this very same predicament. When he began his career in 1806, Russellville, the seat of Logan County, was already teeming with talented attorneys—including future U.S. senator and governor of Illinois Ninian Edwards; George M. Bibb, state legislator and soon-to-be chief justice of the Kentucky court of appeals; and no fewer than four future governors of the state: Charles and James T. Morehead, John Breathitt, and John J. Crittenden. With so crowded and talented a field, Solomon wisely decided to try his luck twenty-five miles to the northeast, in Bowling Green, in neighboring Warren County. There, he established a partnership with Samuel Caldwell, another native of Logan County who for years had served as county clerk. Seventeen years older than Sharp, Caldwell was a man of distinction in the Green River area, having earned renown in the Indian wars and compiled a record of public service that included an unsuccessful run for lieutenant governor in 1808 and service as a presidential elector in 1813, 1817, and 1821.[28]

Caldwell had known Sharp ever since he was a child and was doubtlessly impressed with Sharp's work ethic. Painfully aware of his educational shortcomings, Sharp compensated with an assiduous attention to detail. While some other lawyers "studied Hoyle, more than they did Blackstone," Sharp devoted himself with "unwearied application" to his profession. Several eminent colleagues later testified that "he was remarkable for the extent and accuracy of his various information. His ardor for information was almost quenchless."[29]

The effort paid off. Before long Sharp built a reputation as one of the best lawyers in the Green River district, a man whose "great wealth and talents" were virtually undisputed. Congressman Ben Hardin, a man whose ruthless assessments of others later earned him the nickname "Old Kitchen Knife," thought Sharp "one of the ablest and most eloquent men ever born and raised in Kentucky." In 1812, a neighbor of Sharp's, Joseph Underwood, predicted that Sharp's fellow lawyers in Warren County would unanimously support his bid for reelection to the state legislature, not only because of "personal attachment" but because they wanted Sharp out of the county for at least a few months of the year so they would not have to compete with him for clients. Although he was not a great orator, Sharp possessed a "fine voice" and won over juries with a "style of speech [that] was of the conversational order—plain and concise." By the time he was thirty years old, Sharp's reputation "for ability and integrity was as wide as the state," and within a more few more years, several young men were reading law with him. In 1824, when eighty small landholders in the northern Kentucky county of Campbell were served with writs of ejectment from the seventh federal circuit court in Frankfort, the group sent two representatives to the capital with instructions to "get the best lawyer." After a meticulous search, they chose Sharp.[30]

"Success," Amos Kendall later eulogized, "followed him wherever he turned." Then as now, a successful lawyer was a wealthy lawyer. Tax lists of 1807 credit the twenty-year-old Sharp with but a horse. Only two years later, Sharp owned 3,600 acres of land in three counties; in two more years, he had title to seven slaves. By the time of his death fourteen years later, his net worth of over seventy thousand dollars made him one of the richest men in the state.[31]

Although driven, Sharp was not brash and, at least in his personal dealings, rarely indulged in the belligerent swagger for which Kentuckians were notorious. After his death, it was the consensus of his acquaintances that he "possessed an elevated, a serene and almost imperturbable equanimity"; one editor affirmed that "his temper was not rash, nor violent. His mode of speaking was persuasive and mild." He was, by all accounts, "unassuming," "unpretending," "amiable." Such manners, it was said, "always preserved him from personal altercation."[32]

And yet, for all his personal modesty and amiability, Sharp did not lack enemies. He had, it was said, "too great an avidity for money." Some of the criticism resulted from the fact that he was good at what good lawyers do: "He defended a false position with as much zeal as one which was true, a bad cause with the same apparent sincerity, with which he advocated a good one, the injurer with as much correctness as the injured." Yet, even in relation to other lawyers, Sharp could be exceptionally aggressive in the courtroom. "I had heard a great many men damn Sharp for screwing witnesses too hard," one man later testified. Even his adoring brother Leander admitted that Solomon could be "determined and inflexible." Such behavior earned Sharp "a great many violent enemies" in the Green River district, one of whom—a "respectable man" of Warren County—publicly swore that if he met Sharp "on the road he would shoot him."[33]

One such implacable enemy was Abner D. Hamilton, the father of a man who was put to death as a result in no small measure of Sharp's efforts. In March 1818, John C. Hamilton, the scion of a wealthy and powerful family in Barren County, was accused of the murder of his friend and traveling companion, Dr. Alexander Sanderson, a wealthy planter from Natchez, Mississippi. Judge Christopher Tompkins presided. Hamilton was defended by John Rowan, himself a renowned lawyer and one of the most powerful politicians in the state. Sharp, as one of the commonwealth's attorneys charged with prosecuting the case, "showed [Hamilton] no mercy" and relentlessly helped secure a conviction. On May 17, 1818, Hamilton was executed. Seven years later, the elder Hamilton's intense hatred of Sharp was still well known enough to start rumors that it was he who murdered Sharp. Hamilton felt obliged to buy space in Frankfort newspapers to publicly deny any involvement in Sharp's assassination.[34]

Such a combination of ambition, personality, and native intelligence recommended Sharp to his Warren County neighbors, and in 1809 they elected him to the first of three successive terms in Kentucky's General Assembly. Not surprisingly, Sharp was a Jeffersonian Republican, like virtually every other politician in early Kentucky. More unexpected was that no one ever challenged Sharp's election, for at twenty-one years of age in August 1809, he was well short of the minimum age to serve in the state legislature.[35]

The assembly that young Sharp entered had earned a lively reputation and was never known for its decorum. One English visitor to Frankfort was appalled by the sight of the assembly hall floor "*inundated* with saliva and tobacco juice" and by the sound of "the whole house simultaneously hawking at the close of every sentence." The speaker of the house, meanwhile, "sat in an easy & graceful posture in a raised armchair, an arm over one arm of the chair, & a leg over the other, while the debates were going on." In the early years of the century, the state assembly was not only unseemly but enervated. After the 1810–1811 General Assembly, one spectator complained that "nothing worthy of an intelligent community has been done in the last session of your assembly."[36]

Several themes of Sharp's career and personality are evident in his early political career. He assiduously attended his duties as a legislator, missing no more than a handful of votes in three years. He took great interest in legislation affecting the legal profession, introducing, for example, bills for reforming the mode of summoning juries and the timing of circuit courts. The concerns of his Green River constituents were faithfully attended to: Sharp fought against the immediate repayment of the Green River debt—millions of dollars Southsiders owed to the state government—and objected to the proposed removal of the branch of the Bank of Kentucky from Russellville. Although a slave owner himself, Sharp was unenthusiastic about the attempts to strengthen Kentucky's slave code, voting against a draconian statute titled "An Act for the More Effectual Prevention of Crimes, Conspiracies, and Insurrections of Slaves, Free Negroes, and Mulattoes, and for Their Better Government." And, consistent with his later stance during the relief war of the 1820s, Sharp backed measures designed to help Kentuckians in debt. He opposed, for example, the repeal of an 1809 relief bill passed to abate the effects of the embargo, and he consistently supported a series of occupying claimant laws that protected the property of Kentuckians who had lost their homesteads in legal disputes.

But Sharp's most noteworthy accomplishment in this period was the antidueling legislation he and Ben Hardin guided through the General Assembly in 1811. The bill required that all state officers and attorneys at law take an oath that they had not issued, accepted, or delivered a challenge to fight a duel (after a given date) and would not do so in the future. Dueling was, according to the preamble of Sharp and Hardin's act, an "inhuman" practice, "contrary to the precepts of morality, religion, and civil obligation." Several years later, when the law was challenged, Sharp elaborated on the rationale of the legislation: it was an "experiment," he said, designed to provide the "force of example" to the rest of the state's citizens, and to suggest that the practice of dueling, although "unfortunately so ingrafted into our habits and manners," was premised on "notions of honor and equality, entirely artificial and fallacious."[37]

Yet towering over any quotidian business of the state legislature were the steadily worsening relations between the young republic and the British Empire. Not only were westerners convinced that the British were behind the strengthening resistance movement among the Indians in the Northwest, but their touchy sense of honor that Sharp regretted made Britain's actions on the high seas utterly unacceptable. As the assembly made explicit, "Unless Great Britain shall retrace her steps," there were only two choices: "unqualified base submission, or war." Almost to a person, Kentuckians avidly supported, even craved, war with Britain. The *Kentucky Gazette* reported that "Kentucky seems ready to precipitate itself en masse upon the British and their infernal allies the Indians." Francis Wright added that "the women [of Kentucky] shared the patriotism of the men, vying with each other in repressing their tears and actually buckling on the swords and cartridges and arming the hands of their sons and husbands." An early historian of Kentucky who was but a child during the war, Lewis Collins remembered hearing the news of General William Hull's surrender of Detroit "discussed by a company of married ladies, who unanimously pronounced Hull a traitor, and with great vehemence declared that he ought to be gibbeted, or crucified—ordinary hanging being far too mild a punishment for so monstrous a traitor." The prospective conflict provided an irresistible chance to strike against both of the westerners' ancient enemies; as one Kentuckian, born in 1802, recalled, "Hatred of George III, of British red-coats, and of American aborigines, were the first emotions of my young and patriotic heart."[38]

Sharp's "young and patriotic heart" also fluttered at the opportunity of war with Great Britain and the Northwest Indians. Though personally mild mannered and averse to personal confrontation, Sharp always evinced a pronounced militarism in his public temperament. Indeed, it would be difficult to overstate his admiration for military virtues. While in the state assembly, Sharp voted against allowing conscientious objectors to forgo militia training. Moreover, he constantly and vociferously advocated war with Britain, and his elevation to the rank of colonel in the state militia was always a source of great pride. As one nineteenth-century biographer wrote, Sharp "had a great fondness for military life, its spirit, its activity, and its discipline strongly appealing to his nature."[39]

In these matters, Sharp was typically, quintessentially, western. As Elias Pym Fordham observed in 1818, Kentuckians' "military enthusiasm scarcely knows any limit." The roots of such militarism are not difficult to locate. The habit was first ingrained during the earliest days of settlement, when the only leaders who commanded respect were those most capable of surviving and, more to the point, those who could help others survive—fighters like Daniel Boone and Benjamin Logan. Out in the marchlands of western civilization, necessity trumped custom, and authority divorced from martial ability was less than worthless; it was dangerous. By the early nineteenth century, most of Kentucky's leaders had either fought in the Indian wars or could well remember the ravages of a time when bravery and ruthlessness were virtues. Felix Grundy recalled that, in his youth, "death was in almost every bush, and every thicket concealed an ambuscade. If I am asked to trace my memory back and name the first indelible impression it received, it would be the sight of my eldest brother, bleeding and dying under the wounds inflicted by the tomahawk and scalping knife. Another and another went the same way. . . . Those of us who are here are but the remnant—the wreck—of large families lost in effecting the early settlement of the west." Chilton Allan, born the year before Grundy, speculated that such ever-present danger during the settling of Kentucky gave rise to a "fool-brave . . . spirit which imbued every member, in every class, of all ages and conditions of society." A generation reared on the epic tales of frontier Kentucky's Indian wars yet too young to have participated themselves hungered for war, eager to prove their own worth and valor.[40]

A few weeks after America's declaration of war against Great Britain in the summer of 1812, Sharp was elected to the Thirteenth Congress as a representative from Kentucky's Sixth Congressional District despite that, elected a few weeks shy of his twenty-fifth birthday, he technically was not old enough to serve in the U.S. House of Representatives. Before he could take his seat, however, Sharp enlisted as a private in Lieutenant Colonel Young Ewing's regiment of the Kentucky Mounted Volunteer Militia, a 2,500-man force under the command of Major General Samuel Hopkins, a fifty-nine-year-old veteran who had served on Washington's staff during the Revolutionary War. But Sharp was no ordinary cavalryman, and everyone knew it—he had just been elected to Congress along with Hopkins himself. Ewing, moreover, had been a colleague of Sharp's in the Kentucky General Assembly. And so it was to no one's surprise that twelve days after his enlistment on September 18, Sharp's fellow soldiers elected him major; he joined Ewing's staff the next day.

The expedition itself, however, was a farce from the beginning. After Hull's surrender of Detroit and the fall of Chicago, Governor Isaac Shelby and his advisers feared that the federal authorities would not or could not act "with sufficient promptitude and efficacy" to protect the state from Indian attack. So Shelby immediately dispatched the Kentucky Mounted Volunteer Militia with orders to attack Kickapoo and Peoria villages in Indiana and Illinois, which had allied with Tecumseh. Yet without authorization from the War Department, Kentucky officials had little hope of obtaining adequate supplies for the troops and were thus forced to call on Kentucky women to knit "warm linsey clothes, socks, blankets, [and] linen shirts" for the "patriotic sons of Kentucky." Problems were compounded by the fact that the soldiers had signed on for only thirty days, giving the commanders hopelessly little time to organize their units, train the soldiers, and complete the mission. In such conditions, the *rage militaire* of the day was a very thin reed on which to base the undertaking. Many soldiers opted out of their commitment before they even arrived at the rendezvous point at Fort Harrison, the ramshackle garrison one hundred miles north of Vincennes in the Indiana Territory. Sickness claimed many of those who did show up: "Ther is upwards of one hundred men lying in the osptlle [hospital] at this place," one soldier wrote home.[41]

Although the soldiers did manage to break camp, the expedition could not even find the Kickapoo and Peoria villages. After five days of wandering around the Northwest and a prairie fire that almost engulfed the camp, the five hundred dispirited men who remained informed Hopkins they were going home. It was an inglorious, if not ridiculous, campaign; by Hopkins's own admission, the army had returned "without hardly obtaining the sight of an enemy." But Sharp's forty-two-day tour of duty was enough to secure him a colonelcy in the Kentucky militia—and, in a region obsessed with all things martial, such would prove a considerable boon to the political career he was carefully nurturing.[42]

After a few months' rest in Kentucky, Sharp left for Washington and took his seat in the House of Representatives in May 1813. By then, America had muddled its way through ten months of war with Britain, and Sharp, like most Republicans, was mortified by the general ineptitude of his country's effort. It was scarcely surprising, therefore, that Sharp, long an admirer of Henry Clay, quickly aligned himself with the Speaker and his fellow war hawks. Sharp in fact stayed in the same boardinghouse as John C. Calhoun for the second and third sessions of the Thirtieth Congress. Calhoun in particular was deeply impressed with Sharp; he later wrote, "I have known him long and intimately. He has few superiors of his age in any part of our country."[43]

Sharp, as a first-term congressman, gave no evidence that he was intimidated by a truly impressive array of colleagues. Working alongside established luminaries such as Nathaniel Macon and Timothy Pickering, as well as all three members of the era's "Great Triumvirate"—Daniel Webster, Henry Clay, and John C. Calhoun—Sharp proved himself bold and eloquent in debate and well versed on the issues at hand. His first major speech, in June 1813, a passionate denunciation of Federalist obstruction of the war effort, demonstrated a detailed knowledge of the political and diplomatic intrigues that led to war. In the course of his speech, Sharp—at twenty-five very likely the youngest elected official in the nation's capital—had the temerity to lay the blame for the war squarely at the feet of his Federalist colleagues. Had they not "induced Great Britain to believe we were too divided in our councils to prosecute a war in defence of our rights, she would not have continued her aggressions on our commerce, and we should have had no war." Sharp also upbraided the Federalists for their opposition to the war: "He who opposes the adoption of injudicious measures, is a patriot—those measures once adopted, to oppose their execution is rebellion." New York Federalist Zebulon Shipherd's denunciation of the war, Sharp railed, amounted to "treason against humanity." After the Battle of New Orleans, Sharp delighted in baiting the Federalists, comparing the loyalty of the Louisianans during Jackson's campaign with the "treason" of the Hartford conventionists.[44]

In another early speech, Sharp announced that "national honor" demanded a rigorous prosecution of the war with Britain, a "most potent and perfidious enemy." Of course, such warmongering was expected in a western politician—it was tantamount to political suicide to do anything else, as a U.S. senator from Kentucky, John Pope, was at that moment discovering. But clearly, Sharp was comfortable in the role, as he roundly condemned critics of the war as "proper objects of detestation" and even advocated a preemptive war with Spain, which, he hoped, would not only secure Latin American independence but "afford a school for our Navy." Sharp would intermittently give expression to his youthful zeal and militaristic temperament by reciting verse on the floor of Congress:

> Fresh leaves of martial laurel
> Shall shade the soldier's grave
> Who dies with arm uplifted
> His country's rights to save!

In early 1815, when the news of Jackson's victory at New Orleans reached Washington, an enraptured Sharp again extolled the splendors of patriotic death:

> If humanity shows to the God of the world
> A sight for his fatherly eye
> It is when a people, with banner unfurl'd
> resolve for their freedom to die.[45]

Sharp brought to the Capitol the same audacity and aggressiveness he had honed in the courtroom. After only a few months in Washington, he introduced a resolution asking Richard Rush, the attorney general of the United States, to prosecute Vermont governor Martin Chittenden for treason. Chittenden, a Federalist, had ordered home a militia brigade that his predecessor had sent to New York to assist in the invasion of Canada. Chittenden insisted that the troops were needed at home to defend Vermont and that, in any event, they were improperly serving under the command of regular army officers. An indignant Sharp insisted that Chittenden's edict was an invitation for the Vermont troops to desert their stations and thus amounted to deliberate subversion of the war effort. Although neither Congress nor the attorney general took any action, Sharp's motion was printed and widely distributed. And while Republicans hailed young Sharp for his spirited attack, the Federalists accused Sharp of indulging in "party crimination beyond the ordinary field of debate."[46]

Faced with the sectional obstructionism of the Federalists and the embarrassing inability of the United States to adequately prosecute the war, Sharp, like many of his fellow Republicans, began to reconsider the localistic and minimalist tenets of their Jeffersonian faith. The increased military spending, federal support for transportation improvements, a tariff, and a new national bank all had their origins in a fear of weakness. Believing themselves faced with the option of an impotent republic or a virile nation, American leaders almost invariably, and with remarkable swiftness and relatively little compunction, rethought received republican wisdom and chose the latter. How else but with a strong central government could the country be adequately defended? Only a powerful nation, Sharp insisted, would "induce the citizens freely to march from one extreme to another to meet the enemy." The "grandeur," the "honor" of the nation, he asserted, "could only be attained by an amalgamation of national feeling," while "local state feeling . . . will be the bane of the prosperity of the nation." Should any doubt exist, Sharp spelled it out for his constituents: "We ought to encourage national feeling, not sectional views."[47]

In 1814 this sort of thing still played well in western Kentucky, and Sharp was easily reelected to his seat in Congress, although, strictly speaking, that seat did not exist anymore, for the British had burned the Capitol that summer. (As fellow Kentucky congressman Micah Taul explained, "The Capitol was at that time in ruins, & Congress sat in a house prepared for the purpose about 150 or 200 yards East of the Capitol.") This was the Fourteenth Congress, and this was the advent of National Republicanism.[48]

Though elected in the darkest days of the war, with the British on the verge of destroying Washington, the Fourteenth Congress did not convene until December 4, 1815, almost a full year after the signing of the Treaty of Ghent. This group possessed a "vigor"—to use Henry Adams's suggestive term—that set it apart from "the imbecility of many previous Congresses." It was indeed an impressive group: in addition to Clay, Calhoun, and Webster, also present were William Pinkney, John Randolph, William Lowndes, Richard M. Johnson, and Timothy Pickering—a collection of men that neither lacked ambition nor doubted their own abilities.[49]

The agenda of this Fourteenth Congress, given a presidential mandate by Madison's seventh annual message, was very much shaped by the war and its humiliations. All of the components of the nationalistic program—a new national bank, federal support for the construction of roads and canals, a protective tariff, the continuation of wartime taxes, and especially the buildup of the army and navy—were justified by a determination to never again repeat the indignities of the late war. It was an enterprise at once designed to conquer space, defend borders, and bind together a nation. Sharp explained to his constituents the crucial relation of economic and military power—that such was the expense of war that "the contest among civilized nations is now more frequently decided by gold than by iron." It necessarily followed, therefore, that "the encouragement and promotion of agriculture, of commerce, and of manufactures, not only secures to a people the comforts and enjoyments of life, but also affords them the means of acquiring renown in arms . . . and as money is the sinews of war, the finances of a Government is its most important and difficult branch of administration." And thus Sharp and his colleagues in the Fourteenth Congress braided together patriotism, national defense, and economic development into a cable of national improvement.[50]

Yet as the immediate concerns of war gave way to issues of domestic development, Sharp discovered the limits of his nascent nationalism. Although he gave his assent to all the major initiatives of the Fourteenth Congress, Sharp was ambivalent about this new course he was helping to chart. The tariff, for example, he believed to be necessary only as an expedient, one that would give to the young industries that had taken root during the war the "protecting and fostering hand of Government to give them permanency and prosperity." And though he approved of any measure that promised to help the nation defend itself, Sharp was leery of a standing army, contending that he would not want one more soldier in the army than was necessary to man existing garrisons, adding that "a liberal establishment of military schools" might be a much better means "to support the military character." Sharp, moreover, worried that Congress was getting too far ahead of the opinions of its constituents. "The idea of a perfect commonwealth," he wrote, "is found to consist in an entire unity of interest between the Government and the people. When that unity does not exist, the people are always betrayed by their rulers, whose interest is to oppress them." The Jeffersonian tradition of minimalist government and fear of power that Sharp and his fellow citizens were reared on, it seems, was not easily discarded.[51]

The contradictory pulls of defense and republicanism, of strength and virtue, of expedience and principle, were best encapsulated in Sharp's ambivalence over the rechartering of the Bank of the United States. Beginning in his first term in the Kentucky General Assembly, Sharp served on several committees charged with overseeing banking institutions, and the experience bred in him a chronic suspicion of banks. The "only instinct" of "moneyed institutions," he advanced, "is gain," regardless of the cost to community or country. Thus in 1811, Sharp, along with a majority of his peers in the state assembly, instructed the Kentucky congressional delegation to vote against recharter of the First Bank of the United States.[52]

Five years later, however, Sharp had reconsidered. "It is the part of wisdom in those who administer its Government to accommodate their measures to its new situation," Sharp explained—perhaps a bit defensively—to his constituency in 1816. The problem, as he saw it, was the mismanaged, irresponsible, and almost impossibly prolific state banks that had suspended specie payments and thereby had inundated the country with unredeemable notes that were circulating, as Sharp put it, "in dishonor and depreciation." The resulting inflation, Sharp argued, amounted to a private tax on the public. He was, moreover, infuriated by the hypocrisy of bank officials. By refusing to redeem their notes in specie, the banks in effect were breaking a contract with note holders. Yet those same directors "will post the name of one of their customers as dishonored if he does not meet his contract to a day." All the while, the banks were perfectly capable of resuming payments: "They retain in their vaults the greater part of the specie of the country." In sum, the state banks and their behavior were an affront to "the morality of the country."[53]

And thus by 1816, politicians, searching for a solution to the problem of state banking, found it in a new national bank that would regulate the abuses of local banks. Sharp, in other words—like many of his fellow legislators—voted for the national bank not out of an enthusiasm for entrepreneurship but as a remedy almost homeopathic in its logic: one bank, in effect, was the cure for an epidemic of banks. A national institution that would be held in check by Congress and that would in turn keep state banks honest was a "tried and understood" means of introducing "a general resumption of specie payments and circulation." Moreover, this new national bank would stabilize the finances of the government, "infuse health into the circulating medium of the country, and enable the treasury to refuse all paper in payment of revenue that is not redeemed in specie."[54]

As it turned out, however, the most controversial undertaking of the Fourteenth Congress had nothing to do with the nationalist legislative program. What outraged the American people—and what prematurely ended Sharp's congressional career—was the compensation bill, a proposal to pay congressmen an annual salary of fifteen hundred dollars rather than the six dollars per diem they had been receiving. The legislation was the brainchild of Sharp's fellow representative from Kentucky, Richard M. Johnson. Like the rest of the state's delegation (with the sole exception of Joseph Desha, future governor of Kentucky), Sharp voted for the measure, even going on record publicly thanking Johnson for "bringing forward the proposition." The House, oblivious of the furor they were unleashing, passed the compensation bill on March 8, 1816, by a vote of eighty-one to sixty-seven.[55]

The bill's advocates had grossly misjudged the public temper. As they returned home from the first session, they found themselves almost universally denounced as corrupt and self-serving. The outcry was particularly intense in Kentucky, where the General Assembly passed a resolution denouncing the compensation bill as "intrinsically and justly obnoxious" and demanded its repeal. No Kentucky representative was more pointedly and publicly attacked than Sharp, who was the target of a series of "Public Good" essays printed in the *Russellville Weekly Messenger.* Written by James T. Morehead, a nineteen-year-old law student of John J. Crittenden and future governor of Kentucky, the articles accused Sharp of "legislating for himself" and "displaying an indifference to the promotion of [Kentuckians'] interests, equaled only by his attention to his own." Upon his return home in May 1816, Sharp attempted to defend his vote in front of a large crowd during the Warren County court day. Morehead would have none of it: "All your labor, all your ingenuity, all your arguments of previous preparation," he taunted Sharp, "could not effectuate your design of convincing the public mind of the rectitude of your conduct. . . . Your speech of justification has more clearly shewn the obliquity of your policy."[56]

With all of the congressional seats up for grabs that summer, even the stars of western politics, Richard M. Johnson and Henry Clay, looked vulnerable at the polls for the first time in their public careers. And in the end, of those who voted for the compensation bill, only Clay and Johnson survived the debacle. Two of Kentucky's delegation declined to run again—one of whom, Ben Hardin, flatly refused to canvass the state, "begging pardon for what I do not consider to have been incorrect." Those who ran for reelection were unseated by decisive margins, including Sharp, who lost badly to Revolutionary War veteran David Walker. It was the first defeat of his political career.[57]

Yet the compensation bill debacle did not deter Sharp from once again seeking and securing elective office. In 1817, almost immediately upon returning from the second session of the Fourteenth Congress, he set his sights on reelection to the Kentucky General Assembly. Once home, Sharp found Kentucky convulsed over whether the death of the sitting governor, George Madison, required a new election, or if the lieutenant governor, Gabriel Slaughter, should be allowed to finish out Madison's term.

Despite failing health, Madison—celebrated Indian fighter, veteran of the War of 1812, and brother of Bishop James Madison—had been induced to run for the governor's seat in 1816. Such was his popularity that, upon the announcement of his intention to run, the other candidate immediately dropped out of the race. A few weeks after his pro forma election, however, Madison died, and Lieutenant Governor Slaughter assumed the governorship. There was, for the moment, no call for a new election; the relevant portion of Kentucky's 1799 constitution—article 3, section 18—was ambiguous, stating that in the case of the death of a sitting governor, "the Lieutenant-Governor shall exercise all the power and authority appertaining to the office of Governor, until another be duly qualified." What exactly constituted due qualification—or how or when it could be achieved—was not specified.

In all probability, Slaughter's claim to the governorship would have gone uncontested but for his decision to replace the secretary of state appointed by Madison—Charles S. Todd, son-in-law of Kentucky founding father Isaac Shelby—with John Pope, "a man whose every political act, for the last five years" according to one newspaper, "has been a libel upon the character of his country, and treason against the opinions and feelings" of the people. In particular, Pope's support of the recharter of the Bank of the United States in 1811 and his opposition to the War of 1812—both positions contrary to those of the mass of Kentuckians—earned him "unqualified detestation" across the state. Newspaper editor Amos Kendall, upon hearing the news of Pope's appointment, "was thunderstruck. I considered Pope the leader of the

Federalists, and instantly foresaw a struggle between the parties which must end in the exaltation of the Federalists, or in the prostration of themselves and their leader." The appointment indeed displayed "uncommon stupidity" and amounted to, as one newspaper correspondent put it, "political suicide" on the part of Slaughter.[58]

He should have known better. Slaughter was a veteran of Kentucky politics, having served in the state assembly as both a representative and a senator for over a decade. In 1808 he was elected to his first term as lieutenant governor (defeating, among other candidates, Solomon Sharp's law partner, Samuel Caldwell). In 1812 he ran for governor but was trounced by Isaac Shelby, Kentucky's first governor, who had returned to politics amid the developing crisis with Great Britain. After earning a measure of glory as a commander in the Battle of New Orleans, Slaughter in 1816 again ran for, and won, the office of lieutenant governor. By then, Slaughter was forty-nine years old and was, for a man who had spent most of his adult life in the fluid society of frontier Kentucky, curiously out of step with the popular temper. He distrusted the press and even had the temerity to personally ask the Frankfort newspapers not to report on the new election controversy. Moreover, Slaughter's explanations of America's political system, although accurate enough, were perhaps too candid for westerners. In his annual message of 1817, Slaughter declared that "ours is not a simple democracy" but a representative government bound by checks and balances. Such was absolutely necessary, he believed, for "if every sudden impulse of any community was to be carried into full effect, there would be in such a state, neither confidence, nor safety."[59]

The General Assembly convened in December 1816 and took up the issue of the legitimacy of Slaughter's governorship but concluded that the constitution did not authorize a new election. The question, however, far from receding, became virtually the only issue in the following summer's state elections. After furious campaigning on the part of new election candidates and amid continual and bitter denunciations of Slaughter and his "prime minister" Pope, a "prodigious majority" of the winning candidates committed themselves to supporting a new election, including such luminaries as John J. Crittenden, William T. Barry, George M. Bibb, Joseph C. Breckinridge, Jesse Bledsoe, and, interestingly enough, Charles S. Todd. Aligned with them in this, the Twenty-sixth General Assembly, was former congressman Solomon Sharp. And even amid such an impressive array of once and future talent, the abilities of young Sharp stood out. One correspondent to the *Kentucky Gazette* singled out Sharp for bringing "into our legislature a stock of practical experience and useful talents, with great facility in enforcing his views on a deliberative body, which justly rank him amongst the most respectable men of our country." And so Sharp joined the quarrel, doubtlessly grateful for an issue that deflected attention from the compensation bill fiasco.[60]

Armed with a popular mandate—indeed, armed with what they believed to be literal "instructions" from their constituents—the new election advocates pursued their agenda with force and alacrity. But the state senate defeated a bill passed by the house in December 1817 authorizing a new gubernatorial election. Thereafter, the issue was for all intents and purposes dead. Yet for Slaughter, it was a hollow victory, for the remainder of his administration was one long exercise in futility, complete with a series of overridden vetoes and an official title of "acting governor."

The controversy brought to the fore a number of issues that had been simmering in Kentucky for years. At the heart of the debate were issues that would convulse the state—and the country—for generations: How responsive should the government be to the wishes of the people? Just how direct was American democracy? What happens when the express will of a popular majority can be legitimately construed as contrary to the constitution? And who will interpret the meaning of state and federal constitutions? Matthew Lyon was not merely indulging in empty rhetoric when he asserted that "the first principle of republicanism is involved."[61]

In early 1818, the first signs of a serious economic crisis quickly overshadowed the more abstract concerns surrounding the new election controversy. In its place, banking once again became the issue of the day. Some believed banks were the cure; some believed they were the cause; still others thought they might be both. And Sharp, in what must have seemed to him a cruel reprise of the compensation bill debacle, found himself in yet another politically untenable situation.

Kentucky's adventures in banking had begun in 1802, when the General Assembly conferred banking powers—apparently without the knowledge of some remarkably inattentive legislators—on the Kentucky Insurance Company, making it the first banking establishment west of the Appalachians. Although many Kentuckians were opposed to the institution, it survived repeated legislative challenges, in large part because of the protection of a young but already politically astute Henry Clay. Four years later, the assembly, this time fully aware of what it was doing, chartered the Bank of Kentucky. Partially due to the drama surrounding the simultaneous Spanish conspiracy, which consumed the attention of most westerners, controversy was minimal. But the lack of contention also owed something to the fact that the enabling legislation clearly gave the state legislature the power to regulate the bank. Popular oversight and, if necessary, popular control were exactly what most Kentuckians believed necessary—the bank would be restrained by a nearby and annually accountable state government.[62]

The absence of such restraints helps explain why, ten years later, such an uproar ensued when branch banks of the Second Bank of the United States were established in Lexington and Louisville. Henry Clay warned a fellow supporter of the national bank, "The Bank [of the United States] should not conceal from itself the fact that there is a deep and widespread hostility existing towards it." How could such a distant power be checked? Even as the number of banks increased and their influence spread, Kentuckians had not made peace with such moneyed institutions.[63]

And yet, despite this rapid proliferation of banks, some sectors of the state called for still more. A number of powerful groups, including Kentucky's manufacturers, importing merchants, and ambitious speculators, felt that existing banking institutions did not cater to their needs, and they had advocated since 1810 the establishment of additional, independent banks. Throughout the decade, sympathetic state legislators repeatedly introduced bills creating an independent bank system, but they were all defeated, in part due to the hostility of the Bank of Kentucky, as well as because of a worry that it would be impolitic and unsafe to sanction "the establishment of monied institutions, in the management of which the state was to have no control." Between 1815 and 1817, the assembly attempted to forestall such demands for privatized banking by opening nine new branches of the Bank of Kentucky and augmenting their capital reserve. Yet more and more legislators became persuaded that the idea's time had come. Some believed the independents would serve as a check on the Bank of Kentucky, which many had come to believe had slipped the bonds placed on it. Others maintained that the increased competition would benefit the people, for "a rivalship in banks, like rivalship in all institutions and business," the argument ran, was "necessary for the public good." But much of the newfound support for the new banks came as a result of a looming economic crisis: they would pump money into a currency-poor region; they would stop Kentuckians from going out of state to procure loans; they would keep interest payments in the state.[64]

In fact, rather than being seen as the last wave of the proentrepreneurial banking mania, the independent banks could more accurately be seen as the first attempt of state legislators to shore up the region's steadily worsening economic situation. It was exactly these future advocates of debtor relief in the 1820s—John Adair, George M. Bibb, John Rowan, and Solomon Sharp—who voted for the measure. Sharp himself was instrumental in the passage of the bill; he served on the committee that drafted the enabling legislation, and he consistently defended the bill from hostile amendments.[65]

And so in January 1818, the General Assembly chartered forty-six independent banks with an aggregate capital stock of $8.7 million. Within two years, the independent banks had ground out $26 million worth of bank notes. By 1819, Kentucky, a state in which no banks had existed sixteen years earlier, had fifty-nine banks, more per capita than any other state in the union.[66]

Part and parcel of this support for the independent banks was an attempt to hobble the branches of the national bank, whose policies—at least by the lights of most Kentuckians—were harming the state. The considerable animosity toward the Bank of the United States took the form of a law designed to tax the branch banks out of the state. "You can form no idea of the violence of some of the advocates of the measure," wrote a correspondent to the *Kentucky Reporter*. In case the bank resisted paying the tax, he continued, "two honorable senators pledged themselves in debate, to furnish volunteers from their sections of the state, to aid the officer in demolishing the banking houses and breaking open the vaults." The fact that, within hours of the establishment of the independent banks, "An Act to Tax Banks in This Commonwealth" was introduced into the legislature strongly suggests how closely the two initiatives were related. The real target of the taxation bill, ostensibly directed at all note-bearing institutions in the state, was the Bank of the United States—as everyone was well aware. And once again, it was Sharp who was at the forefront of the fight. In "an animated debate" on the floor, Sharp, along with John Rowan, among others, "advocated the right and expediency" of taxing the national bank. The bill eventually passed, and an eight-thousand-dollar annual tax was imposed on each of the branches in Lexington and Louisville.[67]

A year later, Sharp was easily reelected to the Twenty-seventh General Assembly, and he—along with Samuel McKee of Garrard County and John Logan of Shelby County—stepped up the attack on the Bank of the United States, this time determined to run it out of the state. McKee considered the institution "dangerous on account of its immense power, and injurious to the country on account of its dishonest and bad management," and he denounced its directors as "swindlers." On January 4, 1819, a committee chaired by Sharp reported a bill titled "An Act Imposing a Tax on All Banking Houses Not Incorporated by This Commonwealth." The bill established a sixty-thousand-dollar annual tax (to be paid in five-thousand-dollar monthly installments) on the branches of the Bank of the United States, authorized the sergeant of the court of appeals to break into the bank and take the money from vaults, and allowed him to "summon as many of the citizens of this state as shall be necessary to assist him in the discharge of his duty." The bill's key provision declared that if the branch banks promised before March 4 to leave the state within six months, the tax would not be enforced.[68]

The entire program was closely associated with Sharp, and the legislation of early 1819 was in fact generally referred to as "Mr. Sharp's bill." As far away as South Carolina, Sharp and the initiative were closely identified: in August 1819, John C. Calhoun wrote to Kentuckian Martin Hardin, lamenting that "our friends McKee & Sharp have attacked the national bank." Calhoun hoped in the next session of the legislation that they "will be disposed to view the subject with more moderation, than what they did at the last session of your legislature." Few mistook his aim: "The object distinctly avowed by . . . Mr. Sharp, and others, is to drive the United States Banks out of the State."[69]

The whole effort, however, was rendered moot when, in late February 1819, the seventh federal circuit court issued an injunction restraining the collection of the $120,000 tax on the branch banks. Speaking for the court, Justice Thomas Todd declared that, "the act of Congress being paramount, being the supreme law of the land," the state-levied tax was tantamount to a bill of attainder—a "bill of pains and penalties imposed on the exercise of a right given by Congress." One month later, John Marshall and the U.S. Supreme Court handed down the landmark *McCulloch v. Maryland* decision, to the despair of anti–Bank of the United States forces. Amos Kendall, who would do much to renew this battle in the future, lamented that "the people have in vain looked for relief to Congress and the judiciary, must now look only to themselves."[70]

Amid the political storms of his second stint in the state legislature, Solomon Sharp met and courted Elizabeth T. Scott. "Beautiful and graceful in her person, gentle and affable in her demeanor, sprightly and cheerful in her temper," Eliza, as she was known, was more than ten years younger than Solomon. She was the oldest child of Frankfort's celebrated John M. Scott, the personal physician and close confidant of William Henry Harrison. Dr. Scott had been one of the earliest settlers of Frankfort, and "his house was the rendezvous of all the sociable circles of the place." He had served as an officer under Anthony Wayne during the Fallen Timbers campaign and, eighteen years later, despite failing health, commanded a regiment during the War of 1812. Soon after being forced by his worsening illness to return home, Dr. Scott died, leaving behind four young children and a wife eight months pregnant.[71]

Eliza most likely met Solomon after his reelection to the state assembly in the summer of 1817, when she was nineteen years old. The two were married a year later, shortly after the convening of the state assembly on December 17, 1818. Solomon, however, was a busy man; he worked the day of his wedding, casting a vote for William Logan for U.S. senator, and two days later was back at his desk. Soon after the session ended on February 10, 1819, Solomon and his young bride returned to Bowling Green and began life together.[72]

"Excellent, amiable, and beautiful," Eliza was, apparently, the very embodiment of the "cult of domesticity"—one commentator spoke of her "natural timidity," while another praised "the order, the neatness and elegance, by which her industrious management distinguished her household." She was, moreover, a devout young woman, a Presbyterian "seriously impressed on the subject of religion," a "meek and pious Christian." When she died in 1844, a eulogist asserted that "Mrs. Sharp has that faith which soars beyond the virtues, and fills the heart with the purity of a better world." By all accounts, Solomon and Eliza's marriage was a happy one—she called Solomon "the best of husbands and the kindest of fathers." After his murder, she never remarried.[73]

In early 1819, Solomon Sharp was only thirty-one years old and was, by almost any standard with which he was familiar, tremendously successful. His beautiful and devoted wife came from one of the state's most distinguished families; his legal career was well established and paid handsomely; he owned just under twelve thousand acres of land and thirteen slaves.[74] Politically, despite a reputation that had been moderately tarnished by the rough-and-tumble politics of the new West, he was still a rising star. Sharp was a bundle of contradictions: his humble origins, militarism, and rough edges had proved popular with Kentuckians, even as his discipline and refinement had set him apart from them. He was proud and not easily intimidated, crude yet struggling for a measure of refinement. By turns charming and abrasive, Solomon P. Sharp was the quintessential child of the West.

CHAPTER 2

The Diminutive Fury

Anna Cooke

And yet a headlong, headstrong, downright she,
Young, beautiful, and daring—who would risk
A throne, the world, the universe, to be
Beloved in her own way, and rather whisk
The stars from out the sky, than not be free
As are the billows when the breeze is brisk—
Though such a she's a devil (if that there be one)
Yet she would make full many a Manichean.

—Byron, *Don Juan,* canto 6, stanza 3

To dare to declare war, in however just a cause, against the opinion of one's age and country, a violent and adventurous spirit is required.

—Alexis de Tocqueville, *Democracy in America,* 2:207

Contemporaries thought her a "tigress," a "wretched female," an "evil genius"; historians have labeled her a "diminutive Fury," a "tawdry paramour"; and a small corps of novelists have portrayed her as a beautiful, cultured woman betrayed by the villainy of a heartless seducer. Whatever the merits of these descriptions—whether we see her as a heroine or villainess or an actual person—the fact remains that Anna Cooke was the pivotal figure of the entire episode, for it was she who set in motion the train of events that ended the lives of three people and gave birth to one of early America's most celebrated and enduring narratives.[1]

Anna is a mysterious and intriguing figure—no accurate likeness of her exists, and, as is the case with Sharp, little survives to tell us of the person. The one extended document supposedly written by her—*The Letters of Ann Cook*, published almost immediately after her death in 1826—is a forgery, the first pure fictionalization of the Kentucky Tragedy.[2] A few letters and a scattering of her poetry exist, but together they give us only the briefest glimpse into her mind and personality. Of course, others were quick to comment on her, but, as Robert Penn Warren wrote, "All of the descriptions come after the event, and the face they give us may be taken as a result rather than as a cause of the story."[3] The difficulty is compounded by the fact that the two most detailed depictions of Anna Cooke—one by her adoring husband and the other by the brother of the man who was murdered at her instigation—are hopelessly irreconcilable. It is possible, however, to piece together the outlines of her life and personality.[4]

She was born into the proud and slowly eroding society of Tidewater Virginia in February 1785.[5] The fifth child and first daughter of Giles and Alicia Payne Cooke, Anna grew up in a large household of nine brothers and one sister. Although the family's status in Virginia was later exaggerated in an effort to lend pathos to the Kentucky Tragedy, Giles Cooke's wealth was by no means insubstantial—by the early nineteenth century, he held title to twenty-two slaves, and his Fairfax County estate, located about ten miles southwest of Arlington, encompassed thousands of acres. The wealth and reputation of Anna's mother's side of the family—the Paynes—were greater still and included a connection with Dolley Payne Madison and an uncle who served as one of George Washington's pallbearers in 1799.[6]

Such "high and honorable" family relations granted young Anna access to a quality education, and although there is no record of her formal schooling, Anna's taste for literature and philosophy, as well as her unusually elegant handwriting, suggests substantial learning. Notwithstanding a later South's reputation for anti-intellectualism, the gentry of post-Revolutionary Virginia were remarkably literate: "The taste for reading," the Duke of La Rochefoucauld-Liancourt remarked of Virginians in the mid-1790s, "is commoner there among men of the first class than in any other part of America." Other members of the Cooke family were certainly well read. At their deaths, at least two of Anna's brothers owned dozens of books—a substantial and costly library for the early nineteenth century. Another brother, Peyton Cooke, "wrote a beautiful hand with the old fashioned quill pen."[7]

Their sister Anna belonged to the first generation of American females whose access to formal education was considered essential. In the late eighteenth century, girls' schools mushroomed across the young nation under the novel belief that young women should be trained to be literate, fashion-forsaking republican mothers. To mold the next generation of virtuous citizens, it had come to be thought, girls and young women must be well educated—and not just in social skills and household tasks, but in grammar, history, geography, mathematics, and rhetoric. Although more female academies were established in the North than in the South, many such schools were established in Virginia, and a man like Giles Cooke certainly had the means to send his oldest daughter to one. Not only did Anna most likely have access to a formal education, but her "uncommon energies of mind" suggest that she had a considerable appetite for learning. Her love for literature and poetry is obvious; in one of her few extant letters, for instance, she quotes lines from Alexander Pope's translation of the *Iliad.* A number of people later remarked on Anna's delight in discussing books, and she composed several pieces of poetry.[8]

The earliest years of the new century would have been Anna's glory days—her time to enter what the late-eighteenth-century novelist Hannah Webster Foster described as the "fashionable amusements of brilliant assemblies." It was then, in her late teens, that she would have been immersed in the rituals of courtship, a remarkable, exhilarating, and brief moment in the lives of southern women—or at least those women who, like Anna, "moved in the first circles of society." In an era in which mate selection was more and more becoming a matter of choice, young females—especially those gifted with charisma or talent or beauty—found themselves the center of attention and in possession of considerable power, a marked reversal of the formal and normative relations between the sexes.[9]

The Cookes, should they have resembled other gentry families of late-eighteenth-century Tidewater Virginia, would have stood on the near side of the gulf that separates modern, affectionate, child-centered family life from the patriarchal households that Virginians took for granted before 1750 or so. In that older world, relations within the household were much more formal and emotionally truncated, premised on dependence and reflexive obedience and characterized by relationships that appear to us as emotionally sterile. Such households resembled miniature kingdoms in which domestic tranquility, moderation, and restraint were prized above intimacy and emotional expression. Moreover, the line dividing the family and the community—the boundary between the private and the public—was much less distinct, as households carried out functions we today expect from hospitals, schools, orphanages, nursing homes, and asylums.[10]

In the second half of the eighteenth century, however, the Tidewater gentry remade the emotional and psychological texture of their domestic worlds. Family life was increasingly child centered, affectionate, insular, privatized, intimate, sentimental. And as the range of family functions narrowed, passions were redeployed, and emotional satisfaction was sought and secured more and more at home, among immediate family members, a process that attenuated the connections between the family and the surrounding community. So complete was this destruction of the patriarchal family that by 1831 Tocqueville wondered, "In America the family, in the Roman and aristocratic signification of the word, does not exist."[11]

With the end of the mannered, "aristocratic" family came an intensification of relationships between husbands and wives, brothers and sisters, parents and children. Yet if the emotional intensity was heightened, so too was the risk, for this new world of affection unbound was not the least bit healthier to live in, and the prospect of sudden and unexpected death was no less likely. To love so intensely in an age when life was so tenuous and death so commonplace was to tempt fate. Relatively few among the elite, moreover, looked to religion; if the turn-of-the-century Virginian gentry were postpatriarchal, they were also pre-evangelical, and the sense of resignation to the will of God had atrophied in the preceding decades. As one traveler commented in 1793, "The Virginians are wonderfully indifferent about public worship." Less able or willing to seek solace in faith or to submit to life's vicissitudes and tragedies, the more rationally inclined were left stranded, bereft of the emotional consolation of religion. Little wonder that Virginians of the late eighteenth century, as one historian notes, "seemed less able to control their sorrow when death crossed their families." The increasing sentimentalization of life in the early republic simultaneously raised the emotional pitch of family life and left Virginians less prepared to handle the trauma of a family member's demise.[12]

And thus all evidence suggests that the death of Anna's father, Giles Cooke, in 1805, when she was nineteen or twenty years old, was an extraordinary psychological and emotional blow. The culmination of her season of youth was not marriage to a handsome, accomplished suitor, but a tragedy that her world had left her unequipped to face. Twenty-one years later, Anna was still mourning his loss, writing of "that unknown abode / to which my father's spirit early fled."[13]

Emotionally traumatic, Giles's death was also a financial disaster for a family accustomed to the wealth and fashion of Tidewater Virginia. Within five years, Anna and her mother, sister, and at least five brothers left the land their kind had made for Kentucky's Green River country. They joined the steadily growing class of expatriate Virginians who fled the Old Dominion's "culture of decline" in search of a means to recoup their fading fortunes. For the Tidewater elite, a series of economic crises—soil exhaustion, falling tobacco prices, and a downward spiral of indebtedness—were compounded by social and cultural transformations, including the erosion of deference and the rise of evangelical religion. All combined to push even the once seemingly invulnerable families to the brink of economic ruin and social obsolescence. Like the Cookes, many Virginia families sold their depleted Virginian estates and, with what was left after settling debts, sought a new beginning farther west.[14]

Although the rude and unformed world of western Kentucky's Green River district was a jarring contrast to Tidewater Virginia, the Cookes adapted, garnering a great deal of respect because of their origins. The sons of Giles Cooke resurrected the family fortunes and before long "were among the most respectable in that section of the country." The family's wealth, though reduced, was still substantial: in 1810 the widow Alice claimed twelve slaves, and by the time of his death in February 1819, the estate of the oldest son, Giles Cooke, was valued at $5,516 and included ten slaves. Another son, John W. Cooke, owned a tavern and four slaves, and he served as justice of the peace and state assemblyman from Warren County. (His immediate successor, interestingly, was Solomon Sharp.)[15]

Though her brothers adapted well to the West—recouping lost fortunes as well as social and political influence—Anna's transition to the raw and alien world of western Kentucky was not nearly so smooth. She was, on the one hand, learned enough to question the dictates of her society and, on the other, torn from all she held dear—her father, her home, the world of her childhood and adolescence. In her confusion, disappointment, and anger, it seems she began to doubt the immutability of the early American social order, the justness of the world, and, finally, the very existence of God. "She believed," wrote Leander Sharp, who knew her well before the murder, that "mankind are brought into being with an entire right to dispose of their persons and lives as they please." She was, he continued, "wholly destitute . . . of moral and religious principles" and "believed in no future state of existence. . . . The whole Christian system she denounced as a fraud on mankind, propagated and sustained by cunning and priestcraft." Her husband, in much softer terms, described her as "a sort of Deist." It is very possible that Anna's education exposed her to radical religious ideas in her youth; William Ellery Channing, while living near Richmond, Virginia, just before the turn of the century, observed that "infidelity is very general among the higher classes." Yet whereas such skepticism may have been vaguely disreputable in a man, it was completely unacceptable for the "fairer sex"; such a woman, in Edmund Randolph's words, was "a monster."[16]

Anna, in her day, was not deemed especially attractive, despite the assertions of subsequent playwrights and novelists. According to one of the more or less dispassionate contemporary accounts, "For beauty, she was never remarkable." Even the man whom she eventually married, who killed in her name and wrote at length on her virtues, never described her appearance. The only detailed depiction of Anna comes from her most inveterate enemy, Dr. Leander Sharp, who wrote that she was "in no way a handsome or desirable woman." She was in fact, according to Sharp's doubtlessly unfair depiction, nearly hideous: "small in stature, probably not exceeding 90 pounds in weight, had dark hair and eyes, dark skin inclined to sallow, a large forehead, slender nose, large mouth, low chin, face tapering downwards, had lost her fore teeth, was stoop shouldered." Her personality, Sharp continued, added little: "Her tone of voice appeared to be affected even to childishness, and she was remarkably frivolous in her conversation."[17]

What Anna did in the fifteen years after her arrival in Kentucky is murky; what is most remarkable, however, is what she did not do: become a wife. Her refusal to wed was indeed exceptional, for it flew in the face of all that a young woman was taught in early America—it was a defiance of almost every aspect of a southern belle's socialization. What else could a woman do aside from getting married, raising children, and managing a household? The few appropriate alternatives available in the North dwindled to virtually none in the rural South. And remaining single does seem to have been Anna's choice—it would be hard to imagine that she had no suitors. When her family moved to Kentucky, she was still in her early twenties, the oldest daughter of a respected family from the beau monde of Tidewater Virginia. And if she was not beautiful, even her later enemies would concede that she was "vivacious," while more sympathetic observers thought she "possessed . . . a sprightliness and gaiety, which once made her the delight of the social circles in which she moved, and commanded the admiration of her acquaintances."[18]

Perhaps she was not impressed by the choice of young men of the area, convinced that no young man measured up to her own high origins of which she was so proud; later, she would repeatedly assert that she "had come of one among the best families in Virginia and had passed in the first circle of life." Perhaps she had no wish to trade the power and independence of maidenhood for the subservience of marriage. Tocqueville noted the immense chasm between these two stages of a young woman's life: "In America the independence of woman is irrecoverably lost in the bonds of matrimony. If an unmarried woman is less constrained there than elsewhere, a wife is subjected to stricter obligations. The former makes her father's house an abode of freedom and of pleasure; the latter lives in the home of her husband as if it were a cloister."[19]

Yet Anna's refusal to marry was but one instance of a larger pattern of defiance, for little of her behavior conformed to the emerging prescription for a proper southern woman. She "scoffed at the instruction of society"; all her sorrows, according to one commentator, flowed from her "fatal indifference to public opinion." She was an "unruly woman," one who bristled at the restraints of her gender, time, and place. Such was a rare breed, especially for one of her social status, and it earned her a reputation—probably well earned—of being "an avowed disciple of Mary Wollstonecraft." William T. Barry, chief justice of the "new" state supreme court, believed that Anna's entire life was a warning against such radical ideas, "a living example of the pernicious influence on the female mind of the detestable doctrines of Mary Wollstonecraft whose disciple she is."[20]

So unique, Anna's isolation must have been bitter. She sought out companionship and "was in the habit of visiting many of the most respectable families in Bowling Green." Among these families in the Green River area were the Sharps, and in fact the two families—one rising from obscurity, the other descending from eminence—were well acquainted. Eliza Sharp later wrote that "the respectable connections of Miss Cook were among [Solomon's] most intimate acquaintances," and Leander Sharp claimed to have known Anna as early as 1807. Yet Anna, given her uncommon beliefs and behavior, unsettled many of her neighbors. Eliza later claimed to have found Anna "not only unacceptable, but often disgusting," while Dr. Sharp thought that "her society was sought rather for merriment than instruction, or any other rational enjoyment." The wife of General E. M. Covington prohibited Anna from even setting foot in her house. And little wonder; as Victoria Bynum has written, "so inculcated were the values of purity and chastity among upper and middle-class southern white women that few understood women who were forced or tempted by circumstances to defy the norms of social behavior."[21]

Shunned by her peers, Anna found solace in "drawing, painting, or other amusements." But it was reading she enjoyed most, and in time she had amassed an extensive personal library of works of history, philosophy, and, especially, the illicit novels popular in her day. She had consumed a great number of these works and "delighted to converse upon scenes of romance and fiction." In the early republic, by far the most popular form of the genre—virtually the only form—was the seduction novel. Works such as Susanna Haswell Rowson's *Charlotte Temple* (1794) and Hannah Webster Foster's *The Coquette* (1797) were ostensibly written to caution women against making unwise and immoral choices during courtship, that moment of power and decision. Anna was not unusual in being drawn to novels; suffused with themes of passion and sexuality and tragedy, these sentimental tales were widely read in the early republic, especially by females. Such makes sense, for outside religious tracts, in no other literature were women front and center. It is also logical that Anna would be especially drawn to novels, for most of the plots of these sentimental novels focused on unmarried women who often made bold and unconventional, if disastrous, decisions.[22]

For aging, unmarried white women, any substantial delay of marriage almost inevitably elicited rumors of sexual misbehavior. Those who did not submit to the bonds of marriage were liable to be dealt with harshly. And so it was with Anna, who, Leander Sharp alleged, had "for many years, been guilty of shameless prostitution." Sharp also retailed malicious gossip that Anna "practiced shameless adultery and prostitution while her husband was confined in the jail in Frankfort, for the murder," and that she even propositioned two of the guards who escorted her to Frankfort. But Dr. Sharp did give evidence for Anna's unorthodox sexual behavior, lining up several deponents who swore that Anna was widely known for her "loose character"—that "she had been in the habit of illicit intercourse with men *for ten years*"; that she had been considered "not a little remarkable . . . for great lasciviousness of sentiment and manners." Sharp relayed that Anna was known for taking long, unescorted walks into the countryside, "and when reminded of its impropriety by any of her female acquaintances, and of the remarks to which it might give occasion, she declared she cared not what was said—that, people would always find something to talk about." Anna was, in the opinion of one newspaper editor, "deplorably lost to some of the noblest and most sacred duties of her sex."[23]

We do not have to accept Leander Sharp's characterization of Anna as a "shameless prostitute" to conclude that she was, by the standards of the day, unconventional. That Anna rejected her world's sexual restrictions comports well with what we know about her own penchant to "scoff at the instruction of society." And it also accords with what we know about the South in post-Revolutionary America and, in particular, about the revolution in sexual behavior in the earliest years of the new republic.

The South and especially its backcountry—of which Kentucky was an extension—had always been relatively at ease with human sensuality. Departures from the sexual conventions of colonial and Revolutionary America—premarital sex, common law marriages, serial monogamy, bigamy—were more common in the southern backcountry than anywhere else in British North America. At a time when legal and political officials shouldered much of the responsibility for regulating sexual behavior, it was precisely in those areas where authority was least secure that sexual behavior was most uninhibited. Late colonial commentators recoiled at the sexual license of the frontier. Charles Woodmason, an Anglican minister intent on spreading the gospel to the great unwashed of the Carolina backcountry, was appalled by the "gross licentiousness, wantonness, lasciviousness, rudeness, lewdness, and profligacy" he found there. In 1762, Daniel Boone—the prototypical Kentuckian—returned to his home in western Virginia after an absence of two years to find his wife with a newborn baby girl, Jemima. The father of the child, the story goes, was Daniel's brother. Boone's response? "So much the better, it's all in the family." In 1809, John Clary of Perquimans County, North Carolina, was elected to the state assembly despite the widely known fact that he had recently impregnated his stepdaughter. The South's greater freedom of sexual expression was especially clear to a surprised and delighted twenty-six-year-old Benjamin Gilbert, a Massachusetts native stationed in Kings County, Virginia, during the Revolutionary War. Gilbert found the young women of Virginia to be "exceedingly amouris" and was astounded that "amouris intrigues and gallantry are every where approved of in this state, and amongst the vulgar any man that is given to concupiscence may have his fill."[24]

Intersecting with and augmenting this greater tolerance of sexuality in the late eighteenth century was a continent-wide revolution in sexual behavior among the young. The rebellion against Britain, it seems, had inaugurated a widespread questioning of authority and dependencies of all types, including that of parents over the sexuality of adolescents and young adults. At the same time, expanding opportunities for education imparted a sense that social arrangements were arbitrary and mutable. In sum, an all-encompassing idea spread throughout society that the individual was at liberty to pursue "happiness"—itself freely defined by the individual pursuer. It was a recipe for generational rebellion, and the effects were apparent as the nation's youth quickly translated this individualism and skepticism toward received authority into greater personal and sexual freedom. The key indicator of the late-eighteenth-century sexual revolution—as has been noted by a number of historians—was a marked increase in rates of premarital pregnancy. In terms of sexual mores, it was at once an era of great upheaval and of lax regulation, a period between the externally enforced morality of colonial America and the interior discipline of nineteenth-century America that would be fostered by the Second Great Awakening.[25]

In early 1820, the word quickly spread around Warren County: Anna Cooke—thirty-five, unconventional, and unmarried—was pregnant. In June she delivered a stillborn baby. "Of this child," exclaimed a still-incredulous Dr. Sharp seven years later, "she declared that Col. Sharp was the father!" Anna even specified the date of the supposed liaison: September 18, 1819, on a Sunday while Eliza Sharp was at church.[26]

This, of course, is the origin of the accusation, later brought forth by Jereboam Beauchamp and by Sharp's political enemies, that Sharp had seduced and abandoned a poor, innocent girl. The charge, thus stated, is scarcely plausible. An essential component of seduction, as understood in the early nineteenth century, was the promise of marriage—that is, the seducer persuaded a virginal young woman to surrender under the pretense that they would soon be wed. But in 1819, Solomon Sharp was already married, and everyone, including Anna, knew it. In addition, Anna's youth had long since begun to fade, and in no sense was she naive or ignorant of sexual matters. Dr. Sharp, in his subsequent defense of his brother, lined up dozens of respected citizens of the Green River area who well knew the Sharps and the Cookes to attest that the seduction story was "false," "slanderous," "malicious," and "ridiculous." James C. Cravens, for one, announced that the seduction story "deserves but little notice," for Anna was a "girl of good mind" and had "a full knowledge of Col. Sharp being a married man and living in perfect peace and harmony with his family in the same town."[27]

But the Sharp family ultimately rested their rebuttal of Anna's accusation on evidence of her past sexual improprieties. According to both Leander and

Eliza Sharp, the family's "deep mortification" was allayed when John Keel of Bowling Green (according to Eliza, "a highly respectable citizen and friend") relayed to them a letter written by Anderson Reavis, a young man who, along with Anna, had lived at John W. Cooke's boardinghouse. This document, dated August 18, 1820, completely convinced Eliza "of the foulness of the charge, and of her husband's innocence." Interestingly, the letter, which Leander Sharp later reprinted in his *Vindication,* states only that Reavis, while staying at Cooke's tavern two years before the alleged seduction, had stumbled upon Anna and another man "in a carnal connection with each other." Reavis had gone to feed his horses, and on returning to the house, "before I put my hand on the latch, it was pulled about half open, when I perceived it to be Miss Ann Cook. I then stopped and gave her the door. As she passed me she spoke these words, '*there is nobody there.*' I made her no answer. I then pushed the door open, when I saw a man standing against the partition." As further evidence of Anna's unconventional sexual behavior, Dr. Sharp insisted that a number of men "kept her as a mistress"; one, a mechanic in Bowling Green, "often declared, that he was much more likely to be the father of her child than Col. Sharp." Mrs. Francis Johnson claimed to have witnessed a "most shameful incident," an "assignation" between Anna and a young man who lived in her house. Wade McFaddin swore that Anna had been known to be "a base woman" years before her accusation against Sharp, while D. Turney, who lived at John Cooke's tavern at the same time as Anna, considered her "a woman without virtue or female chastity."[28]

The details of such testimony aside, the interesting point is that the mere charge of Anna's sexual misconduct was enough, in the eyes of the Sharp family and the local community, to clear Solomon. The family's defense gave no direct evidence that he had not or could not have seduced Anna or that he was not or could not have been the father of the child. As Dr. Sharp quite forthrightly put it, Colonel Sharp "rested his vindication, on his own irreproachable character, the improbability of the story at that particular period in his life, and Ann Cook's infamy of character." One critic of the Sharps charged that the "only pretense at apology for this unhallowed act" had been "previous knowledge of the ill fame of this unfortunate young woman."[29]

The picture that emerges is one in which Anna Cooke, because of her violation of early-nineteenth-century sexual boundaries, had effectively forfeited any protection or sympathy reserved for "dishonored" females. The clearest evidence for this, and most damaging to Anna's later story of seduction and innocence betrayed, was the inaction of her brothers at the time of the accusation. She later insisted that she was *feme sole* at the time of her "seduction," a woman bereft of male protection, for "my father, brother, sister and friends were all dead!" She was, she claimed, "a defenseless female," "an innocent," who was "unjustly robbed of character" by "an insidious villain."[30]

It was true that a number of Anna's family members had died in rapid succession. In a remarkable series of misfortunes, between 1817 and 1823, six of her siblings living in Kentucky passed away: Anna's only sister, Elizabeth, died in 1817, followed shortly by her brothers Thomas (1818), Giles (1819), John (1821), Littleton (1822), and William (1823). By 1823, only Anna, her brother Peyton, and their aging mother were left.

Yet contrary to Anna's later claims, at least four of her brothers were alive at the time of her pregnancy in 1819–1820, and three of them lived within a few miles of her. Strikingly, as historian J. W. Cooke has made clear, none of them attempted to exact revenge on Sharp; none of them seemed "to have thought her virtue worth defending." At the time, the brothers' refusal to do anything did not go unnoticed. One pamphleteer taunted the Cookes, "Long have we been amazed at the tacit submission of the relations of this young lady and the torpid forbearance of this injured family."[31]

For the day and age, such "tacit submission" and "torpid forbearance" were indeed remarkable. Throughout the young nation, any sort of sexual predation was very likely to be met with violent reprisal. As Tocqueville noted, "Americans can conceive nothing more precious than a woman's honor." In the South, this morbid sensitivity veered perilously close to psychosis, in which any sexual aggression toward a female member of the family was tantamount, as Bertram Wyatt-Brown has explained, to an assault on a man himself: "Fierce retaliation was therefore mandatory when a daughter, wife or mother had been dishonored." However relaxed early southerners may have been toward certain sexual behaviors, they were extraordinarily rigid in this respect. Ben Hardin, a congressional colleague of Sharp's, declared that seduction was "an outrageous insult" in which "the offender is generally shot down at once, and he is served pretty near right in having the thing administered to him in that way." The outrage, moreover, would not originate solely from the offended family but from society as a whole, as Michel Chevalier quickly learned upon arriving in the United States: "The man who should seduce a woman or be known to have an illicit connection would be excommunicated by the popular clamor." In fact, the "unwritten law" was becoming an acceptable defense strategy that, according to Robert M. Ireland, convinced juries, especially but not exclusively in the South, that "an outraged husband, father, or brother could justifiably kill the alleged libertine who had been sexually intimate with the defendant's wife, daughter, or sister."[32]

Conversely, however, if a woman was not deceived or "dishonored" in some fashion—if she was sexually licentious—then as a matter of course the object of wrath became the woman herself, for such a woman not only surrendered her own virtue but compromised the honor of male family members and brought shame on the entire family. And thus the fact that Anna's brothers did nothing in response to her charges against Solomon Sharp speaks volumes. Indeed, Dr. Sharp claimed that her brother John "was so well satisfied of his sister's lewd conduct that he often expressed to me his regret that he had for a moment entertained an ill feeling towards Col. Sharp." When all was said and done, the brothers not only did not attempt to exact revenge on Colonel Sharp but, as Eliza Sharp later attested, "were willing to testify to the world their conviction of his innocence by employing him in their business."[33]

As J. W. Cooke—himself a descendant of Anna's—wrote, "One can only speculate at the depths of humiliation Anna must have felt at this rebuke. From that moment she may well have begun to think of herself as an orphan." Years later, on the day before her death, Anna wrote of her "brothers brave / who left me early to the storms of fate." Ostensibly, the line is meant to mislead the reader into believing that the deaths of her brothers exposed her to the wiles of a seducer, yet Anna may well have been expressing an honest emotion—her sense that her brothers really did leave her to the "storms of fate" when they did not rally to her side after she accused Sharp.[34]

And thus, "disgusted with the greater part of the world," Anna later wrote, "I entered into retirement." There, surrounded by an impressive library of sentimental literature, Anna immersed herself in a world of beautiful and accomplished women, who, after falling prey to heartless rakes, gave birth to stillborn children. Doubtlessly, Anna related very well to such stories.[35]

Yet a question remains: Did Anna and Solomon have a sexual relationship? We do not know and in all likelihood never will, but a few suppositions may be hazarded. Certainly, nothing—outside the specious claims of Anna and her future husband and the overheated imaginations of later dramatists—suggests that, if such a relationship occurred, it was a seduction in any sense understood by early-nineteenth-century Americans. As one newspaper wrote, Anna was well aware that Solomon was married, and thus "she knew that she could not innocently indulge an attachment for him; and that no promise of fidelity on his part, could be executed, or be sincere." What she seems to have been was a remarkably unconventional woman and, more to the point, a sexually unconventional woman.[36]

But, as earlier historians of the Kentucky Tragedy noted, circumstantial evidence suggests that Anna and Solomon may have had a relationship before 1818. Solomon's home in Warren County was near John W. Cooke's residence, where Anna lived. The two certainly had known each other since at least 1807. We know that Anna was no stranger to the Sharp household after their marriage—despite Eliza's misgivings—and it is very probable that she was a frequent visitor before the marriage as well. They were roughly the same age, although Anna was one or two years older than Solomon. They had similar interests: Both dabbled in romantic poetry—he more than once recited verse on the floor of Congress, and she regularly composed verse literally until the day she died. Both enjoyed reading—Anna's extensive library and voracious reading have already been noted, and although direct evidence of Solomon's reading habits is sparse, we do know that Joseph Underwood, a native of Warren County who was studying at Transylvania University, in a letter home casually mentioned meeting Sharp in a Lexington bookstore. Both possessed dynamic personalities and each delayed marriage a decade or more past the norm; both were mature—in the fall of 1818, she would have been thirty-two or thirty-three, he thirty-one. Her Tidewater background may well have impressed the handsome and successful parvenu Sharp, one of the most eligible bachelors in the state. Anna was refined and "vivacious" and, at least for the day and age, sexually liberated. One contemporary claimed that neither Anna nor Solomon believed "that it was necessary to marry; that persons might co-habit under the impulse of desires." It is speculation, certainly, but it would seem to be plausible that they had a sexual relationship previous to Sharp's marriage.[37]

Another clue is the timing of the alleged tryst that resulted in Anna's pregnancy. When Anna conceived, Sharp had been married for almost a year, and his wife Eliza was eight and a half months pregnant with their first child. Early-nineteenth-century authorities on women's health—such as they were—uniformly discouraged sex during pregnancy. As William Buchan, at the time a widely read authority on pregnancy and child rearing, discreetly put it,

> Curb each loose desire
> Lest added fuel quench the former fire
> lest ye should lose the fruits of pleasure gone
> and love itself undo what love had done.

Deprived of sex during their wives' pregnancies, many men looked elsewhere for relief, and indeed such affairs were common enough that southerners had a special term—the "gander months"—for the later stages of a pregnancy, when husbands were more likely to seek sex outside marriage. The *1811 Dictionary of the Vulgar Tongue* suggests the casual, even facetious manner in which men viewed the "custom," defining the "gander month" as "that month in which a man's wife lies in: wherefore, during that time, husbands plead a sort of indulgence in matters of gallantry." Without sexual access to his wife, Solomon may well have returned to the arms of a previous lover, Anna.[38]

And thus a plausible scenario would posit an intermittent but long-term sexual relationship between Anna and Solomon before he marries. But whether because of Anna's dim view of marriage or because the ambitious Sharp knows that her unorthodox ways disqualify her from becoming the wife he needs to advance in the world, they never marry. Past his thirty-first birthday, Sharp weds the beautiful, young, and well-connected Eliza Scott. After the Sharps settle in Warren County, Eliza becomes pregnant, and Sharp, deprived of sex for months on end, returns to Anna. She too becomes pregnant, but because Anna has never played by the rules of the sexual game, her predicament is viewed as just punishment and her brothers do nothing. Thus abandoned by both her family and her lover, she becomes embittered, "one whose life's bright noon," she later wrote, was "darkened quick by night's black hue."[39]

Anna's descent into darkness paralleled Kentucky's own. After a series of dire economic portents throughout early 1818—slipping prices for agricultural products and a spike in forced debt collections and court-ordered seizures of property—financial ruin descended on the country in early 1819. "Sudden as if by the magic wand of some potent sorcerer," according to one stunned observer, Kentucky was "but the shadow of what it was": "Cold, heart-chilling poverty, with her train of misery and vice, no longer confines herself to the hovel of habitual infamy and squalid idleness, but alike knocks and enters, as does the great king of terrors, into the palace and the cottage. A great terror seems to have come upon the people, and a melancholy sensation of despair seems to have settled on every brow."[40] At first, it was the speculators and merchants and others directly plugged into the national economy who felt the financial crush. But soon, the agricultural majority understood the suffering as well. "The farmer is become as poor as a rat," one contemporary reported; "the labor of the farm costs him more than the produce is worth. He cannot pay the storekeeper, and the storekeeper cannot pay the merchant."[41]

As the terrible depths of the republic's first full-blown economic depression became apparent, Kentuckians desperately searched for the cause of their suffering, and although there was no unanimity, most explanations eventually led to the banks. Some blamed the creation of the independent banks; others blamed the establishment of the Second Bank of the United States; still others blamed the attempt to tax the Bank of the United States. Unfortunately for Solomon Sharp, at one time or another he was closely associated with every one of these initiatives.

The independent banks—whose establishment Sharp had supported—were extraordinarily controversial from the moment of their creation, drawing the fire of those with interests in rival banks, fiscal conservatives, and antibanking purists alike. Denounced as "thieves" and "rag companies," the independent banks never gained the indispensable attribute for any financial institution: confidence. The conservative editor of the *Lexington Western Monitor,* arguing that such financial power was best left in the hands of more experienced and cautious institutions, denounced the independent bank bill as "one of the wildest acts of legislation ever known in our state." Others were outraged at the banks' lack of oversight; it was impolitic and unsafe to sanction the establishment of monied institutions in the "management of which the state was to have no control."[42]

Of course, the Second Bank of the United States—the establishment of which Sharp had also voted for—never lacked for enemies. It was a "MONSTER," an "engine of power," and "one of the greatest curses that ever afflicted our country, and to her may be attributed the principal cause of our present difficulties and embarrassments." Others retained their faith in the national bank and deplored the General Assembly's attempt to run branches out via taxation—an enterprise that Sharp, having second thoughts about the wisdom of inviting the national bank into Kentucky, had sponsored. The tax was, according to one commentator, "outrageously violent in its provisions." The national bank's defenders, which included the editors of several state newspapers, argued that the institution—by supplying financial oversight, by ensuring a uniform currency, and by forcing state and local banks to curtail paper issues and to maintain specie payments—had been a stabilizing force in the state's economy. Moreover, they contended that the attempt to run the national bank out of Kentucky originated not in a disinterested defense of republican principle but in the resentment of selfish and greedy speculators—the "vultures of society" who wished to be free of the regulation and discipline enforced by the national bank. Such is why Sharp, so closely associated with the taxation bill, was berated in the pages of the *Kentucky Gazette.* The attack on the U.S. bank, the letter writer Hampden claimed, was "one great cause of the present reduced price of tobacco, and other productions of agriculture." Still worse, he declared, the measure, by attacking one of the few national institutions that the young nation could claim, would "sow the seeds of discord and civil war amongst the states" and "eventually have produced a dissolution of the union." By attempting to transform the union into "a mere rope of sand," Sharp, along with other supporters of the bill, Hampden affirmed, were no better than the Hartford conventionists. That Sharp as a congressman in 1816 had voted to charter the second national bank carried little weight with his critics, only proving that he was a "trimmer," the nineteenth-century equivalent of a "flip-flopper."[43]

Thus Sharp, for the second time in only three years, found himself in serious political jeopardy. Caught in a political crossfire, he was denounced by all sides, and in August 1819, Sharp, who had never before lost an election to the state legislature, came in third in a field of four. The *Kentucky Gazette* gloated that "the non-election of this trimmer between parties is one of the happiest occurrences that could have taken place in our election."[44]

That fall, as expected, agricultural prices collapsed. But for Kentucky's farmers, it hardly mattered, because no rain fell between May and November 1819, and most of the state's corn, wheat, and tobacco had withered in the fields. The *Frankfort Argus of Western America* reported that "the earth is parched, vegetation has perished, people and stock are suffering for water." By the end of 1819, in some parts of central Kentucky, water imported from seven miles away sold for five dollars a barrel. Low water in the region's rivers brought what commercial activity survived the Panic to a standstill: "For the last seven months our eastern as well as southern commerce has been almost entirely suspended," recounted the *Kentucky Reporter* in January 1820. "We have found it impossible to bring from Pittsburgh or Orleans, many highly essential articles. The same causes have prevented the exportation of our tobacco, flour, whiskey, etc and thereby greatly increased the distress of our citizens." In his December 1819 opening address to the General Assembly, Governor Gabriel Slaughter, a Baptist lay preacher, wondered if the judgment of God had descended on the land: "Are we not admonished by the deficiency of our crops, of our *dependence* upon the ruler of the skies for means necessary to our sustenance, and of the necessity of propitiating by every good word and work the great ruler of the seasons?"[45]

As Sharp retired to his law practice in Bowling Green, Kentucky's Twenty-eighth General Assembly convened in October 1819. Amid the turbulence and desperation, one newspaper related, "The people of Kentucky have their eyes fixed on their representatives, and with palpitating hearts, await in the development of their views, the decision of their fate." That a relief program would be inaugurated was pretty much beyond dispute; the question was what sort of relief. Lawmakers had three basic types of relief legislation from which to choose. First were a cluster of postponement laws, variously known as "replevin laws," "stay laws," or "stop laws," which essentially suspended the collection process and, in the case of replevin laws, allowed the debtor to reclaim previously seized property and thereafter delay repayment of a debt for a given period of time. A second option was a minimum valuation law—what many called "property law"—which stipulated that property sold to satisfy a judgment must bring a certain percentage of its predepression value, rather than whatever the postdepression market would bear. Lastly, proponents of relief could propose inflationary measures, which usually took the form of suspension of specie payments by preexisting banks or, more radically, the creation of state banks for the express purpose of issuing unredeemable bank notes. (Other ancillary relief laws were more ameliorative, including those that put certain classes of property—clothing, bedding, furniture, eating utensils, and tools of trade—beyond the reach of creditors. Kentucky passed such a law in 1815 and added to its provisions in 1820.)[46]

Despite what later historians would assume, relief laws were neither unusual nor radical; during economic crises in early America, the public in fact expected such legislation. Replevin laws, for example, dated from the colonial era and had recently been passed by several states, including Virginia and, in 1792, 1799, 1808, and 1814, Kentucky. Nor was such legislation widely believed to be unconstitutional. In 1792, Kentucky's First General Assembly—which included a good number of men who had only months earlier framed the state's constitution—passed a three-quarters property law with little controversy. As a later Kentucky governor affirmed, "The states had been in the habit of passing [relief laws] from the adoption of the constitution 'without objection.'"[47]

Thus the conventional wisdom in late 1819 held that the assembly would, at a minimum, order the Bank of Kentucky to suspend specie payments, enact a property law, and allow debts to be replevined for at least a year. The first two proposals, however, were ultimately rejected, less a product of a united opposition than of a disunited group of advocates. Rather than closing ranks on one type of relief measure, legislators endlessly squabbled over which would best answer the state's needs. Debate quickly descended into a morass of pointless argument, complete with assemblymen "grossly insult[ing] each other" and "calling each other rude names." An aging Matthew Lyon, certainly no stranger to legislative conflict, exclaimed, "In all my long life I never saw so many opinions among so small a number of wise men pitted against one another."[48]

Finally, on February 11, 1820, after more than two months of debate, the state assembly passed a replevin law that allowed debtors to postpone repayment of debt for twelve months if their creditors would take the notes of the Bank of Kentucky, which had suspended specie payments, thus making its paper more available, and two years if they would not. Yet the replevin law scarcely satisfied a great number of Kentuckians because it contained a class bias. The law chiefly benefited debtors of some consequence, for to obtain a replevin bond one had to secure the endorsement of an established member of the community who would guarantee the debtor's future solvency. As one exasperated correspondent to a local newspaper complained, "The poor man . . . will not be able to collect his debts of the wealthy, but not being able to give satisfactory security, will be obliged to pay all he owes, or take the consequences." The *Lexington Public Advertiser* demanded of the assemblymen, "Have you so long lived at Frankfort in ease and luxury, as to have lost all recollection of the miseries of your fellow citizens?" All in all, as former U.S. senator John Brown accurately assessed, "It is . . . the singular misfortune of the body which has just been dissolved, to have left *every* portion of the people dissatisfied."[49]

Moreover, by merely delaying the repayment of debts, the assembly had done nothing to allay the widespread fear that forced debt collections would so unsettle property ownership that "this once delightful land will become a country of lords and tenants." Representative Henry Daniel, for one, warned that the "country where the bulk of the people do not hold and enjoy property never was nor ever can be a land of liberty." His colleague, Thomas P. Moore, worried that nothing would be left in Kentucky but "wealthy *nabobs* and abject poverty." "Unless there be more protection to property," asked the *Kentucky Gazette,* "how long can we expect to live without seeing a monopoly?" Such concentration of wealth raised fears of a world in which "a few lordly tyrants, exclusive possessors of the soil, would hold the rod of persecution over us, and ultimately cast us into a political slavery more abject than that of the meanest subject of the meanest monarch on earth." Such expressions were neither demagogic nor instances of mere rhetoric: As debt collections proceeded apace, the Bank of the United States shortly became the largest proprietor of real estate in Lexington and Frankfort. The Bank of Kentucky, meanwhile, in a two-day period, brought 275 suits for the collection of $887,154. Merchants initiated thousands more, and within two years of economic collapse, the courts had conveyed to banks, merchants, and other creditors a full one-third of the state's property. The *Lexington Public Advertiser* reported that "there is more money due to the banks than the whole landed property of the state would sell for—so that the whole will belong to the banks."[50]

In such a situation, pro-relief candidates predictably swept the field in the summer elections of 1820, including the governorship. That fall, as the economy continued its downward spiral, the legislature set to work, this time determined not to fall short of the public's expectations. In his annual address to the General Assembly, the newly elected governor, John Adair, directed the legislature to broaden the coverage of the laws: "It will be for you, gentlemen," he announced, "to adopt and enact such measures as will contribute most to alleviate distress, to prevent useless and impolitic sacrifices of property." In addition to strengthening and extending the existing replevin law, the General Assembly on November 29, 1820, chartered the Bank of the Commonwealth and thus laid the cornerstone of the relief program. The bank had virtually no specie; its capital, rather, was land—a resource more tangible than and at least as trustworthy to the farming majority as gold and silver. Moreover, the bank's architects designed it for the benefit not of the speculator but of the small debtor, authorizing the bank to loan no more than one thousand dollars to any Kentuckian, and then only "for the purpose of paying his, her or their just debts, or for the purpose of purchasing the live stock or produce of the country for exportation." Whereas other banks acted as semiprivate "investment clubs" for bank directors and their connections, the legislature chartered the Bank of the Commonwealth for the express purpose of "making loans for longer periods than has been customary, and for the relief of the distresses of the community." The relief system had been democratized.[51]

A year later the legislature—once again overwhelmingly composed of relief partisans—completed the relief system with the passage of a minimum valuation law, by which the General Assembly mandated that any property sold under execution must bring three-quarters of its predepression value. Many Kentuckians had long called for such a law to prevent the prevailing "monstrous sacrifices of real estate." In postdepression markets, property sold to satisfy a creditor's claim brought but a fraction of its former value. In Lexington, for example, a two-story, eight-room house on Main Street was sold for six hundred dollars; another that had been purchased for fifteen thousand dollars three years before sold at auction for thirteen hundred dollars. "All the property of the country seemed doomed to be sold, and yet not pay half the debts. The first plantations were going for a mere song."[52]

Together, the Bank of the Commonwealth and the 1821 property law were designed to remedy the most immediate and most deeply felt consequence of nineteenth-century financial depressions: rampant, wholesale deflation. As Richard Hofstadter perceived sixty years ago, "To one who owes money and finds it hard to come by, economic hardship appears in its simplest guise as a shortage of money." So it was in the wake of the economic collapse of 1819: "So scarce is money of a sound character," one essayist reported, "that you are really disabled from paying your taxes, or procuring the common necessities of life." The letter writer Gracchus accurately summed up the sense of the people, referring to "these times of *pecuniary famine*."[53]

The flip side of a perilously short money supply was that the value of what currency could be procured increased exponentially. One thousand dollars in 1817 might buy fifty to one hundred acres of unimproved land; one thousand dollars in 1820 would buy a lavish estate. In terms of real value, in other words, debtors were being forced to pay back amounts worth many times their original loans. Such a state of affairs was manifestly unfair, according to one state senate committee, which declared that creditors at no time have the right "to take advantage of adventitious circumstances, to demand from [debtors] and coerce *ten times the [original] amount*." To enforce a contract as if nothing had happened in the meantime—that is, to believe in the modern notion, just then emerging, that value was a function of the market price at a given moment—struck many early Americans as little short of madness. As William Gouge, no admirer of relief legislation himself, wrote in 1833, "It is an awful thing to change the money standard of a country: but it is equally awful to refuse to recognize such a change, after it has actually been made." This helps us understand the logic of paper issue, the inflationary tendencies of which were meant to offset rampant and ruinous deflation. It was a logical, equitable means of returning the value of the currency to some semblance of its predepression level—to the value of the money originally lent. Thus, although many later historians would unfairly label the Bank of the Commonwealth a "grand swindling concern," its notes served the purpose for which they were designed.[54]

And so the Bank of the Commonwealth, despite having less than $3,000 of specie in its vaults, attempted to reinflate the economy by issuing almost $2.5 million worth of loans to Kentuckians within a year of its establishment. By May 1821 a correspondent to the *Frankfort Argus of Western America* reported, "Already have I seen unfortunate victims of the times come out of the door of this temple of relief with countenances beaming with hope and joy." Governor Adair credited the institution with saving "a considerable portion of the debtor population of the community from poverty and ruin." With no specie to back up the paper, however, the commonwealth's notes depreciated rapidly. One Kentuckian noted that he had "at least a horse load" of the bank's notes and dryly added that "my neighbors are equally well off." In the end, however, as one supporter admitted, "the money is bad," but "it is better than none," and the commonwealth's bank daily became more popular. One disgusted relief opponent related, "The candidates seem all to think it necessary to ensure their election, to vow allegiance to the Commonwealth's Bank."[55]

Far more unexpected and novel than the relief movement was the formation of an "anti-relief" opposition. Their argument, boiled down to essentials, was that the replevin laws, the Bank of the Commonwealth, and the property law were all "flagrant violations" of state and federal constitutions, socially disruptive, and, as "partial legislation," patently unfair to creditors. Citing article 1, section 10 of the U.S. Constitution, which enforces the obligation of contract, the anti-reliefers—or "anties" as they were called—at once drew on a fear of constitutional degeneration and a deep and powerful current in American political thought that stressed the inviolability of written compacts. "For what was the constitution of the country created?" Hampden cried in the pages of the *Kentucky Gazette*. "If it were intended to yield to times or circumstances, why adopt it? Why place around us barriers, and swear not to overleap them? If the constitution of the country be found insufficient for the great purposes of government; let us in the manner agreed upon, alter, reform, or abolish it." One conservative paper warned, "Whenever the people disregard the written constitution of their country, political evils without number befall them." There was an essential accuracy to the opposition's critique; the framers of the U.S. Constitution had deliberately attempted to eliminate this very sort of state-level legislation.[56]

A still more fundamental fear of the anti-relief faction was that the relief laws were ripping apart the social fabric—weakening the bonds between "man and man" (a phrase endlessly repeated by opponents of the relief program) created by economic transactions. "Legislative interference with private contracts," the anti-relief *Lexington Western Monitor* typically protested, "tends to diminish, if not destroy, that mutual confidence between man and man, that firm reliance on the steadiness of law and the regular course of justice, which are essential to the prosperity of every community." Apocalyptic visions of social and moral anarchy were commonplace in opposition newspapers: "If you suffer your laws to be given to you any longer by the relief party, society will be unhinged, constitutional freedom will be lost, and government will no longer possess those captivating charms which animated and directed our brave ancestors while fighting the sacred battles of liberty." Convinced that Kentucky's commercial infrastructure had rescued the West from barbarism and disorder, anti-relief partisans insisted that their opponents' policies would drag Kentucky back to its earliest days of "savagery and indolence." By destroying the banks, introducing a "currency purely local," assaulting the constitution, and interfering with the creditor-debtor relationship, the relief majority had unleashed "the sovereignty of passion," a "new kind of liberty—the liberty of nature, not of society; of the savage, not of the civilized man." The legislature's disrespect of the law, they argued, would rip apart the very fabric of society:

> We see, or hear, every day of the most daring and most atrocious murders and robberies. From the highest to the lowest in society men are turned out cut-throats and assassins. I hazard nothing in asserting the fact to be that more flagitious and enormous crimes have been perpetrated within the last two years than for twenty years before. Why all this? Because men are taught to contemn good order, and to be regardless of all subordination to the law. Those bonds of civil society which bind us together have been burst asunder, and we are about to revert back to a state of original barbarism.

Thus, the anties proclaimed, the relief system "goes far beyond the simple fraud of substituting paper for money; it is to confirm and establish a revolution."[57]

Such objections, although widely publicized through the state's numerous anti-relief newspapers, went unheeded in the first two or three years after the Panic hit. The opposition could not slow the relief juggernaut; even their most eloquent and talented leaders did well just to get elected. In the summer elections of 1821, one such leader, Robert Wickliffe, polled only 5 percent of the vote in his reelection bid as Fayette County state representative, finishing eighth in a field of nine. The relief program, for the moment, was far too popular for the opposition to bridle.[58]

Yet relief partisans, still holding to Jeffersonian precepts of minimalist, unobtrusive government, shared at least some of the concerns of the anti-relief opposition and were not entirely comfortable with their own program. "In common times," one relief partisan took pains to point out, "we should certainly say away with all property laws—all banking systems, and give us nothing but gold and silver." Governor Adair, as firmly pro-relief as any man in the state government, announced that even though the Bank of the Commonwealth had "saved this community from the severest suffering, and the hazard of civil commotion," all "temporary expedients to regulate the exchanges of paper securities, and all attempts by mere legislative declarations, to affix to them a standard value, are the very worst sorts of political empiricism." The alacrity with which the relief partisans destroyed their own creation confirmed the expedient nature of the legislation. When the Thirty-first General Assembly met in October of 1822 amid signs of economic recovery, Adair opened the session with what Henry Clay—himself ever careful not to publicize his opposition to the relief program—called "quite an Anti-Relief message." Arguing that the relief measures "have completely realized their proposed ends," Adair advocated a return to "normal" economic affairs. On December 7, the legislature overwhelmingly (seventy-one to twenty-five in the house, twenty-two to twelve in the senate) adopted a measure that effectively nullified the property law and dictated that after June 1, 1824, all contracts would be recoverable in specie at a possible replevin of only three months. The assembly further directed the Bank of the Commonwealth to begin withdrawing its notes from circulation and enacted legislation designed to wind down the affairs of the bank. In sum, the relief system as a whole—the replevin law, the Bank of the Commonwealth, and the three-quarters property law—demonstrated not the majority's embrace of a modern, activist government but the extent to which they were willing to go to preserve republican liberty and perceived principles of economic morality. Relief advocates saw their program as a temporary treatment for extraordinary times. Just as physicians of the day did not bleed a healthy patient, even the most ardent relief partisans did not wish to enact a permanent system of legislation that imposed a government presence in private economic transactions. What the relief proponents defended (to stretch the metaphor) was the right to prescribe such heroic therapy when they believed it necessary. To their minds, the anti-relief argument amounted to a denial of the state's ability to prescribe a cure for economic ills and was thus an affront to common sense and morality itself. During times of severe economic crisis, as one General Assembly committee proclaimed, "the government is bound to interfere to protect the citizen or it proves unfaithful to its obligation."[59]

After his defeat in 1819, Sharp returned to his Bowling Green law practice, and the next year, he declined to run for office for the first time in over a decade. But Sharp was not one to stay clear of politics for long, and by the summer of 1821, he was contemplating a run for the state senate. Before the election season got into full swing, however, Governor Adair offered Sharp a pro tem appointment as the state's attorney general. Two other lawyer-politicians, Ben Hardin and George Robertson, had already declined the nomination, probably because the attorney generalship "was not a lucrative office, nor a popular one." Moreover, the position had fallen "into disrepute in public estimation" because of the carelessness of the man who had been attorney general for the past generation: James Blair, father of Francis Preston Blair. Although repeatedly admonished by the judges "to apply his mind more closely to the studying of his cases brought before them," the elder Blair had been "fond of gaiety and company" and possessed a "great aversion to close study."[60]

Despite these drawbacks, Sharp accepted the position with the enthusiastic consent of Eliza, who later wrote, "As my mother lived in Frankfort, his indulgent feelings and anxiety to comply with my wish to live near her, induced him to remove to a distance from his landed property, and relinquish the lucrative practice in which he was engaged." Although Sharp may have abandoned his "lucrative practice" in Bowling Green, moving to Frankfort would not have been so terrible a sacrifice, for both the state high court—the court of appeals—and the seventh U.S. district court were located there, and Sharp doubtlessly saw an opportunity to augment his practice. So that autumn he, Eliza, and their two-year-old-daughter, Jane, moved to Frankfort. After living with Eliza's mother for a short while, they bought a house on Madison Street, directly facing the state capitol. Within a year or so, Solomon's devoted and unmarried brother, Dr. Leander Sharp, followed him to Frankfort.[61]

The attorney general appointment was a high honor and a testament to Sharp's legal reputation, which had continued to grow despite the setbacks of his political career. By 1821, he was widely acknowledged as one of the master lawyers in early Kentucky: "No man ever pervaded with a keener eye, the obscurities of the profession he pursued, or was more entirely skilled in its practice." As four other accomplished attorneys—John Rowan, John Adair, Richard M. Johnson, and William T. Barry—later attested, "As a lawyer he had few equals and no superior in the state." His brother wrote that "his business accumulated beyond that of almost every other man of his profession." In 1821, Sharp, whose entire net worth amounted to $560 only eight years earlier, was worth over $53,000, equivalent to about $1 million today.[62]

Yet on October 25, 1821, the day after the governor submitted Solomon Sharp's name for confirmation, the state senate tabled the nomination pending a select committee's investigation into Sharp's "conduct and personal character." The seduction charge, "fast sinking into oblivion," had been resurrected in a broadside produced by a rogue named John U. Waring.[63]

A talented lawyer who had inherited considerable wealth, Waring had earned his reputation as "the most feared man" in the state. Kentuckians, who as a rule could agree on virtually nothing, almost without exception described Waring as "a man of desperation and violence," "an enemy of mankind," "one of the most malignant and dangerous men that ever lived." Fond of issuing indiscriminate death threats (in the 1830s, he publicly threatened to cut off the ears of Governor James T. Morehead and "pickle them in brine"), Waring was a classic psychopath, a man who "made few friends and many bitter foes": "Nothing delights him more than to provoke his enemy, by insulting language, to strike him, while he holds himself ready at the instant, with a knife or dirk to stab him in return. In this manner he has stabbed six or seven men, of which he makes a boast." While Waring was a resident of Versailles (pronounced "ver-sails"), a small town fifteen miles to the west of Lexington, "his conduct became so outrageous, that the whole town rose upon him as one man, and ordered him to leave Woodford County at the peril of his life." Soon after, Waring moved to Warren County, but very soon he wore out his welcome. As one early Bowling Green resident remembered, Waring "had shot out of the windows and defied the town. They got after him and was about to kill him. They appointed a Committee to wait on him," which escorted him "three miles from town to turn him loose." Such was his notoriety that his death twenty-five years later was met with celebration: "There will be many who will rejoice that the world is rid of a dangerous and desperate man of blood."[64]

Waring's motivations for attacking Sharp are vague. Waring himself claimed to be acting in the public interest, but such would have been the first and last time he did so. Eliza Sharp believed Waring attacked her husband because Sharp had represented a man who was suing Waring. Leander Sharp maintained that Waring's "malignant industry" toward his brother was caused by a determination "to destroy the character of a man who he could not intimidate."[65]

Whatever the reason—interest, envy, or habitual malice—Waring's printing of the broadside spread statewide the charge that Sharp had seduced Anna Cooke, that he had "corrupted the blood of purity, stabbed the best hopes of a fond and widowed mother, cast into infamy and expelled from society a respectable woman, and shrouded a whole family in mourning." Such accusations, as we have seen, were not taken lightly in an honor-bound society, and the senate select committee thoroughly investigated the charge. After days of deliberation in which witnesses were called and documents examined, the committee, in the words of one member, found the charges to be "wholly groundless." On October 30, the senate confirmed Sharp's appointment as the state's new attorney general and thus conferred the state's imprimatur on Sharp's assertion of innocence.[66]

Although it could be argued that Kentucky's patriarchal elite casually dismissed what they considered to be a sexual peccadillo, most recent research stresses how seriously southerners of the early republic took such charges. Thirty years earlier in Virginia, in another case involving accusations of sexual impropriety, Richard Randolph, although he was acquitted (in large part because of an extraordinary defense team consisting of Patrick Henry and John Marshall), was not cleared in the mind of the public, and he was ostracized for the rest of his life. None of this happened in Sharp's case; although Sharp's political enemies intermittently tried to revive the issue, it did not hinder his subsequent political career.[67]

And so, by the early 1820s, Solomon Sharp and Anna Cooke's fortunes could scarcely have been more divergent. Sharp would have had ample reason for pride and optimism: He was the state's highest law official and was blessed with a beautiful wife and a growing family; he had been, moreover, officially exonerated of charges of past misconduct. It surely seemed, his brother later wrote, "that he had nothing before him but a long life of private happiness and public usefulness."[68] Anna, meanwhile, alone with her books, had nothing before her but solitude, despair, and disgrace. Yet she would not be alone for long, for this unruly woman was about to meet an exceptionally unruly man.

CHAPTER 3

Romance and Delusion

Jereboam Beauchamp

Whilome in Albion's isle there dwelt a youth,
Who ne in virtue's ways did take delight;
But spent his days in riot most uncouth,
And vex'd with mirth the drowsy ear of Night.
Ah Me! In sooth he was a shameless wight,
Sore given to revel and ungodly glee
Few earthly things found favour in his sight
Save concubines and carnal companie,
And flaunting wassailers of high and low degree
—Byron, *Childe Harold's Pilgrimage,* canto 1, stanza 2

As Franklin County jailer, John McIntosh would come to know Jereboam Orville Beauchamp well in the nine months the murderer stayed in the dungeon he superintended. Looking back across the debris of the Kentucky Tragedy nearly two centuries later, we must keep front and center one observation of McIntosh's: "I cannot believe any statement made by J. O. Beauchamp to be true which is not corroborated by other evidence."[1]

Like Anna Cooke, Jereboam Beauchamp spent much of his life cavalierly disregarding what was deemed proper behavior by the moral guardians of his day. Believing himself a tragic hero who must create, express, and exhibit his identity without concern for consequences, Beauchamp consciously strove to embody all the reckless traits made alluring by demonic romanticism. He yearned for fame and distinction, declaring just before his death, "This is not an ordinary case, when its history shall be known." As if he feared anonymity and conventionality more than death, he pleaded for recognition that he had daringly transcended the ordinary. He asked, "Have not all its features marked it extraordinary, as the deed was horrid and unparalleled?" Jereboam Beauchamp was emblematic of the manner in which the romantic persuasion seeped into the lives of Americans and helped spark a massive early-nineteenth-century shift in the collective moral sensibility of the young nation.[2]

Thomas Beauchamp was a native of Delaware who brought his young family to Kentucky in the first decade of the nineteenth century. They were among the first settlers of the south-central area of the state known as the Barrens, a flat, treeless region passed over by the first wave of migrants to western Kentucky in the belief that under the "dull uniformity of . . . immense meadows" was soil so poor that "neither man nor beast can reside there." But those daring or desperate enough to take a chance found that the land was more than rich enough to support a productive farm.[3]

Like Solomon Sharp's father, Thomas Beauchamp was a middling farmer—"comfortably independent," as his son would later describe him. And like tens of thousands of other Kentucky men, Thomas Beauchamp was a veteran of the War of 1812, having served, along with Solomon Sharp, in the Kentucky Mounted Volunteer Militia during its misadventure across the Ohio River. (Thomas, in fact, had enlisted in the same company as Solomon's little brother, Absalom.) His stint in the armed forces over, Thomas returned home to Barren County and in 1817 paid two thousand dollars for two hundred acres of land near the Tennessee border that two years later became a part of the new county of Simpson. There he built a home set "close up to the woods," a "small one-story house standing amid a few scattering trees." By 1820, Beauchamp owned a few slaves and a midsize farm worth about five thousand dollars. Thomas had married Sally Smithers in 1797, and the two raised seven sons and daughters. Jereboam, their fourth child, described his upbringing as "pious"; it is very likely the family, attracted to the sense of belonging and community imparted by the camp meetings, was converted to some variant of evangelical Christianity during the "ecstasies" of the Great Revival.[4]

Thomas Beauchamp was a soft-spoken man—during the trial, transcribers repeatedly had trouble hearing his testimony—and his integrity earned him the respect of even his son's mortal enemies, one of whom attested that he was "just, honest and upright." Over the years, Thomas was elected or appointed to a number of minor public offices: Warren County road surveyor in the 1810s, Simpson County justice of the peace in 1823 and 1828, sheriff in 1831. Certainly Jereboam was proud of his father, affirming, "If I have found one man upon the earth, entitled to the name of an honorable or an honest man, my father is that man." The admiration was mutual, for Jereboam, despite his self-confessed "volatile, idle, and wild disposition," claimed to have been his father's favorite child. And given that Thomas would later "well nigh bankrupt . . . himself by expenses incurred in the defense of his son," we have no reason—at least in this instance—to doubt Jereboam's word.[5]

Jereboam was born on September 6, 1802, and, by his own immodest estimate, "early shewed some indications of genius." Thomas's friends, noting the boy's precocious intelligence, urged him to place his son under a better teacher than the neighborhood could offer. And so "Jerry," as his family called him, was sent to study with Dr. Benjamin Thurston, "a man of great abilities and learning" who ran an academy about twenty miles to the east. By the age of sixteen, Jereboam had acquired a solid education, but because of Thomas's inability to similarly provide for his other children, Jereboam determined to strike out on his own. He tried at first "to make a little money by keeping a store," but, finding that he was ill fitted to the life of a shopkeeper, around 1820 Jereboam decided to teach school near Sanford Duncan's Inn, just north of the Tennessee state line. Shortly, he returned to Dr. Thurston's, where he served as an assistant to his mentor and in time resolved to become a lawyer.[6]

As with Anna, there are no extant likenesses of Jereboam; the only descriptions are secondhand and date from decades after his death. Yet they do agree in some particulars: he was of medium height and possessed a "florid complexion," blue eyes, "a turned up nose," and either red or brown hair, each strand of which stood up "like porcupine quills"—although the *Confession* at one point refers to Jereboam's "long bushy curly suit of hair." His speaking voice, according to some accounts, was also distinctive—"sharp" and "shrill." Small wonder that one contemporary remembered that "to see him once one would never fail to recognize him."[7]

If Jereboam's appearance is difficult to reconstruct, his personality most assuredly is not. By almost every account—including his own—Jereboam was "eccentric and ungovernable." The mild-mannered Thomas Beauchamp may not have been much of a disciplinarian; more certainly, Jereboam came of age in a time and place that tolerated or even encouraged displays of audacity, willfulness, and aggression in boys. Yet even by the standards of the early-nineteenth-century Southwest, Jereboam Beauchamp was remarkable for his "vehement and unbridled passions," and many descriptions of the young man strongly suggest that he was not merely undisciplined but a borderline sociopath. One acquaintance, Thomas Smith, thought "Beauchamp's general character was certainly one of the worst I ever knew of his age" and averred, "I . . . never knew him do an act of any kind which indicated magnanimity of soul or real dignity of sentiment." Leander Sharp, who claimed to have known Beauchamp well before the murder, denounced his "wild, lascivious, revengeful, unprincipled and shameless conduct," adding that "avarice was a very predominant trait in his character, and almost all his transactions with men, were marked with the vilest frauds." At least one woman, moreover, swore out a warrant for bastardy against Beauchamp, charging him with fathering and abandoning her child; Dr. Sharp claimed that there were many more such incidents. Tellingly, Beauchamp himself, just before his death, admitted the essential accuracy of such charges, confessing that he had repeatedly rushed into "sin and wickedness, and many times grieved my parents."[8]

Beauchamp was also a violent young man and proud of it. One neighbor, James C. Hays, related that his father warned him to keep his distance from Beauchamp, who, if angered, "would just take out a pistol and shoot you thro' the head." In 1823, one William Mills, fearing that Beauchamp would do him physical harm, swore out a peace bond against him. And during Beauchamp's trial, the prosecution had little problem finding witnesses to attest to his habit of constantly and recklessly threatening others' lives, one of whom swore that Beauchamp rarely went in public without his "guns, pistols, dirks, and knives." Beauchamp himself later boasted of keeping a veritable arsenal in his home—"a loaded musket, with fixed bayonet, a shot gun, a rifle, pistols and other arms, all in excellent order."[9]

By the fall of 1821, the nineteen-year-old Jereboam Beauchamp, this "strange, eccentric, and desperate man," was living in Bowling Green, reading law with Alexander M. Robinson. Although "inattentive to his studies," Beauchamp was, in Robinson's estimation, a young man of "extraordinary intellect" and had in one way or another absorbed a good deal of legal knowledge. One oral tradition has it that Beauchamp, when due to be admitted to the bar, brashly rejected the customary private exam and demanded to be questioned in public. In front of a number of lawyers and other assorted citizens of Bowling Green, Beauchamp was grilled by two well-known and talented judges, Christopher Tompkins on common law and Henry P. Broadnax on international law. "His answers to their interrogatories were so prompt and explicit that it soon became apparent to the company present," the account continues, "that the Judges had caught a whale, so they turned him loose in short order." On April 14, 1823, the Simpson County circuit court granted Jereboam Beauchamp license to practice law.[10]

Although Beauchamp's "vigorous native powers" marked him as a rising star—a "young lawyer of considerable attainments"—he did not establish an office, and he practiced law as if it were but a hobby. Apparently he was not happy in the legal profession; to one acquaintance, he spoke of "quitting the law." On those occasions when he did appear in the courtroom, he sometimes angered the locals with his habit of badgering witnesses. In one instance, Beauchamp, while defending a suspected horse thief, called James C. Hays a "poor or'nary farmer" under cross-examination. (Hays, although he greatly resented the insult, later had to admit that the young lawyer made a "right pretty discourse.") These traits of Beauchamp's—a marked precocity and an aggressive courtroom style—reminded more than a few observers of a another Bowling Green lawyer: Solomon Sharp. In fact, it is possible that Beauchamp modeled his behavior on that of Sharp, whom Beauchamp thought to be a "man of the greatest penetration."[11]

For the story of Jereboam and Anna's introduction and courtship, all we have is the *Confession*, and that, as ever, is a problem. In 1820 Jereboam was eighteen years old and still working for Dr. Thurston when, according to the Beauchamps, there erupted "a general burst of generous indignation" against Solomon Sharp for seducing Anna Cooke. The *Confession* claims that Beauchamp was personally, even "intimately," acquainted with Sharp, and that the young man had wished to study law with him. Yet as seduction "was a species of dishonour, which, from my earliest recollection, had ever excited my most violent reprobation," Beauchamp now refused to consider studying under Sharp: "I would as soon receive into my friendship, an horse thief, as a man . . . who had dishonoured and prostrated the hopes of a respectable and worthy female." This was a typically disingenuous statement; Jereboam Beauchamp himself, as we have seen, had "dishonoured and prostrated the hopes of" at least one young woman.[12]

Shortly after hearing of the putative seduction, Jereboam returned to his childhood home in Simpson County "to spend a few months in a country life with my father." Learning that the celebrated Anna Cooke was living nearby, Jereboam determined to meet her. Undaunted by reports that she refused to accept any company, Jereboam sallied forth to "Retirement," "the romantic little farm" where this "worthy orphan female" had secluded herself. Although Anna initially refused to see him, Jereboam insisted. When she finally appeared, the young man explained that he felt isolated on his father's farm and "had been impelled to obtrude a visit upon her." Although making clear her determination to "avoid society," Anna did entertain Jereboam for a while and sent him on his way with a volume from her "very choice selection of books." On his subsequent visits, however, she flatly refused to see him, leaving Jereboam to cool his heels amid her library. Before long, the *Confession* claims, Anna "had begun to haunt my thoughts and my dreams," but still "she persisted with firmness to refuse" any social interaction. Yet the audacity of her young suitor must have intrigued or flattered her, for finally, "by increasing importunity and persuasion," Jereboam prevailed on her to accept his calls. The two at first limited their discussions to intellectual matters, but before long, Jereboam had confessed his love and "solicited her hand in marriage." Cryptically, Anna insisted that "there was an insuperable barrier" to their love, yet she would be no more specific. "At length," the *Confession* reads, Jereboam "resolved to take no denial, but to know this secret objection. She then told me, with a firmness, which spoke that it was the voice of fate, that the hand which should receive hers, would have to revenge the injury a vilian had done her." The villain, of course, was Sharp, and the injury was his seduction of Anna. Whoever avenged her, the text continues, would earn her undying love. Concerned perhaps that it might appear that Anna—seventeen years older than Jereboam—was manipulating the young man, the *Confession* takes pains to assert that "no conditions, nor any earthly proposition she could have made me could have filled me with so much delight. . . . To hear her thus require what I had so much calculated on and desired was peculiarly pleasing to me indeed."[13]

The story of their initial encounters made for great theater, but many found it less than convincing. Certainly Dr. Sharp later looked on the whole scene with a jaundiced eye: A reckless youth, known for his amours with local girls and said to be "the father of several bastards," heard of a fallen woman who had just moved nearby. Far from "that disinterested feeling of respect towards an injured female, which, he pretends induced him to seek her acquaintance," Dr. Sharp sneered, "he was probably influenced by another feeling more natural to profligate young men." Why else would an eighteen-year-old deviant pursue "a dissolute woman of thirty-five"? Leander Sharp was not the only one to question such an odd pairing; a Frankfort newspaper later speculated that Beauchamp, well aware Anna was a "ruined" woman who had "given herself up to the lewd embraces of a married man," was "*perhaps* attracted by a little *property*, which it was known she possessed." Eliza Sharp, too, later retailed the rumor that "he married her for the property she had and not on account of any personal attachment."[14]

Yet according to the Simpson County tax lists of 1825, the year after Anna and Jereboam were married, the entire Beauchamp estate consisted of 192 acres of third-rate land, two slaves, and three horses, altogether worth $4,226—not inconsiderable holdings, but hardly a worthwhile haul for a gold digger whose own talents as a lawyer could have shortly secured much greater riches. Even Dr. Sharp admitted "it seems indeed astonishing" that Beauchamp would marry a woman of such doubtful reputation and relatively small fortune. Sharp could account for it all only by insisting that "it is one of the most striking instances of the ascendency which bad women sometimes gain over the minds of men." Others followed this same story line. A Louisville newspaper editorialized that Anna exerted "a most uncommon degree of influence . . . over the mind of her husband," while Henry Clay thought the coupling reminiscent of *The London Merchant*, an eighteenth-century English drama in which an older woman seduces and corrupts a naive young man. Thus, in this telling, Beauchamp was a victim of an immoral woman's wiles, caught in the snares of a "keen, experienced, hackneyed adept who intuitively comprehends the best mode of producing effect upon her Johnny Raw. She affects indignant grief, and holds her head high in determination to have nothing more to say, or do with man; to take the veil of retirement, and eat bread moistened with tears." But it is all a show to attract a fool to avenge her "seduction," and "Beauchamp, like a true knight, yields to any terms."[15]

But neither is this explanation persuasive. That Anna, years older than Jereboam, was experienced and capable of manipulating others is undeniable. But had their tie been based merely on one or the other's self-interest—if she was using him to kill Sharp or he was using her for sex or as a shortcut to economic sufficiency—it seems highly unlikely that the two would have stuck together, as they did, to the end. Jereboam, according to Anna, "had been an affectionate husband," and their relationship was emotionally intimate, so much so that she "*knew the inside of him.*" Something very powerful bound together this young, talented, perverse young man and this ingenious, unruly, disgraced woman.[16]

Combing the *Confession* for clues as to the nature of their bond, the first instinct is to strip away the sentimental gloss to find some semblance of verifiable reality, yet a second look suggests that the sentimental gloss, in this instance at least, is exactly the point. The literary style of the *Confession* itself—and especially the ways in which Anna and Jereboam describe each other—gives tangible proof of the couple's shared immersion in a world of sentimental literature. She was a "worthy orphan female" who lived on a "romantic little farm" who spoke with "the voice of fate" that "her heart could never cease to ache, till Col. Sharp should die through her instrumentality"; that "she would kiss the hand, and adore the person who would revenge her." Jereboam was, in Anna's verse appended to the *Confession,* a "spirit divine!" her "heart's lov'd, honor'd Lord," who had "met the direst spite of hell" in order to avenge her dishonor. Such sheer and artless melodrama permeates the text, and it is enormously suggestive.[17]

Romantic literature was his entrée into her world—and vice versa—and literature became at once the base and medium of their relationship. In an erotically charged passage, the *Confession* relates that on the very day Jereboam first trespassed on Anna's solitude, she "spread her library open to me." Thereafter, the two "continued all the evening in my selecting and reading some books . . . which she had pointed out, as favorites of hers, and in the conversation to which this led." Upon leaving that night, Jereboam took one of her volumes with him to ensure that they would meet again. Subsequently, in those early days when she refused to see him, he sat in her library for hours and pored over her considerable collection of books. A mutual love of the word brought these two uniquely deviant personalities together, and their bond was secured by a shared imaginative life; such, in fact, in time gave them the tools to shape the meaning of the entire Kentucky Tragedy. They were kindred spirits not only in their joint distaste for the prevailing prescriptions of proper behavior but in their shared love of literature.[18]

Yet the significance lies not in the mere fact that they were reading but what they were reading: sentimental novels and epic poetry of Byron and his epigones—the yin and yang of early American romantic literature, one that made women the rebellious and doomed heroines of putative morality tales and the other that lionized dashing and handsome young men who disdained the constraints of society.

"This is, emphatically, the age of novel writing," declared the *North American Review* in 1827, and that, as strange as it may seem today, constituted a crisis in the early republic. Authorities from across the political and cultural spectrum—liberals, conservatives, evangelicals, and unchurched alike—denounced novel reading and its alleged effects on America's youth. According to no less an authority than Thomas Jefferson, novels were a "poison" that "infects the mind," that "destroys its tone and revolts it against wholesome reading. Reason and fact, plain and unadorned, are rejected. Nothing can engage attention unless dressed in all the figments of fancy, and nothing so bedecked comes amiss. The result is a bloated imagination, sickly judgement, and disgust towards all the real businesses of life." At the University of North Carolina in 1820, students held a debate over the question, "Ought novels to be interdicted by law?" Such furor, such rhetoric seems bizarrely overwrought from our perspective, yet these critics were not necessarily overreacting. As Cathy Davidson has argued, the well-educated, the ministers, the political elites all accurately perceived that the ever-expanding choice of reading material constituted a severe challenge to their traditional role as intermediaries between texts and audience—and, more to the point, their ability to select and interpret those texts. More and more, readers could choose "among different authorities and take or leave them according to the reader's evaluation of their worth."[19]

The omnipresent theme of novels in the early republic was the seduction—or attempted seduction—of beautiful, naive young women by heartless men. The seduction novel was originally an English import, with Samuel Richardson's *Clarissa* being the earliest and most notable example. Temptation, in the hands of Richardson and his many followers, was secularized, and before long seduction was no longer associated with Satan or his earthly minions misleading humans but with males corrupting females. Yet the fall remained, as these latter-day demons in the shape of men usually succeeded in their diabolical schemes of seduction, leaving in their wake, in the words of Leonard Tennenhouse, "ruined women, stillborn babies, and destinies misshapen by desire." The theme was ubiquitous in early American literature, as authors filled periodicals with such tales: "Innocent Simplicity Betrayed" (1789), "Lothario, or The Accomplished Villain" (1789), "The Flirt: A Moral Tale" (1791), "A Vindication of the Fair Sex against the Charge of Preferring Coxcombs to Men of Worth" (1792), "An Admonition to Those Who Glory in Seducing the Affection of the Fair, and Then Deserting Them" (1792), "Thoughts on Seduction" (1806), "The Victim of Seduction" (1806), "A Young Lady to Her Seducer" (1807), "On Seduction" (1807). "Between 1789 and 1796," according to Tennenhouse, "*Massachusetts Magazine* alone published well over one hundred stories, letters, and poems dealing with seduction," the redundancy of which, he adds, would be difficult to overstate.[20]

If the periodical fiction was most common, the fullest expositions of the seduction genre were those novels so deprecated by the early republic's moral guardians. Of the one hundred or so American novels written before 1820, the clear majority dealt with young women led astray by cold-hearted seducers, including William Hill Brown's *The Power of Sympathy* (1789), arguably the first American novel; *Amelia, or The Faithless Briton* (1789), a story originally serialized in a number of early American magazines and later published as a novel; Tabitha Tenney's *Female Quixotism* (1801), in which a young woman models her behavior after characters she reads of, with predictably disastrous results; and Judith Sargent Murray's *The Story of Margaretta* (1792), the heroine of which, interestingly, avoids the traditional sad fate of seduced females because of her superior education. But the two best examples of the seduction novel are Susanna Rowson's *Charlotte Temple* (first published in America in 1794) and *The Coquette* (1797) by Hannah Webster Foster. *Charlotte Temple,* America's best-selling novel until *Uncle Tom's Cabin* appeared fifty-eight years later, sold approximately forty thousand copies between 1791 and 1810 and was reprinted at least seventy-seven times before 1848. *The Coquette* was phenomenally popular as well and not only remained in print eight decades after its original publication but sold more copies in the mid-1820s than at any other time. This literature, although much of it was written around the turn of the century, continued to be massively popular for decades thereafter.[21]

Although constantly admonished not to read novels (even some novels, ludicrously, warned against reading novels), early American readers blithely made them the era's best-selling form of media. Almost half of one Virginian's substantial library, that of Lady Jean Skipwith, was made up of novels and tales. It was women who wrote most of this literature, and because of the genre's serious and respectful presentation of women's interior lives, it was women, primarily, who read them. By offering an imaginary world that "celebrated rather than suppressed" the female experience, by helping to create and define a community of physically isolated southern women, these works, as Catherine Kerrison maintains, were enormously influential and had even "begun to supplement the traditional conduct-of-life literature."[22]

The ecstasy and the anxiety such writings elicited become more explicable when we recall the early American habit of uniting worlds that we today assume to be essentially separate: social, moral, and literary. Possessed of such assumptions, critics of novel reading believed that such material would engender, in the formulation of a group of young Boston women, a restlessness, an impulse to shirk duties in the expectation of meeting "in life the romantic incidents portrayed by the pen of the Novelist." Moreover, according to a widely reprinted turn-of-the-century article titled "Novel Reading, a Cause of Female Depravity," such fare would encourage women to behave immorally, for novel reading led to impure desires and fostered all that was passionate, emotional, and erotic.[23]

Early-nineteenth-century readers took behavioral cues from their stories, and the line between fiction and fact was (and still is) far more permeable than often assumed. Robert Darnton's documentation of readers' reactions to Jean Jacques Rousseau's famous *La Nouvelle Heloise* strikingly illustrates how deeply this romantic literature affected its audience: "Ordinary readers from all ranks of society were swept off their feet. They wept, they suffocated, they raved, they looked deep into their lives and resolved to live better." One retired army officer, in a letter to Rousseau, professed to have never "wept such delicious tears" as he did while reading of Heloise's fate and even insisted that, on coming to the novel's climax, "I believe I would have gladly died during that supreme moment." As readers "suspended their critical instinct, identified with the characters, and let waves of emotion wash over themselves," they digested the books "so thoroughly that literature became absorbed in life." And it was not just readers of *La Nouvelle Heloise* who blurred the line between literature and reality; Rousseau himself, according to Darnton, "became the heroes that he read about, and he played out the dramas of antiquity in his Genevan apartment." He "never learned to distinguish between literature and reality, having filled his mind with 'bizarre and romantic notions.'"[24]

The picture Darnton paints is one in which both consumer and creator of fictive literature had difficulty discerning where life ended and imagination began. Although Darnton labels this phenomenon "Rousseauism," the tendency went far beyond Rousseau and far beyond France. In America, such was readers' identification with the eponymous heroine of *Charlotte Temple* that a "grave" was created for her in Trinity Churchyard in New York City. For almost a century, thousands of mourners brushed past the nearby monuments to Alexander Hamilton and Robert Fulton to pay their respects to this "bizarre memorial to nobody."[25]

The sentimental novels, far from frivolous diversions, actually seem to have composed a basic and significant component of many Americans' socialization, one they especially drew on during times of crisis. Virginian Nancy Randolph, in an attempt to exonerate herself of charges of sexual impropriety and infanticide, prepared a retrospective defense in 1815 in which she depicted herself as a tragic, passionate, yet ultimately virtuous young woman deserving of her readers' sympathy. Randolph's themes and her phrasing, right down to the epistolary style she adopted, "exactly paralleled popular fiction"—in particular Richardson's *Clarissa* and Foster's *Coquette,* both of which "offered Nancy compelling models for self-creation." In all, there existed in the late eighteenth and early nineteenth century, according to Darnton, "a new relationship between the reader and the printed words. Writer and reader together realized a transformation in a mode of communication that went far beyond literature and that would leave its mark on several generations of revolutionaries and romantics."[26]

Such melodramatic literature was particularly appealing to young women: "Many a little miss just entering her 'teens have I seen stealing to her solitary room," Virginian Nancy Johns Turner Hall remembered; after a while she would find them "wandering about the house, with a broad grin and vacant look of the idiot." Yet sentimental literature struck a chord for readers far beyond dreamy-eyed adolescents roaming the halls of plantation houses or curled up in drawing rooms; it appealed to many Americans confined to society's margins. "Written in defiance of established social and literary tradition and for readers not recognized by many other literary forms," the sentimental novel "encouraged the aspirations of its new readers—aspirations in conflict, at many points, with ideas preached from the pulpit or taught in the common schools." Such were the subversive possibilities of these novels that they were instrumental in the creation and maintenance of what one historian has called a feminine counterculture in early America. Despite constant importunities that females obey the dictates of society, that they "keep within their compass," as one early-nineteenth-century printer enjoined, women as both creators and patrons of these novels defied the thoroughly alarmed authorities of early America. Although this popular culture ostensibly carried conservative messages, it also, in the words of Eve Kornfeld, presented to early Americans "an alternative vision of reality, with subversive implications for American society and republican ideology alike." In particular, such a counterculture inverted many aspects of the male stereotype; rather than virile protectors or wise leaders, men were often portrayed as menacing "moral ciphers" or impotent fools, while women tended to be virtuous if gravely endangered heroines. The literature also subtly undermined and inverted classical republican ideals of stoic male public-mindedness and passionate female interestedness by depicting men as "frequently overwhelmed by their passions and interests" and, in a subtle and subversive manner, portraying women as "active and strong in the defense of virtue."[27]

Knowing what we do of Anna Cooke's rebelliousness and substantial education, her attraction to this literature is hardly surprising. If any doubt remained about what exactly was in that library that she "spread open" to Jereboam, Dr. Sharp made it clear: Anna, he related, "was deeply read in novels" and "delighted to converse upon scenes of romance and fiction." Anna and Jereboam's jailer, John McIntosh, confirmed the report, commenting, "She sometimes conversed upon novels, in which she seemed to be well read." Anna's reading choices were evident to distant observers as well; after the sorry affair had played out, Timothy Flint's *Western Magazine and Review* editorialized, "We can make a very probable conjecture, what kind of books composed Miss Ann Cook's library, and the principles, in which she was indoctrinated"—to wit, "novels, romances, and plays."[28]

Another literature spoke even more clearly to all that was wild and rebellious in the early republic: romantic poetry, the second, masculine-encoded half of literary subversion. Every bit as popular as novels, romantic verse equally disturbed the powers-that-were in early America. Jefferson, immediately following his warning that novels eroded judgment and reason, admonished citizens, "For a like reason, too, much poetry should not be indulged." A year or so later, Washington Irving similarly worried that "the poetic temperament has naturally something in it of the vagabond. When left to itself it runs loosely and wildly, and delights in everything eccentric and licentious."[29]

The most eccentric and licentious poet of the era was also its most prominent, most accomplished, and most controversial: George Gordon, Lord Byron, the high priest of demonic romanticism. He was the lyricist of a generation, and the youth of America adored him almost from the moment Philadelphia printer Moses Thomas published *Childe Harold's Pilgrimage* in 1812. With his American popularity magnified by his opposition to the British cause in the War of 1812, Byron by mid-decade was well on his way to celebrity in the United States, with more than a dozen editions of his poetry in publication. By 1830, ninety-nine American editions of Byron's works had saturated the American market, and seven years later, when Captain Frederick Marryat asked the heads of the great publishing houses of New York and Philadelphia how many copies of Byron's works had been sold, they estimated the number to be somewhere from "one hundred and fifty to two hundred thousand." Such was his influence among Americans that William H. Prescott insisted it was Byron, not Sir Walter Scott, who was "the representative of this epoch."[30]

It is difficult now to recapture the singularity of Byron's work, the sheer audacity of an author who did not strive to inculcate any higher virtues in his readers but rather told of adventures that seemed to positively romanticize deviance. Novels, even if subversive, at least ostensibly carried the message that traditional morality must be upheld; Byron, on the other hand, dared make a hero of a character who "through sin's long labyrinth had run," a "youth, / "Who ne in virtue's ways did take delight; / But spent his days in riot most uncouth"; a "shameless wight" who found favor only in "concubines and carnal companie." He presumed as well to toy with the ruling opinions of polite and patriotic society, ridiculing the enlightened republicanism of Joseph Addison's *Cato* that so touched George Washington. "'Tis not in mortals to command success," the play's hero famously proclaims, "But we'll do more, Sempronius—we'll deserve it." In *Don Juan,* Byron mocks the sentiment and cynically turns its meaning inside out: "'Tis not in mortals to command success, / But *do you more,* Sempronius—*don't* deserve it;' / And take my word, you won't have any less."[31]

No one had ever encountered anything quite like it, and such was the disorientation of Byron's readers that "for some time," author and publisher Samuel Griswold Goodrich remembered, "only a few persons seemed to comprehend it, and many who read it, scarcely knew whether to be delighted or shocked." Yet before long, Byron's verse had "made its way in the public mind," and, at least in the opinion of the literary doyens of the day, precipitated "a fearful plunge" from an "elevated moral tone in literature, into . . . daring if not blasphemous skepticisms." The moral abandon of Byron's poetry was indeed a far cry from the explicit didacticism of most every other Anglo-American piece of literature. Nonetheless, within a few years, "the whole poetic world had become Byronic," and a "bewildered, enchanted" public "followed him, and condescended to bring down their morals and their manners to his degraded and degrading standard." In the hands of the "poet-wizard," Goodrich ruefully observed, "what was at first revolting, came at last to be a fascination."[32]

Other literary arbiters were convinced that Byron's works were eroding their society's morals. Henry Wadsworth Longfellow, for one, sniffed, "No writer has done half so much to corrupt the literary taste as well as the moral principle of our country." To many would-be keepers of virtue in the early nineteenth century, Byron was misleading young Americans—seducing them, as it were—into immorality and self-destruction. F. W. P. Greenwood, a New England Unitarian minister, actually blamed Byron for undermining young Americans' faith, for instilling a "sullen dissatisfaction with the present state" and a concomitant "reckless doubt or disbelief in a future one." William Gibbes Hunt's *Western Review and Miscellaneous Magazine,* published in Lexington, Kentucky, condemned the poet's laughing derision of "all that the world has considered as virtue, constancy, and fidelity in the human character." Moralists like Hunt were taken aback by Byron's lack of seriousness, by his reckless juxtaposition of vice and virtue that could only, Hunt believed, induce in the reader a moral vertigo: "What is grand is followed by what is mean; what is tender is dashed by what is ludicrous and unfeeling; pity is married to satire, and the most sacred affections of the heart to others the most groveling base"; the reader is "whistled back and forth from one point to another," as "good qualities and bad, purity and impurity, pathos and ridicule, love and lust, religion and hypocrisy, are all jumbled together in such a chaos that neither knows the other, and the reader can recognize nothing as he has seen it before." Goodrich recalled that many booksellers refused to retail Byron's "infidel publications" and that ministers, teachers, and parents warned the young of Byron's baleful influence. And yet the effort to stem the tide, to roll back the influence of this patron saint of debauchery, "was all in vain."[33]

One of the more expansive criticisms of Byron and his influence on America appeared in the October 1825 issue of the *North American Review.* "Lord Byron's Character and Writings," by the "Unitarian Pope" himself, Andrews Norton, a professor of theology at Harvard, arraigned Byron for confusing and weakening "the moral sentiments of his admirers." For men like Norton, who thought it was poetry's place to "raise and improve mankind," a "perverted and degraded mind" such as Byron's threatened the very moral fabric of the nation. Norton could only wonder that Byron's "contempt of decency, his depravity, and his impiety" should not have repulsed his legion of fans. Devoid of faith or "strong moral sentiments," convinced of "the worthlessness of man and the worthlessness of life," Byron and his works "have done something to give a poetic interest to a selfish abandonment of duty; to encourage the indulgence of passions, which, in the real intercourse of life, are merely offensive." Norton sadly concluded, "There is a pestilential atmosphere about the ruins of such a mind."[34]

Southern critics were scarcely more kind. In 1838, the *Southern Liter-*

ary Messenger reprinted "Lord Byron's Faults," a twenty-year-old essay by Presbyter Anglicanus, originally published in *Blackwood's Magazine.* The author excoriated Byron, charging that he had "done little more than exhibit to the world, the melancholy spectacle of a great spirit, self-embittered, self wasted, and self-degraded." Anglicanus berated the poet: "With you, heroism is lunacy, philosophy folly, virtue a cheat, and religion a bubble." A few years later, again in the pages of the *Southern Literary Messenger,* Baltimore physician J. E. Snodgrass indicted Byron for having "indulged in fits of passion, and emotions ever-varying—hellishly profane, or hypocritically pious—thoughts which, if they ever found a home in the brains of other poets of the age, they were not sufficiently lost to propriety and virtue to utter them."[35]

In his verse, Byron famously created—or at least gave fullest expression to—a stock character, the "Byronic hero," a figure of enormous influence among the youth of America and Europe. Whether personified by the blithely amoral Don Juan, the reckless Childe Harold, or the brooding and haunted Manfred, the Byronic hero, boiled down to essentials, is a fearless and daring rebel gleefully defying the dictates of society. In its more benign forms, this romantic persona, ensnared within an unjust world, is forced to become a noble outlaw, whose "deliberately anti-social behavior proves worthier of regard than conventional behavior." In its more malignant forms—the ones Byron delighted in devising—the character's moral code degenerates into an antinomian personality whose self-generated moral code brooks no limitations. As the horrified editor of the *Western Review and Miscellaneous Magazine* described Don Juan, Byron's most famous creation, "He cares for nobody and no thing, for no rules and no laws, for none of the common associations of nature, and none of the existing maxims of society." Devoid of any "fixed principles upon any subject," the Byronic persona mirthlessly derides and satirizes "all that the world has considered as virtue, constancy, and fidelity, in the human character."[36]

The singularity of the Byronic moral code found an analog in physical isolation. Aloof from ordinary mortals—whether by choice or tragic circumstance—the hero retreats from a larger and corrupt world, very often accompanied by a beautiful and adoring companion. "Antithetical to every form of instituted culture and authority," the Byronic hero, according to one authority, "attaches himself only to an idealized (female) love object." One of the better examples is the Haidee episode of *Don Juan,* set in one of the "smaller Cyclades," in which the title character and his latest soul mate become "all in all to each other," share "deep and burning moments," and "to each other press, / As if there were no life beneath the sky / Save theirs." In the earlier *Childe Harold's Pilgrimage,* Byron sounds out the same theme:

> Oh! That the Desert were my dwelling place,
> With one fair Spirit for my minister,
> That I might all forget the human race,
> And, hating no one, love but only her!

Yet time and again in Byron's formulations, the lovers' idyll is destroyed by small-minded emissaries of a corrupt world driven to pull down such a hero as this.[37]

An immanent contradiction of Byron's heroes is their simultaneous disdain for others and an all-consuming lust for fame. Such figures are given to an "impassioned misanthropy, a certain sense of superiority," a habit of looking on all others as a "selfish, low minded, cold and unjust" rabble pathetically incapable of fully appreciating genius. Manfred exclaims, "From my youth upwards / My spirit walk'd not with the souls of men"; the Corsair, meanwhile, "hated man too much to feel remorse" for his actions. Such mavericks, according to the *North American Review,* were "utterly discontented with that small portion, which most of us can fairly claim, of the general regard of others," rebels who feared nothing but the prospect of being ignored by the great unwashed. And paradoxically therefore, even as the Byronic hero held mankind in contempt, he constantly, as Norton perceived in his careful dissection of the persona, strove to secure the "admiration and favor" of those same benighted masses.[38]

The Byronic hero's insatiable desire for fame leads to constant pretense, an overweening impulse to strike an appropriately dramatic pose that will "give others that conception of him, which he wished them to entertain." This more or less constant career of projection—what William Prescott defined as the Byronic hero's "vices of affectation"—best encapsulates the immodest need to win the acclaim of others. Perhaps the persona's prime mannerism is haunted melancholy. Tormented by a mysterious guilt, the Byronic hero—"grey-hair'd with anguish" in the words of Manfred, the archetype of this particular mood—broods in a romantic sort of way, one that threw "a charm over that sickly melancholy, to which the young are exposed, from too sensitive feelings, from indolence and timidity, and from desires at once too earthly and too romantic."[39]

In addition, the Byronic hero is perpetually unable to rein in his emotions. The only constant in Byron's work, according to the *Western Review and Miscellaneous Magazine,* is "his devotion to his passions." Such "fierce and wicked" desires ultimately, according to his critics, advertise the supposed virtues of overweening "egotism." And although given to admitting personal failings, the persona's "confessions" are merely the product of vanity, serving not to diminish but to amplify readers' interest.[40]

Like the authors of seduction novels, Byron purposefully effaced the distance between author and creation, between the quotidian and the uncommon, between reality and fantasy. Making clear that his fiction was not entirely fictional, Byron boasted, "Almost all Don Juan is *real* life, either my own—or . . . people I knew." Byron's fans and critics alike adopted the habit, repeatedly failing to differentiate between the poet and the characters who roamed his verse; the worth of one, it seems, was deemed a direct reflection on the other. Over and again, Andrews Norton, for one, unselfconsciously shifted from a discussion of the questionable character of Byron's creations to ruminations on the immorality of the creator, a man "whose principal subject, presented either with or without disguise, was himself." Perhaps Goodrich put it best: "The great fascination . . . , that which creates an agonizing interest in [Byron's] principal poems—is the constant idea presented to the reader that, under the disguise of his fictitious heroes, he is unconsciously depicting his own sad, despairing emotions."[41]

This confusion of reality and illusion had another facet: Byron's verse inspired legions of imitators on both sides of the Atlantic and unleashed a "Byromania," as Byron's future wife Annabella Milbanke termed the phenomenon in 1812. The *Baltimore Emerald* marveled at Byron's influence, going so far as to claim that his "words operate upon other men like their own thoughts." Norton wrote, "When such a writer as Byron expresses strongly what he represents as his own emotions and sentiments, there are many who will adopt them, and apply his language to themselves," including, comically, those who "have affected depravity of which they were not guilty, and have bewailed their sufferings and desolation, with a resolute determination to be miserable." Prescott also noted that "the influence of Byron, of course, has been widely and perniciously felt, as evinced by the passionate rant, affected sentimentality, and dare-devil desperation of a school of imitators." These were the "American Harolds, Manfreds, or Conrads," who arrayed themselves with "turn-down collars and the cynicism of Lord Byron," who stood before their mirrors rehearsing the Byronic gaze "in the hope of catching the curl of the upper lip, and the scowl of the brow," young men who "caught the fashion of deranging their hair or knotting their neck handkerchief or of leaving their shirt collar unbuttoned." Longfellow, looking back on the 1820s, marveled at "what an aping of Lord Byron exhibited itself throughout the country! It was not an imitation of the brighter characteristics of his intellect, but a mimicry of his sullen misanthropy and irreligious gloom." Such was his influence that "every city, town and village had its little Byron, its self-tormenting scoffer at morality, its gloomy misanthropist in song." As one scholar of the Byronic cult aptly summarized, "Byron did not project life into literature nearly so much as he projected literature into life."[42]

Among the many "Byromaniacs" of the day was a young woman born Dorcas Doyen in 1813. A servant girl in Maine, Doyen was seduced at the age of seventeen; thereafter, she became a prostitute and took the name Helen Jewett. She adored Byron and kept a picture of the poet on her wall and well-read and underlined copies of *Don Juan* and *Beppo* on her nightstand. Byron doubtless appealed to such a one who had been a victim of the sexual hypocrisy of her day, one who, born into poverty and obscurity, had willfully reinvented herself as a cosmopolitan woman of the night. Consistent with the Byronic tendency to regard the line between fabrication and actuality as permeable at best, Jewett exploited the story of her tragic "ruin" to attract customers. One such john, Richard Robinson, was himself a devotee of the cult of Byron, given to "grandiosity, bravado, and arrogance, embroidering his remarks with evasion and lies." The two formed a powerful bond that went well beyond business: prostitute and client "both experienced an intensity of feelings, not merely romantic or sexual longing, but dark, moody, depressive feelings as well, that they both enjoyed giving vent to." In early April 1836, Robinson was accused of murdering Jewett, and his trial became one of the great dramas of the 1830s. Although almost assuredly guilty, Robinson won acquittal and headed west; at one point while traveling on the Ohio River, he blurted, "Like Byron, I have drained the bowl of dissipation to its dregs."[43]

This habit of not merely reading romantic literature but, to varying degrees, attempting to live the literature seems to have been fairly widespread. An Alabama lawyer, Thomas W. Farrar, was such "a terror to his section," his biographer relates, that he was drummed out of the city of Montgomery—no mean feat on the rough southern frontier. Before long, he turned up on Shades Mountain in Jefferson County, about one hundred miles to the north. There, in 1827, he slowly and relentlessly chiseled lines from Byron's *Childe Harold's Pilgrimage* into a rock outcropping:

To sit on rocks, to muse o'er flood and fell,
To slowly trace the forest's shady scene,
Where things that own not man's dominion dwell,
And mortal foot hath ne'er or rarely been.

Farrar spent his time at his new home "gambling and carousing" among the remote settlements and the woodlands of Jefferson County. And, far more unusually by the lights of the day, he was accompanied by his wife on his tour of debauchery through remote places where "mortal foot hath ne'er or rarely been." A pattern becomes apparent: two Byron-obsessed, antisocial young people form an intense bond apart from society and flout social norms, including gender roles.[44]

Isaac Starr Clason was a New York actor and poet whose admiration of Byron ran so deep that he composed supplementary cantos for *Don Juan.* Less an artless knockoff than a very capable elaboration on the original, Clason's verse accurately captures the insouciant perversity of the original. Clason's Don Juan, "having roved through half the world's insanities," reminisces on past debaucheries:

I've compass'd every pleasure,
  Caught every joy before its *bead* could pass;
I've loved without restriction, without measure—
  I've sipp'd enjoyment from each sparkling glass.

Like Byron, Clason was no doubt reflecting on his own habits of intemperance, for though "a man of education, taste, and considerable talent," Clason was also "dissolute and profligate." Born around the turn of the century into one of the leading families of New York City, Clason graduated Columbia College before squandering the fortune his merchant father bequeathed him. Although a wastrel, he was a charming wastrel, "a man of attractive manners and brilliant conversation." Clason became an actor and starred in a number of plays at Park and Bowery theaters, including the title role in *Hamlet.* Yet his marriage to a beautiful and talented vocalist ended in bitter divorce. True to the Byromaniac's penchant of braiding life and imagination to the point of indistinguishability, Clason unleashed his bitterness in verse:

There are storms whose lightnings ever glare,
  tempests whose thunders never cease to roll—The storms of love

when madden'd to despair,
the furious tempests of the jealous soul, . . .
Whose blast leaves joy a tomb, and hope a speck,
Reason a blank, and happiness a wreck.

By 1830, after having roved through a good many of the world's insanities, Clason found a new lover on whom he could fix his obsessions and moved with her to London. Four years later, after a slow descent into poverty and despair, he and his mistress took their Byronic bonding to its furthest extreme, committing double suicide in their squalid London boardinghouse by carefully sealing up their room and "inhaling the fumes of lighted charcoal." Authorities found "the deceased . . . lying side by side on a bed," with "a phial of laudanum and a open razor" nearby in case the asphyxiation did not work. It was indeed, as T. Allston Brown insisted, a "wretched career," but it was also a tragic one that revealed a genius just shy of maturity, a talent that, had it had discipline, might very well be better remembered today.[45]

Tellingly—for our purposes—Clason was enthralled not only by Byron but by the story of Anna Cooke and Jereboam Beauchamp. He had in 1833 written an epic poem—long since lost—based on the Kentucky Tragedy. Indeed, Clason and his lover's final act was clearly similar, as we will see, to Anna and Jereboam's death scene. That Clason was drawn to the story of Jereboam and Anna is not surprising, for very likely he recognized in the Beauchamps kindred spirits, personalities who, like Jewett, Robinson, Farrar, and untold others, bore the telltale marks of the Byron devotee.

To understand Jereboam Beauchamp himself, to apprehend "the singular cast of mind and feeling of this extraordinary man," we must make note of Beauchamp's unusually strong mimetic impulses. He possessed a marked talent for acquiring the form if not the substance of whatever he focused on, and such was most likely the key to his academic prowess, especially in a place and time that emphasized rote instruction. It was with "great ease," Beauchamp wrote, "I acquired whatever learning I turned my attention to." This capacity for imitation was not just intellectual but emotional, as he found it easy to perceive and duplicate the moods of his acquaintances. Early in the *Confession* he admits, "Such was the enthusiasm of all my passions, that when I had a bosom friend, all his partialities were my partialities, all his antipathies mine." Beauchamp's strange talent for mimicry found a focal point in the romantic tendencies of his day, which gave him the tools to make the ordinary appear transcendent, the devious romantic, and the depraved pure.[46]

Descriptions of Beauchamp's personality amount essentially to a checklist of the Byronic persona: an overweening quest for fame, pronounced narcissism along with an acute sensitivity to criticism, a marked tendency toward affectation, a chronic unwillingness to submit to the judgment of others, an abiding contempt for the timidity of conventional morality. Indeed, at least according to the *Confession,* it was only with great difficulty that he could suffer all the fools surrounding him: his enemies were "unworthy," "apes," and, during the trial, "perjured reptile worms." Although given to harsh judgments of others, Beauchamp himself bristled at being judged: as one of Beauchamp's acquaintances testified during the trial, "His great depravity of heart always seemed most conspicuous, whenever you formed an estimate of any of his actions." Possessed of an "inconsiderate vanity which made him consider himself superior to the whole world in schemes and intrigues"—a conceit that manifested itself in an omnipresent smirk, a "forced smile upon his countenance"—Beauchamp seldom hesitated to mislead, to lie, or to attempt to manipulate others. Like the Byronic heroes who so enchanted him, he cut himself loose from the moral dictates of society. Freedom, revolution against authority, independence: here they were in their extremity, unencumbered by tradition, authority, or discipline. He was indeed, as Timothy Flint perceived, a "wild ass's colt" living "in deserts in a moral sense."[47]

Like many other "Byromaniacs," Jereboam exhibited an extreme attachment to a lover apart from the "whole world." And again, Jereboam's profile—in his dogged persistence of and subsequent devotion to Anna—comports perfectly with the Byronic profile. A disgusted Dr. Sharp wrote that Jereboam and Anna "have no tie, religious or moral; no interest in the maintenance of a good character which they have forever lost; no inducement to bind them to correct conduct and an observance of the laws, or to restrain them from any act to which they might be stimulated by avarice or revenge." This very abandonment of convention, this unwillingness to abide by external moral codes, only further confirms their commitment to the Byronic.[48]

This "prodigious" vogue of Byron, this epidemic of misanthropic "little Byrons," was more than a literary fad or an affectation among the poet's readers. Byron's work, although created in its own context for reasons distinct from Americans', gave perfect expression to a new romantic worldview that flung itself against the remnants of the republican world of rationality and discipline and duty, of all the virtues advocated by the spokesmen of the founding generation. Byron made liberation, individual display, and the questioning of authority attractive; he invested it all with a sense of charm, mystery, and wonder. Yet, in an important sense, the Byronic cult was not so much a reaction to but a logical extension of the Revolutionary era's antiauthoritarianism, of its rejection of limits and external control. As George Bancroft mused in 1838, "the secret of Byron's power lay in part in the harmony which existed between his muse and the democratic tendency of the age." In William Prescott's estimation, all the hallmarks of the Byronic hero—passion, alienation, "selfishness of egotism," misanthropy, a "haughty spirit of independence," the impulse to seek "solitary communion with nature"—were "characteristic of an age of revolution, when ancient dynasties have crumbled at a touch, and empires have passed away like a dream," when "society has been shaken to its foundations."[49]

Prescott's insight suggests that there was a connection between Americans' embrace of Byron and the social upheaval of the previous decades. Historians such as Gordon Wood, Joyce Appleby, and Daniel Feller have successively illuminated how, in the aftermath of the American Revolution—an event Wood compares to "the breaking of a dam"—old ways and constraints collapsed under the deluge of democratization. According to Appleby, independence brought "an enlarged scope for acting on desires and convictions." In politics, in social relations, in economic endeavor, in sheer physical movement, this sense of boundlessness, possibility, and freedom permeated early American society and imparted a potent sense of individual autonomy and release from the restrictions of the past; early-nineteenth-century Americans, according to Feller, "felt it in their power to determine their future." This remarkably broad framework has helped us to comprehend a vast array of early American developments: the widening franchise, the rejection of traditional Calvinism and the democratization of Christianity, the greater acceptance of market-based economies, the explosion of westward settlement, the appearance of utopian communities, and the increase in sexual experimentation.[50]

Yet what these optimistic accounts of early American reinvention downplay or ignore is the darker side of possibility—that this sense of boundlessness could be as disturbing as it was exhilarating. American society, as Prescott shrewdly observed, had indeed been "shaken to its foundations" by the continuing aftershocks of the American Revolution and its questioning of authority, a force at once terrifically powerful and profoundly unsettling. Many Americans were all too aware of the inherent possibility that the young republic could not find the Revolution's off switch, that a permanent upheaval in all spheres of human activity, including matters of morality and sexuality, was possible. The ascendant sensational psychology, most closely associated with John Locke, suggested a world governed not necessarily by innate moral sensibility but by what society told itself to believe. Romanticism, meanwhile, contained a core imperative that truth and beauty must be created rather than discovered. When all this combined with the furor of materialism, in which concerns for what was good and true were subordinated to an obsession with what was popular and saleable, what moral traditions could survive? Thus loomed the specter of chaos, the anarchic fate of America that European conservatives had long predicted.[51]

Nowhere was this sense of social plasticity more acute or widespread than in the West of the early republic. There, geographic expansion coupled with democratic antiauthoritarianism to create a mutually energizing and extraordinarily explosive compound. Traditional institutions of religion, law, politics, and economics were weakened or obliterated or never created. The consequent "a-institutionalism" that in time transformed into an anti-institutionalism was catalogued by Henry James's remembrance of early-nineteenth-century America:

> One might enumerate the items of high civilization, as it exists in other countries, which [were] absent from the texture of American life, until it should become a wonder to know what was left. No State, in the European sense of the word, and indeed barely a specific national name. No sovereign, no court, no personal loyalty, no aristocracy, no church, no clergy, no army, no diplomatic service, no country gentlemen, no palaces, no castles, nor manors, nor old county-houses, no parsonages, nor thatched cottages nor ivied ruins; no cathedrals, nor abbeys, nor little Norman churches; no great Universities nor public schools—no Oxford, nor Eton, nor Harrow; no literature, no novels, no museums, no pictures, no political society, no sporting class.

America had outrun—in all senses of the word—old ways. To some, it felt like freedom; to others, it felt like being pushed off a cliff. In 1833 New Englander and future transcendentalist James Freeman Clarke, fresh out of Harvard Divinity School, arrived in Louisville hoping to find in the raw West "real freedom of thought and opinion," a place where one was free to express one's "individual convictions." And, indeed, Clarke found "a motley group of modern notions . . . rushing in" to replace the moribund "old Virginian chivalric sentiments." But such was the influx of ideas and sensations that it all approached, he thought, intellectual anarchy: "Public opinion is not an intolerant despotism, for there is no such thing as Public Opinion. The most opposite and contradictory principles, notions, opinions are proclaimed every day. Every variety of human thought here finds its representative. All incongruous, shifting, amorphous. No spirit of order broods over this Chaos." Freeman's observations were not idiosyncratic; one of the key characteristics of westerners, according to one popular guidebook, was an "independence of thought and action." Having "lived almost without restraint," many westerners had "greatly perverted or degenerated" the "virtue of independence." One Englishman wandering through central Kentucky thought that "liberty here means to do each as he pleases." In the nation's capital, Harriet Martineau marveled, "The odd mortals that wander in from the western border cannot be described as a class, for no one is like anybody else." Rather than seeing the region as backward and out of touch with the cultural designs of the day, it would be more accurate to see the West as a uniquely fertile ground for such romantic self-fashioning, for the cultivation of self-generated moral codes.[52]

Some were scarcely surprised that a Jereboam Beauchamp arose out this antinomian chaos; Timothy Flint, reviewing *The Confession of Jereboam O. Beauchamp,* sadly observed, "We have seen multitudes of miniature Beauchamps, who only wanted excitement, opportunity, a clear stage, and fair play, to have enacted a similar tragedy. It is the same germ of character, which gives birth to the numberless pistolings, shootings, dirkings, assassinations duels, which form such a bloody stain on the robe of the west."[53]

Thus the democratic tendencies of the early republic were not just social and political but profoundly moral, and under certain conditions, they transfigured into an antinomian crisis in which belief systems and codes of behavior seemed alarmingly mutable. The era's literature—the material that so enraptured Jereboam and Anna—gave clear expression and encouragement to such tendencies. If Americans could indeed "make the world anew," if culture and society were so mutable, if principles and ideals were at the mercy of the vagaries of environment, then, in the words of David Brion Davis, "each man would be exceptional, a product of unique pressures and influences. He would be a law unto himself." Perhaps inevitably, the uneasiness attending such radical cultural transformation found expression in early America's taste for literature, which itself suggests a country of "successful rebels slightly frightened by their own freedom," a people profoundly concerned that the "quest for liberty could lead to an increasing denial of limits."

And thus the sublime rebellion of the Byronic hero, a superman of sorts—the bastard child of sensational psychology, environmentalism, and materialism. It was a species of antinomianism that was not, of course, new to America but, like the era's seduction literature, thoroughly secularized in a way that America had never seen.[54]

As the *Confession* tells it, as soon as Anna reveals her secret to Jereboam, he rashly determines to journey to Frankfort and challenge Colonel Sharp to a duel. Although Anna begs him to wait until Sharp returns to Bowling Green, where her friends and an outraged public would support whatever revenge he should choose, the headstrong Beauchamp cannot be dissuaded, and he sets off for the capital in October 1821. Outside a Frankfort tavern, Beauchamp finds Sharp, who, suspecting nothing, cordially greets him. The younger man informs Sharp that he has come on important business and asks if he will walk with him. Once outside the town limits, Beauchamp wheels about and furiously confronts Sharp about "the injured Miss Cooke." Sharp turns "pale as a corpse" as Beauchamp announces that he has been "deputed" by Anna to kill him. Yet when Beauchamp challenges Sharp to a duel, the base coward refuses: "My dear friend I cannot fight you on account of Miss Cooke. . . . I never can fight the friend of that worthy injured lady." The tale continues:

> He then step'd back a step, and I thought from the turn of his eye was preparing to run. I sprang forward and caught him by the breast of his coat, and said, now you damn'd villian you shall die. He then fell on his knees and said, my life is in your hands, my friend I beg my life. Spare it for mercy's sake. I let go his coat and slapped him in the face, so hard as to tilt him back on his hands. I then said get up you coward, and go till I meet you in the street to-morrow; and as he arose, I gave him a kick; now said I go arm yourself, for to-morrow I shall horsewhip you in the streets, and repeat it daily till you fight me a duel. He then began to beg again; called me his dear friend in every sentence; told me how miserable he was for his conduct; said his whole estate was at our command, and any thing we chose to require at his hands, if I would let him live, for his wife and child's sake, and then advanced, again to kneel to me. I told him to stand off you villian, or I will take your life for the insult of offering me your *estate*. He said he did not mean to insult me, but any thing under Heaven, he would do which I would require if I would

> spare his life. I told him it was unnecessary to multiply words, for he would have to kill me or I would him, so that he had better at once consent to fight me.

The account has Sharp alternately weeping, whining, flattering, and groveling before Beauchamp; at one point, Sharp even concedes the justice of Beauchamp's vengeance: "Here take my life. I deserve it."[55]

It is difficult to take such rank melodrama at face value, and few scholars who have examined the Kentucky Tragedy with a modicum of skepticism have failed to note the scene's "amusing but unbelievable flavor and tone." Conveniently, there were no seconds or bystanders present to verify the encounter. And although it is certainly conceivable that Beauchamp behaved in such an aggressive and impetuous manner, it seems implausible, to say the least, that Sharp so quickly dissolved into a sniveling and obsequious coward. Englishman William Faux, after observing a duel in Lexington in 1819, wondered at "the barbarous baseness and cruelty of public opinion [that] dooms young men, when challenged to fight. They must fight, kill or be killed, and that for some petty offence beneath the notice of the law . . . to refuse is a stain and high dishonour." It was, moreover, virtually impossible for a man in early Kentucky to get elected to public office—let alone earn repeated reelection—if he shrank from, or merely had the reputation of shrinking from, violent confrontation. The premium placed on physical courage so marked among the earliest settlers of Kentucky remained a defining feature long after, and nowhere more so than among the lawyers and politicians of the state. As recent historians of early Kentucky have well documented, public displays of bravado or courage were the essential means of political ascent, especially for a young man of humble origins like Sharp. For anyone to behave in a manner remotely similar to what the *Confession* describes would have amounted to political suicide and resulted in social ostracism. Well aware of the opprobrium reserved for those deemed cowards, Leander Sharp, when he undertook to vindicate the memory of his brother, made it a priority to amass testimony disproving Beauchamp's claims of Solomon Sharp's cowardice. Young Ewing, Colonel Sharp's commander during the War of 1812, avowed, "I always found him prompt, decisive and manly," while another comrade-in-arms, James C. Cravens, testified, "There was no circumstance of his life which came within my knowledge, that evinced any want of moral courage."[56]

Yet perhaps the best reason to suspect this story is how crucial it was to

Beauchamp's self-exoneration. Only if Sharp had refused to engage Beauchamp in honorable combat could the midnight assassination possibly be excused. According to the *Confession,* Beauchamp murdered an unarmed Sharp in the dead of night not because Beauchamp was a coward but because Sharp was. As one uncritical nineteenth-century popularizer of the Kentucky Tragedy put it, Beauchamp, after Sharp refused to duel him, "considered himself at liberty to avenge [Anna] even by assassination."[57]

The *Confession*'s tale resumes the morning after Beauchamp's putative confrontation with Sharp, our hero prowling the streets of Frankfort with a horsewhip in hand, vainly searching for his victim. (One might think that somebody would have later recalled a strange young man roaming the capital with a horsewhip, looking to flog the state's attorney general; alas, no one was ever found.) Beauchamp is then told that Sharp has returned to Bowling Green, and so he jumps on his horse and rushes back to Warren County, only to discover that he has been duped; Sharp has never left Frankfort. Outmaneuvered, Beauchamp then resolves to lay in wait, ready to beat or kill Sharp at a moment's notice. He watches the Bowling Green courts "with a hawk's eye" for Sharp should he return. Beauchamp even had a "spy" in the town to help him keep vigilant.[58]

And yet, if we are to believe the *Confession,* four years passed without a single chance for Beauchamp to kill or publicly shame Sharp, despite a number of schemes he and Anna claim to have concocted. In one, they seek to lure Sharp to Retirement so that Anna, who has been enthusiastically practicing marksmanship, can kill him herself. Anna writes a letter to Sharp "telling him that notwithstanding the feelings she had manifested towards him, when last she saw him and the sternness with which she had forbid him never to see her again, these had not been the feeling of her heart, but only the momentary effusions of delirium." Sharp replies with a "most feeling letter," promising to visit her soon. When word comes that he is in town, the couple lies in wait. But Sharp never appears, and when the frustrated Beauchamp dashes off to Bowling Green, he finds that Sharp "was two full days on his way to Frankfort!" Undaunted, Anna and Jereboam try yet again to set a trap, this time writing a letter to Sharp under the impossible name "Zebulon X. Yantis," requesting a conference with Sharp to discuss land litigation. Sharp, in all likelihood sensing that something is amiss, sends a noncommittal reply. And thus, after years of miscarried plots and bootless intrigue, the *Confession* asserts that Beauchamp "began to grow impatient."[59]

This dramatic story of a frustrated, four-year quest for revenge makes for great drama, but once again, all indications are that most of it is complete nonsense. Sharp, as the state attorney general, regularly attended sessions of the Warren County circuit court in Bowling Green, and he did so in the February and August terms of 1822 and again in the August term of 1823. As Dr. Sharp later asserted, Beauchamp "had numerous opportunities to execute his bloody design, if he had formed it." More pointedly, Beauchamp was not planning to harm Sharp in these years—on the contrary, he was soliciting Sharp's patronage. In 1823, Beauchamp and an acquaintance named George Work sought out Dr. Sharp and asked if his brother had any notes they could collect for him. Dr. Sharp "gave him one or more notes for collection," and, according to John L. Moore, the clerk of the Simpson County circuit court, Beauchamp successfully collected the money for Colonel Sharp in the case of *S. P. Sharp v. Micajah Clark*. According to Simpson County sheriff Thomas L. Stratton, Beauchamp anxiously expressed a desire "to obtain the further patronage of Col. Sharp." Eliza Sharp claimed that Beauchamp did in fact meet with her husband in Bowling Green several times after his move to Frankfort in 1821—and never "shewed by his conduct, that he harbored the slightest hostility against him." Thus, far from patiently lying in wait for Sharp, Beauchamp "was endeavoring to demean himself as to gain his friendship and further patronage." Moreover, a number of witnesses later swore that Beauchamp was in the habit of expressing a high regard for Colonel Sharp. One, B. F. Simpson, testified that he had heard Beauchamp about this time describe Sharp "as a gentleman and a man of talents"; Thomas M. Smith, a Franklin County lawyer, attested that Jereboam's father had told him that he, Thomas Beauchamp, "knew of no enmity between him and Colonel Sharp"; George Work, who claimed to be "intimate" with Beauchamp, swore at the trial that he had no recollection of Beauchamp's ever expressing any "hostility towards Col. Sharp" and in fact had "an impression on my mind, that I have heard him speak highly of Col. Sharp." As Dr. Sharp summarized in his *Vindication*, "It appears, that down to the year 1824, J. O. Beauchamp had no malice or ill will against Col. Sharp."[60]

In June 1824, in a simple ceremony at Retirement, Jereboam and Anna were wed by William Lynch, justice of the peace. The *Confession* gives contradictory explanations of why the couple waited three years to get married. At one point, it claims that they waited until Jereboam could finish his law studies. Only a few pages later, however, the Jereboam persona claims that the delay was because of his inability to kill Sharp: "I did feel, that I never could call Miss Cooke my wife, till Col. Sharp should die at my hands: and she said, she felt unworthy of me, and would feel that she had degraded me by marrying me, before I have revenged the injuries she had received." Neither excuse makes much sense. Beauchamp was admitted to the bar a year before he was married, and he did not kill Sharp until a year and a half later. The Sharp family later explained the three-year delay of the wedding by pointing out that, for much of their early relationship, Beauchamp was not old enough to get married—he did not turn twenty-one until September 1823—and that his father, "well apprized of Ann Cook's infamous character," refused to give his assent to the pairing. Eliza Sharp added that Beauchamp, who "laughed at the delicacy of his family who would have dissuaded him from forming this connection," tried "to extort a marriage license from the Clerk" by "presenting a loaded pistol to the breast of the clerk who had been forbidden to give him one." Yet a fourth explanation for the timing of the marriage, one that Beauchamp himself apparently gave to both Lynch and a neighbor, John F. Lowe, was that Anna was pregnant. Because Anna never gave birth to a child by Jereboam, Dr. Sharp contended that the pregnancy was a lie of Anna's to get him to marry her. Whatever the reason, the two had now committed themselves to one another, for richer and poorer, for better and much, much worse.[61]

CHAPTER 4

Politics

To me and mine leave Osman Bey;
I've partisans for peril's day:
Think not I am what I appear;
I've arms, and friends, and vengeance near.

—Byron, *The Bride of Abydos,* canto 1

In May 1822, a special session of the Kentucky General Assembly gathered for the primary and relatively simple purpose of reapportioning the state's representation according to the fourth census, which entitled Kentucky to two additional legislators. Governor John Adair, in his opening message of May 14, noted that he was "not aware of the existence of any subject to which the public interest invites your protracted deliberations." Only a few days into the session, however, Judge James Clark of the Bourbon County circuit court provided something for the lawmakers to protractedly deliberate; in the case of *Williams v. Blair,* Clark ruled that Kentucky's 1820 replevin law impaired the obligation of preexisting contracts and thereby violated both state and federal constitutions. The relief-dominated General Assembly instantly wheeled about to face the judiciary's assault on its program and peremptorily summoned Judge Clark to defend his decision.[1]

Clark, in a written defense, maintained that any judge was duty bound to nullify laws that "sober judgment tells him are within the prohibition of the constitution." It was not the judiciary, Clark maintained, but the legislature that had overstepped its boundaries by attempting to intimidate a justice for his considered decision. Such a practice, if tolerated, would undermine the independence of the judiciary, and judges "will in future times become the subservient creatures of the predominant party in the general assembly." American government would then closely resemble the corrupt British-style politics that Americans had rebelled against during the Revolution.[2]

The representatives would have none of it. Ours is a democracy, they asserted. How could one man who was never made to stand before the people thwart the direct representatives of more than half a million citizens? Among the leading defenders of the relief program was Fayette County representative George Shannon, who nineteen years earlier had gained renown as the youngest member of Lewis and Clark's Corps of Discovery. Shannon, now thirty-seven, admitted that relief legislation was indeed exceptional, yet acute distress and imminent ruin dictated the absolute necessity of the laws. To rob the assembly of its ability to periodically shield the state's citizenry from disaster—as Clark's decision would do—would not only expose the people to untold misery but weaken the very foundations of American government. Did not a republic rest on a broad ownership of property? If debt collections were allowed unimpeded, then property would flow from the debtor majority to the creditor minority and create an aristocracy of wealth. And by no means, Shannon and his allies repeatedly and accurately maintained, were such relief measures novel; they had been passed in times of crisis for generations. Relief partisans insisted that the radicals—those who were most clearly departing from precedent—were in fact the judges and their anti-relief supporters. The attempt to overturn legislative relief programs, Frankfort newspaper editor Amos Kendall declared, was based on a principle "new and monstrous." Thus "the interest of the country" required the ouster of Clark, Shannon concluded, for should this vision of judicial supremacy prevail, "a scene of distress, alarm, and embarrassment would ensue unparalleled in the annals of this country."[3]

On Tuesday, May 21, a legislative special committee submitted a report that excoriated Clark for advocating principles "incompatible with the constitutional powers of the Legislative department of this government, subversive of the best interests of the people, and calculated in their consequences to disturb the tranquility of the country." Accordingly, the committee introduced a resolution to remove Clark from office by means of legislative address. The vote in the house, however—fifty-nine to thirty-five—fell four votes short of the two-thirds needed to oust the judge, and the issue was temporarily laid aside as the case was appealed to the state high court.[4]

A year later, as the Thirty-second General Assembly convened in October 1823, the state supreme court—the court of appeals—handed down its ruling. In *Blair v. Williams,* as well as in a companion case appealed from the general court, *Lapsley v. Brashear,* Justices John Boyle, William Owsley, and Benjamin Mills sustained Clark's decision, in effect confirming the illegality of the legislature's entire relief program. The effect was instantaneous and electric; the decisions unleashed one of the more vicious political contests of early America. As anti-relief leader George Robertson later remembered, "No popular controversy, waged without bloodshed, was ever more absorbing and acrimonious than that which raged, like a hurricane, over Kentucky for about three years succeeding the promulgation of those judicial decisions." When the Duke of Saxe-Weimar-Eisenach passed through in 1826, Kentucky "was torn by parties; I was assured that political struggles, often terminating in sanguinary conflicts, were the order of the day. . . . It is said to be almost as dangerous to speak upon the political relations of the state, as to converse upon religion in Spain."[5]

The timing of the uproar is significant; it reveals that the issues at the heart of the relief war went well beyond narrowly defined financial interests. The state's economy, although not yet back to full strength, was clearly recovering by late 1823. The relief party, as we have seen, had already begun to dismantle its own programs: the replevin law had been pared down to a negligible three months, and the Bank of the Commonwealth was burning the notes it had withdrawn from circulation. Yet it was precisely at this point that the relief war mutated into its most volatile phase: the old court versus new court struggle, in which the legislature and the judiciary, in essence, went to war. This court struggle was, to some degree, a continuation of previous battles—among the respective leadership, almost to a person the alignments were identical to what they had been for the four years previous. Yet the issues at hand, which had been primarily economic, now became much more constitutional, and with this change came a heightened conviction—on both sides of the issue—that fundamental principles of republican government itself were at stake: the powers of the legislature and the judiciary, the nature and extent of popular sovereignty, and the propriety and limits of judicial review.

The judicial decisions of 1822 and 1823 reignited a long-standing, smoldering animosity toward the judiciary among ordinary Kentuckians, a bitterness rooted in the state's chronic confusion over land titles and, more particularly, in the basically accurate perception that "metaphysical courts," "aristocratic judges," and "cunning lawyers" had been assisting wealthy landowners and speculators in their land suits against small farmers and were thereby "turning our race of freemen and free holders into a body of tenantry." The indispensable role played by judges in the wave of debt collections and forced sales of the previous five years only exacerbated the resentment. And now these very same "placemen" presumed to assert the still controversial powers of judicial review and set aside law established by the people's direct representatives. Small wonder that a pronounced majority initially sustained the legislature's "judge-breaking" in the belief that the legal authorities were "determined to support the interests of their order at the expense of any other interest in the community."[6]

The leader of the legislature's attack against the judiciary, the "magnus Apollo of the judge breakers" who "rode the whirlwind and directed the storm," was John Rowan. A native of York, Pennsylvania, Rowan was fifty-two years old in 1823, a massive, "leonine" man—six feet, two inches tall and possessed of "large and heavy" features—nicknamed "Old Monarch" by Ben Hardin. A seasoned veteran of Kentucky politics, Rowan had been elected in 1799 to the first of many terms in the state assembly, and he served that same year as a member of Kentucky's second constitutional convention. From 1804 to 1808, he served as Governor Christopher Greenup's secretary of state, and thereafter he was elected to the U.S. House of Representatives. In 1819, Governor Slaughter appointed Rowan to the court of appeals, a position he resigned a year later.[7]

In December 1823, Rowan determined to bring his former colleagues to heel as he authored a set of resolutions condemning the decisions of the court of appeals. In an extensive, twenty-six-page preamble, he reiterated and expanded on the relief party's basic position: the state had, and absolutely must continue to have, an inviolable right to relieve "a great portion of a community who had become indebted by a reasonable anticipation of their resources and were about to be ruined by an unexpected revolution in the state of affairs." In a democratic republic, the judiciary—the least accountable branch of government—had no right to thwart the will of the people's direct representatives. Their "morally indefensible" interference would, in effect, "unnerve" the legislature, "paralyze . . . its power," and throw it into a "state of helpless inaction." The judge's rulings and, indeed, the entirety of the anti-reliefers' strict, formalistic, contractual view of government and society would result in the "extinction in the human heart, not only of all its honorable and honest sensations, of all its love of justice, and of all its charitable impulses, but of all its social tendencies." Another prominent relief man proclaimed, "Our government is not so much *a balance of power,* as a well-connected *chain of responsibility.* . . . We are becoming so very *constitutional,* both at home and abroad, that if our rights and liberties pass through a few more *refining fires,* they will be absorbed in the chemical process." Kentucky's lower house promptly adopted Rowan's preamble and resolutions by a vote of fifty-six to forty.[8]

A year later, in November 1824, Rowan substantially revised and the General Assembly once again adopted his "preamble and resolutions," as they were now widely known, and the document soon stood as the relief party's most developed statement of principle, its de facto platform. Rowan began this remarkable elaboration of his earlier arguments with a fundamental article of American faith—"*The will of the people is the sovereign power of the state.*" Yet he quickly proceeded to advocate truly radical concepts of popular sovereignty premised on Rousseauian notions of a tight-knit community of active citizens unhampered by any check on their collective will. The people, participating in the public realm, composed "a corporate existence, a moral agent, [that] is invested with all the attributes and faculties of moral agency; it is an entirety; it thinks, reflects, reasons, wills, and acts." Such a political collective, moreover, was necessarily and inevitably disinterested; it had no ulterior motives; its only "object is, and must necessarily be, the promotion of the general welfare." Supreme, benevolent, unerring and virtuous, this collective "moral agent" not only was the sole "controlling and paramount power, competent to all the purposes of government," but was expressed exclusively through the legislature, the members of which were, after all, merely servants of this general will. "Government only is free," Rowan thundered in a sweeping denial of checks and balances, "which knows no restraint upon the exercise of its legislative faculties." And thus, when the state judiciary seeks to restrict the legislature, "would not the judges control the people themselves?" Would not the people "cease to be sovereign when they are controlled, and the Judges who control them become the sovereign?" The judiciary's assault on the legislature's expression of the people's will therefore constituted "nothing more nor less than tyranny."[9]

The rights of minorities within this corporate, democratic community, Rowan insisted, were nonexistent: "All that is said . . . about the rights of minorities, is incompatible with the very nature of civil society." The majority, Rowan asserted, was "the channel through which the stream of . . . [the general] will must, to be efficient, flow. The minority is the divergent tendency of a portion of its volume, which, by meeting with resistance in its lateral direction forms a temporary eddy, and again disappears by its confluence with the general stream." In a breathtaking conclusion—one that would have sent Sharp's friend John C. Calhoun reeling—Rowan declared that "the presumption is, always, that the minority is wrong; and the only right which it has, is to escape from that imputation by endeavoring to become, through its enlargement, the majority." Aside from their dubious constitutionality, such radical majoritarian notions at once betrayed the hubris of a faction that had not lost an election in five years and effectually held the party hostage to its continued success: Rowan and the rest of the relief party arrogantly assumed that their political triumphs would continue unabated and that they themselves would never become "a temporary eddy" in their enemies' "general stream."[10]

The general elections in the summer of 1824 served as a referendum on both the judiciary's assault on the relief program and the majority party's hyperpopulism. It was not even close. The voters gave the relief party a two-thirds majority in the General Assembly and overwhelmingly elected pro-relief Joseph Desha the ninth governor of Kentucky. Emboldened, the relief partisans further escalated their attack on the judiciary. After overwhelmingly reaffirming their endorsement of Rowan's preamble and resolutions, the house on December 20, 1824, attempted to impeach the court of appeals judges but fell just short of the requisite two-thirds vote.[11]

Once again frustrated in their attempt to unseat recalcitrant judges, the members of the General Assembly, undaunted, undertook perhaps the most audacious step in antebellum legislative history: they abolished the state supreme court and replaced it with one more to their liking. Relief partisans justified their actions by an ambiguous provision in Kentucky's 1799 constitution that stated that "the judicial power of the state, shall be vested in one Supreme Court, which shall be called the Court of Appeals, and in such inferior courts as the Legislature shall from time to time, ordain and establish." The "judge-breakers," in effect, disregarded the comma after "Court of Appeals" and insisted that the subsequent clause gave the legislature the power to "ordain and establish" not only inferior courts but the state supreme court itself. As Rowan insisted, "The judicial machinery of all the courts, supreme and inferior, is of legislative creation, and is of course subject to remodification by the legislature, as the public good may require."[12]

And thus, after two days of tumultuous debate amid scenes that "resembled a camp night-meeting, in confusion and chaos," in a session stretching into the early morning hours of December 24, 1824, the General Assembly by a vote of fifty-four to forty-four passed a statute designed "to Repeal the Law Organizing the Court of Appeals, and to Reorganize the Court of Appeals." Governor Joseph Desha, awaiting the fate of the measure on the floor of the assembly, immediately signed the reorganization bill. Two weeks later, on January 10, 1825, Desha appointed his secretary of state, William T. Barry, the chief justice of this "new court" and appointed James Haggin, John Trimble, and Benjamin Patton (who died a month later and was replaced by Rezin Davidge) associate justices. Unable by conventional means to tame the judiciary, the legislative and executive branches created their own.[13]

Reactions were immediate and impassioned. The supporters of this "new court" were ebullient, believing they had overthrown a bastion of aristocracy and privilege: "The siege is raised, the *Rubicon* is passed, the *battle is over,* victory is the *people's,*" exclaimed Andrew Hughes, a state senator from northern Kentucky. Anti-relief partisans were, of course, considerably less sanguine: George Robertson, a representative from Garrard County and a leading opponent of both relief and reorganization, proclaimed that on the evening the bill passed, "Satan himself . . . presided over the orgies." Thirty-six state representatives and twelve state senators immediately issued a formal protest, proclaiming, "WE DO CONSIDER IT A REVOLUTION. We consider this unparalleled act as an attempt by the majority to consolidate their power and perpetuate their supremacy, over the rights of the minority." Robert Wickliffe, who quickly assumed leadership of this "old court" faction, portrayed the reorganizers as power-mad radicals: "You have now precisely the revolutionary government that France had—a dominant faction without a check, uniting in their own hands all the powers of government." The old court partisans focused on the dubious constitutionality of the reorganization act itself and thereby shrewdly distanced the court battle from earlier questions concerning the morality and necessity of relief legislation: "It is purely a constitutional question which . . . divides us," the *Danville Olive Branch* explained. "At former elections, we contended at different times whether we should have a relief law, a bank, or the judges broken constitutionally. Now we contend for our constitution, our government, the safety of ourselves and our children." Without complex disquisitions on the rights of minorities, the prerogatives of judges, or the obligations of contracts, the old court supporters hammered away at the reorganizers in terms that even the dullest citizen could understand: "CONSTITUTION OR NO CONSTITUTION is the question." Thus, by mid-1825, the opposition had constructed a powerful yet simple message: "DOWN WITH USURPERS; LONG LIVE LIBERTY; LONG LIVE THE CONSTITUTION."[14]

The eight months between the passage of the reorganization act and the pivotal election of the summer of 1825 were extraordinarily volatile. In March, a weary Amos Kendall wrote to the new U.S. secretary of state, Henry Clay, "Passion is taking the place of reason and you have little conception of the ferocious feelings by which many men . . . are actuated. Violence on one side begets violence on the other, and a degree of heat is rising which not only puts an end to all fair and honorable discussion, but actually endangers the public peace."[15]

Days after the passage of the reorganization act, the *Frankfort Argus of Western America* reported, almost in passing, "The Attorney General has given an opinion that it is constitutional." Personally, Solomon Sharp thought the reorganization act an ill-advised piece of legislation, and he had counseled moderation throughout the December debates. But as the chief law officer of the commonwealth, he concluded that the legislation was in fact constitutional and that he was bound by duty to enforce it. The act's enemies, who had hoped Sharp would register some sort of protest, immediately went on the offensive. "We trust," an old court newspaper in Louisville sneered on the first day of 1825, "Mr. Sharp was not also in danger of being *politely legislated out of office.*" And so Sharp, whose professional duties had, as he had put it only a few months earlier, "happily" kept him above the political anarchy of the relief war, was dragged back into the dark and bloody ground of Kentucky's politics.[16]

On January 27, old court justices John Boyle, William Owsley, and Benjamin Mills, shortly after caucusing with anti-relief doyen Robert Wickliffe and other opponents of reorganization, conspicuously convened into session as a means of protesting the legislature's actions. The court was attended only by old court lawyers, with the exception of Sharp, who "said he would attend merely as he would go to any other *show* where they made no charge." Chief Justice Boyle, presiding, proclaimed "that the court had not met with an intention of entering upon the docket, or doing business—the late act of the Legislature perhaps rendered it inexpedient, perhaps improper," but would hear any motion the court lawyers might have. None made, the court adjourned until the April term.[17]

The next week, Sharp was drawn more deeply still into the conflict when the new court convened and the question arose of who would serve as the clerk of this "reorganized" court—and, more specifically, who would have control of the high court's papers. Achilles Sneed had been the clerk of the court of appeals for the previous twenty-three years and had been given assurances that he would continue his post with the new court. But when the judges of the old court met on January 27, Sneed dispatched a deputy to serve them. Only a few days later, however, Sneed told two of the new court justices that he wished to be their clerk. Seeing that Sneed was trying to play both sides of the fence, new court partisans accused him of treachery, some going so far as to claim that Sneed, were he appointed new court clerk, would attempt to undermine the court from within. And so on February 3, when the new court justices took their oaths of office in front of "a large concourse of lawyers and citizens," Sneed was passed over, and Francis P. Blair, loyal supporter of the new court, was appointed clerk. Sharp, who was present, moved that Sneed be directed to immediately deliver to Blair "all the papers, records, property etc. belonging to the Clerk's office of the late Court of Appeals."[18]

Yet when Blair requested the records, Sneed replied, "I cannot, consistently with my rights nor duties, deliver to you the papers and records of my office." The next morning, Friday, February 4, the new court justices charged Sneed with contempt of court and ordered him to immediately surrender the documents. That afternoon, Sneed and his counsel, John J. Crittenden, appeared before the court, requesting a one-day postponement to prepare an answer to the charges. Although granting the delay, the judges also ordered Sergeant at Arms Richard Taylor to seize the papers. Proceeding at once to Sneed's home only a block away, where he kept his office, Taylor found the door locked and entered through a window, thereby securing a number of documents. On Saturday morning, Sharp charitably suggested that, as the papers had been secured, the charges of contempt against Sneed be dropped. But later that afternoon, Blair discovered that "the dockets, order books, writs and transcripts relating to causes now pending and undetermined" were not among the seized papers. Sharp, by this point having run out of patience, vowed, "I mean to have the papers" and prepared sixteen questions "of the most searching kind," demanding that Sneed explain why he had not turned over all the documents.[19]

On Monday morning, John Harvie, president of the Bank of Kentucky, appeared before the court to deliver Sneed's reply to Sharp's questions. Through Harvie, Sneed maintained that he was still the clerk of the court of appeals, for he had been appointed "during good behavior," and, having faithfully discharged his duties, had been unlawfully dismissed. He furthermore contended that the reorganization act was unconstitutional, that the old court was the lawful supreme court in Kentucky, and that, because he was the only lawful court of appeals clerk, it was still his duty to safeguard the documents. This argument, of course, would have been much more persuasive had Sneed not six days earlier supplicated the supposedly illegitimate new court judges to be their clerk. Sharp, in his eighth question, squarely addressed the issue: "Is not your determination now to retain the Records, books, papers, etc. belonging to the Court of Appeals, in consequence of the Court having passed your claims to the appointment of Clerk, and their having appointed another?" Sneed waved off the suggestion as "impertinent" and attempted to play the sympathy card, claiming to be but a "humble" man whose only desire was "to do his duty; to give no offence; and to await with resignation and submission, the course of events, and the issue of the great political contest." But now, because of the new court's actions, he was "likely to be driven from his office, and compelled, now that he has grown old and grey headed, to seek abroad in the world, for new employments." (Sneed, who was only fifty-two years old, neglected to state that his net worth was over forty thousand dollars—roughly eight hundred thousand dollars in today's money—and that he was in very little danger of being cast adrift in the world.)[20]

Theatrics aside, it eventually came out that the missing documents had been returned to the former clerk's office. Sharp promptly ordered the court officers to return to Sneed's house and seize them. But finding the door once again locked and being "forewarned in [Sneed's] name, by a gentleman there, not to enter," Taylor was forced to go back to the court to get legal permission to forcefully enter the residence. "A verbal order to that effect was *unhesitatingly* given by the court," and the sergeant at arms returned, entered as before through a window, and finally carted away all the needed documents. The judges found Sneed's behavior "highly improper" and fined him ten pounds.[21]

All in all, the affair was not especially well handled by the new court, and the result amounted to a pyrrhic victory, one that provided their enemies an excellent opportunity to pillory them as crude and arrogant usurpers. The ungraceful manner in which the documents were procured—the repeated and forcible entries into Sneed's house—was not flattering to a court whose legality was already dubious. Sharp's role in the episode was not his finest moment either; his pointed questioning of Sneed only underscored a prior reputation for imperiousness and allowed the old court partisans to portray the attorney general as the new court's "arch-inquisitor." The *Kentucky Reporter,* for one, took Sharp to task for trying to "read the heart" of the "aged and venerable" Sneed: "All the sixteen questions are in manner and form, truly revolting to a republican mind." Another paper, the *Maysville Eagle,* tactfully submitted that the behavior of "Mr. Sharp might have been improper, as we frequently see even the best of lawyers sometimes ask improper questions."[22]

In addition, Sharp's position on the reorganization act—a law he personally opposed but officially enforced—revived the old charge that he was a "trimmer," a political "Proteus" who "turned completely round in politics, to catch the popular breeze." The inconsistency, his opponents argued, amounted to nothing less than sheer and typical opportunism on Sharp's part. He had, they sneered, "*cut a summerset,* with his brother, the Doctor, upon his shoulders, fearing he might break his neck in the fall, and became the advocate of revolution; thus degrading the state which he represents, and prostituting the office which he fills, by appearing for the Commonwealth before this band of usurpers." Charges of Sharp's putative "apostacy" and moral duplicity would continue to be aired long after his death.[23]

Sharp's defenders, of course, denied any great inconsistency. Amos Kendall's *Argus* maintained that Sharp "has performed his duty throughout this transaction with the utmost firmness and fidelity." Kendall later added, "It is true that he was opposed to breaking the judges; but it did not thence follow that he should refuse to sanction an act which he believed constitutional, when passed by a majority of the people's representatives." To his adoring brother, Colonel Sharp had heroically displayed "inflexible firmness" during the whole ordeal and, in so doing, had "brought down upon him the most bitter denunciations from the active men of the old Court party."[24]

For a brief moment in the spring of 1825, Kentuckians focused their attention on something other than politics: the visit of the venerable Marquis de Lafayette. Ebenezer Stedman, a semiliterate papermaker from central Kentucky, vividly recalled the universal excitement that the arrival of the sixty-eight-year-old Revolutionary War hero generated: "No Man Before & no man Ever will in all time, have Such Exibations of Love & attention paid him as he had. . . . I cannot give you anny idea of the feeling amounght The people. It seemed to prevade all Classes, woman & children. . . . Evry thing was *Lafayette.*" In Frankfort, officials appropriated almost ten thousand dollars for a gala reception and requested that businesses close their doors during Lafayette's procession through town. In the six tumultuous years of the relief war, Lafayette's visit was the one event capable, at least for a moment, of uniting the fractured state. The *Kentucky Reporter* envisaged with as much longing as prescience, "One spontaneous impulse will assemble the entire population of the district—all being alike influenced by grateful and patriotic feelings."[25]

Solomon Sharp was given the honor of welcoming Lafayette to Kentucky when the aging Frenchman arrived in Louisville on May 11, 1825. The oration itself was nothing remarkable—a brief encomium thanking Lafayette for his efforts in the War of Independence and concluding, "We esteem this the most fortunate moment of our lives, in being permitted to speak the language of a grateful people, for the honor you do them, by this visit." Yet the honor bore witness, if any further proof was needed, to the fact that Sharp was no longer an unpolished young man of ambition. At the age of thirty-seven, he had become a mature and respectable politician, and the young upstart insecure about his abbreviated education had become, in the words of one Louisville newspaper, "a man of original and acute mind."[26]

Lafayette gone, however, the state's political warriors promptly began preparing for the most significant battle of the decade: the approaching summer elections, which would serve as a referendum on the passage of the reorganization act. An especially important race, as both sides fully appreciated, was the contest for Franklin County's two seats in the General Assembly. Because the county was the home of both the state capital and an extraordinary array of gifted politicians, its vote was of great symbolic and strategic importance, and leaders of both parties brought forward their most talented men.

The most powerful leaders of the old court party tirelessly solicited the candidacy of a reluctant John J. Crittenden: "Kentucky expects and she requires of you to put on your armor and take the field," George Robertson cajoled Crittenden in May of 1825; "will you trust the fate of the day to weaker and less counseled champions?" Crittenden was indeed a formidable presence in Kentucky politics, a man whose spectacular rise in many ways resembled Sharp's. Although born near Versailles, in the heart of central Kentucky's Bluegrass region, Crittenden's ambition led him west to the Green River district, where he believed his chances of establishing a successful legal and political career were more promising. It proved to be a shrewd move; by 1825, the thirty-eight-year-old Crittenden, in addition to establishing a lucrative private law practice, had already been the attorney general of the Illinois Territory, a six-term state assemblyman, and a U.S. senator.[27]

Contemporaries described Crittenden as "in neither form nor size uncommon" and possessed of a "homely" face, in part because of his "defective arrangement of teeth." Almost everyone found him to be charming; the fact that a visiting Virginian in 1824 thought him reserved—"civil without being polite"—was surely due to the recent death of his wife, Sallie. Crittenden was, moreover, just eccentric enough to be endearing; as his daughter remembered, "He had a habit of talking to himself with animation. He came down generally before breakfast and walked in front of the house. If alone, he talked and gesticulated earnestly, to the amusement of the children, who were peeping at him through the window. Strangers, guests in the house, would sometimes catch a glimpse of him, and say, 'Why, who is Mr. Crittenden talking to?'"[28]

Crittenden early honed the political skills that later secured him the role of Henry Clay's successor in the U.S. Senate. Warren County representative Joseph Underwood—a man who did not bestow praise lightly—thought that Crittenden "speaks beautifully, chastely, . . . and can when he chooses excite and rivet the attention of his audience." Crittenden was also accomplished in the fine art of persuasion. Perhaps using Thomas Jefferson as a model, Crittenden made it "his custom to entertain the senators and members of the Kentucky legislature every winter, giving about three dinners a week, and thus entertaining, before the session closed, every member more than once."[29]

But more than his charm or professional skills, it was Crittenden's personal integrity that earned him near universal respect. As one contemporary noted, "Mr. Crittenden has a strength of moral character which secures approbation and renders what he says or does, authority with others." This esteem, moreover, transcended party lines, a very rare accomplishment during Kentucky's relief war. Francis Blair, despite his substantial political differences with Crittenden, wrote that he was "a man whose public and private worth has endeared him to all men of all sides in Kentucky." Although he had misgivings about the legislature's program, Crittenden earned the respect of the reliefers by giving "the projected system of finance a fair trial" and even serving as the first president of the Bank of the Commonwealth. Four years later, however, the reorganization act was far too much for Crittenden, and he unequivocally cast his lot with the old court. Early that summer, he consented to become their candidate for the General Assembly.[30]

With their enemies having drafted Crittenden, new court partisans quickly began soliciting Solomon Sharp to become their man. "It was felt," Blair later attested, "that there was no other individual brought out who could contend with the great abilities of Mr. C[rittenden] to vindicate the law before the people or in the House." A Louisville paper remarked, "If any man is calculated to cope with Mr. C[rittenden] in native intellect, it is C[ol]. S[harp]." At first, however, Sharp demurred, professing to have "no wish to engage in the turmoils of our state politics." Even when a delegation of new court partisans came to his house in late May, begging him to reconsider, he told them that "it was neither his interest nor inclination to be a candidate." Finally, however, whether due to the realization that the Sneed affair had irrevocably ended any hope of staying above the fray, the importunities of his political allies, or his own considerable ambition, Sharp relented and announced his candidacy on June 29, 1825.[31]

As Sharp embarked on his campaign that summer, new court supporters feared that their enemies would revive the seduction charge. Amos Kendall, upon the official announcement of Sharp's candidacy, editorialized, "Already we are informed that Mr. Sharp is to be most relentlessly assailed both in his public and private character." Sharp himself was well aware of the possibility; his brother later wrote that "his friends and himself had long before that time been informed, that the materials had been collected, and that he would be publicly assailed with the old story of seducing Ann Cook, if he became a candidate." Yet Sharp could take comfort in the fact that the state senate had cleared him of such charges years earlier. In private, he claimed that, if necessary, he could easily procure documentation—some of it from members of Anna's own family—that would clear his name.[32]

Certainly attempts were made to make the charge an issue that summer. John U. Waring received no fewer than fourteen letters from Frankfort asking for copies of his handbill accusing Sharp of seducing Anna Cooke. The document was distributed; one man, Solomon Snow, attested that while staying at Achilles Sneed's house, his host "received by mail, a packet, or large letter, from Bowlinggreen" containing Waring's 1821 publication. Dr. Sharp later claimed that old court partisans explicitly asked Beauchamp if "his wife's name might be used in an attack on Col. Sharp. Beauchamp, according to Dr. Sharp," coldly replied that "he would put to death any man who did." Whatever the reason, Sharp's putative sexual misconduct, to the surprise of many, did not become an issue during the campaign—the accusation was not aired at all in the newspapers, and a number of observers later swore that "the subject was rarely mentioned."[33]

Which is not to say that Sharp was not the target of strident criticism or that the issue was not obliquely raised—one old court pamphlet, for example, made vague and dark allusions to "the singular system of morality, both public and private, for which he became famous before he left the South of Green river." But in the main Sharp was assailed not for his private affairs but for his public actions, in particular his position on the reorganization act, which, his enemies contended, was a sure sign of Sharp's true, duplicitous character. His harshest critic that summer was the irascible Humphrey Marshall, who in 1825 was nearing the end of his career as one of Kentucky's most controversial public figures and who—at least since his exposé of the Spanish conspiracy in 1806—fancied himself a fearless detector of public corruption. Through his newspaper, the *Frankfort Harbinger*, Marshall assailed Sharp as a "Catiline," a "profligate in morals and a weather-cock in politics; a follower of majorities and a sycophant of power," a man "not fit to be elected by an honest community."[34]

Electioneering in Kentucky was a rough and tumble affair; as the *Kentucky Gazette* explained, the western people "act upon natural ideas of liberty, and require those who tender their services to the public, to appear before the people, who are the only proper judges of the matter." Should a man aspire to public office—"the gift of the people"—then, as one paper expostulated, "the candidates presenting themselves for suffrage become fit objects for eulogy or animadversion, according to their respective merits." Robert J. Breckinridge, the well-bred son of Thomas Jefferson's attorney general, was running for the General Assembly as an old court candidate from Fayette County when he wrote his wife from Lexington: "You would be amused and mad alternately if you were here. See me one moment on a stump—a butcher's block, or a cart, addressing the multitude, pronounced by one set mad—by the other a paragon of sense and power. Handbills—speeches—fun—fight—all manner of things—but it all amuses me."[35]

Although raucous, depraved, and seemingly but a form of entertainment or distraction, politics in Kentucky was a deadly serious business, and the people thoroughly understood the issues. Questions of the decade, remembered one veteran of the relief war, were "canvassed upon the stump, at crossroads, courthouses, and everywhere in Kentucky, until almost every barefooted boy of fifteen was master of the subject." One minister reported, "It is said that in no one of the states are all political questions so thoroughly discussed and understood by the great mass of the people as in Kentucky." One amazed English aristocrat wondered that law and politics was the "chief occupation" of the mass of Kentuckians, which led, he sniffed, to a "meddling busy ignorance."[36]

The climax of the election season came every August, as the men of Kentucky flocked to the polls in a three-day orgy of partisanship, graft, liquor, and violence. In 1830, an astounded twenty-seven-year old, Connecticut-born George D. Prentice, having just arrived in Kentucky to commence research on a campaign biography of Henry Clay, wrote to a New England paper, "I have just witnessed a strange thing—a Kentucky election." For days on end, "whisky and apple toddy flow through our cities and villages like the Euphrates through ancient Babylon." Having visited several towns, Prentice wound up in Frankfort on the last day of the election, and the spectacle horrified him: "Jacksonianism and drunkenness stalked triumphant," he wrote—as if the two were one and inseparable—while "a number of runners, each with a whisky bottle poking its long neck from his pocket, were busily employed bribing voters, and each party kept half a dozen bullies under pay, genuine specimens of Kentucky alligatorism, to flog every poor fellow who should attempt to vote illegally. A half a hundred of mortar would scarcely fill up the chinks of the skulls that were broken on the occasion. I barely escaped myself." Prentice turned away, he reported, "a confirmed believer in the doctrine of total depravity."[37]

The usual frenzy of Kentucky politics was compounded by both the proximate issue of the court battle and the deeper antipathies that had been bred and nursed in the previous six or seven years. The daughter of John J. Crittenden described "a condition of public feeling that was only less violent than civil war. Private friendships were broken up, and danger of strife and bloodshed was imminent." One resident remembered,

> The most vindictive political war raged in Kentucky that was ever known in any country; and it is truly wonderful that civil commotions did not arise under it. They were often expected. At one time I witnessed an election in Frankfort, when it was thought to be unavoidable. Both parties were roused to a perfect pitch of frenzy; both believed a collision absolutely certain; both prepared for it, and both desperately determined to go to all lengths. Never did I have more awful feelings than on the day the polls opened. Every man was armed to the teeth; every man determined, if his way to the polls was obstructed, to cut it out with his arms; and now the struggle commenced. In an ordinary election, the shouts, huzzas, and fights would sometimes create a tumult to be heard a great way off. But now there was no shouting, no noise, no tumult of any kind. Every man voted, not without a general rush to the polls, however, and much crowding. But no man's toes were even trodden on, and it was the most quiet election I ever saw. The "Reliefs" carried the day by a small majority. But there was a general congratulation on all sides at the peaceful

> result, only to be accounted for by the fixed and desperate resolution, evident in every face, and the conviction of every one, that the first blood shed would be a signal for a general melee.[38]

Voters poured into Frankfort; "Horses, Dearborns, Carriages, every thing that could bring a voter, was put in requisition." Kendall guessed that "there might have been 50 voters in the whole county who were not at the polls." As it turned out, he underestimated, for ultimately sixteen hundred votes were cast in a county with approximately fourteen hundred eligible voters. In any case, when the dust cleared, Sharp had received sixty-nine more votes than the second-place finisher, John J. Crittenden.[39]

Although the relief party did well in Frankfort, statewide, in a rapid turn of events, the old court faction soundly defeated its opponents and secured a solid majority in the lower house of the state assembly (sixty-two to thirty-eight), although the new court retained control of the senate (twenty-one to seventeen). The swiftness of the turnaround surprised almost all Kentuckians and absolutely stunned the pro-relief new court partisans, men who had enjoyed a virtual monopoly on state politics since the onset of the Panic of 1819. William Barry, chief justice of the new court, lamented, "The election has terminated differently from the expectation of either party," while Francis Blair despaired, "There never was I think a more extraordinary or more unexpected victory achieved by any party. . . . I am ready to surrender." The old court, of course, was ecstatic: "All fears for the constitution are at an end. . . . The voters have done their duty, vindicated their characters, and put the usurpers down." Crittenden, despite his second-place finish, breathed a sigh of relief as well, writing to Henry Clay, "The general result of our late elections is a triumph, and a just subject of congratulation among the friends of constitutional government."[40]

It was thus, surely, with mixed feelings that Solomon Sharp reviewed the election of 1825. His party was decisively rebuked and had little hope that its victorious opponents would be in a forgiving mood, given the relief party's majoritarian ruthlessness of the previous six years. But Sharp, at least, could take comfort in his election as a state representative. Yet, as matters turned out, this too was a curse, for as a direct result of his decision to reenter politics, Solomon Sharp would soon die.

Throughout the relief war, young Jereboam Beauchamp sided with the anti-relief, old court faction, even though his uncle and namesake, Colonel Jereboam Beauchamp, was a prominent leader of the relief party. It was, in fact, Colonel Beauchamp, a man never known for his learning, who introduced the notorious reorganization bill in the state senate—prompting an incredulous Robert Wickliffe to exclaim that "a man incompetent to write a single paragraph in the bill, was made to father the measure." Colonel Beauchamp, who, like Sharp, owed his title to service in the War of 1812, was a career politician who "could do nothing without mixing politics with it." First elected to the General Assembly in 1802, the year his nephew was born, Colonel Beauchamp represented the central Kentucky county of Washington in the General Assembly for the next twenty-two years and accumulated a good number of enemies along the way. In 1809, his election to the state senate was contested after it was learned that he had "treated with spirituous liquors" an entire battalion at a militia muster. The significance of the episode was not that a politician had dispensed alcohol at a muster but that someone had complained, for such a practice was commonplace, as was easily proven during his trial. He had, most likely, angered somebody who had a fair amount of influence, which would not have been out of character; as John Pope later put it, "especially in political contests [Col. Beauchamp] is often severe and . . . sometimes he goes too far." A broadside denounced Colonel Beauchamp as "famous for nothing but disturbing the peace," and even his own nephew accused him of having "the character of deep intrigue."[41]

Politically, the younger Jereboam Beauchamp was a mirror image of his uncle: "Beauchamp was a very active partizan of the old court in his county," noted one newspaper, "and manifested the most determined hostility to the new court, before and after the elections." Throughout, the *Confession* denounces the relief program, claiming that the debased "moral and political state of society in Kentucky" was a direct consequence of such policies. In the gubernatorial election of 1824, Beauchamp supported the anti-relief candidate, Christopher Tompkins, "a man of the greatest firmness," whom Beauchamp claimed to have known since he was a boy and whose children "had been my early playmates and schoolmates." Beauchamp thought Tompkins "a man of much better qualification and abilities" than his opponent Joseph Desha, a man Beauchamp held in contempt for his lack of "firmness."[42]

Solomon Sharp's return to the political arena did not go unnoticed by the Beauchamps. Later, after the whole bloody episode had played itself out, one newspaper editor opined that the "annunciation of Sharp as a candidate . . . must have awakened in the minds of Beauchamp and his wife, the strongest apprehensions and forebodings for what was to follow. They must have expected to hear the tale of her past imprudence and misfortunes again told and bandied about in handbills and newspapers publications, with additional aggravation, from angry strife and party zeal." And yet, as we have seen, such tales of "imprudence and misfortune" were not openly repeated in Frankfort that summer. The Beauchamps, however—160 miles away in Simpson County—heard an entirely different story. One or more persons told Anna and Jereboam that Sharp was alleging that Anna's stillborn baby could not have been his, for the father was a black man—and that he, Sharp, claimed to have a certificate signed by the midwife who attended Anna proving the charge. Moreover, the Beauchamps were informed, Sharp was not just relating this story by word of mouth but had printed up a handbill repeating the claim of a "colored child," a copy of which—"with Col. Sharp's name annexed," according to one source—was sent to the Beauchamps. The Jereboam persona claims in the *Confession,* "I received a letter from a gentleman . . . informing me of the reports and insinuations which Col. Sharp and his family had circulated, that the child of my wife was a mulatto."[43]

Even the insinuation that a southern woman had engaged in a sexual relationship with a black man was enough to blast her reputation beyond all hope of recovery. It entailed, as one scholar has put it, "the deepest degradation possible for a white woman in the antebellum south." If, as recent historians have well argued, antebellum southerners were not quite as racially neurotic as later generations, the fact remains that such boundaries were very well policed—at least when it came to white women—and those who trespassed were subject to extreme social ostracism. The taboo, it should be noted, was shared by northerners as well; Charles Fenno Hoffman, a New Yorker litterateur fascinated by the Kentucky Tragedy, wrote that the rumor of interracial sex "was enough of itself to fill a far better-regulated mind than [Beauchamp's] with the most deadly purpose." A Rhode Island paper swore, "We think Beauchamp did that, which many a husband would do, under similar circumstances." Not to be outdone, one Kentucky newspaper editor exclaimed that the spreading of such a rumor "merited death, to all who were engaged in it." The charge clearly demarcates the limits of the couple's rebelliousness: they could endure Anna's reputation as a sexual libertine, a disciple of Wollstonecraft, and a religious skeptic—but the sexual partner of a black man? That, apparently, was cause for murder. And thus despite all the Beauchamps' later claims that Sharp had seduced Anna, it was the accusation that she had engaged in interracial sex that triggered the Kentucky Tragedy.[44]

After the murder, both the new court faction and members of Sharp's family vehemently denied the existence of a midwife's certificate claiming that Anna's child was interracial and even that the rumor was aired that election season. Eliza Sharp insisted that the only document she knew of was the letter from Anderson Reavis detailing Anna's sexual dalliances: "This letter . . . given to my husband, *I most solemnly declare,* was the only paper, which, so far as I know or believe, *he ever possessed with regard to this transaction.*" Three years later, John Bass, a law student living with Sharp at the time of the murder, corroborated Eliza's claims, swearing that Colonel Sharp had told him that summer "that the child was the child of some man in the Green River country and that there were letters in the possession of Dr. Payne, that would prove that fact and exculpate him (Col. Sharp) from the charge then made against him." Moreover, Dr. Sharp corralled no fewer than thirty-eight prominent new court supporters who denied that the charge was ever made:

> Neither during the electioneering contest of that year [1825] nor at any other time, previous to his assassination, did we ever hear Col. Sharp, or any of his family or relations, or any other person, say or insinuate, that the child charged to him by Ann Cook, since the wife of J. O. Beauchamp, was a mulatto or coloured child. We further state that some of us were his confidential friends, with whom he often advised, and also mixed much with the people; and in our opinion, it is very improbable that Col. Sharp could have circulated such a statement, or given such a statement for circulation among his friends in Franklin County, without our knowing it.[45]

The midwife herself—Rebecca Dunn—later denied that she been approached before the murder to give testimony concerning Anna Cooke or her child. Interestingly, however, after Sharp's death, in February 1826, Dunn gave an affidavit to Dr. Sharp swearing that "she never saw a white child of such uncommon dark complexion," although she later qualified her assertion, saying that she did not know "whether it was a child of mixed blood." The man who buried Anna's child, French Fort, testified that before interring the coffin, he looked inside and saw to his "great surprize . . . the child was not white, but was evidently coloured." Although neither Dunn nor Fort was certain that the infant was interracial—one scholar has surmised that the baby was cyanotic, a "blue baby"—such suspicions, however inchoate and tentative, would have circulated very quickly in the small world of Warren County, Kentucky, and the Sharps, of necessity interested in the affair, would very likely have been aware of them. It is easy to imagine that Sharp, trying his best to distance himself from responsibility for the child, may have selectively and surreptitiously retailed such gossip in 1825. But all this is conjecture, and certainly, there was no certificate claiming the child was interracial that summer. Very likely, as Kendall later suggested, the subtle distinction between "what *could be done*" and "*what had been done*" was lost in the heated atmosphere of the relief war.[46]

But who wrote to the Beauchamps telling them Sharp was slandering Anna, and, more importantly, why? To the end, Jereboam refused to name his informant (or informants), afraid, he claimed, that "Desha and his satellites" might seek retribution. The letter writer, he maintained, was a man of "pure" and "honorable" principles who relayed the information not out of political malice but from a sense of "disinterested justice." The day he died, Jereboam swore that the person was a "friend of my family," adding, "He was a man on whose word I would and have resigned my life."[47]

Dr. Sharp always believed that old court newspaper editor Patrick Henry Darby was the letter writer and primary instigator of the whole episode and that he had even met with Beauchamp in Simpson County the summer before the murder. But such is highly unlikely, first because the *Confession* describes Beauchamp's informant as a "pure" and "honorable" friend of the family (whereas Darby is repeatedly dismissed as a "fool" whom Beauchamp had never met before he was taken into custody) and, second, and more to the point, because Beauchamp, on his way to the gallows, explicitly exonerated Darby.[48]

One very plausible candidate is Achilles Sneed, the former clerk of the court of appeals who despised Sharp and blamed him for the loss of his very lucrative job. Such a supposition is strengthened by the fact that the night he was convicted for murder, Beauchamp told his uncle that "Col. Sharp owed his death to his activity in wresting the papers of the Court of Appeals from the former clerk." During the 1825 campaign, Sneed was certainly involved in the rumors connecting Solomon and Anna; as we have already seen, a guest of Sneed's that summer attested that someone had sent his host a copy of Waring's 1821 handbill. Leander Sharp claimed to know the identity of "one of the chief agents in instigating Beauchamp" but declined to give the name because "it can now do no good." This most likely is a reference to Sneed, who had suddenly died in September 1825, a month after the election and seven weeks before the murder. At one point the *Confession* refers to the letter writer in the past tense—"He was a man on whose word I would and have resigned my life." On the other hand, just before his execution in July 1826, Beauchamp claimed to have recently "seen the man who gave me the information and conversed with him." Moreover, Beauchamp withheld the name in part because he feared Desha would take revenge, which of course assumed that the person was still alive in the summer of 1826. Probably, more than one person was feeding Beauchamp these rumors; Sneed was probably one of them. The identity of any other persons, if they existed, will most likely never be known.[49]

And then there is the handbill, which, if it existed, points to something far more widespread than either a misunderstanding over a midwife's certificate or one man's desire for revenge. To the end, Beauchamp insisted that he had received "an anonymous letter enclosing a handbill, which purported to have been prepared by Col. Sharp, in which he vindicated himself from the charge of seduction, by publishing a certificate that the child which Ann Cook, then Mrs. Beauchamp, had charged to him." Such a document would, in fact, be evidence of a quite deliberate plot "to work on the minds of Beauchamp and his unfortunate wife," for no one in Frankfort—neither new court nor old court partisans—had ever "heard even the most distant hint of a handbill being published by Colonel Sharp." But because Anna claimed to have destroyed all the papers they had received soon after Beauchamp's return from Frankfort, the only evidence for its existence is the assertion of Jereboam Beauchamp.[50]

The consensus among the new court party was that "the accusation made against Col. Sharp and his family to fire the mind of Beauchamp and his wife, was engendered by the monster (or monsters if there were more than one) who made the communication, doubtless for a bad purpose, if not to produce the dreadful catastrophe which had occurred." To Dr. Sharp, it all amounted to a political assassination: Certain members of the old court party, inflamed over Sharp's role in the seizure of the court records of the old court and fearful of his influence and power, incited Beauchamp to murder his brother. "The letter-writer *intended* to provoke Beauchamp to some violent course" to produce "the ruin or the death of my brother." And interestingly, both Beauchamp's father Thomas and Anna herself agreed with Dr. Sharp's assessment—Anna, according to one witness, said that Jereboam "was not the only person who ought to be made to suffer for that crime," for others had "induced" him to kill Sharp by communicating these tales that "exasperated him in the highest degree." Thomas M. Smith, a Franklin County lawyer, swore that Jereboam's father had told him that "if his son was guilty, he had been induced to it by some one in Frankfort."[51]

Beauchamp, far more volatile than anyone suspected, now determined to seek Sharp "in whatever corner of the world he might be hid." Although the *Confession* presents this as the final straw that put Beauchamp on the road to Frankfort in November 1825, it was almost certainly the only reason he killed Sharp. Beauchamp himself did not adhere to sexual convention; he had no compunction about soliciting Sharp for legal work; he had not been lying in wait for Sharp for four years. Only after he heard the allegation that his wife had slept with a black man was he ready to kill.[52]

The *Confession* depicts Beauchamp's decision to assassinate Sharp as the product of "the most mature deliberation"; it claims that he made the "dispassionate calculations" with "as much calmness as I would determine an ordinary matter of business." With typical bombast, the Beauchamp persona exclaims, "Never was a murder planned with such studied precaution since the world began." Sharp's putative refusal to engage Beauchamp in personal combat dictated Beauchamp's choice to kill Sharp in the dead of night rather than challenge him to a duel. For good measure, Beauchamp tacked another pretense onto the *Confession:* had he killed Sharp in a duel or in any other public manner, "the fury of the New Court faction," combined with "the wealth of the Sharp family," would have created a "tremendous monster" that would have had him put to death regardless. Yet Simpson County constable John F. Lowe testified that Anna told him the assassination was the result of her insistence: "Beauchamp wanted to kill Sharp in public, but . . . she had got on her knees to him not to do it in public; . . . she had laid the plan; and still insisted it was a laudable act. . . . She had devised the plan." Although the *Confession* denies that Anna kneeled before Jereboam, begging him to murder Sharp covertly, when asked just before his death why he killed Colonel Sharp, Jereboam "hesitated sometime, and then said, 'my wife persuaded me to kill him.'"[53]

So there it was: sent information that Sharp was claiming Anna's baby to be a mulatto, Anna convinced Jereboam to murder Sharp. This is what set the Kentucky Tragedy in motion, this is why he assassinated Sharp as he did, and this is why Anna ultimately joined Jereboam in his dungeon: he had murdered Sharp at her behest.

After initially planning to kill Sharp during the August elections, Beauchamp claimed to have been forced to postpone the assassination until early November, when the General Assembly convened. To provide an alibi for his presence in Frankfort, Beauchamp contrived to have himself called to the capital on ostensibly urgent and irksome "business of consequence." In the summer of 1825, Beauchamp gave some plats and certificates to his cousin from west Tennessee, Thomas Beauchamp, the son of Colonel Jereboam Beauchamp, and instructed him to record them in the register's office in Frankfort. Thomas, however, passed the certificates on to a friend, Elias Smith, who in turn asked Colonel Beauchamp if he would take them to Frankfort. Colonel Beauchamp agreed, but when he arrived at Smith's residence to pick up the documents, he could not get them, for they were locked up. Beauchamp knew none of this, and when he showed up at the land office in Frankfort the morning after the murder, the papers were not there.[54]

Yet another component of this plot, the *Confession* claims, was Beauchamp's issuing a warrant for his own arrest, thus giving him an excuse for being absent from Simpson County for a week or so. It was a bastardy warrant—an extraordinarily strange choice for one who was on his way to murder a man for sexual misconduct. And H. B. Montague, the justice of the peace who issued the warrant, later deposed that it was not Beauchamp who swore out the complaint but a woman named Ruth Reed—"a poor orphan girl, left without a mother to guide or counsel her." The warrant, dated October 29, 1825, alleges that the child was born on June 10, 1824, the very month Anna and Jereboam were wed—and three years after Jereboam and Anna had begun their relationship. And thus bizarrely, as Dr. Sharp wrote, the very moment that Beauchamp "was seeking the life of Col. Sharp, under the pretense that he had seduced and slandered an unprotected, inexperienced orphan girl, of 35 years old! he was himself exposed to apprehension under a warrant for seducing a young and thoughtless orphan, whom he had literally and truly ruined!"[55]

This is yet another example of Jereboam Beauchamp's routine misdirection, and it points anew to the difficulty in unraveling the Kentucky Tragedy. To do so, we must understand this intersection of political slander and partisan enmity, gendered expectations and racial taboo, literary-inspired personae and unstable personality.

CHAPTER 5

Murder

In a moment, we may plunge our years
In fatal penitence, and in the blight
Of our own soul, turn all our blood to tears,
And colour things to come with hues of night.
—Byron, *Childe Harold's Pilgrimage,* canto 3, stanza 70

Situated along a double bend in the Kentucky River, Frankfort, as one visitor indelicately put it, "stands in a hole." New Yorker Charles Fenno Hoffman was more charitable, in 1833 describing the state's capital as lying "so deeply buried in a gorge of hills that almost the first view you have of the town is by looking into its chimneys." The river, Hoffman continued, cuts "its way through precipitous limestone banks, makes a bend here through a complete circus of romantic-looking knolls about three or four hundred feet high: between the base of these and the bank of the river on either side is a level amphitheater, upon which the town is built."[1]

Frankfort was improbably named for a Jewish pioneer named Stephen Frank who was killed by Indians while on a salt-making expedition in 1780. Afterward, a shallow gravel shoal that was used to cross the river became known as "Franksford" and, eventually, Frankfort. In 1786, the Virginia legislature created the town on land owned by General James Wilkinson, Revolutionary War officer, inveterate schemer, and—in John Randolph's immortal denunciation—a "mammoth of iniquity." Six years later, when Kentucky joined the Union and a commission was set up to determine the state capital, the town fathers of Frankfort outbid the rival towns of Petersburg, Leestown, and Lexington by offering town lots, building materials, and well over three thousand dollars.[2]

As Frankfort was located astride a major river and lay on the outskirts of the immensely fertile Bluegrass region, it was not outrageous to believe that the capital would shortly become the state's leading settlement. In 1796, Frenchman Victor Collot opined, "It is probable that in ten years time this town will have twice the population and wealth of Lexington." Yet the anticipated boom never came, and by the turn of the century, the town's population of 628 was less than half of Lexington's. Twenty-five years later, Frankfort's population still hovered around 1,700, 40 percent of whom were enslaved. And although Frankfort could boast of some progress and a few badges of gentility—a public water system, a couple of prominent estates (U.S. Senator John Brown's Liberty Hall and the governor's mansion, both built in 1796), and the state penitentiary (established in 1799)—the capital still bore the physical and social markings of a small town not far at all removed from the coarse habits of the frontier.[3]

Those who dearly wished for Frankfort to be something more were appalled by the town's lack of refinement: one early-nineteenth-century observer regretted that "a spirit of gaming and drinking prevails among the young men of this place." Louis Marshall, Chief Justice John Marshall's brother, remembered, "Frankfort was one of the worst places, at that time, I have ever known. John Brown kept a wench. All the leading men about Frankfort were corrupt." Little wonder that Mary Breckinridge, widow of Thomas Jefferson's second attorney general, dismissed Frankfort as "that polluted place." Another, far less genteel woman, Agness Templin, thought Frankfort a "wicked" place teeming with "profane" company and compared her son who was studying theology there to Lot in Sodom and "Danielle in Babolun." Still others were not so much offended as bored; well into the antebellum years, residents grumbled, "There is nothing of any interest in this little town. Now and then a dogfight, or a loose horse, will gather a crowd and produce some excitement; but even these slightly stirring things are of rare occurrence."[4]

But Frankfort was not just another Kentucky hamlet. By the 1820s, the capital, despite its deficiencies, was the residence of a remarkable array of young and talented politicians, including John J. Crittenden, George M. Bibb, Francis P. Blair, Amos Kendall, and Solomon P. Sharp. "There was then no fashion, or attempt at it in Frankfort," remembered one contemporary, "but more substantial intellect than anywhere else in the State." Frankfort—with its remarkable concentration of political talent, its never-realized potential, its extremes of languor and debauchery—was antebellum Kentucky in microcosm.[5]

Late every fall, as the legislature convened, the sleepy, debased village would suddenly awake to a frenzy of sociability and political intrigue. Soon after the convening of the General Assembly in 1828, Horace Waring wrote his brother Henry, "This little town is now all life, all glee—the amusements here are of the first order, viz, theatrical exhibitions, grand assembly halls, private parties and a variety of other amusements consume the leisure hours of the members of the legislature, the visitors, and the citizens of Frankfort." In November 1825, the usual excitement attending the beginning of a legislative session was considerably heightened both by the ongoing relief war and by the new court party's stunning reversal in the August elections. Even jaded veterans of state politics were amazed that such "an immense crowd from all quarters of the State had assembled to witness the meeting of the legislature." And it was not just the men who were caught up in the furor. A visitor from Virginia wondered that "the ladies of the neighborhood were in the daily habit of visiting the House of Representatives, by which means, they were acquainted with the leading arguments, urged by both parties, and you seldom fail to find them enlisted on one side or the other." The stunned traveler reported that "all who breathed the atmosphere of Frankfort, who lived in the neighborhood, or who visited the scene felt its exciting influence." Six years of political bitterness and anger, it seemed, had been distilled and brought to bear on this little town in late 1825.[6]

Such was the town that Jereboam Beauchamp rode into after a five-day, 160-mile journey on the evening of November 6, 1825, about a half an hour after sunset on a moonless night. Beauchamp sought lodging at two of Frankfort's celebrated inns—"commodious and conducted in the best manner," according to one travel guide. Perhaps the most renowned was the Mansion House, run by Colonel Richard Taylor, the sergeant at arms for the new court who had broken into the house of Achilles Sneed during the battle for control of the court of appeals' documents. The Mansion House also served as the informal headquarters of the new court party, which made Beauchamp's choice to seek accommodations there remarkably curious. Why would someone who had so meticulously prepared to murder a leading member of the new court faction—a man whom Beauchamp himself described as "the leader, the orator and saviour of his party"—elect to stay at the new court's informal center of operations? Beauchamp, apparently, had not so carefully planned this murder.[7]

Taylor's son James was working the desk that Sunday night and later recalled that "a gentleman with a handkerchief round his head" entered the tavern, claiming to be ill and asking for a private room. Taylor informed Beauchamp that not only were the private rooms taken but most guests were sleeping two or three to a bed. After Beauchamp declined his offer of "a pallet in the dining room," Taylor suggested he try Weisiger's Tavern a couple of blocks away. There, Beauchamp once again requested a private room but received the same answer: "All the small rooms were taken up; he could get lodging but not a room." When Beauchamp demurred, the barkeeper Robert Sacry suggested that he stay at a private residence and "recommended him to Mr. Scott's."[8]

"Mr. Scott" was Joel Scott, who had come to Kentucky in 1785 as a young boy and settled with his family in Scott County. He became a mill owner and merchant in Georgetown and, in January 1825, was appointed superintendent of the state penitentiary. Scott inherited an institution "wretched beyond description," its inmates in such a condition that "cannot be described with the use of decent language." Shortly, Scott transformed the penitentiary, which had cost the state thousands of dollars a year to maintain, into a makeshift factory staffed by prisoners that in the next decade turned a profit of approximately thirty thousand dollars. Scott was also an avid new court partisan—four months earlier, in the wake of the August elections, the old court faction charged Scott with dressing inmates in civilian clothing and marching them to the courthouse to vote for the new court slate (which may help account for the county's two hundred surplus votes). Moreover, Scott was a very close friend of Beauchamp's intended victim; Scott had, along with Leander Sharp, witnessed the drawing of Solomon Sharp's will a year earlier.[9]

And thus—in one of many bizarre events that threatened to turn the Kentucky Tragedy into a farce the first time around—Beauchamp at about seven o'clock that Sunday night wound up on the doorstep of Joel Scott, warden of the state penitentiary, stalwart supporter of the new court party, and an intimate friend of Solomon Sharp. Answering the door, Scott told Beauchamp that he "did not keep entertainment, public nor private," but once the young man recounted how crowded the inns were and that the clerk at Weisiger's had recommended him, Scott relented, adding that he "would entertain any man under such circumstances." The warden invited Beauchamp inside and asked him to take a seat. Beauchamp "took off his hat and brushed off the handkerchief he had on his head," Scott later testified. "I asked him if he was unwell; he said, no, he had rode through the barrens, and the woods were on fire, and the smoke and dust made his head ache a little." Around nine o'clock, after dinner and a bit of small talk, Beauchamp stepped out to feed his horse.

Twenty or thirty minutes later, he returned, and Scott showed him to his room, whereupon the guest "took a book out of his pocket and observed he would read awhile."[10]

Across town, Sharp was spending his last night politicking, touring the taverns and paying his respects to the arriving members of the state assembly. Sharp knew his party was in a difficult situation. After the new court debacle that summer, it dawned on many true believers that they had overreached in both their radical majoritarianism and their attempt to tamper with a coordinate branch of government. Now they began to cast about for a compromise, and Sharp—known for his ambivalence toward judge-breaking in the first place—was the man to whom they looked to broker a settlement. Moreover, after John Rowan's elevation to the U.S. Senate, Sharp was poised to "take a stand at the head of the New Court party." Delighted to be back in the center of things, Sharp, for the next several hours, conversed "with the members at various rooms, with uncommon cheerfulness and vivacity." Around eleven o'clock, the exhausted Sharp returned home and shortly went to bed.[11]

Back at Joel Scott's, Beauchamp prepared. He had brought along yarn socks to muffle his footsteps and make sure he left no tracks, an old wool hat, and a black silk mask, which, he seems to have believed, "gave him the exact appearance of a negro." He would need the disguise, for that night "the stars gave light enough wherewithal to discern the face of an acquaintance on coming near him and closely noticing his face."[12]

Accounts of Beauchamp's whereabouts for the next several hours differ substantially, offering a prime example of the difficulty in ascertaining what happened in the Kentucky Tragedy. The *Confession* claims that Beauchamp crept out of Scott's residence about nine thirty, "although the family were all up and passing about the house," and proceeded down to the river, where he discarded his coat, hat, and shoes and donned his disguise. Well before ten o'clock, Beauchamp claimed, he had found the Sharp mansion on Madison Street. Seeing that his intended victim was not home, he crept over to the Mansion House a block away, where he spied Sharp through a window. Losing sight of his victim and fearing he had gone home, Beauchamp scurried back to Sharp's house, only to find that he was not there either. About an hour later, the *Confession* continues, while Beauchamp was reconnoitering the back side of the house, Sharp came home through the front door. Beauchamp then crossed the street to the public square, crouched among the ruins of the statehouse, which had burned the year before, and waited for three hours. He had, he claimed, "habituated my mind to philosophise and reason upon the subject of killing Col Sharp, till I thought I could kill him with as much tranquility of feeling, as I could whip a servant that I thought deserved a whipping."[13]

Dr. Sharp disputed Beauchamp's account of events, maintaining that he could not have crept out at nine thirty, because Scott—a close friend of his—was in the habit of bolting his door from the inside when he retired for the night, and Beauchamp could not have gotten back inside if he had left before his host had gone to bed. Only if Beauchamp had gone out late at night and left the door unlocked, Dr. Sharp maintained, could he have reentered the house after the murder. Moreover, in his testimony during the trial, Scott himself claimed that he heard Beauchamp leave his room sometime between one and three o'clock in the morning. Scott's account also squares with the testimony of the two night watchmen, Elias M. Crane and James Downing, who were on patrol the morning of November 7. Both men swore that around one or one thirty, they came across a man fitting the description of Beauchamp slowly walking down St. Clair Street between Scott's and Sharp's residences. Three credible witnesses, in other words, placed Beauchamp shortly before the murder not where he claimed to have been—crouching among the ruins of the statehouse—but roaming the street of Frankfort.[14]

The discrepancy is significant, for as Beauchamp himself later admitted, he "knew extremely little about the town, never having been in it but once or twice before; that 4 or 5 years ago, and then almost wholly in the night." So how, if Scott and the night watchmen are to be trusted, did Beauchamp, this stranger to Frankfort who had only a few minutes in the dead of night to get his bearings, manage not only to locate Sharp's residence but to ascertain which of the five doors on the first floor of the house Sharp was most likely to answer? Had he knocked on the wrong door, he would have awoken one of the many people in the house: Dr. Leander Sharp, Eliza's brother Dr. William Henry Harrison Scott, John Bass (a law student of Sharp's), the Sharps' slaves, and the couple's three small children. The door Beauchamp did knock on, the one closest to where Solomon and Eliza were sleeping, was, according to Dr. Sharp, "barely visible from the street and many of the people of Frankfort did not know of its existence." Moreover, Solomon and Eliza had only days earlier begun sleeping there, so that the ailing Bass and Eliza's brother could use their bedroom. "The murderer knew," Dr. Sharp reviewed, "precisely where his victim was."[15]

According to Dr. Sharp and a great many of his brother's political allies, the only explanation was that Beauchamp had an accomplice—very likely the same person who had told the Beauchamps that Sharp was spreading rumors about the race of Anna's baby—and that the murder was in fact a political assassination. As Dr. Sharp presented his case in the *Vindication,* Beauchamp lied about when he left Scott's house to conceal the fact that he had an accessory, someone who not only showed Beauchamp which house was Sharp's but "pointed out the room occupied by Col. Sharp and the door by which it could be most securely approached."[16]

At first glance, Dr. Sharp's argument seems compelling. But a closer look, as well as a consideration of other sources, suggests that his suspicions were, in all likelihood, unfounded. For one, it was not at all difficult to find Sharp's house. As Beauchamp himself admitted, "It was the easiest thing in the world to point it out, so that a stranger could not mistake it. He had simply to be told it was the nearest house to the state-house, for it stands only the width of the street, from the then state house, and almost right across the street from it." J. W. Coleman, the historian who had a better understanding of the logistics of the murder than any other writer, dismissed the issue out of hand; Sharp's mansion was, he wrote, "one of the handsomest and best-known residences in Frankfort, and even to an out-of-town stranger at night, was not difficult to find." But how did Beauchamp know which door to knock on? If he had indeed spent four or five hours prowling about the residence, then he most likely would have been able to ascertain, first, that there was a door in the alleyway and, second, that the Sharps were sleeping near it. As he wrote in the *Confession,* he had lurked about the house for so long that he could "see all that was going on in it, and could see what rooms were occupied and what were not, as well as if I had lived about the house." Across town, meanwhile, Scott most likely had failed to bolt his door that night and may well have heard Beauchamp not leaving but returning to his room. And as to the night watchmen's testimony, it is plausible that Beauchamp, forced to wait so long for a chance to strike, had not stayed close to the house all that time—he may well have gotten cold feet and taken to wandering the streets of Frankfort.[17]

But perhaps the best evidence against the existence of a conspiracy is Beauchamp's own bumbling. Despite the effort to portray the killing as masterfully premeditated, the *Confession* unintentionally betrays a nervous and indecisive young man. One would think that an accomplice, one familiar with Frankfort and its political alignments, would have told Beauchamp not to try to rent a room at the unofficial headquarters of the new court party. And surely any remotely knowledgeable coconspirator would have dissuaded

Beauchamp from staying the night with a man who was both the superintendent of the state penitentiary and a very close friend of Solomon Sharp's. In any case, only moments before his own death, Beauchamp, when asked how he had found Sharp's house, admitted the prosaic truth: "I found it myself without any assistance."[18]

After midnight, Jereboam Beauchamp lurked outside Solomon Sharp's house, a "two and a half story red brick house, built flush with the sidewalk," facing the west side of the public square on Madison Street. Beauchamp watched as C. P. Bacon came to the house and asked Dr. Sharp to attend an ailing slave of his across town. Beauchamp later claimed to have been relieved to see the doctor leave, for although he yearned to kill him as well "for the part he had taken in this slander about the black child," Anna had begged him to spare his life, for "she always said to see him deprived of his brother, whom he literally worshiped, was the greatest revenge she could possibly imagine or wish to be exercised upon him." After the murder of Solomon, Anna cruelly calculated, "it would be a charity and the greatest humanity to the Dr. to kill him also."[19]

Near two o'clock, Beauchamp—masked and armed with "a small old-fashioned butcher knife, ground sharp on the back as well as edge"—approached the side door in the alleyway between Sharp's house and the residence of General Samuel South. He knocked three times, "loud and quick," awakening both Solomon and Eliza. "Who's there?" Sharp asked. "John A. Covington," replied Beauchamp, aware that Sharp knew a number of Covingtons in the Green River district. Eliza had never before heard the "sharp" and "shrill" voice—one that, she later recalled, "made such an impression on me that I was sure if I ever heard it again I should know it"—and begged Solomon not to open the door.[20]

> Quickly Col. Sharp's foot was heard upon the floor. I saw under the door he approached without a light! I drew my mask from my face, and immediately Col. Sharp opened the door, I advanced into the room and with my left hand I grasped his right wrist, as with an iron hand. The violence of the grasp made Col. Sharp spring back and trying to disengage his wrist, he said, "what Covington is this?" I replied, "John A. Covington, sir." "I don't know you," said Col. Sharp. . . . I said to Col. Sharp in a tone as though I was deeply mortified at his not knowing me; "And do you not know me sure enough."

> "Not with your handkerchief about your face," said Col. Sharp. . . . I then replied in a soft conciliating persuasive tone of voice, "Come to the light Col. and you will know me." And pulling him by the arm he came readily to the door. I stepped with one foot back upon the first step out at the door, and still holding his wrist with my left hand, I stripped my hat and handkerchief from over my forehead and head, and looked right up in Col. Sharp's face. . . . He sprang back and exclaimed in the deepest tone of astonishment, dismay, and horror, and despair I ever heard, "Great God!! It's him!!!" And as he said that he fell on his knees. . . . I let go his wrist and grasped him by the throat, and dashing him against the facing of the door, I choaked him against it to keep him from hallowing, and muttered in his face, "die you villian." And as I said that, I plunged the dagger to his heart. Letting him go at the moment I stabbed him, he sprang up from his knees and endeavored to throw his arms round my neck, saying "pray Mr. Beauchamp," but as he said that I struck him in the face with my left hand; and knocked him his full length into the room. By this time I saw the light approaching, and dashed a little way off and put on my mask. I then came and squatted in the alley near the door, to hear if he should speak. His wife talked to him, but he could not answer her.[21]

Shortly before his execution, Beauchamp revisited the moment in verse. In this telling, Beauchamp momentarily pauses as he feels "the flash of pity through my soul." But he soon recovers, and as he "plung'd the poison'd shaft of death, / Which calmed my hearts black vengeful storm," Beauchamp savors the moment: "With fiendly laugh I mock his groan."[22]

Eliza Sharp's recollection was far less melodramatic. After knocking on the door, she testified, the stranger claimed that he had gotten into town late and, finding the taverns full, was looking for a place to stay. The half-asleep Solomon fumbled with the lock. The door finally opened, Beauchamp barged in, announcing, "I am John A. Covington, don't you know me?" When Mr. Sharp answered, "I don't think I do," Beauchamp shot back, "Then damn you, you soon shall know me," and stabbed the defenseless man.[23]

Seeing her husband assaulted, Eliza ran back through her bedroom, out onto the back porch, and into the bedroom shared by her brother and Bass. "My sister came into our room and said somebody was in the room murdering her husband," Dr. Scott later testified. "I got a candle and went in, and found Col. Sharp dying." Close behind, Bass "enquired of Mrs. Sharp if she knew who had done the deed or who did she suspect had done it? She answered in substance, that she knew not who had done it and knew not whom to suspect."[24]

Dr. Sharp was immediately retrieved from the Bacon household. At first assuming his brother merely had a "fainty fit," Dr. Sharp was not particularly alarmed. Then he drew near the house, saw the commotion, and was met outside by Dr. Scott, who told him the awful news. "I went in," Leander later recalled, "and found him laying stretched on the carpet, and my sister [Eliza] sitting with his head on a pillow in her lap. He was just drawing his last breath." Rather than having "plunged the dagger to his heart," Beauchamp had stabbed Sharp in the stomach, about two inches below the breast bone. And although there was little blood, when Dr. Sharp examined the wound, he knew at once it was mortal. The shattered Leander moaned, "O my dear brother gone." He later wrote, "I scarcely know what followed." By the time John Harvie, president of the Bank of Kentucky, arrived on the murder scene, he found Dr. Sharp "insensible." Anna had indeed ruthlessly and accurately predicted that the murder would devastate Solomon's adoring younger brother.[25]

George M. Bibb, one of Kentucky's premier jurists and a leader of the new court party, lived only a few blocks away. On arriving at the Sharps', he recoiled at the scene: the corpse of Solomon Sharp laid out on the bed, Leander Sharp lying on one side and Eliza on the other, her head on her husband's chest "in an agony of grief." Around the room, Sharp's three small children—six-year-old Jane, two-year-old John, and one-year-old Solomon—were all "crying most piteously." When another neighbor, Amos Kendall, arrived, "the shrieks of [Sharp's] little daughter pervaded the stillness of the night and echoed throughout the dark and melancholy mansion. His wife had lost the power of uttering her grief, and as she laid on the dead body of her husband and embraced his yet warm but lifeless form, every sigh seemed as if it would burst her heart." One bystander, an old pioneer "accustomed to the distressing scenes through which the early settlers passed" and "familiar with examples of Indian warfare and Indian butchery," swore that he "had never before witnessed a scene so heartrending."[26]

Not long after, the anguished and disoriented Eliza aimlessly wandered about the house. Straying outside, she suddenly screamed; a masked man was "standing on the pavement, with his hands on the window sill, as though he was peeping in at the window." It was Beauchamp, who had lingered so that someone would see him and "take me for a negro with my black mask on." He ran, and although he was pursued, "by the time they got out of the house, I was out of the lott." In the darkness of the early morning, Beauchamp easily escaped his pursuers. He then retrieved his coat, hat, and shoes down by the river and bundled his blood-stained clothes, tied them to a rock, and sank them in the Kentucky River. Nearby, he buried the murder weapon.[27]

Behind him, Beauchamp had left a shattered family. Eliza later that morning "fell into fits," became delirious, and would "again and again visit the fatal spot, and with an eye of phrenzied expectation." Over the next several months, she suffered long bouts of "temporary estrangements in her intellect." For the remainder of her short life, November 7 would be an especially painful day—it was not only the day her husband was murdered but also her birthday.[28]

Sometime around three o'clock, Jereboam Beauchamp stole back to Joel Scott's residence, "creeping up the stairs as softly as a cat." After lighting a candle and burning his mask in the fireplace, he reflected on what he had done: "Such were the happy feelings which pervaded me, and the perfect resignation which I felt to the will of Heaven, having accomplished my long settled purpose, that in five minutes after I laid down, I fell fast asleep and slept soundly."[29]

CHAPTER 6

The Politics of Murder

> There was in him a vital scorn of all:
> As if the worst had fall'n which could befall
> He stood a stranger in this breathing world,
> An erring spirit from another hurled;
> A thing of dark imaginings. . . .
>
> —Byron, *Lara*

The news of the murder of Solomon Sharp spread quickly in the early morning hours of November 7, causing a sensation "deep beyond description," a gloom among the townspeople "of the deepest cast." A young Robert J. Breckinridge wrote his wife, "Every thing is hustle and consternation at an act which is unprecedented in our country and almost too horrid to be credited, on the very evidence of our senses." The assassination of a prominent statesman would have been disturbing in any event, but for a man to "receive the dagger in his bosom" as he was opening "his door and his heart to receive a guest" was a perversion of hospitality, "a blow at all that is sacred to social and civil life." In a world just then developing notions of marriage as akin to Edenic bliss and the home as a haven from a heartless world, the murderer had invaded sanctuary, had despoiled the nearest approximation of paradise that people of the early republic could envision. Observers responded with a palpable sense of outrage and, in typical western fashion, called for swift and merciless punishment. Writing to his father Henry, Theodore W. Clay described the killing as "one of the most atrocious and unheard of acts of murder" and noted that "language could not find terms strong enough to condemn it in, or could the law be too severe in avenging the rights of humanity." Andrew Jackson, who had known Sharp since childhood, lamented the murder as a loss "not only to his family, but to his country." Ever sanguinary, Jackson declared, "The only attonement for this cruel and unheard of murder is the blood of his slayer."[1]

Joseph Underwood, a thirty-four-year-old state representative from Warren County, was a close friend of Sharp's despite their substantial political differences. Having visited with Sharp only hours earlier, Underwood awoke early Monday morning to the horrible news:

> I would not at first believe it, but the horrible fact was soon verified so as to leave no doubt of its truth. An indescribable rush of thought & feeling agitated me. Our old acquaintance, the conversation we last had, his fine health, his cheerfulness, his kind inquiries after his friends in Warren, his animated countenance, his talents of the first order as a lawyer, his office as legislator, his wife, his children all suddenly exchanged for an unexpected bloody grave; the daring deed, the fiend-like assassin, the mysterious motive, all flashed thru my mind in quick succession producing sensations which are without name. I went to see the body, it was pale & dead. I saw it enlivened by the soul tho overnight the contrast & that so sudden, resembles an awful dream. My senses told me it was real & I gazed with sorrow while my mind insensibly wandered in a train of thought on that unfathomable subject, the creation & final destinies of man, & the strange conflicts which the base passions bring about in this world & the littleness of the causes which lead to the most calamitous events & indeed the littleness of fame talents & wealth on earth compared with those unknown scenes which an immortal soul may expect beyond the tomb.[2]

Official responses reflected this sense of shock and mourning laced with fury. John J. Crittenden authored resolutions lauding Sharp's public service, which were promptly passed by the General Assembly, while the new court of appeals eulogized his "genius, patriotism and energies" and proclaimed the court to be in mourning for thirty days, as did Frankfort's seventh federal circuit court. (Conspicuously, the "old" court of appeals was silent on the matter.) The members of the legislature donned crapes on their left arms and unanimously authorized Governor Desha to offer a three-thousand-dollar reward for the apprehension of the murderer, while the trustees of Frankfort contributed another one thousand dollars.[3]

Kept at home until the next day, Sharp's body was carried across Broadway to the Presbyterian church in which the legislature had been meeting since the capitol had burned the previous November. There, in a "nice black coffin," the corpse lay in state, and at two thirty on Tuesday afternoon, services commenced. In front of the legislature, official dignitaries, and a "large concourse of citizens," Jacob Creath delivered the funeral sermon (one that prematurely crotchety Underwood—having recovered from his existential meditations—described as "a miserable one & convinced me that Creath had no talents altho he has been much puffed as a first rate baptist preacher"). Afterward, a procession escorted the body a mile and a half northeast of town to the Bellevue burying grounds, where Sharp was interred in a place of honor reserved for former statesmen.[4]

The search for the culprit began immediately, but in the absence of eyewitnesses, the prospect of apprehending the murderer initially seemed remote. "The villain has not been discovered," Theodore Clay wrote; "there seems to be no hope for it." Among the suspects' names that surfaced early was that of John U. Waring, the sociopath whose efforts to derail Sharp's nomination for the attorney generalship were well known. Yet as it happened, Waring was fifteen miles away in Fayette County, recovering from a gunshot wound, a souvenir of yet another ugly incident involving a man whom he had previously stabbed. Abner D. Hamilton was also briefly suspected because of Sharp's role in securing the murder conviction and execution of his son, John C. Hamilton. The speculation was serious enough to prompt Hamilton to buy space in the *Frankfort Argus of Western America* to categorically deny he was in any way involved in the murder. For good measure he promised to give the party who started the rumor "his just due" should the "scoundrel dare exhibit himself."[5]

Very soon, however, Jereboam Beauchamp became the sole focus of suspicion. The first to suspect the young man was Joel Scott, even before he was aware of Beauchamp's connection to Anna Cooke. When Scott heard the news of his friend's assassination, he raced over to Madison Street before daybreak. Told the murder had occurred around one or two in the morning, Scott, believing he had heard Beauchamp leave the house that night, wondered aloud if his guest was the murderer. Scott immediately returned home accompanied by Henry Payne and Benjamin Taylor. It was still not daylight when Scott went up to Beauchamp's room. "Beauchamp was standing by the bed, dressed, except his coat. 'Sir,' said I, 'there was a horrid murder committed in town last night, at Col. Sharp's; some man had gone to Col. Sharp's and called him up, and had killed him.' He said 'it was a most horrid case,' rather casting down his head and looking on the floor. I repeated the remark, that it was a horrid case, and observed that probably there could not be such a case found in history. He said nothing." At the trial Scott swore that Beauchamp's "*countenance* and *manner* was such, as to convince me, without any manner of doubt, that he was the guilty man." And yet the *Confession* gives a very different version of the meeting, one in which Beauchamp suavely deflects all of Scott's suspicions: "I heard Mr. Scott come stamping up stairs to my room. He opened my door and said, good morning Mr. Beauchamp. I returned the salutation with a very pleasant politeness, but Mr. Scott abruptly said, 'don't you think some man went to Sharp's last night and killed him?' I put on a face of great astonishment, and replied, 'great God, is it possible! What, Col. Sharp?' . . . My manner I saw quite removed, for the moment, his suspicions." In this instance, at least, Beauchamp's account is more trustworthy. Both Taylor and Payne later testified that Scott's suspicions were allayed after his initial discussion with Beauchamp and that Scott, in fact, "requested them to go back and stop the report" that Beauchamp might be the murderer.[6]

Beauchamp, meanwhile, went downstairs just after sunrise, swallowed a shot of whiskey for breakfast, and rode straight to the land register's office. The clerk on duty there, Harrison Fenwick, later swore that Beauchamp "had no other business that I recollect, but to return a survey, which I refused to receive, because there was no warrant." The papers that Beauchamp had sent in April had never been filed. His plan had broken down, and he was stuck in Frankfort without an alibi or, as he put it, "the least shadow of business." Frightened, Beauchamp went back to his lodgings, where Joel Scott was waiting, his suspicions revived on learning that Beauchamp was Anna Cooke's husband. Scott peppered Beauchamp with questions as to why he was leaving town so quickly and why he was not staying to witness the meeting of the legislature. Beauchamp could only weakly reply that he needed to visit some relatives in Bloomfield—a small town about twenty-five miles to the southwest of Frankfort. Although he later claimed that he had been imperturbable and able to coolly calibrate his conduct "with a deliberate view to the effect it would have in evidence," a more accurate assessment would be that Beauchamp, caught without an explanation for his presence in the capital and already the object of suspicion, fled Frankfort in a panic about half an hour after daybreak.[7]

Although Kendall and other new court partisans would continue for months to speak of "the mystery which shrouds the motive of the murderer," when it was found that the husband of Anna Cooke had arrived in Frankfort the night before the assassination and had suddenly left the next morning, many people came to simply assume Beauchamp's guilt. Indeed, before the day was out, "a rumor was already circulating in town, affirming, in the most confident terms, that Beauchamp was the murderer." And when it was learned that Beauchamp had failed to mention Sharp's death to a number of people he had met on the road leading out of Frankfort, suspicions were heightened further. On hearing this single fact, Ben Hardin "without a moment's hesitation . . . pronounced Beauchamp the assassin." And so, with the weight of evidence mounting, "it was determined to send for him," and a group of armed men started after Beauchamp about ten o'clock on Monday night.[8]

Three days later, on Thursday, November 10, Beauchamp arrived at Retirement just before sunset:

> She was walking down the grove, upon the road I was to come, anxiously expecting my arrival. So soon as I saw her thus alone, I hoisted my flag of victory. She ran to meet me, and as I alit from my horse I gave her the flag, and she fell prostrate on her face before me. She then burst into tears and lifted her voice in gratitude to Heaven, that she was revenged for all the misery a villain had brought upon her family. Then clasping her arms about my knees, she called upon the spirits of her father, her brothers and her sister to bless me and to intercede with a just Providence, to protect me from all harm for the righteous deed I had done.

The two retired to a secluded spot on the farm so Jereboam could narrate "all the circumstances of the glorious deed"; well into the evening, Anna reveled in the details of Sharp's murder. "I do not believe there ever lived upon the earth," the *Confession* claims, "two more happy beings than we then were."[9]

Beauchamp's behavior on his return home—specifically his inability to resist striking a dramatic pose—would in time provide his prosecutors with a good deal of damning evidence. His little sister, Malinda, saw him wave his "flag of victory" and, unfortunately for her brother, later mentioned it in the presence of their neighbor, John F. Lowe, who happened to be a Simpson County constable. When Lowe, who was playing cards at the Beauchamps' house that night, asked Beauchamp why he had returned home waving a flag—a fairly melodramatic display for someone who had just returned from registering a land claim—Beauchamp replied, apropos of nothing, "*For victory.*" Beauchamp then informed Lowe that he had come "to believe more in a God than I used to," for now he saw that "there is a God that will give vengeance to them that ought to have it." When another guest, Absalom Stratton, asked if Beauchamp had completed his business in Frankfort, the young man gave a similar cryptic and incriminating response: he had "*authentically*" accomplished his task—"*to his satisfaction.*" The next day, Beauchamp continued his melodramatic and puzzling outbursts, telling yet another visitor, Richard Hallaway—Retirement, it seems, was awfully crowded—that "things had happened as right into his hands, as ever into a man's hands in the world." Preposterously, the *Confession* boasts of Beauchamp's "tranquil, unsuspicious conduct" on his return home.[10]

The following evening, the four men dispatched to retrieve Beauchamp arrived at Retirement. When they announced he was a suspect in the murder of Colonel Sharp, Beauchamp "put on a face of great astonishment" and "promptly avowed my ready determination to go immediately to Frankfort, if there was any thing said there, prejudicial to my reputation." His one condition was that he would accompany his pursuers back to Frankfort not as their prisoner but only as an honorable man determined to dispel any doubt of his innocence. The men accepted his provision.[11]

The patrol had brought along two pieces of evidence: the measurement of the footprint found in Sharp's garden and a handkerchief discovered in the alley outside Sharp's door. Told of the track, Beauchamp claimed to have been "very much pleased," for he was not even wearing shoes when he killed Sharp and thus knew "they had gotten some other persons track." Yet the measurement approximated Beauchamp's shoe—"it did not differ in length scarcely any," Beauchamp later exclaimed. Upon seeing this, his pursuers "cried out . . . 'exactly! exactly! To an hairs breadth!'" The men also asked for Beauchamp's dirk, which he gladly handed over, knowing that he had buried the murder weapon back in Frankfort and that the width of the blade would match neither the tear in the handkerchief nor the fatal wound on Sharp's body. The guard apparently glimpsed this as well, for when Beauchamp asked for his dirk after they had traveled down the road a bit, the guard claimed not to have it; "they had thrown it away, sure enough." Such was Beauchamp's anger, the *Confession* claims in a stupefyingly delusional aside, that he feared he "would kill all . . . of them."[12]

If Beauchamp did not worry much about the footprint or the dirk, he was acutely concerned about the handkerchief the guard had brought along. Early the morning of the murder, "when it was scarcely light enough to see," a handkerchief was found lying near the door through which Beauchamp had entered by Eliza Sharp's twenty-year-old sister, Arabella Scott. The piece of cloth—old and filthy, "blue with wide stripes" with the corner cut off—had "two holes that were plainly cuts, obviously penetrated with a knife." In addition, "there were some spots of blood upon it, with stains of yellow extending beyond the actual blood." Arabella, after showing it to her brother John, gave it to their twenty-five-year-old brother, Dr. William Henry Harrison Scott, who, assuming that "it belonged to some of the negroes," incredibly, "threw it down." Shortly, Colonel Taylor found it, and several persons once again examined the item. When the guard started after Beauchamp that evening, they took it with them.[13]

Although the *Confession* claims that Beauchamp had left the handkerchief in his room at Scott's and that it was used to frame him, in truth he had left the handkerchief at the murder scene and knew that it was a damning piece of evidence. Such was why Beauchamp now took advantage of the guard's carelessness and destroyed the handkerchief. On the second night out of Simpson County, Beauchamp and his escort—a "set of devils" whom he believed he "could dupe or deceive in any way"—stopped at Buster's Tavern outside Munfordville, a small town about sixty miles south of Louisville. After the guards had drunk liquor until they were all "very heavy and sleepy," Beauchamp made sure that he shared a bed with the one who had possession of the handkerchief, a man named Carroll. Another guest at Buster's, John Anderson—"quite an intelligent, honorable young gentleman," according to Beauchamp—later testified that "after supper, the gentleman who had the handkerchief, went and laid down upon the bed prepared for Beauchamp, with his coat on, and the handkerchief in his left hand pocket, and went to sleep. Beauchamp went and laid down on the same bed, behind the gentleman. After Beauchamp had lain two or three hours, about 12 o'clock, he jumped up." Anderson saw the restless Beauchamp "put his hand in his pocket, and lean over, and I thought put something into the fire. I observed the fire, but saw nothing. Beauchamp then drew me into a conversation calculated to divert my attention from the fire. The room was warm and did not want any additional fire." Beauchamp in fact had pilfered the handkerchief and, under the pretense of tending the coals, had thrown it in the flames. "It was consumed in a moment," he later wrote, without anyone having "the least idea or suspicion."[14]

The next day, as the group stopped in Munfordville for breakfast, Beauchamp proclaimed that the handkerchief would exonerate him and asked to see it. Carroll checked his pocket and exclaimed, "It's gone!" The guard, unable to locate the prime piece of evidence, "began to look one to another, with a blank foolish look, that was truly diverting; insomuch that some in the house actually broke right out into laughter at them." Beauchamp enjoyed the moment immensely, once again proving—to himself at least—that he was superior to all the mediocrities around him. In all, the trip back to Frankfort can only be described as ludicrous; before the procession had made it halfway to Frankfort, they no longer possessed either the possible murder weapon or the only piece of evidence that might have tied Beauchamp to the murder scene.[15]

The procession arrived in Frankfort on Tuesday evening, November 15—eight days after the murder—and Beauchamp was lodged at the home of one his pursuers, Constable William Jackson. Beauchamp "found the whole country in a flame, and although prejudice was at its zenith against me, without a shadow of proof, yet things were beginning to work exactly to my wish, and as I had planned. Amos Kendall, Editor of the Argus, and oracle of the New Court faction, had begun already to howl piteously over Sharp, as a martyr in his country's service, and in the cause of the people, as he called the cause he advocated in politics." On Wednesday morning, with "the popular excitement . . . at its highest rage," Beauchamp appeared before the justices of the examining court, John Brown and Oliver P. Waggoner. Beauchamp's shoe print was again compared to the track found in Sharp's garden. Although many present proclaimed it to be a match, George M. Bibb, who had carefully measured the print near the murder scene, proclaimed that Beauchamp's shoe "never could, by any possibility, have made the track he measured in Col. Sharp's garden." The material evidence against Beauchamp, already meager, was quickly disappearing: no matching footprint, no handkerchief, no murder weapon, no eyewitness. The prosecution's case was indeed precarious, and Colonel Sharp's brothers, Leander and Fidelio, worried that the court of inquiry would not find enough evidence to warrant a trial. "They had not now," Beauchamp gloated, "the slightest pretense of proof against me; not one single circumstance, to raise even the suspicion of my guilt." Such was Beauchamp's confidence in his imminent exoneration that he seemed, perversely, to relish the spotlight. When the commonwealth's attorney petitioned the examining court for more time to summon witnesses from Simpson County, Beauchamp affected to be pleased, avowing that he wished the matter to be fully investigated: "I . . . arose and stated before the assembly, that I would be far from seeking to be acquitted, or to leave the place while it was suggested that proof could be any where had against me, and that I was quite willing to remain in custody, and allow full time for the friends of the deceased to collect any evidence they might deem important, if any existed." Yet when Beauchamp's temporary attorney, Thomas B. Monroe, requested that Beauchamp be allowed to stay in a private residence until the trial, the court refused, denied bail, and remanded the young man to jail. However thin the evidence may have been, however confident Beauchamp professed to be, the circumstantial evidence, the young man's behavior after the murder, and his connection with Anna Cooke convinced many people that they had the right man.[16]

Well before Beauchamp was brought back to town, the murder of Sharp was becoming politicized. Just two days after the murder, Amos Kendall wrote, "Col. Sharp's talents, the station which he held, the time selected for the horrid deed, and the fact that he was not known to have a personal enemy, cause suspicions to flash across the mind that the assassin was not actuated wholly by personal considerations." The insinuation that Sharp's murder was a political assassination hit a raw nerve among old court partisans, and they immediately launched blistering counterattacks: Kendall was but a "practiced and unlicenced libeler"; his remarks were the "wicked and wanton effort" of a "corrupt, babbling dwarf." The indignant editor of the *Lexington Whig* denounced "this idiotic and fiend-like imputation" and accused Kendall of being a "traitor to his country" who "should be shunned as a monster." Patrick Henry Darby, the editor of the *Frankfort Commentator,* strained to reach new heights of bombast: "It appears to us to require the mind of the assassin to conceive, and the hand of a murderer to pen, the very conception of such a charge." Clearly, the old court supporters maintained, Beauchamp's motivation was personal—he killed Sharp to avenge his wife's dishonor. The *Kentucky Reporter,* only days after the murder, named Beauchamp a prime suspect based on his desire for "personal revenge," while the *Commentator* surmised that Beauchamp's personal animosity toward Sharp had "excited the bad passions which prompted him to do the deed wherewith he is charged."[17]

Yet as much as the old court party tried to portray the accusation as the aberrant and incautious ravings of the hyperpartisan Kendall, the suspicion and the fear that Sharp was murdered for political reasons was neither begun nor solely promulgated by the editor of the *Frankfort Argus of Western Amer-*

ica. On the day of the murder—well before Kendall's initial suspicions were published—Lunsford Pitts Yandell, a medical student at Transylvania University in Lexington, wrote, "It is suspected that the infuriated friend of some one of the opposite party has perpetuated the atrocious deed. This will be the prevalent belief, and will excite into increased action the party feeling of the country." Leander Sharp maintained that "multitudes in Frankfort openly expressed such a belief and the impression spread through the state with the tidings of the dreadful event." Unfounded rumors spread that there was a conspiracy to assassinate Governor Desha and that an attempt had already been made on the life of Lieutenant Governor Robert B. McAfee. Thus Kendall could accurately respond to his critics, "No man can deny the prevalence of suspicions that the assassin was actuated by political considerations. We have heard them uttered through our streets; we have heard them echoed from every section of the state as the tidings have spread." And though Kendall demurred that "this suspicion is involuntary and probably unfounded," he disingenuously added that new court supporters "see through all history, the bloody track of the political assassin."[18]

Whether or not Beauchamp's murder of Sharp had political causes, it certainly had political consequences and in fact became, as one nineteenth-century biographer asserted, "not merely . . . a private but . . . a public calamity." Sharp's death dealt yet another severe blow to a new court party already staggered by the defeat in the summer elections. "I looked to Col. Sharp with *confidence* to be the leader of the party," Francis P. Blair lamented, "and considered him as *the point of their strength,* around which they would rally." With John Rowan elevated to the U.S. Senate and other new court luminaries either defeated or in retirement, Sharp would have been his party's most experienced advocate in the state house of representatives, the one who could have most effectively countered the substantial array of talents that the old court party brought to bear: John J. Crittenden, Benjamin Hardin, George Robertson, Joseph Underwood, and Robert J. Breckinridge. A justifiably worried Amos Kendall wrote, "Although there are many young men of the highest promise, on the side of liberal principles, in the House of Representatives, there is not one among them whose age and experience, whose knowledge of the proceedings of legislative bodies, qualify them to take the lead in public business." In sum, Sharp's loss was irreparable: "When the political friends of Col. Sharp awoke on the morning of the first day of the session and learned that he was struck dead in his chamber; when they found that the head to which they had committed their arrangements had ceased to think, . . . a sense of the destitution ran through every bosom, which cannot be described. It turned hope itself to dismay. It paralyzed every effort on one side and now every thing is carried by acclamation on the other."[19]

The partisan implications of Sharp's death only fueled the speculations that the murder was in fact a political assassination. Why was Sharp, one of the most prominent leaders of the new court party, killed the night before the convening of the legislature? How did the presumptive assassin, a man unfamiliar with Frankfort, manage to locate his victim's house? How did he know which of the seven doors leading into Sharp's house would be the one that Sharp would most likely answer? And how did the murderer know that Sharp and his wife had in the previous week given their bedroom in the front of the house to an ill law student and were themselves sleeping in a guest bedroom near a partially obscured door opening on the alley? Beauchamp at once grasped the possibilities of this line of thought. While trying to deflect suspicion from himself, he wrote, "There is a manifest improbability rebutting all presumptions of my guilt in this, that I had not been in Frankfort since Col. Sharp lived in the house in which he was kill'd. I knew extremely little about the Town, never having been in it but once or twice before; that 4 or 5 years ago, and then almost wholly in the night. . . . This difficulty presents itself to the mind of every body."[20]

Though he would later glory in the fact that he had stabbed Sharp to death, Beauchamp, for six months after his arrest, heatedly denied having committed the crime: "I am innocent of the murder of Col. Sharp: of any feeling of malevolence towards him." He even feigned surprise as to why anyone would suspect him of—as he himself put it—"so black a crime." He asked George Bibb to visit him to "tell me, as a man of candor, on what your opinion against me, and that of the thinking part of the community, is based." Why, it was absurd to believe that he could kill "a man so highly and justly esteemed" as Solomon Sharp. As to the rumors that he killed Sharp out of vengeance for Anna's putative seduction, Beauchamp protested that he possessed "the most decided determination never to make the wounds of that family bleed afresh, by reviving unpleasant feelings which time had measurably consoled."[21]

Beauchamp embraced the idea that the more politicized the murder became, the better his chances for acquittal, and he therefore did his best to inflame such suspicions. The real murderer, he claimed, was attempting "to prepossess the public mind against me" in order to prove that a "most atrocious deed was committed from personal, not political views!" He tried to portray himself as a political casualty of the court struggle: "I am," he claimed, "one of those most unfortunate victims of popular excitement & party zeal, which republics have had in all ages to offer as it would seem, occasionally as a sacrifice to the Immortal Gods for the blessings of liberty." In ordinary times, Beauchamp continued, he would not even have been taken into custody, but "such is the rage of popular excitement, & the peculiar turn which this case is likely to take, that I have reason to fear even for my life." In a typically melodramatic outburst, Beauchamp beseeched John Crittenden, "Is there no Cicero, no Henry in Our Republic to stem the torrent of party zeal, and fearlessly stand forth in the defence of oppress'd innocence & the just rights of man?"[22]

With questions swirling over Beauchamp's ability to locate his victim, with the assassination being ascribed to political, not personal, animosities, Beauchamp grew hopeful: "This tune caught my fancy exactly; and while things went on thus, I began to feel pretty safe." However, rather than diverting suspicion away from Beauchamp, "this tune" led many observers to another conclusion entirely: Beauchamp had an accomplice, who, for his own political motives, had inflamed Beauchamp's personal hostility toward Sharp, had told the young man that Sharp was spreading awful rumors about his wife, and then had informed Beauchamp of the best time and place to kill Sharp. Beauchamp, in this formulation, was a mere patsy goaded into murdering Sharp by "busy and designing men"—a "ferocious band" of old court partisans—who, wanting Sharp dead, had poured "falsehoods" in Beauchamp's ears "in relation to the recent conduct of Col. Sharp." Beauchamp professed to be astounded at the turn of events and, in typically immodest terms, proclaimed that they were "as unlooked for, and as unprovided for by me, as the burning of Moscow was by Bonaparte." In truth, Beauchamp was infuriated by the implication that he—a transcendent genius on the order of world historical figures—was merely a tool, a dupe of others more clever than he. In a move that seriously diminished his chances of acquittal, "the new court faction . . . lashed me and the old court party together." And the means to do so all but dropped in their lap.[23]

Patrick Henry Darby—described by Beauchamp as "one of the greatest fools I ever met with in the world"—casually stepped into this political miasma of intrigue and misdirection and made it worse still. It is not often that a historian comes across a figure of such striking clarity. Virtually without dissent, everyone who crossed Darby's path found him to be morally and physically repugnant, given to perjury and disturbing "the good order of society." Possessed of "an ugly face," Darby had an almost preternatural talent for evoking disdain and hatred. He was, to give only a few examples, a "vindictive and indefatigable monster," a man who "has no principles," a "damned scoundrel." Noted Tennessee jurist John McNairy attested, "I fear that with him the end would justify the means," while Felix Grundy thought that he had "known no man so mischievous, troublesome, and dangerous." Another Tennessee acquaintance did not believe that "public opinion . . . accords to him the possession of a single virtue." Even the clergy piled on; Darby's former pastor in Nashville remembered him as "a very imprudent, immoral man," while the Reverend Hardy McCryer thought Darby a "sore visitation to any civilized and Christian land."[24]

Little is known of Darby's origins. Born in 1783 to humble circumstances in either Ireland or western Pennsylvania, he was the younger brother of noted geographer William Darby. After spending time as a young man in the Louisiana, Arkansas, and Illinois territories, by 1811 Darby was practicing law in Hopkinsville, Kentucky. As a sideline, he would buy up disputed land titles from absentee claimants and then evict the occupants, a practice that so disturbed the peace of the community that "a law was passed by the General Assembly in 1819 to prevent his further operations." Having made few friends in this manner, Darby thought it wise to remove to Clarksville, Tennessee, where he again set up practice and again promptly alienated the locals. This time, Darby managed to reach a new low, even by his own standards: he sold a client of his—a free black woman—into slavery. Shortly after, learning that there was an error in the act that incorporated the town of Clarksville, Darby attempted to throw all of the titles to the town into dispute. Outraged, prominent residents told Darby to leave town within an hour or "be taken over the river and whipped as long as there was a beech limb in the bottom." Thus, "by his forwardness and insolence, he soon made himself hated by every body, and it was not long before he found it necessary to decamp."[25]

By 1822, the thirty-nine-year-old Darby was in Nashville, editing an anti-relief newspaper he called the *Constitutional Advocate.* He soon came to the attention of Andrew Jackson, who hired Darby to represent him in a land case and thereafter supported Darby's unsuccessful campaign for the state legislature. Predictably, Darby in due time angered Jackson, who later wrote, "I never did admire the principles of Mr. Darby. . . . His want of judgement and imprudence, will injure any cause which he attempts to advocate." In 1824 Darby was disbarred in Tennessee for publishing information on a pending lawsuit in which he was involved. Soon after, to the regret of few, Darby left the state. The speaker of the Tennessee assembly avowed (on the record) that he "had rather see earthquakes, famine, and pestilence visit the land, than for that man again to come among us."[26]

"In an evil day for Kentucky," Leander Sharp later deadpanned, "Mr. Darby determined to make this state his future residence." Yet Darby, despite his strange talent for alienation, also possessed a "sparkling mind" and exuded a "particular assurance" and thereby quickly managed to insinuate himself into centers of powers in early Kentucky. Soon after being admitted to the Franklin County bar, Darby earned the admiration of the old court partisans for his refusal to take the oath before the new court justices. After practicing law for a year or so, Darby reentered the political fray by buying out Humphrey Marshall's *Harbinger* in September 1825 and resurrecting the title *Constitutional Advocate*. Darby maintained Marshall's old court political sympathies and, before long, was carrying on an editorial rivalry with Amos Kendall that, even by the standards of the time and profession, was extraordinarily acrimonious.[27]

After Beauchamp's arrest, Darby, his "delight in the agitations of a storm" once again fully on display, claimed to have heard Beauchamp, a year or so earlier, threaten Sharp's life in Brandenburg, a town on the Ohio River. While Beauchamp was still being held at William Jackson's residence, Darby paid the suspect a visit. As Beauchamp later wrote, he was speaking with John Rowan—who had agreed to advise but not represent him—when "pop, Darby obtrudes his ugly phiz, right into the room." Beauchamp, after Rowan informed him that this was the man who claimed to have heard Beauchamp threaten to kill Sharp, "immediately rose, and abruptly asked 'Mr. Darby, Did you ever see me before Sir?'" Darby, struck speechless, could only fidget while a stern and contemptuous Beauchamp demanded, "Look at me—I will lay off my cloak—did you ever see me before?" Darby hesitated and then averred that he had seen him in Brandenburg the previous May. Yet Beauchamp was easily able to prove that he was nowhere near Brandenburg at the time the alleged meeting took place, and Darby was forced to retract the assertion, now claiming that he "had great difficulty in fixing the location" and that the man he spoke to was not Beauchamp. (Threatening the life of Solomon Sharp, apparently, was common.) Darby, however, was not done; shortly after the confrontation at William Jackson's residence, he told at least three people—one of them Congressman Ben Hardin—that he had actually visited Beauchamp's house in Simpson County. Here was Darby's most explosive assertion, one that convinced Eliza and Leander Sharp that Darby was an accomplice to the murder. (Later, Darby once again repudiated his own statements—he had visited another lawyer's house, not Beauchamp's.)[28]

For Beauchamp, Darby's reckless assertions only "made the matter an hundred times worse, and, in a great measure, really confirmed the suspicion, that he . . . was concerned in the murder." By early 1826, the Sharp family and a great many new court supporters were convinced that old court advocates Patrick Henry Darby and Jereboam Beauchamp had conspired to kill Solomon Sharp.[29]

On March 22, 1826, the burgeoning political controversy—fueled by a toxic mixture of Darby's bizarre behavior and Beauchamp's misdirection—became exponentially bitterer when a letter signed by Solomon's widow, Eliza Sharp, appeared in the *Argus of Western America*. There, Eliza flatly declared Patrick Henry Darby to be "the chief instigator of the foul murder which has deprived me of all my heart held most dear on earth." She accused Darby, "my husband's most active enemy" during the previous summer's political campaign, of telling Beauchamp—"for the purpose of stimulating him to revenge"—that Sharp had forged public documents during the election affirming that Anna's child was interracial. Darby, she charged, had met with Beauchamp the night of the murder and given him the crucial information about her home that allowed Beauchamp to find and kill her husband. Darby, in sum, was Beauchamp's "accomplice and sentinel." Eliza's charges, already outlined by Amos Kendall and other new court partisans, were later fleshed out and given further documentation by Solomon's brother, Dr. Leander Sharp, in his *Vindication*. The crux of the charge was that Darby's involvement in the assassination proved that "the murder had in it more of *politics* than of *vengeance*."[30]

Eliza's accusation centered on a visit that Darby had inexplicably paid the Sharps "on the very day which preceded the fatal night," even though "Darby had long avoided the society of my husband." Just before taking his leave, Darby, according to Eliza, asked Solomon "where Mr. Bass, a young gentleman who was sick in our house, lay." Solomon told Darby that he and Eliza had switched rooms with Bass, but the question struck Eliza as odd, as, indeed, did the entire visit—especially considering the substantial political differences between the two men. Puzzled by the call, Solomon guessed that Darby "came to his office to spy out what he was preparing for the legislature."[31]

Immediately after the murder, Eliza believed she understood the true purpose of Darby's visit and his unusual questions: he was reconnoitering the murder scene, ascertaining where the Sharps slept to better direct Beauchamp to the proper door. “It then occurred to me, that the room in which Bass lay, was that which had been occupied by us until within a very few days.” And thus Sharp’s answer to Darby’s query “gave the very information that was necessary to guide the murderer to our new bed room which was in the back part of the house.” This is why, the morning of the murder, while still “in the first paroxysms” of her grief, Eliza repeatedly accused Darby of the murder: “My mother and Dr. Sharp, from prudential motives, begged me again and again, not to use his name. I did not then, nor do I now believe, that he was the man who entered the house and stuck the fatal blow . . . but my mind was strongly impressed with the idea that he was in some way concerned in it.”[32]

Eliza was convinced—as was her brother-in-law, Dr. Sharp—that Beauchamp, on the night of November 6, met with Darby, who gave him the information necessary to find and kill Sharp. This is how, Eliza wrote, a man who had never

> had any opportunity to become acquainted with the peculiar construction of our house, and the rooms as occupied by different inmates . . . had learned enough of the house to apply at a private door, in a secret alley which entered close to the door of our newly occupied bed-room, instead of applying at the front door or at the door of our former bed-room, then occupied by Mr. Bass, Dr. Sharp, and Dr. Scott, which opened on the back porch, or at any other outer door of the house, all of which were more likely to be approached by a stranger.

Darby’s behavior after the murder only confirmed Eliza’s suspicions. Darby, she argued, too quickly averred that he had heard Beauchamp threaten the life of her husband; moreover, when Darby and Beauchamp spoke at William Jackson’s, it was the distinct opinion of some who witnessed the encounter that, by “the looks they exchanged,” the two “knew each other well, and had met more familiarly under different circumstances.” When Darby then proceeded to claim that he had actually been to the Beauchamps’ house, the Sharps’ suspicions transformed into certainty. Although careful to assert that she did not “impute his death to a party,” Eliza unequivocally linked the murder of her husband with the partisan conflict then rocking the state: “The hatred which led to the murder, was engendered in the late electioneering strife. This conviction I uttered in the first moment of my grief, and it returned upon me at every lucid interval of my understanding.”[33]

The old court quickly retaliated. Eliza Sharp, they charged—in a very interesting choice of words—had been "seduced" into authorizing "a publication so useless and so wanton under the sanction of her name and character," and thereby had become "the victim of . . . wicked purposes." Darby himself charged that the letter was not written by Eliza but was "the joint production of Francis P. Blair and Amos Kendall" and further amended by Joel Scott. Later, under oath during the trial, Eliza affirmed not only that she wrote the document but that she still believed every word of it to be true. Kendall deposed that the letter "came to the office as I was informed and believe in the hand writing of Mrs. Sharp." Although he aided "in correcting" the letter, his understanding was that she had written the communication "without consulting any human being." John M. Bass swore that he saw the letter in manuscript form—in Eliza's handwriting—and that she asserted, "Here is a piece which I prepared for the press and intend to publish in the next Argus."[34]

Patrick Henry Darby, seemingly wishing to prove correct Eliza's charges that he was a "vindictive and indefatigable monster," exclaimed that it was not he who instigated Beauchamp but the Sharp family and their political allies, by spreading the rumor of Anna's black child: "Eliza T. Sharp, Leander J. Sharp, William Henry Harrison Scott, Francis P. Blair, Amos Kendall, the Bibbs and their associates . . . were the persons, who, by their foul and malignant slanders, to gratify their own pride, and subserve their own purposes of interest and ambition, did (though not intending or expecting such an effect or consequence) provoke the feelings that drew the dagger." New court publications returned fire: The editor of the *Frankfort Patriot* demanded, "Can the spirit of party rage run so high to destroy all the natural sensibilities, all the charities of life? . . . Have we not reached the period when the natural tenderness of generous men for the feebler sex has lost its influence?" Kendall, meanwhile, asked, "Has it come to this, that a man who has been literally driven from a foreign state for his malevolence and his vices, shall be tolerated in attacking the reputation of the murdered and the mourner in this chivalrous land, and yet be hugged to the bosom of a powerful party, lauded and defended?" This, in Kendall's neologism, was "Darbyism"—slandering a dead man and his surviving family, "a thing so shocking to every feeling of justice, humanity and honor" that "barbarism, vandalism or any other word is too feeble to express the horrible idea."[35]

Awaiting trial, Beauchamp solicited the services of a number of lawyers, none of whom were in a hurry to defend a man accused of assassinating

Kentucky's former attorney general. His first choice was John J. Crittenden, whose reputation was such that "criminals from other counties were always trying first to engage him to defend them." Even as Beauchamp was being taken away from their home, Anna had urged him to contact Crittenden. And so in November Beauchamp wrote two long, maudlin letters to Crittenden, begging him to serve as his counsel: "Can you, oh Crittenden, refuse to give your voice at the prayer of a fond supplicating wife, to see that *Justice* is done to one whom all others appear anxious to oppress! I cannot believe it." With brazen dishonesty Beauchamp implored Crittenden: "If circumstances are unfortunately so very unfavourable towards me, that your judgement is convinced beyond a doubt, that I have murdered your friend, in the name of Heaven throw every grain of influence and exertion which your are master of into the scale against me, & let me meet the fate I so justly deserve, if I am guilty." Crittenden did meet with Beauchamp, but having also been asked by the Sharps to aid in the prosecution, he was, as he later wrote, "much embarrassed as to the course I would pursue." In the end, he declined to participate on either side. Then, in succession, Beauchamp turned to George Bibb, Thomas Triplett, Lewis Sanders, and Thomas Monroe, each of whom refused to take the case.[36]

Finally, Beauchamp found someone to represent him: the habitually contrarian John Pope. Born in 1770 in Prince William County, Virginia, Pope was brought to Kentucky as a young boy, his family settling a few miles east of where Louisville stands today. When he was about ten years old, John's right arm was crushed in a cornstalk mill and had to be amputated above the elbow. Thereafter, Pope turned his energies to academics and compiled an impeccable record. He attended Dr. James Priestley's Salem Academy at Bardstown, along with several other future leaders of the state, including Joseph Hamilton Daveiss, John Rowan, and Felix Grundy. In the mid-1790s, Pope moved to Lexington, where he studied law under George Nicholas, the father of Kentucky's first constitution. There he once again rubbed shoulders with the best and brightest young men of Kentucky—William T. Barry, Jesse Bledsoe, Isham Talbot, and Robert Wickliffe, as well as his old friends Daveiss and Rowan. Pope also expanded his political and social influence by an uncanny knack for marrying well—his first wife was a niece of Patrick Henry; his second was the sister of Louisa Catherine Johnson Adams, wife of John Quincy Adams.[37]

By 1826, the fifty-six-year-old Pope—"very handsome," albeit "a little fleshy"—had been one of the leading politicians in Kentucky for more than two decades. Throughout, however, he had also been the most controversial political figure in the state, primarily because of his intermittent sympathies for the Federalist Party and his well-earned reputation as a maverick. One colleague remembered him as "a good speaker and a very plausible reasoner—but very unstable in . . . his politics." Persistently adhering to a prepartisan political tradition, Pope insisted that a statesman should never align himself to more than a "slight degree" with any faction. In the late 1790s, Pope associated with the small and beleaguered band of Kentucky Federalists who openly admired Alexander Hamilton and fiercely opposed the Kentucky legislature's condemnation of the Alien and Sedition Acts. Only two years later, however, Pope voted for Thomas Jefferson as a presidential elector, and in 1807 he was elected as a Republican to the U.S. Senate. Such actions proved him, to his admirers, to be a man of principle; to his detractors, a disloyal opportunist. Yet whatever popular esteem he had garnered almost evaporated after he voted for the renewal the Bank of the United States in 1811 (contrary to the explicit instructions of the Kentucky General Assembly) and, still more controversially, opposed the declaration of war with Great Britain the following year. "Lucifer fell from Heaven," the *Kentucky Gazette* admonished, "and so has John Pope fallen from the elevated place which he once held in the affections of his fellow-citizens." Another paper estimated that Pope's actions "were unacceptable, to say the least of them, to more than nineteen twentieths at least of the people in this state." For a time, Pope was persona non grata—in 1813 he could not even get reelected to the state legislature, losing by a humiliating margin of 1,208 to 434. Four years later, this popular revulsion toward Pope—and in particular his appointment as secretary of state—sparked the ugly new election uproar of 1816–1817. Although he managed to hold on to his office, Pope, at the end of his tenure, returned to his law practice in 1820 and stayed clear of political office for the next few years. In 1824 he supported his wife's brother-in-law, John Quincy Adams, for president; four years later, however, he was in Jackson's camp, and he secured an appointment as territorial governor of Arkansas in 1829. Perhaps inevitably, Pope had a falling-out with Jackson and closed out his political career with three terms in the U.S. Congress as a Whig representative.[38]

However uncertain Pope's political loyalties, he had no doubt as to his own talents. "I have embarked in political life and mean to make a business of it," a thirty-eight-year-old Pope wrote to Ninian Edwards in 1808. "I occupy much higher ground here [in Kentucky] both on the score of talents and republicanism than either you or myself expected," he thought, adding that "except Breckinridge no man from the West ever had more popularity in Congress." In 1823, he made the ludicrous prediction, "I expect to be the next governor." As the old court–new court crisis reached its climax in 1825–1826, Pope, still deeming himself above such grubby party distinctions, believed he was the man to reunite the state. Having been elected to the Kentucky senate the previous summer, Pope proposed a compromise: the old court would be dissolved, but its judges given new commissions, and three more justices should be appointed to the court, bringing the number up to six. The idea went nowhere, for the old court now anticipated victory and betrayed no inclination to compromise.[39]

Pope's arrogance, maddening inconsistency, and political delusions all combined to elicit deep antipathies and often provoked passionate denunciations: "He is a rough drunken vulgar old man, and he will not stick to the truth!" one Kentuckian exclaimed. Yet however egotistical, however politically imprudent, Pope was a man of substantial legal skill, and Beauchamp was fortunate to procure his services. Pope was assisted by Thomas J. Lacey and Samuel Q. Richardson, a thirty-four-year-old land lawyer educated at Transylvania University, himself "a violent, brave, and dangerous man."[40]

On March 20, 1826, a Franklin County grand jury convened and, "after a long and careful investigation, returned a true bill" against Beauchamp. Investigating the possibility of a conspiracy, the grand jury concluded that there was no evidence that Beauchamp had had an accomplice. A special session of the Franklin circuit court was scheduled for the second Monday in May, May 8, for the sole purpose of trying Jereboam O. Beauchamp for the murder of Solomon P. Sharp.[41]

Solomon Porcius Sharp. Photograph of a portrait by Matthew Harris Jouett, ca. 1820. (Courtesy of the Filson Historical Society, Louisville, Kentucky.)

Anna and Jereboam Beauchamp. Dating from decades after the murder, these illustrations are purely conjectural. No likeness of Anna or Jereboam was made during their lifetimes. (Reprinted from *The Avenger's Doom, or The Singular, Thrilling, and Exciting History and Lamentable Fate of J. O. Beauchamp and Miss Ann Cooke* [Louisville, KY: Barclay, Orton, 1851].)

"Judge Breaking" by Hannibal Sratchi depicts the chaos of the old court–new court conflict. New court combatants wield clubs labeled "Replevin," "Preamble and Resolution" (John Rowan's new court manifesto), and "Patrick Henry" (the pseudonym of a particularly controversial new court author). On the left, Amos Kendall blows a bugle labeled "Argus." Old court partisans respond in kind with "Protest" (their response to the reorganization act of 1824), the state constitution, and "Lapis v. Blue-Skin" (*Lapsley v. Brashear,* the case that overturned the relief laws). The epigraph reads, "With many a stiff thwack, many a bang / Hard crab-tree and old iron rang," lines from Samuel Butler's *Hudibras,* a Restoration-era epic poem that satirized the excesses of English Puritanism. (Courtesy of the Kentucky Historical Society, Frankfort.)

(right) John Rowan, the leader and intellectual force of the relief party–new court movement. (Courtesy of My Old Kentucky Home State Park, Kentucky Department of Parks, Bardstown.)

Francis P. Blair. Solomon Sharp's defense of Blair's appointment as the clerk of the new court marked Sharp's return to the political arena in early 1825. (Courtesy of Blair House, U.S. Department of State, Washington, DC.)

The Joel Scott residence, once located on the corner of Miro and High streets in Frankfort, Kentucky, was where Jereboam Beauchamp stayed the night he assassinated Sharp. (J. Winston Coleman Jr. Kentuckiana Collection, J. Douglas Gay Jr./ Frances Carrick Thomas Library, Transylvania University, Lexington, Kentucky.)

(above) The Sharp residence on Madison Street in Frankfort, Kentucky. The doorway in which Beauchamp attacked Sharp was located off the alley to the left of the house. The residence was demolished in the 1970s, and the site is now home to the John C. Watts Federal Building and U.S. Courthouse. (J. Winston Coleman Jr. Kentuckiana Collection, J. Douglas Gay Jr./Frances Carrick Thomas Library, Transylvania University, Lexington, Kentucky.) *(below)* "Plan of Col. Sharp's House." (Reprinted from J. G. Dana and R. S. Thomas, *Beauchamp's Trial: A Report of the Trial of Jereboam O. Beauchamp before the Franklin Circuit Court in May 1826 upon an Indictment for the Murder of Col. Solomon P. Sharp* [Frankfort, KY: Hodges, 1826].)

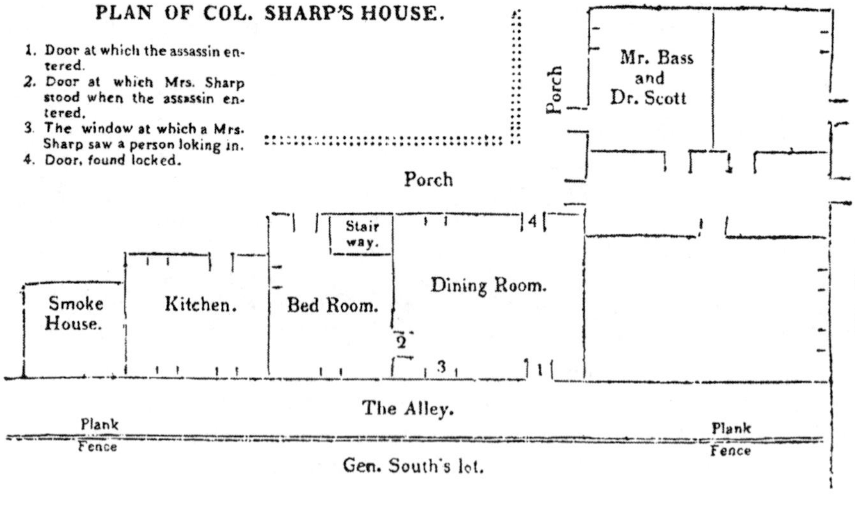

Patrick Henry Darby, one of the more notorious figures of the early West. (Portrait by Matthew Harris Jouett, 1788–1827; Honorable Patrick Henry Darby; oil on panel; 28 5/8 × 23 3/4 in. [72.7 × 60.3 cm]; bequest of Maria Louise Darby and Nanny Flournoy Darby, 1958.7; Speed Art Museum, Louisville, Kentucky.)

The brilliant and mercurial John Pope, Beauchamp's counsel. (Courtesy of the Arkansas History Commission, Little Rock.)

Amos Kendall, who carried on a furious newspaper war with Darby in early 1826, helped stoke fears that the assassination of Sharp was politically motivated. (Courtesy of the Library of Congress, Washington, DC.)

"Great God, it is Beauchamp." Several melodramatic depictions of the Sharp murder appeared as true crime stories in the sensationalist press from the 1830s to the 1850s. (Reprinted from *The Avenger's Doom.)*

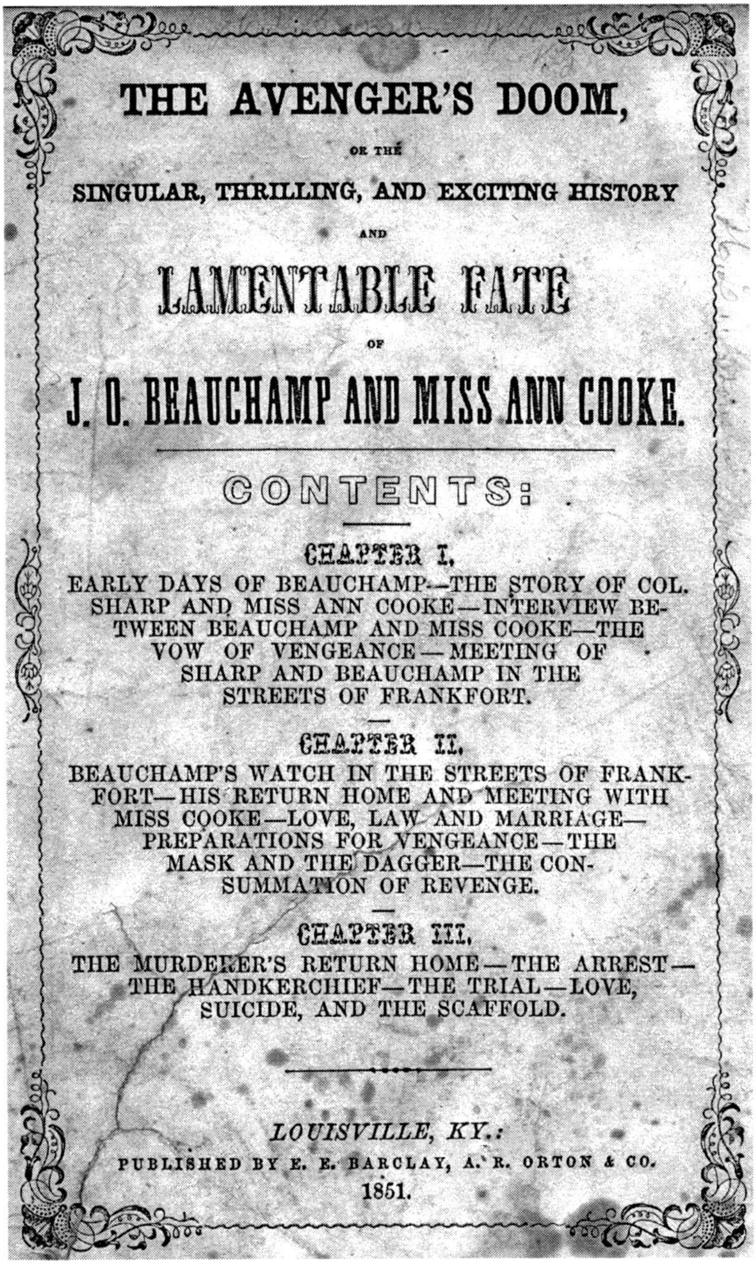

THE AVENGER'S DOOM,

OR THE

SINGULAR, THRILLING, AND EXCITING HISTORY

AND

LAMENTABLE FATE

OF

J. O. BEAUCHAMP AND MISS ANN COOKE.

CONTENTS:

CHAPTER I.

EARLY DAYS OF BEAUCHAMP—THE STORY OF COL. SHARP AND MISS ANN COOKE—INTERVIEW BETWEEN BEAUCHAMP AND MISS COOKE—THE VOW OF VENGEANCE—MEETING OF SHARP AND BEAUCHAMP IN THE STREETS OF FRANKFORT.

CHAPTER II.

BEAUCHAMP'S WATCH IN THE STREETS OF FRANKFORT—HIS RETURN HOME AND MEETING WITH MISS COOKE—LOVE, LAW AND MARRIAGE—PREPARATIONS FOR VENGEANCE—THE MASK AND THE DAGGER—THE CONSUMMATION OF REVENGE.

CHAPTER III.

THE MURDERER'S RETURN HOME—THE ARREST—THE HANDKERCHIEF—THE TRIAL—LOVE, SUICIDE, AND THE SCAFFOLD.

LOUISVILLE, KY.:

PUBLISHED BY E. E. BARCLAY, A. R. ORTON & CO.

1851.

Throughout the antebellum era, publications such as *The Avenger's Doom* romanticized the Kentucky Tragedy, depicting Anna and Jereboam as martyrs to the code of honor.

Title page of William Gilmore Simms, *Beauchampe, or The Kentucky Tragedy: A Sequel to* Charlemont (Chicago: Maxwell, 1888). Building on the stories of the Beauchamps, a generation of dramatists recycled a story shaped by literary cliché and produced, predictably, still more literary cliché.

CHAPTER 7

The Trial

He knew himself a villain—but he deemed
The rest no better than the thing he seemed;
And scorned the best as hypocrites who hid
Those deeds the bolder spirit plainly did.
He knew himself detested, but he knew
The hearts that loathed him, crouched and dreaded too.

—Byron, *The Corsair*

The trial, to read the *Confession,* was an utter travesty, and Beauchamp the victim of a "tornado of prejudice." Beauchamp railed that the prosecution's case was littered with "the most barefaced falsehoods imaginable," that "misrepresentation flowing from prejudice or worse motives" tainted the testimony of the state's witnesses. He was convicted, it seems, only because of massive and flagrant bribery: "The whole treasury of the Commonwealth was thrown open as a reward to villians to swear away my life!" It was "wholy upon circumstances, subsequently raised and fabricated, that I have been convicted." Alone in his cell, before the trial had closed, Beauchamp poured out his vitriol in verse:

Then rave ye angry storms of fate!
Spit on your vilest blasts of hate!
   Ye purjured reptile worms!!!
Disdaining aught to yield—my soul,
Shall gladly fly this earthly goal,
   Safe to my Anna's arms.

Anna, too, depicted Jereboam as a political martyr, a victim of "perjur'd hatred's poison'd sword," the object of the "wrath of a venal band" who "rais'd the war cry . . . And marshalled all the force of all the land, / Against one lone, oppressed, unfriended man."[1]

A number of scholars have taken the Beauchamps' specious allegations of fraud, perjury, and tampered evidence at face value. "The disappearance of evidence at the trial, obvious examples of perjury and perhaps bribery," according to Robert Bamberg, "all reinforce our sense of the confusion and political intrigue which existed at the time." J. Winston Coleman Jr. has maintained that "the evidence was juggled, exhibits disappeared and could not be produced; there was bribery and perjury." Yet the clearest examples of evidence tampering (the destruction of the handkerchief) and attempted perjury (an attempt to suborn a witness, as we shall see) were Beauchamp's doing. The most suspicious testimony presented by the prosecution—that of Patrick Henry Darby—was easily exposed by defense lawyers as nonsense. For almost two centuries the Beauchamps' claims of perjury and unfairness have formed a key component of the "Kentucky Tragedy." Yet, once again, a close examination of the evidence reveals not that the trial was a miscarriage of justice, but that the Beauchamps believed themselves capable of tailoring people's perceptions for their own ends.[2]

Bizarrely, Beauchamp at times seemed to enjoy his own murder trial. Throughout the proceedings, observers remarked on his "perfect composure and self possession" and his "firm and composed, sometimes cheerful" appearance. While prosecution and defense wrangled over testimony and evidence, Beauchamp, understanding better than anyone what actually happened, delighted in his privileged position: he alone, he liked to think, knew who was lying or truthful or mistaken. Like any good aspiring Byronic hero, Beauchamp believed himself intellectually, emotionally, and morally above the ordinary run of mankind and absolutely delighted in this Olympian perspective. He constantly brandished a "forced smile upon his countenance" that, along with his confident, even insouciant air, infuriated his enemies. Savoring the scene of dozens of people attempting to navigate the webs of misdirection and lies he had spun, Beauchamp found the trial to be "an amusing occasion to sit silently by and take a philosophical consideration of human nature," a chance to determine which witnesses gave "a true colouring" to Beauchamp's actions and which were carried "along with the current opinion . . . like many weak minds."[3]

The drama took place in the Franklin County courthouse, a modest structure built twenty years earlier on the southeast corner of Frankfort's public square, not a hundred yards from where Beauchamp had murdered Sharp. The trials held there were often public spectacles and attracted all ranks of citizens. John J. Crittenden's daughter recalled that in the 1820s "ladies were in the habit of attending criminal trials" in Frankfort and often traveled great distances to witness them. Beauchamp's was the most notable trial in at least a generation. One local paper reported that throughout the hearing, "the Court-House has been crowded with citizens and strangers, and the most intense interest is manifested by every person acquainted in the least with the history and progress of the prosecution."[4]

The presiding judge was Henry Davidge, whose cousin, Julia H. Tevis, described him as a "Kentucky gentleman" who "lived above commonplace things," possessed of "that perfect self-possession born of a feeling of superiority." Davidge was indeed a man of painstaking erudition and undoubted self-assurance whose equanimity and reserve earned the respect of polite society in Kentucky. On the bench, he was stern and resolute; he never allowed "the slightest disrespect to his official character [and] governed the jury with unflinching severity."[5]

Davidge's political sympathies were well known. He had served several terms in the General Assembly as an opponent of the relief system and was horrified by the legislature's attempt to tame the judiciary; according to Francis Blair, who served as the trial's clerk, Davidge was "as much an anti–judge breaker as anybody in the Commonwealth." Blair also retailed the rumor that the judge's considerable debts had reduced him to little more than a tool of the old court faction: "If he were to fail in the slightest to obey" the old court party leadership, they "would desert him and he being a perfect Bankrupt could not give security and would be unable to hold his office." Yet, if the new court partisans worried about the political biases of Davidge, such concerns may well have been offset by the fact that Davidge had known well the murder victim. At one point during the trial, when Beauchamp's lawyer took the jury over to Sharp's house, Davidge, "already acquainted with the premises declined going."[6]

The prosecution was led by Charles Scott Bibb, the son of George M. Bibb and the grandson of Charles Scott, Kentucky's governor from 1808 to 1812. He was assisted by the Kentucky attorney general, J. W. Denny, and, at the request of the friends and family of Sharp, by Daniel Mayes, the Sharp family lawyer from the Green River area. Beauchamp gave an uncharacteristically generous and eerily disengaged assessment of the commonwealth's attorneys:

"I was most ably prosecuted," he wrote after being sentenced to death; "Bibb spoke in the spirit of his native honor, humanity, and fairness," while Mayes, although "betraying a rancorous prejudice against me, . . . traced me out, in all my subtle studied precautions, for the commission of the murder, with much accuracy."[7]

The defense denied not only that Beauchamp had killed Sharp but that he had any ill will toward the man at all—despite the fact that everyone knew that his wife had previously charged Sharp with seduction and abandonment. Yet Beauchamp's lawyers stayed well clear of Anna's charge of seduction, for any mention of sexual predation would have likely led the jury to the conclusion that Beauchamp had exacted revenge on Sharp. The prosecution also avoided the highly volatile issue because of the wishes of the Sharp family—who had always denied that there had been a seduction and did not wish to revive the memory of the ugly incident—and doubtlessly because the prosecutors feared that any mention of seduction might convince the jury that the murder was justifiable. The result was a weird ballet of avoidance in which both sides assiduously steered clear of an obvious and explosive subtext of the entire case. During the trial, when one prosecution witness obliquely referred to the preexisting "delicate situation" between Beauchamp and Sharp, the commonwealth's attorney quickly moved on. At another point, Darby began to allude to the seduction charge but was interrupted by Pope, and the subject was quickly changed, neither side objecting.[8]

Another consequence of this development was a highly unusual gap in the prosecution's case: it never attempted to prove motive. So, for example, although the state clearly demonstrated that Beauchamp had repeatedly threatened Sharp's life, the reason remained nebulous—which left some observers wondering that "nothing was developed which could throw the least light on the motives of the murderer."[9]

If the prosecution ignored motive, the state's newspapers certainly did not. New court supporters, of course, believed the motive to have been political—that someone, most likely Patrick Henry Darby, had goaded Beauchamp into assassinating the new court's most valued, experienced, and skilled leader. The old court, meanwhile, maintained that Beauchamp, acting alone, had committed the murder for personal reasons brought about by Sharp's own immorality. Some faulted Beauchamp not so much for killing Sharp but for doing so in the dead of night rather than challenging him to a duel. Darby mused, if only Beauchamp, "in the character of a proud, bold, and magnanimous man, put [Sharp] to death in the street, in open day; and rested for his justification upon the justice and feeling of mankind, the world would never have convicted him of murder." He added, "If he dies for the deed, he will die not so much for the death of Col. Sharp, as for the manner of doing it! He will die, because . . . he is a mean, cowardly, prowling, and insidious wretch!" If a man was to seek such "primal justice," he must always respect "the manly and chivalrous feelings of mankind"; Beauchamp's reckless mode of vengeance only "renders society unsafe and insecure."[10]

And thus both sides in this partisan war of words simply, almost casually, assumed Beauchamp's guilt. As a result, during the first two days of the trial—Monday, May 8, and Tuesday, May 9—the court's attention was consumed by the extraordinary furor surrounding the case. "With much apparent warmth and zeal," Beauchamp's lead counsel, John Pope, argued that the "improper publications" of the region's newspapers had "tended greatly to prejudice the public mind" against Beauchamp. Moreover, the offer of reward money tendered by both the state legislature and the town of Frankfort, the defense argued, had "induced certain persons . . . to resort to all means and exert every influence to procure his conviction that they may receive and realise the rewards as offered by the Legislature and Trustees." Pope darkly warned that these interested individuals were persons of influence, and the defense "has most reasons to dread their operation on his trial." One of the principal witnesses—Darby—"has been mainly concerned in exciting and carrying on said publications as made in this Circuit." Taking umbrage, Darby "severally interrupted" the proceedings, protesting that "he was ready now, and at all times, to defend and justify himself." After Pope gave Darby a "severe castigation," he moved for a postponement of the trial until after the August elections. Although Davidge agreed that the publications were improper, he would only push the trial back to July. Beauchamp and his lawyers, after conferring throughout the afternoon, decided to proceed at once.[11]

The formal indictment of *The Commonwealth of Kentucky v. Jereboam O. Beauchamp* being read, potential jurors were interviewed. In all, the attorneys called and examined forty-eight men, twenty-eight of whom were dismissed for having formed or expressed a prior opinion of the case; another eight were rejected out of hand. The twelve jurors finally chosen composed a fairly representative cross-section of the white male population of Frankfort. One of them, Edward Minter, possessed a net worth of twenty-five dollars, while another, Thomas Collins, claimed an estate worth just under ten thousand dollars. Another man, Colonel Thomas Lillard, was a Franklin County justice of the peace and had been a member of the first county court in the 1790s. At least half were small slaveholders, and most were farmers with modest landholdings, although two were merchants—neither especially prosperous—and another was a tavern owner.[12]

Preliminaries completed and attempts to forestall the trial unsuccessful, testimony commenced on Wednesday afternoon, May 10. The prosecution's case was largely circumstantial, but such was not at all unusual. Throughout the nineteenth century, jurors rarely had the luxury of forensic science or eyewitness accounts, and therefore almost all murder cases hinged on indirect evidence. And if there were no eyewitnesses at this trial, there were plenty of witnesses; in only four and a half days, prosecution and defense brought to the stand no fewer than sixty-one people—the commonwealth thirty-five, Beauchamp's lawyers twenty-six—many of whom testified more than once.[13]

The state's first order of business was the unexpectedly easy task of establishing Beauchamp's habit of announcing his intent to murder Solomon Sharp. A veritable bounty of testimony was available: Simpson County constable John F. Lowe swore that Beauchamp had recently refused to talk about Sharp, for "by God, the man I intend to kill, I never say any thing about"; John Hays testified that Beauchamp told him, "If ever I get a chance, I will send him to hell, where he ought to have been many years ago."[14]

The prosecution attempted to put Beauchamp at the scene of the crime despite the lack of an eyewitness or any extant material evidence. The best they could manage was Eliza Sharp's recollection that it was Beauchamp's voice she heard calling her husband to the door that night. Her testimony had a powerful effect; Eliza took the stand with a veil over her face and answered the counsel's questions "in a low tone of voice, not always distinctly heard." Being forced to relive the night that had shattered her family "naturally produced in her the most excruciating sensations, and in the hearers a lively sympathy."[15]

Eliza Sharp swore that the "sharp, shrill voice" of the murderer was so distinctive that she would forever recognize it. After Beauchamp was apprehended, his uncle Colonel Beauchamp proposed that she hear Jereboam speak, hoping it would help exonerate his nephew. Beauchamp himself endorsed the idea, imagining that he had disguised his voice so well that night that he had little to fear. So Joel Scott, "at the request of old Jerry and young Jerry," arranged for Eliza to surreptitiously come to the jail. On hearing Beauchamp speak, Eliza "became very much agitated," and now, on the stand, she testified, "I thought I should have fainted." The voice she heard that night, Eliza swore, was Jereboam Beauchamp's: "I could not possibly be mistaken."[16]

As Jereboam had announced himself at the Sharp's door that night as "John A. Covington," the prosecution tried to establish Beauchamp's habit of mistakenly referring to John W. Covington, a friend of the Sharps, as "John A. Covington," a person that did not exist. Captain William C. Bradburn, who owned a shop in which Jereboam had sharpened a knife a week or so before the murder, attested that Beauchamp repeatedly made the mistake of saying "John A. Covington." Two other acquaintances of Beauchamp's, Jesse Bunch and Isaac Covington, the brother of John W., both swore that Beauchamp referred to "John A. Covington" the very day he was arrested.[17]

Although the defense expended a great deal of energy trying to rebut this testimony, it only partially succeeded. One defense witness swore that he heard Beauchamp speak of John *W.* Covington, but another, on cross-examination, admitted that he had a "slight impression" that Beauchamp "miscalled" Covington's middle initial. In the *Confession*, Beauchamp himself maintained that he deliberately chose the name "John A. Covington" as a means of deflecting suspicion—so well did he know the Covingtons that anyone would realize that he would not have made such an error. In truth, however, Beauchamp viewed this evidence as particularly damaging and went to great lengths to try to counter it. When, as we will see, Beauchamp tried to suborn a witness, he specifically tried to ensure that it would be said in court that he always referred to Covington accurately; this "*must* be sworn," Beauchamp insisted, "if all the rest is abandoned."[18]

To demonstrate that Beauchamp was prowling around Frankfort the night of the murder, the prosecution called to the stand two night patrolmen, Elias M. Crane and James Downing, both of whom saw a man fitting Beauchamp's description walking the streets in the early morning hours of November 7. According to the pair, they saw a young man at about one thirty, "with a cloak around him," walking slowly down St. Clair Street toward Sharp's house with "his arms . . . folded up." Downing claimed that the man stood out in his memory because "it was observed in conversation among us . . . that if we could not find any negroes, we would take up some of the judge breakers. We meant to have some fun out of them. When we found it was a stranger, we did not interrupt him."[19]

The prosecution then called a number of witnesses who testified to Beauchamp's actions on his way home from Frankfort. Josiah Wilkins, Thomas Middleton, and William Johnson all swore that Beauchamp had failed to mention to them the news of Solomon Sharp's murder. The defense, however, effectively countered this testimony with a number of witnesses who swore that Beauchamp did indeed speak of the killing on his way home. J. M. Brown, a resident of Bardstown who was related to Beauchamp by marriage, swore that Beauchamp had told him of the murder. Two other men, John T. Brown and J. H. Montgomery, likewise affirmed that Beauchamp had casually mentioned Sharp's assassination and that neither suspected that Beauchamp had any connection to the crime.[20]

Much more damning were Beauchamp's bizarre comments and behavior upon his return home—his waving a red flag and, when asked why, blurting "For victory"; his boasting that "things had happened as right into his hands, as ever into a man's hands in the world"; and his declarations that he had completed his business "by God, to my satisfaction," and that he had learned that "there is a God that will give vengeance to them that ought to have it." It was exceedingly strange behavior for someone who had not even accomplished the mundane goal of registering a land claim.[21]

The prosecution focused a great deal of attention on the erstwhile handkerchief and brought forth a number of witnesses who testified that Beauchamp was wearing a similar one before the murder. Unfortunately, the handkerchief, thanks to the guile of Beauchamp and the carelessness of his escort, no longer existed, and the prosecution's witnesses had trouble describing it very clearly—it was successively described as "blue with wide stripes," "madras," "cotton cross barred," "muslin"; some claimed that it had holes in it; others said that it did not. Beauchamp later mocked "the wild and variant speculations upon the subject of the appearance of the camelian-like handkerchief."[22]

Although Beauchamp melodramatically spouted that "the handkerchief . . . was used to take my life with," the reality was that his defense team did a very good job of countering this evidence. They brought forward convincing witnesses—among them John Harvie, president of the Bank of Kentucky, and George Bibb, one of the more celebrated statesmen of early Kentucky—who both testified that, on coming to Sharp's house, they thoroughly searched the premises and saw no handkerchief. Harvie testified that he examined the scene looking for "some object—a knife, a handkerchief, or something that might serve as a clue to the murderer"—and had found nothing. When Pope asked him how closely he searched the premises, Harvie returned, "I never examined a bundle of papers in the Bank of Kentucky with more particularity." Likewise, Bibb attested that as soon as it was light, he twice examined the alley without finding any relevant material evidence whatsoever. About breakfast time, Bibb went home, and Samuel South, Sharp's next-door neighbor, came and told him that a handkerchief had been found: "When I went back with Gen. South, the handkerchief was placed in the situation where it was stated Col. Taylor had found it. I am confident it could not have been there when we searched the alley." Another witness, Judge Robert Trimble, saw the handkerchief soon after it was found and thought that the blood stains were not fresh.[23]

This testimony, Beauchamp crowed, "threw a dark shade of suspicion around the Sharp family, for having fabricated the handkerchief altogether." Although this is a gross overstatement, the defense had nonetheless cast substantial doubt as to the authenticity of this key piece of evidence. The truth of the matter, as Beauchamp later disclosed to his guard at the jail, Benjamin Edrington, was that he actually had two handkerchiefs, one that he wore on his head to help conceal his features and another that he tied around his hand to keep the blood from staining his clothes. Beauchamp, according to Edrington, admitted, "As Sharp was in the act of falling, [Beauchamp] threw up his hand and caught the handkerchief that he had around his head, and in trying to save the one that was on his head he lost the one that was on his hand, and after he got out of the house, he found he had lost it." This, apparently, was the handkerchief that Arabella Scott found. The account also explains why Beauchamp risked loitering at the murder scene. Bibb's and Harvie's testimony, meanwhile, can most likely be explained by Arabella's finding the handkerchief before the two men, in the confusion of the early morning, could examine the alley.[24]

The defense was also able to cast doubt on the footprints in the Sharps' garden. Because the tracks leading to the house were distinct and close together, while those leading away were farther apart, many assumed the tracks to have been made by the murderer. Yet John Harvie doubted it, for he "saw nothing in the track indicating precipitancy or caution." In any case, George Bibb testified that the "first moment" he examined Beauchamp's footprint, he "was satisfied it was not the track which I saw in the garden."[25]

The defense made short work of Joel Scott's testimony that Beauchamp acted suspiciously when told of the murder. According to Benjamin Taylor and Colonel Henry C. Payne, both of whom accompanied Scott back to his house to interrogate Beauchamp, Scott did initially suspect Beauchamp, but when he returned from interviewing his guest, he told them that "he was perhaps premature in putting forth suspicions." Scott's doubts "were removed by the manner in which the man received the information," and he even suggested, according to Taylor, "that we should go back, and remove the impression made by the manner in which he had made the suggestion."[26]

The state then made the mistake of trying to prove that Beauchamp had journeyed to Frankfort to kill Sharp a month before the actual murder. Dr. Sharp claimed that he heard "some body working at the knob of the door" of Sharp's house after midnight "some time in October." Leonard J. Fenwick, who was living at the Mansion House, professed to have seen Beauchamp there on October 9. "I was writing, and posting books up stairs, and came down in the morning and looked at the Register, and saw the name of Jere Beauchamp on it, and asked Fountain, if old Jere Beauchamp was there, he said, no, and took me by the arm, and led me away, and pointed to a man near the fireplace" whom Fenwick tentatively identified as Beauchamp. Although two other men, Richard T. Fountain and Thomas Y. Bryant, essentially corroborated Fenwick's testimony, the defense easily laid bare the accusation for the nonsense it was. Under cross-examination Fountain was forced to admit that he had no proof of Beauchamp's visit, for the pages of the Mansion House register for October 10 through 13 had been torn out; more to the point, the defense clearly established that on October 10 Beauchamp was 160 miles away, at the Simpson County courthouse, and that, five days later, he had attended a sale in his neighborhood. As Beauchamp later boasted, the whole charge was a "most barefaced and completely detected fabrication."[27]

Another embarrassment for the prosecution was the testimony of Patrick Henry Darby, who took the stand on the second day of testimony and proceeded, characteristically, to cause trouble. A witness for the state, Darby was now, under oath, forced to recant previous assertions that he had heard Beauchamp threaten the life of Sharp in Brandenburg and that he had actually visited the Beauchamps' house in Simpson County. Now Darby had a new tale: While traveling from Nashville in the fall of 1824, he had stopped at a well about two hundred yards outside Duncan's Tavern, right across the Tennessee state line in Simpson County. "While I was there," Darby testified, a man "rode up, dressed in light coloured homespun clothes," a man he now thought was Beauchamp, "though I have no such a distinct recollection of his person as to say whether he was the man or not." As Darby told it, this person said he had married Anna Cooke and wanted to employ Darby to sue Solomon Sharp, who had promised the young man "a thousand dollars, a negro girl, and two hundred acres of land" as recompense for Sharp's affair with the woman he eventually married. After telling Beauchamp (or whoever he was) that he thought the case was hopeless, Darby continued, the young man "flew into a violent passion, a rage," vowing to shoot Sharp in the streets of Frankfort.[28]

Pope mercilessly cross-examined Darby, making it painfully clear that Darby himself was suspected by some to have a hand in the murder, that he might wish to see Beauchamp convicted to deflect suspicion from both the old court party and himself, that he had earlier told different stories, and that he had actually traveled to Simpson County collecting affidavits that would help convict Beauchamp. By the end of the ordeal, "so contradictory were his declarations, and so strange his conduct," Darby had only managed to further weaken the prosecution's case.[29]

Although there existed a general, almost casual, assumption that Beauchamp was guilty, the prosecution could not have been optimistic midway through the trial. Beauchamp's behavior had been suspicious the morning of the murder and after he arrived home, but the handkerchief and the voice evidence were inconclusive, and the track in the garden did not match Beauchamp's shoe. Pope and his assistants, moreover, had eviscerated the charge that Beauchamp had attempted to kill Sharp in Frankfort the previous October and had cast serious doubt on the testimony of both Joel Scott and Patrick Darby.

And then Beauchamp himself virtually handed the case to the prosecution. On Thursday morning, the second day of testimony, a neighbor of the Beauchamps'—Simpson County constable John F. Lowe—on being called to the stand, produced a letter and a document he claimed Beauchamp had authored. Beauchamp evidently admitted to his counsel the nature of the items, for Pope immediately and strenuously objected to their introduction, insisting that although the documents might implicate Beauchamp in a "different and distinct offence," they were but "confidential communication[s] made by the prisoner to *his wife*, which had been surreptitiously, or accidentally, obtained by the witness." The prosecution ominously countered that "where a prisoner introduces *falsehood* into his defense, it is an indication of guilt." For considerable portions of the next two days, Judge Davidge heard arguments over the admissibility of this evidence before deciding early Saturday morning that the letter and document could be read to the jury. It was the turning point of the trial, for after the contents of these materials became known, even Beauchamp's most dedicated supporters began to doubt his innocence. Colonel Beauchamp later admitted, "I never thought him guilty, until after I saw or heard the document read which he sent to Lowe. I then began to think him guilty."[30]

John Fair Lowe, a forty-year-old native of Surry County, North Carolina, was apparently as close to Jereboam and Anna as anyone. The Beauchamps turned to Lowe when, shortly after their marriage in 1824, Anna fell ill and needed help. And it was Lowe to whom the Beauchamps once again turned when they tried to manipulate the outcome of the trial. "You have in all my knowing," Beauchamp wrote Lowe in early March, "ever befriended me faithfully. And will you now desert me, when I so much need your friendship?"[31]

The Beauchamps had tried to persuade Lowe—a law officer—to commit perjury in the upcoming trial. Such deceit was necessary, Beauchamp explained to Lowe in the March letter, for despite his innocence—"it is all foolish suspicion that is against me, and nothing more"—"villains" were roaming the state, offering bribes to "creatures base enough" to swear to his guilt. Such "unworthy enemies"—men who would utter "barefaced lies"—threatened him with the prospect of being "murdered publicly." "If you were in my situation," Beauchamp implored, "I would never stand aloof."[32]

And so, in addition to the letter, Beauchamp prepared a second, more damning piece of evidence—a remarkable, seven-thousand-word script with which Anna, in the Beauchamps' elaborate scheme, was to direct Lowe. Anna, by pressing "the substance . . . upon his mind," would coach Lowe's testimony so that he would be able to make a statement "in his own way." Back in Simpson County, Anna frequently invited Lowe to their house in an attempt to persuade him to help—so often, in fact, that he worried that "people would think he went to see her for improper purposes." (And indeed, as Frankfort merchant D. C. Humphreys remembered years later, Anna "was suspected to be in unlawful intimacy" with Lowe.) As had Jereboam, Anna tried to influence Lowe with professions of friendship, at one point pathetically exclaiming, "Oh! Mr. Lowe, I want a friend—will you be my friend?" After Lowe assured her that he was, Anna "implored him to save her husband." When Lowe finally "gave her encouragement," Anna—despite Jereboam's explicit instructions not to "even let Lowe look upon my handwritings"—gave Lowe the document to study. He told her "he would take it, and think of it."[33]

These instructions for perjury must have stunned Lowe. He was to swear to a whole array of falsehoods designed to exonerate Beauchamp: that Beauchamp himself believed the whole story of Anna's "seduction" to be "a fabrication of John U. Waring's"; that Beauchamp had no quarrel with Sharp and was in the habit of speaking well of him; that Beauchamp did not even wish to go to Frankfort and had asked Lowe to go in his stead; that the night of Beauchamp's return from Frankfort, he had behaved normally; that Beauchamp, when told that two people had caught a glimpse of the assassin at the murder scene, exclaimed, "I thank God for that . . . for if they saw the murderer, they will know I am not the man"; that when one of the guards who apprehended Beauchamp tried to get him to say he knew John A. Covington, Beauchamp swore, "No, I only know John W."; and that one of the guards offered Lowe a bribe of one hundred dollars to say that the handkerchief was Beauchamp's.[34]

Beauchamp went so far as to invent dialogue for Lowe. If asked to recall the night of Beauchamp's return from Frankfort, Lowe was to say that when he and Beauchamp went to tend their horses, Beauchamp suddenly remembered the big news from Frankfort: "Oh! I did not tell you! Col. Sharp has been murdered. . . . I think I heard them in the street talking about the murder, and saying something about one John A. Covington, and I inferred, perhaps him and some fellow there by the name of John H. Covington had had some difference." Lowe was to ask, "Could it be possible politics had got to such a rage as for him to be killed out of the way on that account?" A saddened Beauchamp would reply, "No, a body ought to hope not," adding that "it was as likely some of his own slaves as any way."[35]

The script, Beauchamp planned, would not only clear himself but throw suspicion onto Patrick Henry Darby. Lowe was to testify that when Darby traveled to Simpson County, he tried to bribe Lowe into swearing that Beauchamp was in the habit of referring to John W. Covington as "John A. Covington," and then attempted to give Lowe a handkerchief doctored to look exactly like the piece of evidence lost at the tavern on the way back to Frankfort. Just before an enraged Lowe nobly ran the villain off his land (the story continued), Darby offered yet another bribe if Lowe would keep quiet about the whole affair. As Beauchamp contrived this ridiculous scene, as soon as Darby left, Lowe went to Anna and told her the whole story: "She cried for joy and begg'd me for heavens sake to let no one know it till trial."[36]

Thus the Beauchamps not only asked Lowe to commit perjury but wanted him to frame another man. This design "to implicate an innocent man" appalled the *Niles' Register,* while the *Frankfort Spirit of '76* marveled at "the attempt . . . to blast the reputation of an innocent individual, and fix upon him the charge of murder." But perhaps the most stunning aspect of the whole affair was Beauchamp's brazen belief that he could get Lowe to risk his own reputation and freedom in order to implicate Darby. Here, once again,

Beauchamp displayed an almost staggering combination of ignorance and audacity, of imprudence and impudence.[37]

Darby, certainly, took exception to the whole affair; in the courtroom, as the document was read to the jury, he "rose from his chair and looked Beauchamp full in the face the greater part of the time." And when, immediately afterward, Lowe was called back to the stand and asked if he and Darby had had any conversation remotely similar to that outlined in the document, Lowe swore, "I never spoke to the gentleman in my life," and proceeded to make clear that virtually everything Beauchamp had written was sheer fiction.[38]

The introduction of this evidence marked the true turning point of the trial. Beauchamp's claims of unfairness and perjury aside, his blatant and foolish attempt to suborn Lowe proved to be, as Hezekiah Niles put it, "the most powerful witness against him." The *Paris (KY) Western Citizen* likewise insisted that the document "proves clearly . . . that Beauchamp is the real murderer"; another paper, although admitting Beauchamp's "extreme ingenuity," insisted that "the malignity of the attempt to suborn the witness to clear the guilty and implicate the innocent, is only exceeded by the foul murder itself."[39]

After his clumsy scheme had collapsed, Beauchamp could only rail impotently at the "treachery and double villainy of John F. Lowe" and claim to believe that Lowe had conspired with Darby to secure a conviction: "Lowe had all the time been acting traitor for Darby, to ensnare me." Beauchamp churlishly dismissed Lowe as "a very ignorant man" who, he alleged, at his request had previously committed perjury "upon the trial of a warrant I was interested in, out of mere friendship." Possessed of "a corrupt heart and of no honor," Lowe "has seldom any firmness in his friendships; nor can he be bound by any tie; which may be depended upon, but self-interest." Small wonder that Lowe, after Beauchamp's execution, sued the publisher of the *Confession* for twenty thousand dollars for "the malicious putting forth of the false and libelous publication."[40]

All of Beauchamp's later writing about misrepresentations, falsehoods, bribery, and politically motivated injustice aside, what, more than anything, secured his conviction were his own actions. Had he not melodramatically and cryptically boasted on his return home of "getting the job done"; had he been careful to mention the murder to everyone he spoke with on the way home; above all, had he not tried to rig his own murder trial, the prosecution's case would have been far weaker. Beauchamp's behavior testifies to his belief that he could fabricate reality and manipulate perceptions, and it was this hubris that secured his fate. Yet the same impulse would later serve him well, if posthumously. Beauchamp's affectations, his attempt to suborn Lowe, and, as we will see, the *Confession* itself should be understood as very similar attempts to manipulate others and shape the perception of events.

In early America, a time when oratorical skills were highly regarded, the closing arguments provided the climax of any important trial. Certainly the substance of the case was put forward and evidence "sifted, weighed, and interpreted," but style mattered tremendously as the attorneys faced off in a rhetorical duel designed to sway the emotions of the jury. These encounters also, by today's standards, took up an exorbitant amount of time—in Beauchamp's case, almost half of the trial. The prosecuting attorneys were relatively brief—Bibb spoke for over two hours, followed by Mayes, whose remarks lasted four hours more—but Lacey, Pope, and Richardson successively harangued the jury from late Tuesday afternoon until Friday morning. Yet surprisingly, given the quality of the argumentation, the intense interest in the case, and the meticulousness with which the rest of the trial was recorded, no one transcribed either side's closing remarks.[41]

The consensus of those present was that the defense attorneys' summation was "conducted with distinguished ability," that their closing arguments were "very ingenious, generally eloquent," that "every effort was made to save the prisoner which zeal and talents could dictate." The speech of Pope, the lead defense attorney, was especially anticipated, for although a remarkably controversial figure, he was also widely acknowledged to be one the state's more accomplished orators. Eleven years earlier, Amos Kendall, having just arrived in Kentucky from New England, had witnessed Pope's efforts to save another young man charged with murder. Although the eloquence of Pope's address and his ability to appeal to the juror's emotions amazed Kendall, he also thought that Pope had a tendency to meander, to be "led from his subject by many irrelevant ideas which seemed to strike him on the occasion, and at length made his discourse tedious." Kendall, leaving the courtroom at sundown, was later astonished to learn that Pope had "continued his argument till nearly ten, and, though he had spoken six hours, did not finish!" (Pope's client in that case was found guilty and, after an unsuccessful appeal for a new trial, was executed.) Decades later, in the 1840s, General D. L. Adair witnessed another closing argument of Pope's—"the most remarkable to which I ever listened." Pope, by then seventy-three years old, "entered the crowded court-room—venerable and very striking in appearance—swinging his armless sleeve." Although Pope began feebly—"in the outset it was halting, his words came with difficulty, his sentences were not rounded, his gesticulation was unimpressive, his voice husky"—he soon warmed up, growing increasingly and singularly eloquent. "All defects disappeared—his voice grew musical and his speech flowed in full and impassioned volume." In the end, Adair thought, "The effect of the speech was wonderful. It converted almost every one who heard him."[42]

Beauchamp, too, was impressed by his lead counsel. Pope, he later wrote, "made an eloquent and able display, and it was one of the best defences I ever heard." And, true to form, Pope antagonized at least one member of his audience; as soon as he had finished his speech and was leaving the bar, Darby—upset at whatever Pope had said and no doubt still smarting from his brutal cross-examination earlier in the trial—tried to beat the one-armed man with his cane. Beauchamp, becoming agitated—"What feelings overwhelmed my understanding!" he later wrote—jumped out of his seat and charged Darby. The guards subdued Beauchamp, while "Darby was seized away by the crowd."[43]

Order restored, Attorney General Denny presented the prosecution's rebuttal and, "with great power," countered "the various points made by the other side, confuting most of the arguments they had advanced with apparent ease, recurring to the prominent facts proved, connecting them, and pressing them upon the attention of the jury, in a manner which seemed to render the conclusion of the defendant's guilt irresistible." Even Beauchamp admitted that "Denny concluded the argument with ability, and spoke in a very fair and impartial manner."[44]

At five o'clock in the afternoon of Friday, May 19, the closing arguments finally exhausted, the jury commenced deliberations. They were not gone an hour before returning with their verdict. Guilty. According to the next week's *Frankfort Argus of Western America,* there was not "the least hesitation in a single juror." As the verdict was read, "the countenance of the prisoner was unmoved"; Beauchamp, according to another source, "lost not his fortitude or self command." Beauchamp himself boasted that the verdict "made no change in my feelings, because I had habitually calculated upon it; and was at all times, so far reconciled to die, after I had killed Col. Sharp, that death had no power to daunt me." Those nearer to the young man, however, could see that Beauchamp "betrayed sensible emotion," that "*he had 'that within, which passeth show.'*" Sentencing was scheduled for the next morning, and the court adjourned.[45]

The next morning, just as Davidge was to announce Beauchamp's sentence, Pope moved for a postponement until Anna Beauchamp could be brought forward; "the court readily assented." After Jereboam's trial had begun, a warrant had been issued for Anna's arrest so it could be determined whether she should be prosecuted for involvement in the murder. Why Pope wanted Anna examined at this point is unclear, but very likely he was attempting to garner sympathy for his client, hoping that the sight of the couple might make leniency more likely or would perhaps even save Beauchamp from execution. And so Judge Davidge relinquished the bench to John Brown and E. S. Coleman, both justices of the peace for Franklin County, to hold a preliminary hearing to decide if Anna was an "accessary before the fact, to the Murder of Col. Sharp." Pope served as her attorney. Jereboam sat by her side.[46]

Only a handful of witnesses were called, among them Colonel Absalom Stratton, who testified that Anna had exulted in the death of Sharp, declaring that "heaven had avenged her," and Jesse Lane, who swore that Anna declared that "she could or would have stabbed [Sharp] herself." But once again the key witness was John F. Lowe and his testimony concerning Anna's role in planning the murder. According to Lowe, it was Beauchamp's determination to kill Sharp, and Anna had merely "induced him to determine on doing it in a different manner." He testified that she had "got on her knees and begged" Jereboam not to kill Sharp publicly but to assassinate him under cover of darkness. In the end, Lowe testified, "It was [Jereboam Beauchamp's] own project" to murder Sharp.[47]

Justices Brown and Coleman, "after conferring together, remarked, that they felt some difficulty in the case; but all things considered, they were disposed to discharge her." According to the *Louisville Gazette,* Beauchamp "discovered so much sensibility at the acquittal of his wife, when he himself was under sentence of death, as to clasp her to his arms in open court." Dr. Sharp was dismayed: "She was plainly proved to have been an accomplice, and yet was she set at liberty."[48]

Although acquitted, Anna refused to leave her husband's side and, as Jereboam put it, "immured herself with me in my dungeon." (It was indeed a dungeon; "the only entrance was through a trap door above," accessible only by a ladder.) Many commentators have wondered why, but she had no other choice. She was a pariah—not only a fallen woman but one implicated in a notorious murder. She had nowhere else to go.[49]

On Monday, May 22, Judge Davidge, after delivering to Beauchamp "an address and exhortation, as is often done on such occasions," proceeded "in a very feeling, yet firm manner, to pronounce the sentence of the law on the Prisoner." The Commonwealth of Kentucky would execute Jereboam O. Beauchamp on June 16. "With considerable composure and apparent calmness," Beauchamp stood up and requested "*time to write something* for the benefit of those nearer and dearer to him than *life itself*." It was Beauchamp's last gambit to avoid the hangman.[50]

CHAPTER 8

Prison and Execution

As boy, I thought myself a clever fellow,
  And wish'd that others held the same opinion;
They took it up when my days grew more mellow,
  And other minds acknowledged my dominion:
Now my sere fancy 'falls into the yellow
  Leaf,' and imagination droops her pinion,
And the sad truth which hovers o'er my desk
Turns what was once romantic to burlesque.

—Byron, *Don Juan*, canto 4, stanza 3

Though consigned to a dungeon and sentenced to hang, Beauchamp had by no means resigned himself to die. In the next seven weeks, he and Anna, by both their words and actions, would lay the foundations of the myth of the Kentucky Tragedy in an attempt to avoid execution. From late May to early July, the two conspired to craft a document meant to shape perceptions of themselves and what they had done, even as they tried to excite suspicions that Sharp's murder was a political conspiracy. The Beauchamps consciously appropriated and reshaped the memes of romantic literature, then synthesized them with precepts of southern honor to create a wild and vengeful Byronic hero, the star of a fanciful morality play designed to generate a demand for Beauchamp's reprieve. But the Kentucky Tragedy was not built solely on the *Confession* and its romantic tropes; it was the Beauchamps' behavior—their literary-inspired performances—as much as their writing that won over their audience. They, in effect, put on a production—a play based on the characters they had fashioned. Anna and Jereboam Beauchamp not only scripted their story but also staged it. [1]

On Sunday, May 21, Jereboam wrote his mother, Sally, "My friends are trying several ways by which they confidently hope to save me yet." The day before, John Pope had tried to convince Judge Davidge to issue an arrest of judgment, based on the grounds that "there was no law in force in Kentucky authorizing the court to pronounce sentence of death" because the reorganization act of 1824—the remarkable legislation that had created a "new" court of appeals—had inadvertently repealed a 1796 law that detailed punishments in capital murder cases. In addition, Pope asked for a new trial on the grounds that the documents proving Beauchamp's suborning of Lowe were improperly admitted as evidence. Early Monday morning, Davidge promptly rejected both motions, asserting that first, even if the reorganization act had repealed the act of 1796, the common law was still in effect, and second, the court had already "considered well the admissibility" of the script for Lowe. When Pope announced that he was taking his appeal to the state's highest court, Davidge merely "smiled at this suggestion," knowing full well that the court of appeals did not have jurisdiction over criminal cases.[2]

Nonetheless, two days later Pope stood before the "old" court of appeals, reiterating the argument Davidge had rejected, that "there was no law in force in Kentucky which authorized the court to pronounce sentence of death against the prisoner." But Pope had an even more daunting task—that of convincing the justices he had a right to be in front of them because the reorganization act had repealed all laws relative to the court of appeals, and thus "there was no law to prevent this court from taking jurisdiction of *criminal* cases as well as *civil.*" Of course, as Pope well knew, if the reorganization act was valid, then the old court of appeals—the very court he faced at that moment—did not exist. So he was forced to maintain that only portions of the act were binding, that "the reorganizing law was constitutional, so far as it purported to repeal former laws, although every other part of it should be considered by the court to be unconstitutional." Such a transparently selective, legalistic, and truly torturous reading convinced no one. Robert Wickliffe, appearing as a friend of the court (the prosecuting commonwealth's attorneys were all new court men and refused to practice in front of the old court), maintained, as had Davidge, that the common law, "relative to murder, was in full force in Kentucky." Furthermore, Wickliffe continued, the reorganization act was "unconstitutional and void from A to Izzard. Not one solitary section of it should be regarded by this court." Not surprisingly, the court agreed, and the next morning it rejected the appeal without so much as an explanation.[3]

Beauchamp's only hope now was a pardon from the governor, even though Desha had repeatedly asserted he would do nothing of the sort. Yet Beauchamp believed he could change the governor's mind by exciting "the sympathies of the country," and he immediately set out to create a grassroots movement for a reprieve. Beauchamp was convinced his ploy would work, for he believed Desha "was not a man of firmness" and "popular clamor alone, governed him ever."[4]

Beauchamp commenced his enterprise on May 22—the very day the old court refused his appeal—by writing to Amos Kendall and asking for his help in appealing "to my country, in mercy to let me live." Beauchamp knew that Kendall, as the editor of the state's leading newspaper, would be "greatly and extensively influential in inclining my countrymen to such a course of humanity." Beauchamp insisted he did not deserve execution and pledged, "I shall appeal to the magnanimity of my countrymen to suffer me to live out the measure of my days which nature may assign me, in a foreign land"—perhaps "Greece or South America." In exile, Beauchamp apparently fantasized, he could strike a Manfred-like pose and beguile a new audience with a perpetual state of self-abasement for the sins of his mysterious past. The very notion, however, that the state's legal authorities would exile a convicted murderer was bizarre—no precedent existed for any such punishment, outside Greek mythology and the era's romantic literature.[5]

Although Kendall ignored the plea, Beauchamp set about his work. On June 5, he informed Governor Desha that he was "preparing an appeal to my country for its mercy to mitigate its sentence of death upon me," adding that he would not ask "your Excellency for an exercise of the high prerogative of pardon, unless I can first gain the voice of my country in my behalf." Beauchamp freely admitted that he wanted his appeal to be "diffuse[d] throughout the state" so that the people may learn that "this is not an ordinary case."[6] The result—*The Confession of Jereboam O. Beauchamp*—was the cornerstone of the Beauchamps' attempt to prolong his life. It has rarely garnered the full suspicion it merits.

That a convicted criminal would issue a confession in the early nineteenth century was not at all unusual—it was, in fact, all but customary. "Virtually every condemned crook, con man, or other criminal," writes Cathy Davidson, "recorded the outlines of his or her life before ascending to the gallows." Although many of these confessions were the means by which convicted criminals strove to memorialize themselves, to leave behind some substance of their existence other than popular hearsay and social obloquy, such was not, at least initially, Beauchamp's purpose; rather, the aim of this confession was to obviate the need for a memorial.[7]

Before the text is dissected, a crucial point needs to be made: contrary to everything that has been written about the Kentucky Tragedy, the *Confession* was not the work of Beauchamp but of the Beauchamps. It is implausible, to say the least, that the assertive Anna—seventeen years Jereboam's senior, better educated, more widely read, and at his side the entire time—meekly sat by Jereboam's side as he composed the document on which his life depended. Such an assumption would be, in fact, directly contrary to everything we know about this strong-willed and singular woman. The *Confession* itself, moreover, strongly suggests that the two saw one another, at least by the lights of the day, as equals. Anna and Jereboam's relationship, according to the text, was based on equality and respect (itself a hallmark of romantic literature): "We reasoned together as intelligent beings on all occasions, neither assuming any superiority; but each conscious of the others affections and confident the ideas of each would be duly weighed and appreciated by the other." It is not at all surprising that Anna's input would be obscured, for the *Confession*—designed as it was to obtain a pardon for Jereboam—needed to be presented as solely the work of the murderer. Yet all signs point to the conclusion that the two closely collaborated in the fashioning of this story. And thus, just as Beauchamp insisted that the murder of Sharp was "neither imputable to the one or the other of us, but to both," so too was the *Confession;* it was not "his," it was "theirs."[8]

To gain popular support, to portray Jereboam's behavior as sympathetically as possible, the Beauchamps well understood that they needed to strike a resonant chord with the public, to assign a significance to the episode that, as Jereboam had put it to Kendall, "the world would appreciate." Accordingly, the *Confession,* in essence, undertakes a synthesis of the two dominant themes of romantic literature: the seduction tale and Byronic verse epics. It was no simple task, for the two archetypes of these literatures—the wronged sentimental heroine and the passionate, brooding Byronic hero—were fundamentally incompatible. The heroines of the sentimental novels were victims of seduction, whereas the Byronic hero—especially in the Don Juan incarnation—was a seducer extraordinaire. Only in their challenge to polite society did the two models converge.[9]

That the Beauchamps would hang their story on a fictional framework was not such an imaginative leap, for both the pathetic and demonic forms of romantic writing self-consciously worked to efface the boundary between literature and reality. Seduction novels inevitably claimed to have been based on true stories. The heroine of *Charlotte Temple*—originally subtitled *A Tale of Truth*—was supposedly inspired by the life and death of Charlotte Stanley, a woman who had been abandoned by John Montresor, the chief engineer of the British army in America. Hannah Webster Foster, meanwhile, based Eliza Wharton, *The Coquette*'s title character, on Eliza Whitman, a young woman who died in a Massachusetts tavern in 1788 after giving birth to a stillborn child. Just as anxious to obscure the line separating fact from fiction was the era's romantic verse. Byron himself, as previously noted, boasted the "real life" nature of his works, a claim that his reading public uncritically accepted. (Byron, incidentally, infused his creations with this inability to discern imagination from actuality; Don Juan's mother, Donna Inez, "had a devil of a spirit, / And sometimes mix'd up fancies with realities.")[10]

The Beauchamps, in a sense, closed the circle; just as a fact was once turned into fiction, they transmuted fiction back into "fact," and early Americans delighted in this seeming confirmation of their entertainment. That Jereboam and Anna could take these unpromising elements and fashion them into a coherent and plausible tale is ample proof of their audacity and, let it be said, their considerable skill. As Timothy Flint discerned in his review of the *Confession*, "there is abundant evidence that each possessed a gifted and uncommon mind." The Beauchamps' strange ability to shape perceptions of the Kentucky Tragedy for almost two centuries is a result of the fact that the couple, well versed in the literature of their day, knew the themes that would resonate with their audience: seduction and villainy and defense of honor—all of which they manipulated in the service of attempting to secure Jereboam's pardon.[11]

Put another way, the *Confession* was but the first of a number of fictional Kentucky Tragedies written throughout the nineteenth century. This artificiality of the *Confession*, its reliance on literary stereotypes, has not gone unnoticed by previous students of the episode. Almost sixty years ago, J. Winston Coleman, in the first attempt at a substantive history of the Kentucky Tragedy, perceived that the *Confession* amounted to a "studied effort to make [Beauchamp] the chief actor and hero of a sensational and romantic drama," the purpose of which was to transform Beauchamp "from the role of a brutal murderer into the noble champion and martyred protector of female virtue" and thus procure "a pardon from Governor Desha or at least a reprieve." (Coleman, however, made the mistake of completely dismissing the *Confession* itself—"so replete with bare-faced lies and crude inventions that it is entitled to little or no weight as source material"—and thereby failed to pursue any number of significant themes.) Literary scholar Dennis Duffy, in a brief but insightful treatment of the Kentucky Tragedy, perceived that the Beauchamps "themselves could hardly wait to turn the facts into fiction, and fiction of a lurid cast." Leslie Fiedler and Arthur Zeiger also glimpsed the fabrications behind the *Confession:* "Surely the tale of seduction and murder and suicide enacted by Anna and Jereboam and Solomon Sharp does not precede self-conscious literature, but follows it lamely—representing at last a special brand of naive and sentimental decadence, life tearfully imitating something less than art." A fuller, if more tentative, discussion of this dynamic comes from Dickson Bruce: "In one sense, Beauchamp's *Confession* may have represented the first literary version of the events, not simply in its self-serving and often fictional content, but in the ways in which Beauchamp, or his collaborators, drew heavily on literary conventions and devices for the final document," most obviously "those literary conventions that had been associated with the tradition of sentimental seduction novels dating back to the eighteenth century."[12]

These authors are absolutely correct in identifying one of the two pillars on which the Beauchamps built their story: the seduction tale. The *Confession* begins with an admonitory essay, precisely in the manner of sentimental seduction literature. Just as Susanna Rowson, for example, commences *Charlotte Temple* with an affirmation that her book will be worthwhile "if the following tale should save one hapless fair one from the errors which ruined poor Charlotte," so too does the Jereboam persona announce at the outset of the *Confession,* "If my death teaches a respect for the laws of my country, my example will be not less serviceable, in teaching a respect for those laws of honor, to revenge the violation and outrage, of which, I so freely die." Indeed, the text insists, Jereboam's murder of Solomon Sharp offered a "loud and lasting warning" to a "certain class of heroes, who make their glory to consist in triumphs over the virtue and the happiness of worthy unfortunate orphan females." Now, thanks to Beauchamp's heroism, such wretches might "pause sometimes in their mad career, and reflect, that though the deluded victim of their villany, may have no father to protect or revenge her, yet some friendly arm may sooner or later be nerved by her, to avenge her blighted prospects."[13]

The basic plot of the numerous seduction novels of the age—an orphan girl's seduction at the hands of a heartless reprobate—is faithfully duplicated in the *Confession.* Anna and Solomon met years earlier, when she was the daughter of a proud and prosperous family and he was a young man mired in "poverty and obscurity." The Cookes "patronised and supported him, in his whole career, till at length the scale was turned." Yet the treacherous Sharp repaid the Cookes with betrayal; he "seduced one whom he should have protected as a sister"—the young, virginal Anna. Alas, no one—at least in the Beauchamps' fantasy—was left who could avenge her: "Father, brothers, and friends, by a strange succession of calamities had been swept into the grave, and had left her almost without one soul on earth, save her dear old mother, to whom she could look for consolation and comfort." And so Anna, disgraced and devastated, "retired with her broken-hearted mother, never again to mingle in society." Ensconced in "a romantic little farm," Anna "sternly refused to make any acquaintances, or even to receive the society, or visits of her former acquaintances." The wages of sin, the inevitable result of the fall, was death, here enacted symbolically as Anna was "buried in a living grave."[14]

The Beauchamps imbued the *Confession* with the rank melodrama to which readers of romantic literature were accustomed. Jereboam finds Anna "in her sorrow and immolation"; the couple form an emotional bond "such as mortals seldom feel"; when Anna tells Jereboam of the "insuperable barrier" to their love, she does so "with a firmness, which spoke that it was the voice of fate," that "she would kiss the hand, and adore the person who would revenge her," that "her heart would never cease to ache, till Col. Sharp should die through her instrumentality." Jereboam vows that he could "never for a moment . . . suffer a villain to live, who had been the seducer of one I pressed to my bosom as a wife." When he departs for Frankfort on his unsuccessful mission to battle Sharp in 1821, Anna "burst into tears at parting and invoked the protecting arm of heaven." When Jereboam hunts down the "whining coward," the confrontation itself, as depicted in the *Confession,* reads like a script, complete with stage directions: "I bade him begone from me . . . (starting toward him.)" When apart, the Beauchamps communicate by means of "a secret method of writing, known only to ourselves." Anna poisons the point of the knife with which Beauchamp kills Sharp. Jereboam, as if he avenges seduced maidens on a regular basis, exclaims, "I always like to look a villain in the eye." Rather than admit the ease of locating Sharp's house, the *Confession* declares, "I had learned from a source which the offer of life would scarcely wring from me, where Col. Sharp lived." On his return home, Jereboam waves a red flag. When he realizes that the guard escorting him back to Frankfort has conveniently lost his dirk, Beauchamp's fury is such that he fears he "would kill all six of them." (The *Confession* does not explain how one man who has just had his weapon taken from him would accomplish such a feat.) In sum, here are all the key attributes of the sentimental novel as inventoried long ago by Carl van Doren: "sentimentalism, bathos, easy tears, high-flying language, melodrama, moralizings without stint or number."[15]

Further confirming the literary underpinnings of the document are the dramatis personae of the Beauchamps' fantasy, all portrayed in broad, stereotypical strokes. Solomon Sharp, in the hands of the Beauchamps, is transformed into a one-dimensional creature of such unremitting vileness that the preservation of the moral order necessitates his murder: an "unprincipled politician" who undertook a "mad career" of seducing "orphan females"; "a coward fiend" who refused to give Jereboam satisfaction when he challenged him to a duel; a "wretch," possessed of the "vilest heart / that ever human blood did animate."[16]

The headstrong and idiosyncratic Anna, meanwhile, is reduced to an "injured female," a "daughter of grief," "a child of evil fate," whose tale is one of "matchless woe." (Only when the *Confession* refers to her as a "troubled soul" do we approach reality.) Significantly, the text takes pains to depict Anna's role as a daughter and, more specifically, as an orphan, for narratives of early American seduction novels, as the Beauchamps understood, very often took place in the shadow of one or both parents' deaths. As Rodney Hessinger has pointed out, the heroines of seduction tales "often suffered the fate of seduction because they lacked parental guidance." Here, of course, the Beauchamps were again tailoring reality to conform to their audience's expectations, eliding the fact that Anna was thirty-three years old at the time of her putative seduction and that, although her father was deceased, her mother still lived—as did her brothers, who, if the tale were true, would have faced social ostracism had they not defended her.[17]

Yet the Beauchamps' depiction of Jereboam is most interesting, for it demonstrates that they did not blindly mimic sentimental seduction literature but managed to create something new. Time and again in the era's great seduction tales, the elemental lust for vengeance remained unsatisfied as villains went unpunished—or at least unavenged. It is not that miscreants such as Montraville and Mademoiselle La Rue in *Charlotte Temple* and Major Peter Sanford in *The Coquette* do not pay for their sins. Montraville is tortured by the memory of what he has done—"to the end of his life [he] was subject to severe fits of melancholy"—while La Rue winds up a street beggar in London; Major Sanford, after the death of Eliza, is undone by "confusion, horror, and despair," doomed, as the character himself puts it, to forever feeling "the disgraceful, and torturing effects of my guilt in seducing her!" In *The Power of Sympathy,* the seducer goes unpunished for a full generation, until two of his children commit suicide as a result of his misdeeds. But in every case, the villains, those who preyed on young women, only indirectly pay for their sins, and, although a guilty conscience and nature itself ultimately exact a frightful toll on the seducer, conspicuously missing in these tales were virile, vengeful men. Almost all male characters in early seduction literature were either young and debauched or old and impotent.[18]

To rob a maiden of her virginity, whether by force or fraud, was, as the cliché had it, "worse than murder": "Where is the father of any sensibility or honorable feelings," the Beauchamps asked, "who would not infinitely rather a villain would silently put his daughter out of the world, than to seduce and leave her to drag out a wretched degraded existence tenfold more painful to the father than her death?"[19] If seduction was worse than murder, then the seducer was worse than a murderer and deserving of still more extraordinary punishment. Yet the stories of seduction did not supply an immediate, emotionally satisfying retribution for the crime.

This void left an unrequited longing for vengeance, as encapsulated by "To a Seducer," a poem by Georgia poet Henry Denison printed in the *Argus of Western America* only three months before Sharp's murder. The piece contains all the usual ingredients—a merciless seducer, a ruined maid, a heartbroken family—but underscores the response of a virtuous young man who, coming on the scene, prays for a day of reckoning:

Great God, I cried, and must it be?
  Shall this sweet flower be left to languish?
And will no bolt be cast by thee,
  To blast the wretch who caused the anguish?
Far from a parent's fostering hand,
  By wily arts induced to wander,
Now fades her lately blooming charms,
  From parents dear and friends asunder,
Great Heaven! If suffering virtue call,
  To thee upraised for vengeance ever,

O let the direst curses fall,
On the seducer's head forever.[20]

The narrator of *Charlotte Temple* had likewise given to voice this vicarious wish for reprisal: "Gracious heaven! I wish for power to extirpate those monsters of seduction from the earth." In *The Power of Sympathy*, William Hill Brown depicts seducers as inhabiting such a deep circle of hell that murderers, duelists, gamblers, suicides, and misers "thank fate their crimes are not of so deep a dye." But notably, neither Rowson, Brown, Foster, nor most of the genre's other authors supplied such an avenger, leaving the reader's desire for atonement unrequited.[21]

The Beauchamps sated this thirst for retribution by inserting a wild and vengeful Byronic hero into the stock tale of virtue robbed. Jereboam was accordingly transformed into a "spirit divine!" whose worth and honor—according to the Anna persona—"shall be / my soul's sweet theme 'til I am cold in death." He was the hero she longed for, a champion who bravely

met the direst spite of hell
and mock'd their purjury, and scorned to yield
aught of his tranquil air; and happier fell
than ever hero did on glory's field.

In avenging her, Jereboam had "revived / The happiness she long had lost." In a letter to a lady in Frankfort, Anna emoted, "He was my all on earth—without whom I would never have lived in any event." The Byronic mood reaches an absurd climax in Beauchamp's verse appended to the *Confession*. Composed during the trial before Anna was summoned, the composition envisions her spirit bringing peace to his "troubled mind," shielding him from the world's "venomed spite." Beauchamp defies the "angry storms of fate" and raves against those who would destroy this magnificent man. Warming to his task, Jereboam rants that he

mounts above
Misfortunes highest waves
He cries—prisons for *clay!* the etherial soul,
Triumphant soars! disdain control,
And mocks a perjured world!
The shaft's too late! He soars too high!

He rides in triumph through the sky,
Not caring whence 'twas hurled.[22]

The Beauchamps' entire enterprise, in fact, was a variant of the "Byronic confession," defined by literary critic James Soderholm as "a mode of presentation in which disguise and disclosure intermix and where the aim is not forgiveness or self-expiation, but rather rhetorically evoking various responses in one's audience in order to manipulate one's own image." This form of autobiographical writing was pioneered decades earlier by Jean Jacques Rousseau but perfected by Byron, whose entire oeuvre, as Andrews Norton pointed out, has, "in fact, the character of 'Confessions.'"[23]

The predominant trait of the Byronic hero was emotional intensity, and the Beauchamps, accordingly, carefully constructed just such a headstrong, impetuous figure as the protagonist of the *Confession*. In the first two paragraphs alone, he is described as "eccentric," "ungovernable," "wild" (twice), and "volatile." While pursuing Anna, Jereboam, although initially rebuffed, cannot help but pursue her further, so does she "haunt my thoughts and my dreams." Receiving Anna's hand in return for a promise to exact vengeance on Sharp, "in my ardour I determined to fight Col. Sharp before our marriage." Later, during the trial, when Darby lunges toward Pope after his closing argument, the Beauchamp persona exclaims, "Oh! Almighty God, what feelings overwhelmed my understanding! I forgot my situation, and rushed out at Darby, the jailer holding one arm, and some of the guard the other."[24]

Yet if the Beauchamp persona is passionate, he rises above the ordinary concerns of mere mortals: "I never regarded death much," the *Confession* insists at one point, later reiterating that "death had no power to daunt me." When he hears the guilty verdict, Jereboam insists, "It made no change in my feelings." The persona, in fact, towers over the commonplace and frivolous worries of the multitude: "My fate has moved all . . . more than it has me." Far above the commonplace morality of ordinary mortals, he could kill a man "with as much tranquility of feeling as I could whip a servant that I thought deserved a whipping."[25]

The *Confession* repeatedly takes pains to dismiss the nondescript masses, the mere presence of whom only serves to underscore Jereboam's exceptional nature: the guards sent to apprehend him in Simpson County, for example, were but "a drunken careless set of fellows, who I could dupe or deceive in any way." The multitude lacked a certain, magical quality—"firmness"—that the Beauchamps prized: "I knew how few indeed there were," the Jereboam persona remarks of the trial, "who would have firmness enough to tell a man's manner, or what he said about a murder, just as it took place." Superior to the rank and file, the Jereboam of the *Confession,* like some ethnocentric anthropologist observing a tribe he considers savage, professes that the trial "really afforded me . . . an amusing occasion to sit silently by and take a philosophical consideration of human nature."[26]

Jereboam, to read the *Confession,* was a prodigy; "I early shewed some indications of genius" and caught people's notice with "the great ease with which I acquired whatever learning I turned my attention to." (The text's abundant grammatical and spelling errors suggest that it was not "with great ease" that he acquired the fundamentals of the English language.) Likewise, the *Confession* immodestly refers to the script prepared for Lowe as "ingenious." These delusions of grandeur come to a climax when the *Confession* compares Beauchamp to Napoleon—the very embodiment of everything that the romantic era admired. The Anna persona's poetry appended to the *Confession* goes further still, proclaiming that Beauchamp was a "more than mortal man!"[27]

The fictive Beauchamp, apparently, even possessed a preternatural ability to divine the future. Throughout the *Confession,* he claims to have "foreseen" any number of events: that killing Sharp would infuriate the new court partisans and that the murder in Frankfort would be "hazzardous"; that "it was impossible to avoid being arrested for the murder." Such was his gift for "prophetic certainty," such were his "foresight and success, in so planning the murder," that he returned from Frankfort "within 15 minutes of the exact time I had told my wife I would get home." The Anna persona, too, got into the act, supposedly warning Sharp years before she met Jereboam "in the spirit of prophecy" that someone should avenge her.[28]

The *Confession's* depiction of the Beauchamps' homestead, Retirement, as an idyll in which two remarkable souls commune far from the rest of humanity is also a predominant romantic conceit. This trope of withdrawal from society was a cliché not only of seduction literature—the shamed and humiliated victim of seduction being condemned to a form of social death—but also of Byronic verse, in which the hero, having rejected the conventional and timid morality of the common run of humanity, withdraws with his lover to an "island paradise." Retirement, in the hands of the Beauchamps, became just such an Edenic retreat, in which Anna and Jereboam banished themselves from what they referred to as "the whole world." Yet, as such literary treatments made clear, such a two-person utopian community was inevitably doomed. And sure enough, the *Confession* relates, the Beauchamps soon "received a letter from a gentleman" that told of Sharp's circulation of the story that Anna's child was interracial.[29]

Here the questions arise: To what extent did the Jereboam persona and Jereboam Orville Beauchamp coincide? How do we separate the pose from the person? Indeed, was there separation? It is often difficult to tell where imposture left off and self-willed character transformation began. Many young people did attempt to tear down the wall between life and imagination, and much of Beauchamp's actions strongly suggest that he did as well. At the same time, however, significant distance existed between the projected character and the actual person. Although the Beauchamp persona boasts, for example, that he "never regarded death much," the entire project of the *Confession* proves that Beauchamp regarded death a great deal. Similarly, a marked discrepancy exists between the Beauchamps' depiction of Retirement as a retreat from the "whole world" and its actual condition. Contrary to their claims, Anna and Jereboam actually led a quite active social life. Richard Hallaway and his wife, who lived about a mile away, regularly exchanged visits with the Beauchamps. John F. Lowe testified that after Jereboam left for Frankfort to kill Sharp, Lowe and his brother visited Beauchamp's house, and "there were a number of persons there." When Jereboam returned from murdering Sharp, he found a house full of visitors, including Lowe and two other neighbors, Mary Prescott and Martha Dowell, as well as Beauchamp's sister Malinda and his sixteen-year-old brother Asher. The next morning when the posse arrived, yet another guest, Colonel Absalom Stratton, was visiting.[30]

The Byronic mask slipped at other times as well. The *Confession* swears, "I had calmly come to the resolution that I would rather die than fly my country." Yet only weeks earlier Beauchamp had written to Kendall that he "shall appeal to the magnanimity of my countrymen to suffer me to live out the measure of days which nature may assign me in a foreign land." A month later, Beauchamp again pleaded with Governor Desha to be allowed "to go in to perpetual exile." All of this not only demonstrates Beauchamp's habitual prevarication but supplies yet another telltale sign of the Byronic hero, who, in Perry Miller's characterization, "must perish bravely in the final encounter, or else remove himself into mysterious exile." Perhaps the clearest proof, however, of Beauchamp's insincerity was his claim that he had killed Sharp to avenge a seduction—"the vilest act of which human nature was capable"—while he himself had Ruth Reed's bastardy warrant sworn out on him. A chronic poseur, Beauchamp, like Byron, was "the sum of his masquerades."[31]

The Beauchamps played with the tropes of sentimental literature and Byronic romanticism, manipulated them and used them for their own purposes. And yet there was one more idiom the couple had mastered. The *Confession* carries on at great length about "honor" and "dishonor"—the words appear eight times in its first six pages alone. Seduction, the Beauchamp persona claims, "was a species of dishonour, which, from my earliest recollections, had excited my most violent reprobation." His story, he believed, would teach a respect for "laws of honor" and deter wretches like Sharp who were bent on "dishonoring" women. The *Confession* itself was necessary, in part, because Beauchamp's family felt "dishonoured" by his conviction. When the posse came for him, Beauchamp refused to be taken as a prisoner, agreeing to accompany the men back to Frankfort only as a "gentleman" called on to "meet the charge." In his correspondence with John Crittenden, Beauchamp professed to be worried only about his reputation, the ultimate concern of any honorable man: "*I fear not for my neck.* My life is not what I come to Frankfort to save. . . . But what may not a man fear for his character, and prospect of respect in life, (without which I can never esteem life a blessing,) when he is informed that gentlemen of your character and influence believe him a murderer." In yet another testament to Beauchamp's audacity, he appealed to honor even as he tried to suborn John Lowe: "Will you not save me from worse than murder, when you can do it so easily, and so honorably too[?] In fact a man's honor binds him to save his friend from injustice." Beauchamp insisted that "the first call of honor is fidelity to a friend." So too, in the poetry appended to the *Confession,* Sharp is depicted as assailing "the heart of virtue" with "dishonour's blow." Anna and Jereboam's grave would stand as a monument to "love and honor."[32]

Far too often such assertions have been taken at face value. J. W. Cooke writes, "Both Anna and Jereboam acted in accordance with what they believed to be the claims of honor. This code . . . required that womenfolk be protected from the wiles of seducers; should a woman's chastity be violated, the violator must be punished. That was exactly what Beauchamp believed himself to be doing when he plunged his knife into Sharp's heart." One collection of Kentucky Tragedy documents, Jules Zanger's *Casebook on the Beauchamp Tragedy* (1963), even reprints *The Code of Honor,* an 1837 guidebook of honor and dueling written by the governor of South Carolina, John Lyle Wilson. More recently, Dickson Bruce has written that "in many ways . . . the Kentucky Tragedy represents a classic case of an honor killing."[33]

Beauchamp's contemporaries, less enamored with his posturing, clearly perceived that his commitment to the precepts of honor was uncertain at best: "He repeats the mysterious word, 'honor,'" wrote Timothy Flint, "until he fancies himself an *honourable man.*" As we have seen, Darby, in a repugnant but sadly accurate screed, suggested that Beauchamp's undoing was not in committing murder but in failing to obey the rules of honor as a means of "gaining satisfaction." Darby explained that if Sharp was indeed the source of "grossly aggravated calumnies" directed against Anna, if Jereboam—instead of stalking him at night like "a mean, cowardly, prowling, and insidious wretch"—had "in the character of a proud, bold, and magnanimous man, put [Sharp] to death in the street, in open day, and rested for his justification upon the justice and feeling of mankind, the world would never have convicted him of murder." And thus if Beauchamp "dies for the deed, he will die not so much for the death of Col. Sharp, as for the manner of doing it! . . . The wrong to Beauchamp and his wife, merited death, to all who were engaged in it. But when men outrage the laws in the punishment of such acts, to be supported in it, they must, at least keep the manly and chivalrous feelings of mankind, on their side." Had only Beauchamp abided by honor's dictates, then he could have killed with impunity.[34]

But Beauchamp had no use for the precepts of honor—although it was a language he spoke fluently and a belief system whose rituals and incantations he knew well. Beauchamp was neither honorable nor dishonorable; he was "a-honorable"—for if honor necessarily encompassed an overweening concern with a community's expectation and opinion, then Beauchamp, who conceived of himself as exempt from the social rules that guided lesser men, thought himself above honor, or at least beside it. To any who bothered to peek behind the facade, the hollowness of his assertions was obvious, his pretensions to honor absurd: What man of honor, by the reckoning of the nineteenth-century South, ambushed his enemy in the dead of night? What man of honor repeatedly lied about his conduct and misled his own allies and family members? Dishonesty represented a very serious offense in southern society; merely to insinuate that someone had misled another was to court a duel, for deceit was the preserve of con men, hucksters, and slaves. Yet Beauchamp habitually lied, and, moreover, it was precisely when he was lying that he was most inclined to appeal to someone's honor.[35]

In fact, much of Beauchamp's behavior amounted to a more or less sublimated attack on an honor-based social system that demanded of its supplicants, as Bertram Wyatt-Brown asserts, a rejection of "authority of the self" in favor of "symbols, expletives, ritual speeches, gestures, half-understood impulses, externalities, titles, and physical appearances." Heavy demands, indeed, and perhaps "half-understood" as a rule, but Beauchamp discerned the constructed nature of the cult of honor and, indeed, much of the ethical system of his day and age. The problem, at least for Beauchamp, was that honor was an extraordinarily restrictive code, "a hard law" whose inherent contradictions "held men in shackles of prejudice, pride, and superficiality." Honor constricted an individual's choices, hedged his will, restrained his ego, operated as a form of social control; such limitations neither Jereboam nor Anna could abide.[36]

The Beauchamps' actions demonstrate their identification not with the dominant honor-bound culture of their day but with a romantic counterculture to that society. These two clusters of social imperatives—the cult of honor and Byronic romanticism—were antithetical: one hinged on the opinion of the community; the other professed to be immune from the sentiments of others and at its extreme became a form of moral antinomianism. Whereas honor demanded, above all, obeisance to social scripts, Byron and his ilk extolled the pleasures of defying rules and expectations imposed by others. Whereas the southern man of honor was bound by overprescribed social roles and inescapably obsessed with society's judgment, the "Byromaniacs" aspired to a freedom from what they considered to be the absurd and inflexible social constraints, especially those relating to gender norms and sexuality.[37]

Yet, if the Beauchamps defied their society's core ethic, the southern world of honor ironically provided the couple shelter to develop their artifices. In the Old South, appearances mattered greatly; if they could not be trusted in a culture that seldom bothered to look much more closely, then all that was solid would melt. Such a world, one that relied so much on public image, put a high price on deception detected. Lying, or being accused of lying, was grounds for violence and even death. Southern culture, of course, had its share of dishonesty and deceit, but it radically raised the stakes of calling attention to such faults: "Now listen—here it all is in a nutshell," Mary Boykin Chesnut famously warned, "men may be dishonest, immoral, cruel, black with every crime. [But] take care how you say so unless you are a crack shot and willing to risk your life in defense of your words." Within this all-or-nothing social code—respect an individual's facade or be ready to put your life on the line—a young person, especially one as notoriously unstable and belligerent as Jereboam or as unruly and intelligent as Anna, could find a good deal of space to construct his or her own code of ethics, even one that would nurture the growth of one's own sense of superiority to others' morality. Ironically, the Beauchamps' freedom to reject their culture's dictates was made possible in part by an honor-based society that was ostensibly very restrictive.[38]

The Beauchamps took this language of honor, the lingua franca of the South, and manipulated it for their own ends. In the make-believe world of the *Confession,* the honorable Beauchamp exacts justice on Sharp, a man without honor who disregards the better dictates of society. This is exactly backward; it was Jereboam and Anna who flouted the dictates of society and then turned those dictates back on their world and made themselves alluring.

With the *Confession* in production but time running perilously short, the Beauchamps composed an epitaph for the tomb in which they vowed to be buried together. (Although the lines were attributed to Anna, here again, as with the *Confession,* the far more likely possibility is that the couple coauthored them.) The proposed inscription, predictably, was imbued with the mannerisms of romantic literature. It begins with the Beauchamps imagining their gravesite:

> Entomb'd below in each others' arms,
> The Husband and the Wife repose,
> Safe from life's never ending storms,
> And safe from all their cruel foes.

Anna was a "child of evil fate," seduced by a "villain's wiles." Yet the magnificent Jereboam, "her heart's lov'd, honor'd Lord," moved by "her tale of matchless woe," took revenge and "laid her base seducer low / And struck dismay to virtue's foes." Like many a novelist and poet of the era, the Beauchamps address their audience directly, demanding sympathy for the righteous reprisal that Jereboam exacted:

> Reader! If honor's generous blood
> E'er warmed thy breast, here drop a tear,
> And let the sympathetic flood,
> Deep in thy mind its traces bear.

Three more times the epitaph insists on tears from the reader, for the Christlike Beauchamp has died for young women everywhere: "For thy defense the husband here, / Laid down in youth his life and fame." The echoes of sentimental literature are unmistakable. In *The Power of Sympathy,* the inscription on the tombstone of Harriot Fawcet reads, "O pass not on—if merit claim a tear / or dying virtue cause a sigh sincere." Eliza Wharton's tombstone in *The Coquette* proclaims that "the tears of strangers watered her grave."[39]

The epitaph was part of the Beauchamps' campaign to win a pardon; it was written not to adorn their headstone but to prevent the necessity of a headstone. The Beauchamps submitted the inscription to the *Argus* in Anna's name a month prior to Beauchamp's scheduled execution, but Kendall, having no wish to give the Beauchamps' antics more attention or credibility, refused to publish it. The epitaph did not see the light of day until old court newspapers published it a week after Jereboam's execution.[40]

As a part of their attempt to arouse sympathy, the Beauchamps composed a number of personal letters. On June 13, Jereboam melodramatically declared to Lucy McCrearey and her daughter, Phebe—Tennessee acquaintances of his—"*I have shed the blood of my fellow man, but my conscience is clear before my God!!!*" He added that he had "given a loud and lasting warning to that class of heroes of modern times, who make their glory to consist in prostrating the pride and happiness of worth widowed matrons, by the immolation of their delusioned and ruined daughters." For good measure, he added, "From you Miss Phebe, and from your worthy cousins, I am sure I shall receive the tear of approbation and of pity for my early fate." His lines were well rehearsed; the already threadbare demand for tears would appear again, while other phrases—"a loud and lasting warning" issued to "a certain class of *heroes,* who make their glory to consist in triumphs over the virtue and happiness of worthy unfortunate orphan females"—are repeated verbatim in the preface to the *Confession.*[41]

For a brief moment, the Beauchamps' campaign seemed to be working. The couple's fabrications roused the pity, if not empathy, of many townspeople. Anna, in particular, according to a young Virginian passing through Frankfort, "was treated by some of the ladies with all the kindness and sympathy of persecuted and injured innocence. Presents, vanities, and delicacies were sent to her at the gaol with the compliments of the ladies." Dr. Sharp, meanwhile, was horrified to hear that "these blood-stained felons ate and drank like a King and Queen." As benefactors showered the pair with "every species of luxury and delicacy"—one sympathizer, apparently, even slipped Jereboam a file to help him escape—Dr. Sharp fairly spat, "Did they approve of the crime?"[42]

More than sympathy—and exactly as the Beauchamps had hoped and planned—some began to actively support clemency. "There were many in the country who were ready to petition for his pardon," Dr. Sharp maintained. "Petitions were started in some quarters and were procuring many signatures." A number of women presented Governor Desha with an appeal in which they claimed moral authority in the matter at hand and asked that Jereboam be pardoned. The Beauchamps were casting themselves as the misfortunate protagonists of a tragedy that had not yet completely unfolded. According to their plan, the audience was given a sense that they could participate in the melodrama, could demand a pardon, and could even prevent the tragic denouement, becoming themselves heroic.[43]

Yet if the Beauchamps wrote the *Confession* to procure a pardon, why was the document not published before Jereboam's execution? It was not for a lack of trying. In mid-June Beauchamp sent for Jacob H. Holeman, a respected Frankfort printer and former state printer, and read to him a portion of the manuscript. Holeman initially agreed to publish it, but he brought the document back the next day, categorically refusing to help. Jereboam then tried to convince his guard Benjamin Edrington "to take it and have it printed; but on reading it, he also declined having any thing to do with it." Jereboam next turned to his uncle. When he gave Colonel Beauchamp the manuscript, the uncle demanded, "In the name of God, if there is any thing in it that is wrong, strike it out and do not implicate an innocent person." Jereboam adamantly swore it was all true, and Colonel Beauchamp agreed to take the manuscript. As the older man was leaving, Jereboam "called to him to stop untill he gave him the title page." When the colonel read what Jereboam had hastily scribbled, once again he "cautioned his nephew, if it was not correct[, not] to have it published. But J. O. Beauchamp still persisted." The proposed title page, which the colonel duly submitted for copyright purposes on June 17, 1826, read,

The Confession of Jereboam O. Beauchamp
Being an account of the most important circumstances which led to and attended the murder of
Col. Solomon P. Sharp
Who was assassinated in Frankfort, Kentucky of the night preceding the convening of the session of Legislature of 1825 by
One Patrick Henry Darby
And
Jereboam O. Beauchamp
Written by J. O. Beauchamp immediately on being condemned for the murder.

Here is the reason Holeman and Edrington would not touch the manuscript: In an effort to buy Jereboam some time to arouse the sympathy that might secure a pardon, the Beauchamps were still trying to inflame suspicion and fear that the murder was a political conspiracy. Weeks earlier, on the day following his sentencing, Jereboam had told his uncle that he had had several accomplices in the murder of Sharp, including Patrick Henry Darby. John McIntosh, Jereboam's jailer, was in the dungeon at the time and "overheard the greater part" of this oral "confession." "The conversation was in a loud whisper," McIntosh later deposed, and although Anna tried to divert his attention in order "that I might not hear it," he distinctly heard "Col. Beauchamp ask him whether or not, any person was concerned with him in the murder of Sharp." In addition to Darby, Jereboam fingered several others, although McIntosh was unable to hear their names.[44]

In his letter to Lucy and Phebe McCrearey, Beauchamp claimed that Darby "was with me in the assassination of Colonel Sharp" and asked the two if they could confirm a meeting between him and Darby at the McCreareys' house where they had "called each by name." (Lucy, Phebe, and two other members of the McCrearey family later attested that, although they had known both Beauchamp and Darby, they "had no recollection of ever seeing them together.") In late June, with rumors swarming of the Beauchamps' charge of conspiracy, Darby visited the dungeon. Although the Beauchamps had already exonerated Darby in the manuscript of the *Confession,* Jereboam "concluded I would torment the perjured wretch a little longer, and I therefore strenuously accused him to his face, before the whole audience. . . . He went off with the fullest conviction that I would die solemnly avowing that he was with me in the assassination." Darby spent much of the next few weeks "writhing with agitation and alarm."[45]

In late June, a week and a half after Colonel Beauchamp took the *Confession* and tried to find a publisher outside Frankfort, he "redelivered to J. O. Beauchamp the manuscript," telling his nephew that no one would print it. With only a week before Jereboam's scheduled execution, this was the greatest blow to the Beauchamps' hopes: their story would not be read by the public before the scheduled hanging, and there would be no groundswell of support for a stay of execution. Thereafter, the Beauchamps' gambits became increasingly desperate: within a couple of days, Jereboam offered the guard a bribe of one thousand dollars to let them escape and wrote a letter to his uncle begging him to smuggle a saw into jail. He even tried to contact both Eliza and Leander Sharp to convince them that "he had been deceived into the murder by false information given him by Mr. Darby," and he actually asked if the Sharps would, as an incredulous Dr. Sharp later wrote, "petition for a pardon!"[46]

On July 4, three days before his scheduled execution and with no hope of getting the *Confession* published in time, Beauchamp again wrote Governor Desha, requesting yet another thirty-day respite "for the sole purpose of completing the publication" that would give "a full and minute account of all the causes which led to, and the circumstances which attended the assassination of Col. Sharp." Needing more time to publish the story, Beauchamp begged for an extension of his quite literal deadline "to hear the country's determination of my appeal," to see if they would "permit me to go into exile." Beauchamp added, in an unsubtle bid to pressure Desha, "I cannot, nor will I, ever leave an incomplete disclosure to be taken advantage of by my enemies and yours." At nine o'clock that night, Colonel Beauchamp delivered his nephew's petition to the Governor's Mansion, where Desha, already in bed, read it. Arising, the governor went downstairs to tell the elder Beauchamp that he believed the letter to be "an attempt to induce him to grant the desired respite by the advantages he [the governor] was to receive from the young man's publication" and that under no condition would he issue a pardon. And thus the uncle went back to the jail and told Jereboam that "he must prepare to die."[47]

A number of observers commented that Beauchamp, until the very end, did not seem to grasp the seriousness of his predicament. Darby thought that Beauchamp "does not fully realize the situation, in which he is generally supposed to stand; but indulges a buoyant hope that he shall experience the executive clemency." Three days before his scheduled death, however, it finally and irrevocably dawned on the couple that Jereboam would actually be executed for the murder of Solomon Sharp. It was then that he and Anna "commenced those acts of desperation, which . . . had all along been apprehended." In their first desperate act, the couple went native: "We will die, calling on the name of that Jesus, whom we have both once in our lives reviled, to intercede with the Father for his sake to pardon us, although the chief of sinners." Jereboam exclaims in the last page of the *Confession,* "I believe in the Lord Jesus Christ. Oh! How my soul leaps out to my blessed Jesus." They prayed that the Lord would "direct, inspire and influence our minds" so that "we may discern what it is his will we should do, and we would endeavor to do it." Jesus, apparently, told them to commit suicide, for Anna and Jereboam that very night took an overdose of laudanum. Trying to justify the taking of their own lives, Jereboam pledged, "We will pray while we lift the fatal cup to our lips."[48]

Anna had long since determined that if Jereboam was executed she would die with him. In May, when she joined Jereboam, she had smuggled into the dungeon a vial of laudanum hidden "in her bosom . . . knowing that no search would be there made." When it became apparent, seven weeks later, that their confession would not appear in time to win over the public, Anna made little attempt to hide her intention to kill herself, telling a number of people that "she would die with him and be buried in the same coffin" or, failing that, "would not survive him three days." Soon after Desha had denied a stay of execution, Anna announced to John McIntosh that he should "get a shroud for her and a coffin big enough to hold her and her husband." Jereboam claimed to have tried to persuade Anna not to take her own life, to "await the will of heaven," but she would have none of it, avowing that she would die with him, even if she had to starve herself to death.[49]

And so throughout Wednesday, July 5, Anna and Jereboam prepared. They packed their belongings—"papers, bedding, and clothing"—and designated to whom they should be bequeathed. Afterward, Anna composed verse dedicated to Francis R. Hawkins, a "soul of sympathetic mould" who had shown generosity to the Beauchamps and, more important, had shed a tear "of virtue . . . for virtue wronged": "To feel the angelic pity's touch / Of sister woman's kindly hand, . . . soothes the dying hour of one / Whose lot has been the sport of fate." Anna also wrote a letter to a woman in Frankfort: "This day's sun will set, to rise no more upon my unfortunate husband and myself. But we die happy and contented." Assuming the pose of an adoring wife whose very existence was given meaning by an everlasting devotion to her husband—"without whom I would never have lived"—Anna gushed, "I glory to die with the lord of my bosom's love, who so freely dies for me." She and Jereboam, Anna wrote, anticipated their "destined hour to quit this world" with "happy cheerful tranquility—nay joy." Composing her will, Anna left all her property to her father-in-law, Thomas Beauchamp; there was no word of farewell to her mother, her brother Peyton, her sisters-in-law, or her nieces and nephews. To them she had nothing to say.[50]

That night, moments before taking the laudanum, the two—typically and incredibly—proceeded to narrate their own suicides. Jereboam compulsively added to the *Confession:* "Our spirits will in a few moments," he wrote, "leave these bodies, and wing their way to the unknown abode which our God may assign them!" Anna, meanwhile, was "carefully dividing into equal portions" the laudanum "with as much composure, as she ever shared with me a glass of wine." At once self-dramatizing and self-justifying, Jereboam wrote, "I now prepare to take a fatal portion of *Laudanum* . . . with the clearest dictates of my judgement; and after months of prayer, to the Author of my being, to permit me to do it." Anna, meanwhile, surrendered to her obsessive need to compose verse and composed an ode to Jereboam, her "Lord of bosom's love": "Thy worth, thy honor and thy love shall be, / My soul's sweet theme 'til I am cold in death. . . . And wedded to his side my form shall lie." In a poem composed the day before her death, Anna wrote,

> This night by God's all ruling will,
> We close our eyes to wake no more,
> But hope our vital spirits still,
> Will happy live and God adore.

Typically, it is unclear whether they were to adore God, or God them.[51]

At about midnight the two knelt in prayer and swallowed an overdose of laudanum. Before the drug could take effect, Beauchamp returned to his narrative: "My beloved wife and myself have now drank the poison which will shortly launch us into eternity. We can neither of us, refrain from singing with joy, so happy are our anticipations, for the scene we will ere morning's sun awake in." They resumed their prayers: "Great God, forgive and bless us, and take us to thyself, for the sake of thy blessed Son. Amen. Amen." Hours later, as the two prepared to die, they choreographed their own death scene, carefully arranging their bodies as if they were staging a tableau vivant so popular in the nineteenth century: "We . . . laid down and placed our bodies in the fond embrace, in which we wished them interred. My Wife laid her head on my right arm, with which I encircled her body, and tied my right hand, to her left, upon her bosom. We also, as we laid side by side, confined our bodies together with an handkerchief, to prevent the struggles of death from severing us." Habitual poseurs, Anna and Jereboam also left "Directions for Our Burial" in which the two explained how they wished their corpses to be laid in their double-wide coffin: "We wished to be placed with my Wife's head on my right arm, and that confined round upon her bosom."[52]

Whatever their faults—and they were many—Anna and Jereboam deserve credit for having the gall, the will, not to break character even at the very end. Or perhaps they had lost themselves in their own masquerades.

Whatever the case, such effrontery is the most compelling reason that so many have taken the *Confession* and the epitaph at face value. It is tempting, and indeed logical, to see all this as substantial proof that their story was true—that Anna was an innocent victim of seduction and that Jereboam killed Sharp in the name of honor and all that was deemed holy in the early nineteenth century. But, in reality, the two were engaging in their habitual misdirection and self-dramatization even up to the moment of their deaths; they were starring in their own production.

For whatever reason, whether taking too much or not enough or the wrong type of laudanum, Anna and Jereboam's suicide attempt failed. On Thursday morning, McIntosh, finding Anna extremely ill and all their worldly goods packed up, suspected they had taken poison, although Jereboam denied it. Governor Desha, on learning of the situation, urged the jailer to remove Anna from the jail. "This he determined to do," the *Argus of Western America* reported, "but on mentioning it to Mrs. Beauchamp, she declared she would not leave her husband unless she were dragged from him by force; and the difficulty and apparent cruelty of doing it under such circumstances, induced the jailer to let her remain." Assuming that they had no other means to attempt to take their lives, McIntosh left the two together, but only under the watch of the guard, Benjamin Edrington. As the day progressed, the pair finally confessed that they had, in fact, attempted suicide. Jereboam "expressed great regret and repentance for the act, and when McIntosh again expressed a determination to separate them," Anna and Jereboam both, on their honor, "swore that if he would let them remain together, no further effort to take their own lives should be made." Why anyone at this point would trust the Beauchamps' "honor" is beyond explanation, but the jailer nonetheless acceded to the request. The two "remained quite feeble during the day" as a steady procession of preachers arrived at the dungeon to talk to Jereboam. He sent them all away, promising he would speak with them later.[53]

That afternoon, Jereboam began to ricochet from contrition to anger to resignation. According to one newspaper account, within a few hours he asked forgiveness for his suicide attempt, then became enraged and called McIntosh and Edrington "fools for wishing to prevent his taking his own life," and finally "became reconciled to the jailer" and "wrote an article thanking him for his kind treatment." At about ten o'clock that night, Beauchamp again picked up his pen and, in an extremely shaky hand, wrote a postscript to the *Confession:* "Near 24 hours have elapsed, without the laudnum [*sic*] having had any effect!!" Yet the two still had some of the drug left, which Anna swallowed, but she soon vomited. After taking yet another, smaller dose, Jereboam noted, "My Wife is now asleep; I hope to wake no more in this world!"[54]

Early the morning of the execution, Friday, July 7, "the drums were heard beating, the report of a musket was occasionally heard, and men in uniform were seen mingling among the citizens." As the sun rose, it became apparent that Anna had survived the second and third doses of laudanum. "She is so fearful," Jereboam wrote, "of being left alive, with no means to take her life; and no one to consolate and strengthen her after my death."[55]

Soon Thomas Beauchamp, accompanied by his brother Colonel Beauchamp, came to speak with his son for the last time. Both men were "much affected" when they met Jereboam, who promptly told them of his and Anna's determination to kill themselves. When Jereboam begged the colonel for his dirk, the uncle physically recoiled, protesting "that in giving it to him he should feel himself an accomplice in their crime." But Jereboam's request was completely unnecessary, as we will see, for he and Anna already had a knife. He wished, it seems, in yet another example of his chronic impulse to dramatize events, to elicit a response from his audience.[56]

Soon afterward, no fewer than four of the most prominent Baptist preachers of the West arrived at the dungeon: Porter Clay, a younger brother of Henry Clay; Silas M. Noel, the head of the Baptist church in Frankfort, a former circuit judge and the former editor of a well-known religious periodical, the *Gospel Herald;* seventy-nine-year-old William Hickman, by some accounts the first minister to settle in the trans-Appalachian West; and the "argumentative, Calvinistic, and really eloquent" George Waller, once described as "amongst the most laborious and influential ministers in the West." Jereboam, however, citing Anna's fragile condition, would not allow the preachers into the dungeon and would speak with them only through the grating above. The young man professed to be completely confident that "his sins were forgiven and that he should be happy beyond the grave." He swore, moreover, that he had "the greatest abhorrence for the crime of suicide which he had attempted to commit, and declared that he regretted it more than any other act of his life." On leaving, one of the ministers remarked that "no devoted Christian . . . ever talked with more perfect resignation and reliance on Heaven's mercy."[57]

Yet once again, Beauchamp had fooled his audience and given further testament to his habit of deception. After convincing the ministers of his remorse, he asked them to come back at noon. But he planned to be dead by then, for he and Anna, far from regretting their suicide attempts, had resolved to try once more to kill themselves. As Darby later remarked, "They died as much Pagans as any two Indians of the forest."[58]

By midmorning all visitors had departed, leaving only Edrington, Anna, and Jereboam in the dimly lit dungeon, where "the little light of day which usually penetrated into it, was shut out by a blanket hung against the grate" and a "feeble candle gave the only light which shone in this fearful abode." Anna, severely weakened by successive doses of laudanum, asked Edrington if he thought suicide a forgivable sin. "He told her he thought not; that it was one of those crimes which did not leave time for repentance and could not be forgiven. He begged her to dismiss all such thoughts."[59]

Shortly after eleven o'clock in the morning, Jereboam and Anna whispered together for some time and then asked Edrington to leave the dungeon under the pretense that Anna needed privacy. After climbing the ladder, Edrington was positioning the trapdoor so he could see below when he heard "a deep sigh." Jereboam immediately called for him, and, quickly descending the ladder, Edrington discovered the two lying together. Anna's arm was laid across the chest of Jereboam, who was "laying on his back, apparently in great alarm and in loud and earnest prayer," crying, "O thou God of Justice, have mercy upon us; O thou God of Justice, have mercy upon us; O thou God of Justice, have mercy upon us." Not quite grasping what had happened, Edrington merely took a seat until Beauchamp ceased his babbling. Finally quiet, Beauchamp "seemed to be entirely composed," and he requested the guard to "tell my father, that my wife and myself are going straight to Heaven—we are dying." When Edrington laconically replied, "No, I reckon not," Beauchamp murmured, "Yes, it is so—we have killed ourselves." Finally catching Beauchamp's drift, Edrington jumped to his feet, assuming that the two had again swallowed laudanum. As he approached Anna, however, he saw something in her hand. "He raised her arm and found it to be . . . a common case knife sharpened at the point and bloody about half way up."[60]

They had both stabbed themselves and had done so in a manner eerily similar to Beauchamp's murder of Sharp. As Jereboam explained a few moments later, he had taken the knife, declared, "My dear, now I die," and brought down the blade. But Anna, having fortified herself with a shot of toddy, deflected his arm, snatched the knife from his hand, and plunged it "a little to the right of the centre of her abdomen." Jereboam had managed to stab himself "about the centre of the body just below the pit of the stomach," but his wound was not as severe as Anna's, and it was not fatal. Having flubbed his grand exit, Jereboam soon after admitted that he had been "seized with a kind of terror" after the first blow and could not bring himself to strike again, whereas Anna had "no compunctions" about committing suicide. Jereboam, meanwhile, rationalized that it was "the will of God that I should die under the gallows." But the truth was that Jereboam did not have the nerve Anna possessed. Two nights before, when they had first attempted suicide, Jereboam had marveled at Anna's "serene aspect! I should be lost in amazement and astonishment at her strength of mind! which can enable her so composedly to meet death!" As Francis P. Blair put it, Anna had "infinitely more spirit" than her husband, dying "like a tragedy queen with the knife in her hand, without the gallows to drive her to desperation."[61]

Edrington immediately called for help, and Anna was taken upstairs to a bedroom in McIntosh's house. Repeatedly asked what had happened, Anna only responded, "I struck the fatal blow myself, and am dying for my dear husband." Although mortally wounded, she had up to this point made no sound—"she did not sigh, nor groan, nor shew any pain." But shortly she began to writhe "in the agonies of death," and when "her screams reached the ears of Beauchamp in his dungeon," Jereboam became greatly agitated: "Is that my dear wife?" he asked. "Do bring me word, what she says." Yet even as Anna suffered, Jereboam continued his weirdly obsessive narration. "Your husband is dying happy!" the *Confession* reads, "For you I lived, for you I die! I hear you groan! I hope you may yet be recovered—if you are, live till it is God's will to take you, and prepare to meet me in a better world!"[62]

Upstairs, three doctors examined Anna's wound, and all agreed it was mortal, "especially in her present debilitated state." Yet Jereboam was told she would recover as he was led through the jailer's quarters on his way to the gallows. He pitifully begged to see Anna, contending that it was "cruel" for him to die without saying goodbye to his wife. Relenting, the guard carried him into the room and laid him on the bed beside her. Placing his hand on her face, Jereboam asked, "My dear, do you know that this is the hand of your husband?" When she did not respond, "he felt of her pulse" and knew the truth. "Physicians, you have deceived me," he exclaimed, "she is dying." Transforming his wife's deathbed into a stage, he turned to the women in the room and blurted, "From you ladies, I demand a tear of sympathy." A few minutes later, feeling Anna's pulse slow and then stop, Jereboam, melodramatic to the end, proclaimed, "Farewell, . . . child of sorrow—farewell child of misfortune and persecution—you are now secure from the tongue of slander—for you I have lived; for you I die." Kissing Anna twice, Jereboam announced, "I am now ready to go." A local newspaper reported, as if it were reviewing a play, that "the closing scene was truly mournful and affecting." The Beauchamps would have been flattered.[63]

Normally the state executed condemned criminals inside the prison yard in Frankfort's public square. For more notorious offenders, however, when the crime had generated an unusual amount of interest and a large audience was expected, gallows were erected on the outskirts of town, at the juncture of Lexington and Glenn's Creek roads.[64]

Public executions in early America were pageants designed to reinforce the moral order of the community and express the ineffable force of law, carefully staged dramas devised to impart an array of lessons to an audience brought forth and transfixed by the promise of violent death: the state shall punish vice; religious authorities shall ensure that the moral order be reestablished; the offender with his death shall atone for his sins against man and God. If everything went according to script, the criminal would see the error of his ways and warn the spectators to never tread his awful path.[65]

Just a few years before Beauchamp's execution, Henry Cogswell Knight, a New England poet and future Episcopal clergyman, wandered into Frankfort just as such a gruesome performance was about to be enacted—the execution of "a notorious bully" turned murderer named Wharton Ransdale. "In order to give you an idea of the fearful simplicity of a public execution in this state," Knight reported, "I will detail what I now lament to have ever witnessed." It took place on a day in August "so hot," Knight wrote, "as to parch my hands, as I sat upon my horse in the sun." At about eleven o'clock in the morning, "the light-horse artillery and infantry drew up before the brick prison" in the center of Frankfort. An hour later, a cart containing a shroud and a coffin and drawn by a "little mean scraggy yellowish-white deathlike horse" appeared to take the condemned man to the gallows. Shortly,

> Ransdale walked down the steps, pale as a spectre, dressed in a clear white shirt, waistcoat, and pantaloons, with his collar open, so as to exhibit the fatal noose upon his neck. . . . He seated himself of his own accord on his coffin, alone in the cart. The guard having formed a hollowed square around the vehicle, it was led along for half a mile on the public road overlooking the town. When the cart, surrounded by pale thousands, arrived up under the low cedar one-

> legged gallows-tree, it halted. The neighbouring hills were crowned with witnesses—all in breathless silence.

At least three preachers were in attendance, one of whom prayed with Ransdale while the others "faithfully harangued the people" and, at the prisoner's request, took special care to warn the young "to shun bad company and whiskey." At last, Ransdale himself, who had "become penitent, and willing to die," addressed the crowd, "warning them by his example, forgiving his enemies, and craving their forgiveness." A few moments later, the condemned man sat on his own coffin "and sang a hymn aloud, and alone; and a melancholy sound it was, to hear a fellow mortal in full health, and strength, sing his own funeral dirge." As he was being positioned on the gallows, "Ransdale stood a moment with his hands upraised as high as he was able in prayer; and then, when he had ceased, and heard the tall grim black leader smite the horse, with a moral courage worthy of a better destiny, he ran and jumped forcibly into the air. For a little time, he swung to and fro without the slightest struggle; then drawing up, and clinching his hands slowly, and stiffly spreading and raising his feet a little once, he gave up the ghost." As Knight looked on, he "shuddered, and yet wished, for once, to behold the end of the law."[66]

Seven years later, on July 7, 1826, on those same grounds, the massive audience expected a similar, "good" execution in which the malefactor would accept and repent of his sins, would warn others not to do as he had. He would even, perhaps, like Ransdale, offer a glimpse of the better, more honorable man he would have been in another life; it would have lent the whole affair a bittersweet air of lost possibility. But here, as in so many other instances, Jereboam Beauchamp refused to follow convention. He had written his own script, and, as ever, it deviated significantly from what mainstream society expected.[67]

All that morning, as if a festival or a revival were in the making, "people came pouring in from the country in every direction," forming an "immense crowd" that packed the streets of Frankfort all the way to the gallows about half a mile away. The presence of musicians lent the gathering a carnival-like atmosphere. By eleven thirty, the word spread that the Beauchamps had stabbed themselves, and thereafter "every rumor of the dying pair" flew through the amassed people, and "a general movement was observed among the crowds in the streets towards the jail."[68]

By twelve thirty, Beauchamp's military escort had assembled outside the prison. Beauchamp was carried out of McIntosh's house in a blanket and laid in a covered dearborn, where the Franklin County sheriff put the rope around his neck. Just as the wagon was leaving the prison grounds, Beauchamp, "in a severe tone," exclaimed, "I want to see Darby. . . . I want to acquit him." Darby, who happened to be nearby—he was, after all, a reporter—approached the wagon. The condemned man smiled and extended his hand, but Darby did not move. Beauchamp, as Darby later recounted, then "said that he had sent for me, for the purpose of saying to me, in the presence of those who surrounded him, that I had no agency whatever, in the murder of Col. Sharp, nor in the instigating causes which had led to it." Darby, however, was in no mood for forgiveness: "Beauchamp," he said, "you have endeavored to do me all the injury you could. . . . For a young man, you are the most abandoned I have ever seen. I hope you will die, because I know you are not fit to live." Utterly unfazed, Beauchamp accused Darby of "vile perjury," adding, "I cannot conceive your motive." Apparently Jereboam had convinced himself that Darby's initial story, that the two had met at Duncan's Well, was the reason for his indictment and, ultimately, his death sentence. "Mr. Darby," Beauchamp continued, "you never saw me . . . anywhere until you saw me a prisoner at Jackson's in Frankfort." Before Darby could reply, "Beauchamp waved his hand to him, indicating that he wanted to hear no more, and said, 'Drive on.'"[69]

And so Beauchamp acquitted Darby and thereby laid to rest any widespread or rational suspicion that he was at the center of a political conspiracy to murder Solomon Sharp. "Beauchamp's acquittal of Darby," Dr. Sharp had to admit, "has made a strong impression upon the country, and induced many to think that he is innocent." Kendall, who had done more than anyone to raise suspicions over Darby's role in the murder, wrote later that week, "In justice to ourselves, we do not hesitate to say that we believe his man innocent of any participation in the murder of Col. Sharp. This we say not to conciliate his friendship or deprecate his vengeance. We scorn the one and defy the other. But we say it because IT IS JUST." Yet Dr. Sharp never abandoned his increasingly threadbare theory that Darby had been Beauchamp's accomplice, insisting that Jereboam, once his own fate was sealed, had decided to altruistically conceal the guilt of his political allies. Such a tortured explanation, more a product of despair and loss than of logic, convinced virtually nobody. Fears of a political conspiracy behind the murder of Sharp died, for the most part, with Beauchamp.[70]

The soldiers, the wagon, and the crowd wound their way through the streets of Frankfort to the sound of beating drums. "This music is delightful,"

Beauchamp mused, no doubt fantasizing about how noble his composure would appear in the next week's newspapers; "I never moved more happily in my life." Seeing "some windows filled with ladies, shedding tears," Beauchamp asked that the side curtains of the dearborn be raised so he could "wave his hand to them in token of respect." He bowed his head to the people along the streets as his procession passed. One newspaper in its review of the scene pronounced his demeanor as "peculiarly affecting and manly" and commended him for the "great fortitude and composure" with which he faced death. It was almost as if this was exactly what Beauchamp always wished for; he was the star, the recipient of tears and admiration. It was his last and greatest performance, and it went far to cement his posthumous victory.[71]

As the dearborn made its way to the execution grounds, Beauchamp asked John McIntosh to sit next to him. The jailer used the opportunity to ply Beauchamp about a number of unanswered questions, and Jereboam, for once, replied with some candor, most likely because McIntosh "was ever honorable, magnanimous and humane to me, and to my wife." How had Jereboam and Anna procured the laudanum and the knife? Anna had smuggled the laudanum into the dungeon, and he had "kept a knife which was sent in with his food, some months ago and concealed it." How, if it was not with Darby's help, had Beauchamp found Sharp's house? "I found it myself without any assistance," replied Beauchamp (thus, typically, contradicting both his own account in the *Confession* and Lowe's testimony during Anna's examination). Who had told Beauchamp that Colonel Sharp was circulating rumors that Anna's child was black? Here, Beauchamp "gave the jailer an inquisitive look and said, 'I got it in the anonymous letter I received from Frankfort,'" but then immediately contradicted himself: "I have since seen the man who gave me the information and conversed with him. He informed me that Sharp had told him with his own mouth, that the child charged to him by my wife, was a colored child." When McIntosh replied that he "should like to know that man's name, Beauchamp smiled and said, 'O no; you have been kind to me and I would gratify any reasonable request of yours, but that man has been the friend of my family, and his name I will never disclose. I have hinted at it in what I have written, but not so that it will be understood.'" Whether any of this was true, whether such a person existed, we will, in all probability, never know.[72]

As the wagon began to ascend the gallows hill, Beauchamp caught sight of Colonel Thomas Lillard, one of the jurors at the trial. Beauchamp called him over, smiled, and offered his hand: "You rendered a righteous verdict," Jereboam intoned, "but it was on perjured evidence." Once more, he claimed that it was the false testimony that brought him down, again underscoring that, in Beauchamp's mind, he was defeated only by the treachery and dishonesty of his adversaries. Lillard knew better but let the comment go. He did, however, pointedly ask Beauchamp who had convinced him to murder Colonel Sharp. Beauchamp "hesitated sometime, and then said, 'my wife persuaded me to kill him.'" As he had earlier admitted in the *Confession,* "I can refuse her nothing she prays of me to do."[73]

Over five thousand people—more than three times the population of Frankfort—had gathered around the execution grounds. As the wagon came to a stop in the shadow of the gallows, Beauchamp complimented its construction, pronouncing it to be "a good strong one." A veritable corps of preachers, who had long since arrived, "surrounded him, enquiring the state of his mind," asking if he was sure he would meet Jesus. Beauchamp "seemed wholly unmoved" and replied that "his sins were forgiven on Thursday morning." He refused to say whether he would commit the crime again and, tiring of the theatrics that were not of his making, repeatedly and impatiently demanded to be executed: "I want to go to my wife." Although rumor had it that Beauchamp, like Ransdale and many others, would speak to the throng—would provide those gathered with the thrill of being warned against sinful ways—he refused to do so.[74]

After being lifted from the dearborn and stood up, the weakened Beauchamp asked for a glass of water. As a runner went for the drink, Beauchamp turned to the musicians and asked them, apropos of nothing, to play a lively reel, "Bonaparte's Retreat from Moscow." The puzzled band members were taken aback and played the song only after Beauchamp repeated the request. Historians have struggled to understand Beauchamp's bizarre choice; one has speculated, "Perhaps a slow version of it was played." Yet the verdict of a local newspaper—that the request further demonstrated "the singular cast of mind and feeling of this extraordinary man"—is much closer to the mark. In one sense, he was obviously juxtaposing his destiny with that of the icon of romantics everywhere, Napoleon, whom Beauchamp saw as a fellow genius brought low by overreaching. Jereboam, like Napoleon in Russia, had gambled and lost, and he too would pay for it. And now, with his Josephine dead, Jereboam would go out like the world historical figure he was in his own mind.[75]

But the request, more fundamentally, was a part of Beauchamp's subversion of his own execution, a means of sabotaging the drama in which he was supposed to star. He understood that a ritual was being enacted, that a performance was being staged, but he refused to play a role that he had not scripted. That is why he attempted suicide—to deprive the drama of its leading man, to avoid, as Beauchamp himself put, being hanged "as a spectacle for fools to gaze at." Failing that, he waved to the ladies and refused to appear frightened or contrite in the least. He admired the construction of his own gallows; he refused to cooperate with the preachers; he would not address the audience; and at the very end, he had the band play a completely inappropriate tune. No dirge for him, and he certainly was not going to sing it himself. It all was at once subversive and self-dramatizing, a means of diminishing those around him and magnifying his own Byronic persona.[76]

The water was brought to him, he drank, and "in a firm voice" he announced that he would get to his feet when they were ready. The hangman gave the signal, Beauchamp arose, and "the rope being fixed, he said, 'drive off, I am ready to die.'" The cart started, and "at half past one o'clock he was launched into eternity."

> He exhibited symptoms of life from some minutes; but his struggles were feeble. After hanging fifteen minutes, the body was taken down and delivered to his father. In a few hours, the afflicted old gentleman with his scarcely less afflicted brother, started with the two bodies for Bloomfield in Nelson County, where Beauchamp had requested to be buried. There, in accordance also with their request, a coffin was prepared big enough to hold them both, and they were placed in it with his right arm around her neck. In that condition they were committed to the earth, until the last dreadful day.[77]

Having effaced the boundary between life and literature, the Beauchamps pushed further still and made life itself romance. And their audience was thrilled.

The theme that runs through their lives, their writing, and their performances is an understanding and manipulation of the constructs of their society—not only of literary clichés and dramatic conventions but of social imperatives and expectations, demands that they had never felt obligated to obey themselves. And at the very end, when they felt they could no longer control the production, they, in essence, exited the stage on their own terms. Anna's suicide and Jereboam's subversion of the execution ritual have in common a singular determination to thwart society's expectations and excite a response from their audience. Whether they cared that they had left behind the wreckage of three families, we do not know.

CHAPTER 9

Memory and the Invention of a Tragedy

And when, at length, the mind shall be all free
From what it hates in this degraded form,
Reft of its carnal life, save what shall be
Existent happier in the fly and worm,—
When elements to elements conform,
And dust is as it should be, shall I not
Feel all I see, less dazzling, but more warm?
The bodiless thought? The Spirit of each spot?
Of which, even now, I share at times the immortal lot?

—Byron, *Childe Harold's Pilgrimage,* canto 3, stanza 74

The Beauchamps' design to evoke sympathy worked—too late to save the couple, as it turned out, but in time to ignite the mass creation of an enduring myth of America's romantic age. Credulous and voyeuristic, Americans across the country accepted the Beauchamps' excuses for their sins—honorable, if reckless, vengeance exacted in the defense of an orphan's honor. And thus Jereboam's revenge killing—revenge not for seduction but because Sharp's political enemies told Beauchamp that he was spreading the rumor that Anna's child was interracial—was replaced by a saccharin tale of innocence defiled and manhood asserted. But Americans did not just passively consume the story; they made it their own. Before the *Confession* appeared, even before people knew more than the barest outline of events, newspapers across the country gleefully peddled literary cliché in the guise of reportage. The Beauchamps' fabrications, in other words, released into the public domain, took on a life of their own. Like an open source program, the story was continually modified and redistributed, in time becoming something far more detailed and elaborate and even further removed from reality. Subsequently, with the blissful collaboration of unwitting accomplices, the story became history. If the *Confession* was not just the work of Jereboam but of him and Anna, the broader Kentucky Tragedy myth was not just the creation of the Beauchamps but of America.

Sharp's murder, the political firestorm in the wake of Jereboam's arrest and trial, Anna's suicide, and Beauchamp's execution all, in the summer of 1826, became "a subject of peculiar and intense interest throughout the U. States," according to one Maine newspaper. In Rhode Island, the episode "excite[d] an interest, a sympathy, and a horror almost beyond parallel," while the August 1, 1826, issue of the *New York Spectator,* was "almost exclusively devoted to the publication of a history of the last days of Beauchamp and his wife, and the horrid tragedy which concluded their career of infamy and guilt."[1]

The whole nation watched, intently, if through a glass darkly. From the start, the sheer weirdness of it all compelled observers to reach for literary and theatrical frameworks. On August 1, the *New Hampshire Gazette* set forth that "the tragedy of Beauchamp, in Kentucky, is probably one of the most horrible stories that private history could produce. The reality of this narrative far outstrips imagination." "No poet, no novelist," the *Philadelphia National Gazette and Literary Register* affirmed, "has conceived a story more harrowing, nor framed a lesson more powerful against the indulgence of a licentious passion." The papers constantly returned to the drama metaphor. The *Baltimore Patriot* thought the episode's moral lesson to be "equal to that of the best play extant," while the *Vermont Gazette* related that "the curtain has dropped upon the close of the bloody drama." A Massachusetts paper pronounced that "the real horrors of the Kentucky tragedy are not surpassed by any imaginary ones of the deepest German Drama."[2]

Distant observers did not know what had actually happened in Kentucky, nor did they care to find out—time and again, when accurate information surfaced that did not correspond to the plotline, it was ignored or shouted down. Dr. Sharp, in particular, wrote letter after letter to newspaper editors and dramatists, tying to stem the tide, trying to relay an account a bit closer to reality. It went for naught, for more important to observers was the dramatic or didactic potential of the episode. To some, it was just more titillating to believe that an innocent, if irresponsible, young woman had been led astray by the machinations of a cold-blooded seducer and afterward was avenged by a reckless and headstrong knight-errant. To others—the self-appointed guardians of the nation's morality—the Kentucky Tragedy presented a chance to lecture an increasingly mobile and rootless young generation on the dangers of deception and illicit sexuality. The story was, one editor cautioned in an interesting choice of words, "pregnant with views of human character and means of instruction. It is a beacon, a light, to warn us from the indulgence of passion, to teach us to shun the paths of vice, and to show us to what inevitable crime and woe, the first guilty step leads. Here is a volume against seduction, promise breaking, murder and suicide." The *Baltimore Patriot* thought that the story of the Beauchamps brought home "with the irresistible force of truth" the consequences of "indulging the passions, and imposing upon them no moral restraint." In the crucible of such social imperatives—an ironic and truly American combination of sensationalism and a concern for morality—any concern for accuracy fell by the wayside as Americans retold the Kentucky Tragedy according to what they wanted young people to believe, what they had seen on the stage, and what they had read in their literature. "We have bought and read, and paid our dollar to see acted on the stage," wrote the nearly tumescent editor of the *Baltimore Patriot,* "many a tragedy not half so interesting, either in plot or catastrophe, as the tragedy of the Kentuckian."[3]

Observers not only shoved events into literary categories but also seemed to lose track of where reportage ended and literary criticism began. On April 5, 1826, even as Beauchamp awaited his trial and well before anyone had come to a reasonably clear understanding of what had happened, Isaac Munroe, the editor of the *Baltimore Patriot,* cried that "this act, in its plot, cast and catastrophe, is one of the most perfect tragedies ever enacted in real life." Three months later, after events had actually run their course, Munroe opined—apparently without any sense of a distinction between fact and fiction—that "the tragedy of the murder of Col. Sharp only required a little more variety of plot, scenery, and persons, to make it completely Shakespearean." Other editors not only compared the events to drama but actually remarked on them as if they were drama critics evaluating a work of fiction. The *Philadelphia Democratic Press* criticized a Kentucky newspaper's account of the Beauchamps' last days as "deficient, in one particular; we are not made sufficiently acquainted with the scene of action. The dungeon, its size and shape and dimensions, should all have been vividly brought before us. . . . Additional interest would have been given if the persons and countenances, and even the dresses, of the miserably infatuated and devoted couple had been sketched."[4]

Frustrated with the "deficiencies" of the initial newspaper accounts, writers simply invested the already lurid Kentucky Tragedy with still more sensationalism. The *Philadelphia Democratic Press* assumed the role of omniscient narrator, presuming to know the feelings of Anna: Beauchamp's "hand dyed with the blood of her seducer and calumniator had become infinitely more dear to her than ever. . . . To sleep in the same coffin, to sleep on the arm which had poniarded her destroyer, seems to have been the only hope she entertained of futurity." An even more egregious fabrication appeared in the *Georgetown Metropolitan.* Supposedly a dispatch from a correspondent in Frankfort, the "letter" conveniently supplies the backdrop of the story: Colonel Sharp courted the young, volatile Ann, and "when a woman like her gives her heart, all else is but too apt to follow." After she became pregnant, Sharp left her to marry another. Although devastated, Ann moved on with her life and married the honorable and loving Beauchamp. Their idyll was broken by the devastating news that Sharp was spreading the rumor that the child charged to him was fathered by a black man:

> This information was conveyed to Beauchamp in a letter, which letter Mrs. B. got and read. Just as her husband was entering the door. As soon as the damning intelligence met her eye, she sunk in a chair for a minute or two;—and suddenly recovering herself, she extended her arms upwards, her dark eyes flashing fire terrible as the lightning of Heaven—"Oh, my god! This demands *vengeance! Vengeance!* See, see," said she, handing the letter to her husband—"*Charlotte Corday* struck a tyrant down, and she was lauded in history, if I kill the villain I shall be . . . branded as a murderess?" Beauchamp took the letter and read it; and then taking his wife's hand, and looking her full in the face, said, in a slow and emphatic manner—"my much injured, my much insulted Ann, *his doom is sealed!*"

After traveling to Frankfort and killing Sharp, Beauchamp returned home. Ann threw "her arms wildly round his neck," and "vehemently asked '*is it done?*' Then putting both her hands before her face, she said, 'God is just and I am revenged'; and sitting on a chair, she sobbed most piteously for half-an-hour." After the trial and Beauchamp's death sentence, Ann joins him in his cell and resolves to die with him: "You generously shared my unhappy destiny in life. I will show you how cheerfully I will unite mine your's in death. Do you not remember . . . how Aria, when her husband Paetus Cecinna was accused only of a conspiracy against Claudius stabbed herself, and handed the dagger to him, who followed her noble example? Do you not recollect, too, how Cleopatra refused to outlive the fallen fortunes of the great Antony?" Reverting to the third person, this "report" has her proclaim that "the mind of Ann Beauchamp is made up; and she disdains to listen to the arguments of the sophists and fools, who would endeavor to move her from her purpose." The couple resolve to kill themselves with an overdose of laudanum; Ann drinks first, and then, "handing him the phial, [she] said: 'Recollect, my dear, with what a determined spirit Socrates drank the hemlock!" (This Ann, apparently, could do nothing significant without an accompanying historical reference.) After the drug fails to have its effect, "she took his hand, and smiling with a kind of mournful composure, said 'come, my dear husband, the knife must do us the friendly office after all.' . . . He then drew forth the knife, and stabbed himself! She seized his hand, as if anxious to perish at the same moment, and plunged it into her body!" And as if there were others present at that moment, the "correspondent" concludes, "The whole scene was one of such an agonizing character that tears fell from every eye. It will be long, indeed, ere I forget it."[5]

These impromptu fictionalizations of the Kentucky Tragedy developed what at first appear to be two variations of the story, both of which hinge on the figure of Anna: one in which she is cast as a scheming crone who ensnares a young man and incites him to commit murder, and another in which she is depicted as a beautiful young maiden driven by dreadful events to bloody revenge. But these two story lines are actually the same—two chapters of one tale.[6]

Many amateur dramatists depicted Anna as a devious and manipulative harridan who drives a naive young man to commit unspeakable crimes. A number of literary figures existed on which to base such a character, including, of course, Lady Macbeth; one editor thought that Anna "made her husband the same tool that the wife of Macbeth did him." Yet by and large it was a Hanoverian-era English play that supplied the prism through which many early Americans viewed the Kentucky Tragedy: George Lillo's *The London Merchant, or The History of George Barnwell* (1731). One of the very first to do so was, of all people, U.S. Secretary of State Henry Clay. On August 2, 1826, he wrote to Josiah Stoddard Johnston, a senator from Louisiana, "You will have seen the tragical end of Beauchamp and his unfortunate wife. We live in an age of romance. Ask Mrs. Johnston if the story might not be wrought up into a fine popular tragedy—one similar to Geo. Barnwell?" Although originally published in England a century earlier, *The London Merchant* was hugely popular in early-nineteenth-century America—for generations, it was a stock play of early American theater—and was widely praised for its moral instruction. The melodrama is a seduction story, but interestingly, it is a male seduction story in which an older, malevolent, and designing woman named Millwood corrupts a virtuous and impressionable young man, George Barnwell. However—and the point is crucial—the root of Millwood's evil, and the reason so many people associated it with the Beauchamp affair, was her own seduction and abandonment years earlier.[7]

In the story, George Barnwell, "the delight of every eye and joy of every heart that knew him," is a servant of the honorable merchant Thorowgood. Millwood sets her sights on young Barnwell in order to rob his employers; as the villainess tells her servant Lucy, "We can take advantage only of the young and innocent part of the sex, who, having never injured women, apprehend no injury from them." Millwood seduces Barnwell, and afterward the young man, writhing "on the rack of wild desire," is under her control: "You shall command me always," he confesses; "I will stay here forever, if you'd have me." Barnwell's downfall rapidly ensues as he begins to embezzle from Thorowgood, although his guilt is concealed by the merchant's beautiful and virtuous daughter, Maria, who is secretly in love with him.[8]

Sinking into an abyss of consummate depravity, Barnwell tries but fails to free himself from Millwood's clutches: "Life is not to be endured without her. She's got such firm possession of my heart, and governs there with such despotic sway—ay, there's the cause of all my sin and sorrow!" Should the audience not understand where all of this is headed, Barnwell cries that "the storm that lust began must end in blood." Finally, Millwood, craving still more plunder, persuades Barnwell to kill his rich uncle. Lucy then turns on her mistress in an attempt to stop the murder, but she is too late, and Barnwell assassinates his wealthy relative. Overcome with despair and guilt, however, the young man fails to steal the money, and, on his return, an outraged Millwood not only curses him for a fool but turns him in for the murder. The miserable Barnwell exclaims, "Death is all I wish," and lays bare the moral of the story: "Be warn'd, ye youths who see my sad despair, avoid lewd women."[9]

Millwood, however, does not escape—her servants tell the authorities everything. Cornered, she excoriates men with a perfect fury: "Well may I curse your barbarous sex, who robbed me of [perfections of mind and body] ere I knew their worth; then left me, too late, to count their value by their loss. Another and another spoiler came, and all my gain was poverty and reproach." By taking men's treasure, she has only done to them what they have done to her; her sins are "no worse than those committed daily by rich and powerful men. Men of all degrees and all professions I have known . . . all were alike wicked to the utmost of their power. . . . Women are your universal prey," who, "with cruel arts you labour to destroy; a thousand ways our ruin you pursue, yet blame in us those arts first taught by you." She spits out a final malediction: "I know you and I hate you all; I expect no mercy and I ask for none."[10]

Once Barnwell is arrested, his pathetic predicament "drew tears from every eye." Pitiful scenes from the dungeon predictably follow: Thorowgood forgives Barnwell, and Maria confesses her love for him. Barnwell and Millwood go the gallows together: he "composed" and "humble," she "wild, ruffled with passion, confounded and amazed," cursing her very existence. "Is this the end of all my flattering hopes? Were youth and beauty given me for a curse, and wisdom only to insure my ruin? They were, they were. Heaven, thou hast done thy worst."[11]

At the heart of the tale is a warning that the debasing of a female leads to moral havoc—that once woman, the sentinel of virtue, is corrupted, the very fabric of decency and goodness begins to unravel. Millwood personifies the unleashed fury of a morally unbound femininity: "A woman without virtue," she proclaims, "like a man without honour or honesty, is capable of any action." Precisely because women have such immense power over men, they must be treated with respect. At one point in the play, after Millwood declares, "We are but slaves to men," her honorable servant Lucy responds, "Nay, 'tis they that are slaves most certainly, for we lay them under contribution." Lucy later lectures Blunt, a dull-witted fellow servant, "You men are much easier imposed on in these affairs than your vanity will allow you to believe."[12]

Early Americans distant from the scene clearly saw the Kentucky Tragedy through the prism of *The London Merchant.* In the *Philadelphia National Gazette and Literary Register* of July 1826, for instance, Anna is transformed into Millwood incarnate: "The wretched female, it appears, was originally corrupted by the person who was the first sacrifice in the tragedy—a man of elevated rank in the profession of the law and the society of his State." In "the rancor of disappointment," Anna became a "tigress" whose "fierce spirit" thirsted for vengeance and "gave a truly demoniac character to her whole scheme of existence"; "ambition, love, and revenge, appear to be predominant traits of her character and feelings." Beauchamp, of course, is cast as Barnwell, over whom Anna held sway "as if by the spell of an enchantress." A "slave" to Anna, Jereboam was "doatingly fond of this evil genius" and had been, "at least for two years, if not more, under the constant excitement of his wife, to the murder of Col. Sharpe." It was, one paper summarized, "one of the most striking and awful combinations of desperate revenge, hardened guilt, and fatal result, which have ever been offered, whether in real life, the drama, or the pages of romance, to the wonder and detestation of mankind."[13]

Other observers preferred to back the story up a bit, to invent a pre-seduction Anna, a character who would lend a more sentimental flavor to the story. "Miss Cook," many papers declared—without any proof or attribution whatsoever—was "a young and lovely woman, with fine sylph-like figure; a countenance the most sweet and expressive" and "remarkable for . . . the excellence of her character." Though her family was not as well off as their neighbors in Virginia, Anna's education was such that "her genius and mind towered far beyond her more wealthy associates." Alas, once removed to Kentucky, this "innocent and beautiful creature" fell under the spell of Solomon Sharp, the very personification of evil. He was a "treacherous wretch," who, after seducing Anna, "gave her in marriage to another," promising "some landed property to the pair, but did not fulfill his word." (One paper, the *Pittsburgh Statesman,* actually reported that Anna was "an orphan girl, living in his family, and under his protection.") His malice still not slaked, Sharp "sought, by the foulest calumny, to make her whole future life miserable; he said that the woman he had seduced, was so lost to every feeling of chastity, honor, and fidelity, that she had had a Black child! This was capping the climax of wrongs and disgraces which, with no niggard hand, he had heaped upon this most unfortunate of women."[14]

In reaction to these unspeakable crimes, Anna was made into the "demented heroine," an Ophelia-like victim of unbearable circumstance that appears time and again in antebellum literature. And thus the newspapers transformed Anna Cooke Beauchamp into a stock literary figure of the day: maddened by her betrayal, she "thought upon her wrongs," "dwelt on the means of vengeance," and "in a short time became possessed with the spirit of a daemon." The editor of the *National Advertiser* made explicit the lesson:

"A high spirited woman," should she be "dishonored, insulted, defamed, as it appears in this case, the usual check of the mind is thrown off, and all the most vindictive passions of nature, collect in a focus to bring the object to destruction." The *Georgetown Metropolitan* reported that "her whole heart was now fixed on revenge, so much so that her countenance underwent a great change, losing all its sweetness and placidity, and her husband said, at times he almost feared to look on it."[15]

The outraged Anna soon determined that "nothing short of *the life* of Sharp could satisfy her great revenge." And thus the young maiden, possessed of a "sweet and expressive" countenance, transformed into a scheming and vindictive, Millwood-like creature. Soon, she "found a willing instrument" of her vengeance: Jereboam Beauchamp, who in these tales was "a student at law in the office of Col. Sharpe," on whom Sharp had dumped Anna after he was finished with her. Although some papers portrayed Jereboam as one who courageously defended his love from the calumnies of Sharp, a noble avenger in whom "were centered all her affections in life, and even her hopes after death," others made him into a Barnwell-like, hapless dupe of Anna: "She urged, she counseled, she persuaded, she guided, and she forced, it is said her unfortunate partner to become the murderer of Sharp."[16]

The most developed example of these flights of fancy masquerading as reality—one that synthesized elements of spirited femininity and infuriated vengeance and thereby unified the various depictions of Anna—was *The Letters of Ann Cook, Late Mrs. Beauchamp, to Her Friend in Maryland, Containing Short History of the Life of That Remarkable Woman,* hurriedly brought to press in Washington DC at the end of 1826. We have no idea who wrote *The Letters of Ann Cook,* in part because so few people ever doubted that Anna composed them. Its publication was initially met by a modicum of skepticism, but any suspicions were soon overwhelmed by readers' desire to have their assumptions and prejudices confirmed. Within a matter of days, the editor of the *Washington National Journal* jumped from doubt—"If these letters be genuine they serve to exhibit the character of that extraordinary woman in a new light, and will be read, I think, with the deepest interest by all who have heard of her fate"—to rapturous endorsement: "I have read these letters with the deepest interest, and cannot bring myself to doubt their genuineness." Adopting a similar degree of credulity, many scholars have accepted *The Letters of Ann Cook* as a legitimate primary source. The work was reprinted in its entirety in the most extensive published collection of documents relating to the episode—Loren Kallsen's *Kentucky Tragedy: A Problem in Romantic*

Attitudes—and historians' responses have ranged from guarded pronouncements that the letters "in places . . . have the ring of authenticity" to declarations that they are "obviously authentic."[17]

Yet to anyone with a cursory knowledge of the life of Anna Cooke Beauchamp and the events she set in motion, *The Letters of Ann Cook* is a self-evident forgery, written by someone who knew little or nothing of Anna and had merely taken scattered newspaper accounts of the events in question and fleshed them out into a melodramatic narrative. The document, for example, is riddled with geographical inaccuracies: The first seven letters were supposedly written from Loudon County, Virginia, although Anna and her family hailed from Fairfax County. Of the last seven allegedly sent from Kentucky, four were from "Laurenceburg," Kentucky, where Anna never lived; two were from Franklin County, where Anna never stayed until her self-imposed incarceration; and one was from the Frankfort prison, where Anna and Jereboam were never confined. In fact, given the number and extent of the distortions as well as the self-evidently contrived tone of the work, the wonder is that anyone—then or now—could believe this mawkish and saccharine drivel authentic. What *The Letters of Ann Cook* amounts to is a short novel written in the epistolary style made famous by Samuel Richardson's *Pamela* and later adopted by Hannah Webster Foster in *The Coquette*. The technique was particularly well suited to the Kentucky Tragedy, for, as a genre, epistolary novels—by affecting to present actual documents to the reader without the intervention of an omniscient narrator—were themselves contrived to efface the boundary between fact and fiction.[18]

The "letters," according to the volume's putative, unnamed editor, were written to his wife, Ellen, who "had been a schoolmate and early friend" of Anna's. Like *The Coquette*'s Eliza Wharton, the Ann Cook of the *Letters* is a passionate, intelligent, and desirable young woman whose recent loss of her father has left her devoid of male protection and thus vulnerable—at least by the logic of her day—to the attentions of a pitiless seducer. She grew up, we learn, in polite Virginian society, a young woman who "loved the amusement passionately," and was everywhere "an object of attraction, an idol—flattered, caressed, and sometimes adored." She was, as well, a sensuous young woman. The author, intent on injecting an added measure of eroticism into his or her story, has Ann ask Ellen at one point if she can "remember the little wood in which we so often concealed ourselves, and the clear stream where we were accustomed to bathe in the afternoon, though in momentary apprehension of being discovered." Ann later reminds Ellen that she "often praised me for the beauty of my figure." She is, as well, fond of solitude—a dangerous proclivity according to the moral arbiters of the early republic: "I would often prefer being alone, for while alone I can indulge the wild and romantic visions that crowd upon me." Such visions, which give her "strong and powerful excitement," are sharpened by her penchant for faintly illicit literature: "I read and read again the works of Shakespeare, Milton, Thompson, Gray, [and] Goldsmith." But her favorite is Alexander Pope's *Eloisa to Abelard:* "I have always loved to dwell on the character of Heloisa," the ill-fated medieval heroine who, for the love of her tragic paramour, allowed herself to be consigned to a convent.[19]

From her earliest days, Ann is depicted as a tempestuous young woman imbued with a reckless inability to abide injustice: "My feelings are acute, and tremblingly alive to every thing like insult and neglect." As a little girl, she pushed into a creek a "wicked and mischievous boy" who "told a deliberate falsehood on my sister." At fourteen, she pelted a man on the head with a large rock after he had severely whipped a slave child. But it was the seduction of her sister Mary ("Poor Mary! Ill-fated girl, she was the victim of treachery") that first unleashed the full force of Ann's fury. After Mary languished and died "literally of a broken heart," Ann revenged her sister as well as "the honour and injuries of my family." Taking a pair of pistols, she invited the reprobate for a walk: "I stopped him, and presented one of the pistols—Wretch, I said, . . . defend yourself—for you or I must fall. He was thunderstruck and paralyzed. Never saw a being so overcome with fear. . . . Coward! Said I, base and dishonourable coward." As he approached, Ann shot him. Leaving him on the ground, she told a neighbor where he was; "he is, I learn, recovering." She vows, "I would not hesitate to tear the heart from him who should thus attempt to trifle with my peace," and adds, "I believe, Ellen, if I had been a man I should have been something of a warrior."[20]

Compounding the family's problems is the growing financial crisis of her father, who had, "by trusting too much to a deceitful friend," lost all his property, and soon thereafter died. Ann—the last surviving child in this tale—and her widowed mother move to Kentucky. Despondent at the loss of her father and "thrown upon a strange land, poor, friendless, and almost destitute," Ann develops a more pronounced preference for solitude. Finally, after being persuaded to attend a party at a neighbor's house, Anna is swept off her feet by "Colonel S——," a man who "stands high at the bar and in society" and whose "countenance was peculiarly intelligent—his eye sparkling, and full of mind, and his whole appearance graceful and prepossessing." The attraction is immediate; she finds him "singularly fascinating," and they "danced together frequently, and he was constantly by my side during the night, and waited on me home." The very next day, Sharp's nefarious scheme to rob Ann of her "greatest treasure" begins to bear fruit; "when he approaches, or seats himself by me, I feel the blood gushing to my heart—it tingles through my veins—my whole frame trembles with emotion, and I can scarcely speak. He, too, seems to be equally moved and agitated." Seeing Sharp at another gathering, Ann "continued to drink, deeper and deeper, the maddening draughts of love"; she soon blurts to Ellen, "We were surely born for each other."[21]

Sharp beguiles Ann with the writings of Byron—a shrewd choice, apparently, for Ann thinks Byron "just the man to captivate the female heart—at least, such a heart as mine." Moreover, he introduces her to "the skeptical works of Hume, Voltaire, and Paine" in a devious attempt to undermine her scruples. It works, thanks to the failure of her parents to properly inculcate religious principles in their daughter. Thus, despite Ellen's repeated entreaties for Anna to "seek religion, to read the bible, and to meditate much upon the divine precepts it contained, and the Heavenly consolations it afforded," Ann remains unmoved: "To religion," she writes, "I have never paid much attention."[22]

Bereft of a moral compass, inundated with the attentions of a handsome and accomplished suitor, Ann surrenders. "Ellen! . . . *I have yielded.*" Sharp, after plying her with wine, took Ann home, and "we were alone in the room; and—and—I blush to tell it; but my dear Ellen, I scarcely knew what I did; my senses were bewildered—my heart overflowed. I confided in his honour—in his love. . . . He loves me—he doats on me, and will not, cannot, betray me. Oh! No! No! Impossible." The affair continued for several months, and Ann became Sharp's kept woman: "Like Heloisa," Ann writes, "I thought not, and cared not, about the marriage tie." Before long, she was pregnant.[23]

Anyone remotely familiar with the drift of early-nineteenth-century seduction literature knew what was coming next: abandonment. Even as he availed himself of Ann's charms, Sharp was plotting an advantageous marriage to another: "Great God! Ellen, can you believe it? I was told that he had addressed and was then actually engaged, to another woman." Ann, "in the lowest abyss of misery, prostrated to the earth, the victim of the basest treachery," was now "abandoned by the world—forsaken and cast off by him for whom I would have sacrificed every earthly hope." When she confronted him, she recalls, Sharp

> took me by the hand. "Ann," said he, "I must leave you; I do it with great reluctance, but we must part, to meet no more." . . . "Hold," said I, roused to a pitch of phrenzy, "man of treachery! . . . Throw me not upon a pitiless world, with a broken heart and ruined reputation. . . . I have no one in the wide world to rest upon but you; for you I have sacrificed, and would sacrifice, my health, my character, my life. Have pity on me then, and do not—oh! Do not abandon me to utter wretchedness. . . . I will be your servant, your menial, any thing, to be remembered and loved."

Sharp dismissed her pleas as "folly" and "madness" and, promising to provide for their child, "rushed precipitately from my room." Ann completely lost her composure: "I raved incessantly of S——and my child; my fancies were wild and horrible." Tormented beyond endurance, she fell "senseless on the floor, and was borne to my bed, without the appearance of life. A raging fever seized my brain, and for weeks I remained in a state of delirium—in almost cureless madness."[24]

Like Millwood, the forsaken Ann lashes out at males everywhere: "This is a horrible world, Ellen; man is a monster that disgraces it." Very soon, Ann's despair mutates into anger, her misery into revenge: "I brooded over the injuries I had endured, till every particle of attachment was rooted from my heart, and I began to abhor the very sound of his name." Once again, on cue and according to script, woman pushed beyond endurance becomes a vengeful and bloodthirsty virago. Yet the anonymous author of *The Letters of Ann Cook*, by reasserting the frailty of women, has Ann, for the moment, pull up short of the reckless furor of Millwood: "I am a poor, weak woman, the plaything of passion, the sport of feeling." Only one thing saves her; only one tie binds her to this world: "*I am a mother*. . . . Its smile is the smile of a seraph."[25]

Before Sharp abandoned Ann, he introduced to his mistress the very instrument of her vengeance: a young man named Beauchamp. As Ann plunged into despondency, it was Beauchamp who was "almost constantly with me," who "had been indefatigable in his endeavors to alleviate my sufferings." After Sharp abandoned Ann and she "became indifferent about life," only "the assiduity and tender attentions of the kind and generous Beauchamp" saved her. Yet catastrophe again visits Ann; at only six months old, her infant child dies. "I wept not—I spoke not. I felt as if I had been born to sorrow." Before long, Beauchamp proposes, and she listlessly accepts: "You know my history . . . and my shame, if you are willing to receive to your bosom a poor outcast, whom the world has stigmatized as guilty and polluted, with a wounded heart and a blighted name, then take me. I am yours forever." Although Beauchamp loves her dearly—Ann confesses to an "almost unbounded" influence over him—she can never think of him as more than a friend: "I feel no joy in his embrace—no pleasure in his smile."[26]

And then Ellen receives a final letter from prison—"the last letter I shall ever write you." Beauchamp, who had burned to punish Sharp, had at last gained satisfaction: "I have been revenged, terribly revenged. The cause of my ruin, my shame, and my miseries, is no more. He has fallen by the hand of my husband, the noble avenger of my wrongs, and the defender of my character." Although Ann had been prepared to forget Sharp's seduction, "this monster—this fiend, in human shape, had circulated reports every where that the infant I brought into life, was the—the—Oh! I shudder at the very mention of it—*the child of a negro father.*" And so Beauchamp murdered Sharp. But he was apprehended, put on trial, and sentenced to die—"and I shall die with him," Ann vows.[27]

Although Beauchamp had wished to call Sharp out, to exact his retribution in public, Ann "thought that was too hazardous, and not a revenge sufficiently refined for the injury I had suffered." So she exhorted him to assassinate Sharp, to "plunge the dagger into his heart while folded in the arms of her for whom he deserted me." And so he did: "Was it not a noble, heroic, unparalleled deed?" Ann asks Ellen. After his arrest, Beauchamp was put on trial and "convicted, with an imprudent haste, and a cruel expedition I did not think possible." Ann has joined her hero in jail and vowed to die with him: "Shall I survive him who, in the flower of youth, in the prospect of future eminence, could sacrifice life, for the much injured and persecuted partner of his bosom? No! No! . . . I will snatch him from the ignominious fate they have allotted him. I will lead the way to death by setting him the example." Ann ends with an exhausted avowal: "Oh! Ellen, I have been long, long, sick of life, it has been a weary and painful journey to me, and I hail its termination with a pleasure I cannot express, although under circumstances that society may deem horrible."[28]

The letters overflow with amateurish and transparently contrived foreshadowing. Early in the narrative, Ann gushes, "I did myself sometimes foolishly dream that I was destined to play a distinguished part on the theatre of life," and "it has always struck me that I was born for some great object, and I must fulfill my destiny, be it what it may." Even before Sharp betrays her, she tells of a dream of hers in which she kills him with a dagger. At other points she muses, "I often feel a strange foreboding of future calamity" and "I do not think I shall live long." In one unintentionally humorous passage, Ann writes, "The other evening at twilight, I was surprised to see the colour of the flowers of a much lighter red, resembling blood, and hanging their withered heads to the earth. What does this portend?" A few pages later, Ann tells the story of an old man in the neighborhood who mistakenly shot his own son. The father, realizing what he had done, dropped dead on his son's corpse, and they were buried in the same grave.[29]

Like any seduction tale worthy of the genre, *The Letters of Ann Cook* strains to make clear its didactic purpose. The "editor" begins with the obligatory warning: "This awful tragedy will, I trust, have a beneficial moral tendency, by exhibiting the dreadful effects of seduction and treachery, and the consequences which flow from the first fatal aberration from the paths of virtue and innocence." If young females hoped to avoid the destiny of this "ill-fated and misguided woman," they should note well four fatal mistakes that a headstrong woman like Ann might make: first, they should never allow themselves "to be too much under the influence of feeling and passion"; second, they should never trust "too confidently on their own strength"; third, they should never have faith in "the honour of man"; and last, they must not indulge in "solitude." Ann, it seems, was permitted to "give too great a reign to her sensibilities and feelings, rendered morbid by solitude, and acute from indulgence." The proper course and remedy for all of this was for young women to attend to their religious training; for if only had Ann's "mind been early and properly imbued with a sense of religion, her misfortunes might have been avoided."[30]

Paradoxically, the "editor," despite these admonitions and a vague condemnation of Ann and Jereboam's actions, defends the pair and the essential nobility and necessity of their conduct. Typical of these early dramatizations of the Kentucky Tragedy, *The Letters of Ann Cook* moralizes, "When we consider the greatness of the injury, and the magnitude of the aggravation, we cannot but sympathise in the fate of those who executed it, and feel inclined to cast over their guilt and their frailty the mantle of extenuation." Ultimately, the blame is laid squarely at the feet of the victim himself: "The dreadful end of Colonel Sharpe . . . strikingly admonishes the young and vicious to be cautious how they trifle with the affections of a tender and confiding female. The misfortunes and horrors that made up the tragedy lately exhibited in Kentucky must be attributed to his criminal seduction of the ill-fated writers of the following letters; and on his head should principally rest, as the original cause, the odium and the censure of society."[31]

In the fall of 1826, Jereboam Beauchamp's brother-in-law, Gervis Hammond, delivered the Beauchamps' manuscript to William H. Holmes, a resident of Bloomfield, Kentucky, who had the aspiration—if not the ability—to become a publisher. In December, five months after the execution, Jereboam and Anna's failed attempt to save themselves appeared as *The Confession of Jereboam O. Beauchamp, Who Was Executed at Frankfort, Ky on the 7th of July, 1826 for the Murder of Col. Solomon P. Sharp, a Member of the Legislature, and Late Attorney General of Ky.* Holmes's pamphlet was a slipshod production. One contemporary reviewer dismissed it as a "mean looking and half illegible work," and a modern scholar observes that the *Confession* was "obviously neither revised nor proofread by its author, is carelessly printed on coarse paper, is illegible in parts, and is full of typographical errors."[32]

Judging by its initial reviews, one would not anticipate the enormous influence the *Confession* would have in the decades to come. The *Middlesex (CT) Gazette* thought it a "detestable volume" and noted that "many reasons might be shown why this disgusting stuff had better be suppressed." A Tennessee paper wrote that the *Confession* was "written with great plainness and simplicity, in an energetic, but loose, incorrect style, displaying some knowledge of mankind, great coolness, perseverance, and decision of character, and no small obliquity of moral principle." In all, the production revealed "an unblushing avowal of the most cool, deliberate, and unbending system of revenge and of blood-thirsty violence. Not an admission of guilt, not a compunctious visiting of conscience, is to be discovered throughout all its details of crime."[33]

Despite its amateurish production and poor critical reception, the *Confession* was enormously popular. The escapades of the Beauchamps themselves and the subsequent embellishments of eastern papers had "excited so much curiosity" that the pamphlet was soon on sale at bookstores across the state and had "been read by three quarters of the readers in the western country, and by thousands elsewhere." A summary of the *Confession* published in the *Nashville Banner* was reprinted in dozens of newspapers throughout the nation in the winter and spring of 1827. One New York City paper was so overwhelmed by demands "for the continuation of Beauchamp's Confession, that we are resolved to gratify the public by further extracts." Some were skeptical, but doubts were quickly dismissed: "Although abounding with adventures almost too romantic for real life, [the *Confession*] cannot be read without interest, and scarcely, we imagine, without an inclination of the mind to regard them as true."[34]

With the rise of the sensationalist penny press in the 1830s, a number of glosses on the *Confession* appeared in "true crime" publications like Henry St. Clair's *United States Criminal Calendar* (1835), P. R. Hamblin's *United States Criminal History* (1836), George N. Thomson's *Confessions, Trials, and Biographical Sketches of the Most Cold Blooded Murderers* (1837), and Henry K. Brooke's *Tragedies on the Land* (1840). In the 1840s and 1850s, spurred by a slate of novels based on the Kentucky Tragedy, standalone editions of the *Confession* were produced in Louisville, Frankfort, New York, and Philadelphia.[35]

At every step in the creation of the myth of the Kentucky Tragedy, the plotline was contested. One English periodical, the *London Magazine,* after perusing the dispatch that had Anna claiming to be a latter-day Cleopatra, archly wondered how the narrator "happened to be so accurately informed of the particulars of a scene which he could not possibly have witnessed." The editor could scarcely understand America's infatuation with the Kentucky Tragedy: "The Americans are vehement admirers of things on a great scale, not excepting great crimes. Any excessive atrocity commands their respect, provided only that the actor plays his part with hardihood, and delivers abundance of bombast." The editor was amazed that Americans could admire a couple whose "greatness of mind induced them to butcher the colonel" and found the Beauchamps' provocation—the story that Anna's child was interracial—to be inexplicable: "We have to observe now the terrible consequences of blackening young ladies' babies in the United States. One may safely swear in America that black's white, but not that white's black." Mocking the supposed moral that Americans took away from the ordeal—the danger of seduction—the *London Magazine* submitted its own lesson: "If young ladies have not white children before marriage, they will not find themselves necessitated to kill colonels for swearing that white's black; and then their husbands will not come to be hanged for obliging them; and they will not have to poison or stab themselves in prison, to the unspeakable admiration of persons of sentiment."[36]

There were skeptics closer to home who refused to be beguiled by the Beauchamps' fantastic tale. One observer in Philadelphia flatly denounced any excuse proffered for such "black and infamous crimes," while another wrote of Anna's epitaph, "Whatever may be thought of their merit as *poetry*, it is certain that they are cunningly contrived to palliate her guilt and excite compassion for her fate. The theory of revenge, taught in them, is as *diabolical*, as the spirit with which she pursued the destruction of her enemy, and sacrificed the character and life of her husband. It is not 'a tomb of love and honor' in which they repose, but one of murder and suicide, the fruits of horrible infatuation and implacable malice." In a lengthy piece, the *Albany Argus and City Gazette* objected to the sympathetic characterizations of Anna, asserting that "there is no direct proof that her early aberrations were the result of an association with Sharp . . . nor does it appear, in evidence, even allowing such an association, that they were produced any more by the perfidy of Sharp than by her own misconduct." Even if the seduction rumors were true, "by what rule of law could [Sharp] be condemned to death, or by what rule of ethics could she become the executioner?" Any further doubts as to the Beauchamps' lack of character were confirmed by "an act of the most despicable and revolting cowardice": their attempt "to suborn and perjure a witness, in order to bring the disgrace of their own crime and an ignominious death, *upon an innocent man!*" The Beauchamps' behavior, in sum, was "derogatory to Christianity and sound principles, to the obligations of society, and to the paramount authority of the laws." "Justitia," writing in the *Boston Daily Advertiser*, condemned one paper for remarking that Anna had been "one of the most unfortunate of women": "Can any thing be ill-judged, more pernicious, than the publication of stuff like this? For ourselves, we are no longer at a loss to account for the state of society which seems to exist in Kentucky, when the most atrocious criminals die not only unhonoured in their death, but even enjoying the sympathy of their fellow-citizens, as if they had died innocent of the shocking crimes of which they were convicted."[37]

At a distance, apparently, the dramatic possibilities were especially conspicuous, as if the Kentuckians were a cast of characters enacting a stock of literary clichés, and they, the observers farther east, were writers and directors of melodrama. Yet it was those at a remove from the events, and not the Kentuckians, who had been manipulated, for the alacrity with which commentators—and, later, novelists and playwrights—ran with the story suggests the degree to which the Beauchamps' concoctions shaped their fellow Americans' view of the events.

Many Kentuckians also objected to outside papers running riot with the story. Reverend Silas M. Noel, an acquaintance of the Sharp family, insisted that "those catch-penny scribblers (in other States), whose interest it is to make out a *good* story, have overreached themselves." The *Frankfort Commentator* took exception to "the extraordinary sympathy" that "distant prints" were lavishing on Anna and Jereboam. Such misinformation "is mainly to be attributed to the erroneous descriptions which have been given of Mrs. Beauchamp—as '*a young, a beautiful, and an artless girl.*' . . . This is an imaginary character. . . . For beauty, she was never remarkable. . . . Was she *artless?* Let her corrupt overtures to the witnesses against her husband, and her address in managing those overtures answer. Let the epitaph, written by her, to be engraved on the tombstone, and which was certainly genuine, answer." Such were the distortions that even Patrick Henry Darby felt compelled to come to Sharp's aid: "Great injustice has been done Col. Sharp, in some publications, which have represented him as having induced his student (Beauchamp never was such) to marry his paramour, ignorant of her true character and condition, to conceal her shame and his own guilt." Another writer, identifying himself as "A Member of the Kentucky Delegation," tried to debunk *The Letters of Ann Cook*. After cataloguing the publication's manifold misstatements of fact and myriad implausibilities, he pronounced the work "the most shameful fabrication which I have ever seen issued from the American press." The author, moreover, perceptively noted the *Letters'* stylistic similarities to sentimental fiction: "The whole tale with all its disgusting circumstances, may do well enough for the Miss Owenson class of novels, but has no existence in real life." Refusing to be disillusioned, one correspondent to the *Providence (RI) Literary Cadet* took umbrage at the puncturing of a story he or she immensely enjoyed: "That these letters are genuine, we have many reasons for believing." The author promised to give proof in a later issue of the paper but, tellingly, never did.[38]

Timothy Flint, in a lengthy review of the *Confession*, also refused to be seduced by the Beauchamps' blandishments. Although Flint felt compelled to point out the "stern lesson" the story held for "that basest of all characters" (that is, "a deliberate, and persevering seducer"), he refused to accept the story at face value. Beauchamp's brashness was not romantic and alluring; it was but senseless dissipation, the product a "want of the rod, and parental restraint, and . . . just learning enough to excite fermentation in the brain and effervescence at the heart." Anna, meanwhile, was not a wronged heroine but "a keen, experienced, hackneyed adept, with the same class of principles with Beauchamp, but more intelligent and enlightened." After goading Jereboam into murdering Sharp and seeing him convicted for his crimes, Anna, "with the high minded purpose of a Roman matron, and the unshrinking nerve of a female Werter, is determined to die with her husband." Throughout the sad affair, Flint saw, the Beauchamps' behavior was sheer affectation. The fact, for example, that Anna "actually commits suicide, and dies before her husband" was not evidence of her integrity or devotion but merely "astonishing proof [of] how far people can become the dupes of a part, merely got up at first for stage effect."[39]

Over the decades, as the Kentucky Tragedy became ever more firmly ensconced in America's collective memory, all but forgotten were the protests of those who knew well the spuriousness of the episode's central document, who realized, as Benjamin Edrington did, that "very little of what [Beauchamp] said contained the truth." Dr. Sharp wrote that "the people in Frankfort and its vicinity, knew, the moment they saw [the *Confession*] that it was a tissue of bungling fabrications and downright falsehoods from beginning to end." Darby, who was intimately acquainted with Beauchamp's penchant for dissimulation, announced that "*no credit whatever* ought to be given or confidence placed in anything the book contains, unless the fact stated, is so corroborated by other facts and circumstances that is known to exist." One late-nineteenth-century biographical sketch of Solomon Sharp made plain the injustice: "The hand that in the darkness of night struck the treacherous blow was no more worthy of confidence than the lying tongue of the same body; still the flimsy story told by the murderer made to do duty as exemplifying the cause of the assassination or in order to gain sympathy for himself and palliate his heinous act, has been handed down to posterity, while the facts which all the circumstances arrest as true and which point to the murders as the result of a conspiracy to attain political ends, have been lost sight of."[40]

Others challenged the *Confession*'s distortions by more formal means. Two of the "perjured reptile worms" that the Beauchamps had complained of—John F. Lowe and William C. Bradburn—filed libel suits in Simpson County against Gervis Hammond, who had "falsely, wickedly, and maliciously procured and collected a certain libelous manuscript called the confession of J. O. Beauchamp and caused and procured the same to be published." Lowe and Bradburn charged that the *Confession* had "blasted" their characters "throughout the whole world," and each demanded twenty thousand dollars in compensation. Hammond, completely unable to substantiate the Beauchamps' claims, "evaded the service of the warrant, bid adieu to his two daughters, leaving them with their grand-father, Job Hammond, and fled to Mexico, where he after a time became a Catholic priest."[41]

But of course it was Dr. Leander Sharp, more than anyone else, who tried to correct the Beauchamps' falsehoods. Shortly after Jereboam's execution—and prior to the publication of the *Confession*—Dr. Sharp issued a "powerful appeal" to Joseph Hutton, an actor, poet, and schoolteacher from New Bern, North Carolina, who was composing a drama based on the murder and trial titled "The Power of Passion." Hutton suspended his work pending Sharp's appeal, which, apparently, was convincing, for the play never appeared. In August 1826, Sharp wrote to the editors of *Niles' Register* and the *Baltimore Weekly Register*, contesting their reporting of the episode, protesting, as Hezekiah Niles summarized, that "Colonel Sharp never seduced Mrs. Beauchamp; never procured her a husband; never made any promise of land to her or her husband; never charged her with having had a colored child; and that all these thing have been fabricated by his brother's political enemies!" Dr. Sharp announced his intention to "vindicate the reputation of his deceased brother"; his account was published within a year as *Vindication of the Character of the Late Col. Solomon P. Sharp.*[42]

Dr. Sharp had begun the *Vindication* upon Beauchamp's arraignment in November 1825 due to Sharp's fear that "a sufficiency of evidence could not . . . be procured to send him for a further trial." In early 1826 the doctor undertook the first of several trips to the Green River country, where he, assisted by his brothers Fidelio and Absalom, collected depositions to be used both to convict Beauchamp and to defend Solomon's character. That March, Eliza Sharp announced in her *Argus of Western America* essay that Dr. Sharp had "procured those evidences" that he would, "in due time, lay . . . before the public in vindication of his brother's fame." Learning that Beauchamp's *Confession* would be published in late 1826, the doctor postponed the publication of his work until he could incorporate the necessary rebuttals. Finally, in mid-1827, the *Vindication* was published in Frankfort by Amos Kendall. However, despite all of Dr. Sharp's effort, his work was not made public. As Dr. Sharp himself explained in an 1829 letter to the *U.S. Telegraph*, "by the advice of my counsel, I have suspended its publication until the termination of certain suits brought against the widow of the late Colonel Sharp, myself, and others, for an alleged libel." Because the Sharps had continued to insist that Darby was an accessory to the murder, Darby had instituted libel suits against Dr. Sharp, Eliza Sharp, Amos Kendall, and Colonel Jereboam Beauchamp. He had a good case, for however well the *Vindication* documents the truly bizarre nature of Anna and Jereboam as individuals, it falls far short of proving that Beauchamp received any assistance from Darby or explaining why Beauchamp exonerated Darby on his way to the gallows. We do not know why Dr. Sharp kept the *Vindication* under wraps for the rest of his life—even after Darby died in 1829, and with him the threat of the libel suits; perhaps Eliza persuaded him not to publicize it, finding the prospect of reviving the controversy over the death of her husband far too painful.[43]

For decades afterward, even as a torrent of novels and plays flooded America, the Sharp family continued to protest Solomon's depiction as a heartless miscreant and the Beauchamps as star-crossed lovers. When a Louisville theater in 1858 staged the play *Sybil*—an adaptation of William Gilmore Simms's melodramatic novels based on the Kentucky Tragedy—Colonel Sharp's second son, Solomon Leander Sharp, now thirty-four years old, vehemently protested. The play gives the Solomon Sharp character the perfectly unsubtle name Rufus Wolfe, alternately described as a "wretch," an "arch-fiend," and "a villain—a base, consummate villain." In the pages of the *Louisville Journal*, the son asserted that both the play and the spate of novels then so popular "are all so gross a slander upon the truth of history and the character of a man who filled important trusts in the State of Kentucky." Sharp submitted a number of documents—including numerous depositions his uncle Leander Sharp had accumulated—that both attested to his father's upstanding character and set forth the family's argument that Darby had instigated Colonel Sharp's murder by pouring "infamous lies" into the ears of Beauchamp. Sharp concluded, "There are hundreds in Kentucky whose memories will bear me out in the truths above stated." Typically, the effort went for naught; the fruit of Solomon Leander Sharp's efforts was a one-day postponement of the play.[44]

Why was the American public so eager to disregard the protests of those who knew well the Beauchamps' story to be false? One reason was the more or less commonplace and commonsensical notion that any confession given under sentence of death was to be trusted. There existed, according to one student of the genre, an "old assumption that only the most alien of individuals would leave the world having last uttered a falsehood. To remind readers that a confession had been extracted from a person on the brink of death was to offer a warrant for that confession's truth." A Maine newspaper related that "recently the confession of Beauchamp, the hero of the tragedy, has found its way into a great number of the respectable newspapers of the day; and it being the production of a man 'whose days were numbered,' and who was about to expiate under the awful sentence of law, the crime of foul and midnight murder, has been received as a candid and impartial statement of facts." True to form, a recent historian of the Kentucky Tragedy asks, "How can we dismiss as worthless the last testament of a man who is shortly to meet his God?"—failing to consider that the *Confession* was conceived as a means to postpone the appointment.[45]

But there existed a much broader and deeper reason why the protests of those who knew better were drowned out, why Americans embraced and assimilated the questionable story with such alacrity: the Beauchamps hewed closely to the romantic narrative conventions of the day and thereby tapped into enormously powerful social forces. Early Americans not only expected but desired to discover and vicariously experience such "romantic incidents." The Beauchamps knew what early Americans wanted to hear and gave the public what it craved, a story that at once seemed to corroborate the sensationally popular didactic fiction they had been devouring for decades and to gratify the public's thirst for passionate and reckless antiheroes.

In a fascinating and determined attempt to make life imitate art, Americans—influenced by the countless melodramas depicting the horrific consequences of seduction—instantly appropriated the Kentucky Tragedy and crammed recalcitrant reality into comfortable literary frameworks that inculcated values of chastity and piety and moral rectitude. The events vindicated their fiction—and in an era in which a cloud of disreputability still lingered about romantic literature, such was a powerful impulse. Americans wanted to believe that such melodramatic events really did happen, such characters really did exist, such passions really were unleashed. Sharp did not seduce Anna, but the Beauchamps, with the enthusiastic collaboration of the media, seduced America. We of the early twenty-first century, although liable to believe ourselves too savvy to be susceptible to such blandishments, are every bit as eager as early-nineteenth-century Americans to nullify the boundaries between entertainment and more serious endeavor. We should be more careful.[46]

CHAPTER 10

The Kentucky Tragedy

And, after all, what is a lie? 'Tis but
  The truth in masquerade; and I defy
Historians, heroes, lawyers, priests to put
  A fact without some leaven of a lie.
The very shadow of true Truth would shut
  Up annals, revelations, poesy,
And prophecy—except it should be dated
Some years before the incidents related.

—Byron, *Don Juan,* canto 11, stanza 37

Over the past 180 years or so, most people have been introduced to the Kentucky Tragedy by literature. Novelists, playwrights, and purveyors of folklore—not historians and not, by and large, the historical record—have shaped the memory of the episode and have given it meaning. If there is indeed, as C. Vann Woodward suggested, an "ancient rivalry" between history and literature for control of the past, then here, at least, literature has surely prevailed and continues to distort and romanticize the episode. A 2001 Valentine's Day newspaper headline read, "Together Forever: Honor Avenged Led to Death for 19th-Century Bloomfield Couple."[1]

In the thirty-five years between the Beauchamps' deaths and the Civil War, the murder of Solomon Sharp was easily one of the most enduring episodes in America's collective memory. For decades, wave after wave of plays and novels and yet more plays based on those novels washed over an America riding the crest of the romantic movement. By the latter nineteenth century, however, the event ceased to intrigue Americans, and, with one eminently forgettable exception, no attempts were made to dramatize the Kentucky Tragedy until the mid-twentieth century. Then the episode once more came into vogue with the publication of the most accomplished dramatization of the events—Robert Penn Warren's *World Enough and Time*—as well as the first serious attempt at a history and three document collections.[2]

The antebellum American attempts to novelize Beauchamp's sordid murder of Sharp include *The Letters of Ann Cook* (1826), an epistolary novella, as we have seen, masquerading as nonfiction; Charles Fenno Hoffman's *Greyslaer* (1840); William Gilmore Simms's *Beauchampe* (1842), revised and reissued fourteen years later in two separate volumes as *Charlemont* (1856) and *Beauchampe* (1856); Hannah Davis Pittman's *The Heart of Kentucky* (1908); and Robert Penn Warren's *World Enough and Time* (1950). In addition, at least seven plays were produced—*Beauchamp* (1833); Thomas Holley Chivers's *Conrad and Eudora* (1834), revised a few years later and retitled *Leoni* (ca. 1838); Edgar Allan Poe's *Politian* (1835); Charlotte Mary Sanford Barnes's *Octavia Bragaldi* (1837); *Greyslaer* (1840), a stage production of Hoffman's novel; and *Sybil* (1858), John Savage's adaptation of Simms's *Beauchampe.* Although only *Octavia Bragaldi, Greyslaer,* and *Sybil* were ever performed before audiences, those three were staged extensively throughout America as well as Australia and England.[3]

What, at least in part, brings all of these fictionalizations of the Kentucky Tragedy squarely into the domain of the historian is that the authors—all of them—persistently maintained that theirs was an absolutely true story, a claim that their audiences uncritically accepted and that many subsequent scholars have been far too quick to corroborate. The first extant dramatization of the events, an anonymous play dating from 1833, was purportedly "founded upon the real tragic events and facts." Nine years later, William Gilmore Simms alleged that his novel *Beauchampe* was the "genuine article," based solely on "vital truths . . . relating to Beauchampe, and the famous Kentucky tragedy." Although other dramatists—Chivers, Poe, Barnes, Hoffman, Savage, Pittman, Warren—made similar assertions, it was Simms whose claims of veracity were the most elaborate: "However strange the facts may appear . . . they are yet unquestionably true." His drama, he continued, "has been very carefully prepared from and according to the evidence; the art of the romancer being held in close subjection to the historical authorities. I have furnished only the necessary details which would fill such blanks in the story as are of domestic character." Contemporary reviewers swallowed such assertions whole; the *Charleston (SC) Mercury*, for instance, wrote that Simms's work had "adhered most closely to historical fact," while the *United States Democratic Review* assured its readers that the book "is no fictitious creation" but "a true tale, still fresh in the recollection of those who lived upon or near 'the dark and bloody ground' where it transpired." Later scholars failed to correct the egregious error. William P. Trent, a late-nineteenth-century biographer of Simms, proclaimed *Beauchampe* to be "an almost literal account of the killing of Colonel Sharpe by Colonel Beauchamp," adding, "Simms gives these details with relentless accuracy."[4]

Although some of these works garnered a measure of critical approval and popularity—*Greyslaer*, in particular, went through a number of editions—what was most noteworthy and consistent about them, as judged by contemporaries and later critics alike, was their lack of success as dramatic works. However many times talented authors revisited the theme of the Kentucky Tragedy, none—at least until the mid-twentieth century—managed to attain excellence (or even competence) by any serious literary standard. Some—Chivers and Simms among them—felt compelled to revise their first attempts, whereas Poe, after wrestling with *Politian* for years, finally abandoned it; when later asked what became of the work, he laconically replied, "There *is* no more of 'Politian.'"[5]

Perhaps Americans did not have a taste for tragedy. Hoffman's tale, the one successful gloss on the Beauchamp affair, was the sole work to tease a happy ending out of it all. Poe had another explanation for the collective failure: "The *facts* of this remarkable tragedy, as arranged by actual circumstance, would put to shame the skill of the consummate artist." But Poe was mistaken; the "facts," as we have seen, were arranged not by circumstance but by the Beauchamps. The problem was that these dramatists were rehashing a previously contrived tale, a performance already staged. In the end, the romantic story of seduction and revenge and honor defended was not scripted by William Gilmore Simms or Edgar Allan Poe or Robert Penn Warren; it was written by Anna and Jereboam Beauchamp. They concocted all of this years earlier, for the two, steeped in the literature of the era, knew exactly what Americans wanted and expected to hear, and with that knowledge, they tapped into the cultural touchstones of the era's literature: seduction and honor and reckless heroism. It was the Beauchamps—through the *Confession* they wrote, their tombstone inscription that summarizes it, and their own performances—who shaped the perceptions, arranged the memory, and controlled the meaning of the Kentucky Tragedy. And like dutiful if unaware retainers, novelists and playwrights could only manage to ineffectually recycle literary cliché.[6]

For seven years after the deaths of Sharp and the Beauchamps, rumors swirled of impending dramatizations. The first recorded suggestion that the debacle could be transformed into melodrama came, as we have seen, from Henry Clay. He was not the only one to whom the idea occurred. Deferring to Dr. Sharp, Joseph Hutton abandoned his play "The Power of Passion," but soon thereafter, the "Milford Bard" of Delaware, Dr. John Lofland, began to compose his own dramatization of the Kentucky Tragedy. Subtitled "The Victim's Vengeance," it was, in the words of the bard himself, "founded on the bloody circumstance which took place in Kentucky, when Pity stood over bleeding Morality, and wrote with blood and tears, the downfall of Virtue." Like Hutton's work, however, Lofland's drama never appeared. Another attempt to fictionalize the episode was an epic poem, "Beauchamp," reportedly composed in the early 1830s by Isaac Starr Clason, Byronic actor, poet, and suicide. According to the nineteenth-century literary auteur Evert Duyckinck, "The manuscript was never seen by any of his family, though he was heard to repeat passages from it. The poem is probably irrevocably lost."[7]

Of the early dramatizations of the Kentucky Tragedy that survive, most are plays: the anonymous *Beauchamp,* Chivers's *Conrad and Eudora* and *Leoni,* Poe's *Politian,* and Barnes's *Octavia Bragaldi,* all of which were begun in the decade after the deaths of the Beauchamps. Although some have claimed that *Conrad and Eudora* (1834) was the first dramatization of the Kentucky Tragedy, the honor belongs to *Beauchamp,* published a year earlier. The drama, purportedly composed by "A Resident near the Scene of Action," does demonstrate an acquaintance with local politics and personalities. Yet although the author promises to reveal previously unknown information, he adds virtually nothing to the already familiar story. The work amounts to a fairly conventional and artless knockoff of the *Confession:* Sharp seduces Ann "as doth the wily adder charm the innocent bird flittering in the air." Ann withdraws from the world until learning that Sharp, the unmitigated villain, is claiming that "the child to which this lady gave birth was not the offspring of a white man." Her wrath is unleashed—"die then he must." She procures the aid of the heroic and fearless Beauchamp, and Sharp is soon and justly murdered. Sharp's political henchmen exact their vengeance by rigging the trial, and Beauchamp is sentenced to die. Ann joins her hero in jail and kills herself, and Beauchamp is hanged. Put another way, the author of

Beauchamp found that he had little to do outside writing supplementary dialogue and concocting a few minor scenes; the Beauchamps had already done his work for him. Key scenes—for example, Beauchamp's putative attempt to challenge Sharp to a duel—are lifted straight from the *Confession.*[8]

The only remarkable feature of *Beauchamp* is the author's familiarity with the political background of the affair. Patrick Henry Darby, for example, becomes Darbey and is rehabilitated into a no-nonsense, perceptive, and even prophetic figure. Telling of Sharp's misdeeds, Darbey announces, "Murder will out, and this wiley consellor will have to marshal all his wits, to avoid that justice he has so often cheated." Upshaw (John Upshaw Waring) is a tempestuous but ultimately clear-eyed man who grieves that Beauchamp, "this brave youth," is to be executed "for doing a virtuous act." Francis P. Blair, meanwhile, becomes Francis ("a damn'd puppy," according to Upshaw, who is "always sticking his nose in great men's———"). Amus (Amos Kendall) conspires to politicize the murder for the benefit of his party and even lusts after Ann: "The widow of a man that's hanged, you know, makes the best wife in the world." The entire production, as Dickson Bruce rightly perceives, is "essentially a *drame à clef* from an Old Court point of view."[9]

Thomas Holley Chivers is better known today for his squabbles with Edgar Allan Poe than for anything he wrote, and for good reason. Chivers's never-performed *Conrad and Eudora* is easily the most unfortunate attempt to stage the Kentucky Tragedy. Striving for poetic heights, Chivers created overwrought and pretentious verse that is almost impossibly bad. One character speaks of "the Poets, all, run mad, at run-mad love!" Another muses, "We cannot feel the joys we have enjoyed, / And only know the joys we now enjoy." A mother reminds her daughter that she has "nurs'd thee, child!—and, from these lacteal springs, / have I, at midnight, fed thee,—half asleep!" Yet Chivers cannot be completely dismissed, for in the midst of this near perfect rubbish, one occasionally stumbles across a line of such undeniable power and eloquence as "I live to view the mirror of his blood." And then we understand what Poe meant in 1841 when he called Chivers "one of the best and one of the worst poets in America."[10]

Chivers was born in 1809 in Washington, Georgia, the son of a small but prosperous planter. At eighteen, he wed his sixteen-year-old first cousin, who, for unknown reasons, left him within a year while expecting their first child. Reeling from the scandal, Chivers fled his home state and enrolled in the medical school at Transylvania University in Lexington, Kentucky. After graduating with distinction in 1830, he briefly practiced medicine before turning to writing. He published a collection of poems in 1832 before completing *Conrad and Eudora* in 1834.[11]

Chivers's biographers have assumed that he acquired some insight about Cooke, Beauchamp, or Sharp as a student at Transylvania—that while in central Kentucky he must have met someone who had witnessed the events or who knew one or more of the principals. Yet *Conrad and Eudora* does not contain any information about the episode not available in other sources. Indeed, Chivers's acquaintance with the basic facts of the case was fairly shaky, for as he himself later admitted, "When I was a student of Medicine in Transylvania University, some person gave me a pamphlet containing the Confession of Beauchampe. . . . I then made a sketch of the outlines of a Play which I intended to write upon that remarkable occurrence; but before I had finished it, some person took the pamphlet away from me, and I then wrote the following play." Not only did Chivers lack special insight into the lives of the characters, but he did not even have basic source materials at hand.[12]

The title characters, Conrad and Eudora, are modeled on Jereboam and Anna; Sharp becomes the diabolical Alonzo. Chivers, unfortunately, kept the setting in Frankfort, which lends the work a distinct absurdity, as people named Alonzo and Eudora spout faux Shakespearean lines such as "Thou did'st defer his death, to give me pain!" and "I see—thy countenance is full of storms!" The play opens with Alonzo—ambitious, heartless, lustful—trying to seduce the young, virginal Eudora, whom he has just met: "Why not, in this pleasant world delight / Since Pope has said, 'whatever is, is right.'" At one point, Alonzo, his excitement getting the best of him, comically blurts, "I long to be where I have never been!" When Eudora demurs, Alonzo declares his everlasting devotion, and the naive girl can only wonder that "such love should kindle up so soon!" With her father dead, bereft of a dowry, Eudora has "one bright jewel . . . more precious far, than gold!"—of which Alonzo, although engaged to another, soon robs her. With no one to exact revenge, she sinks into despair. "That I had died when I was but a child! . . . The lying lips of wanton lust, / Betray'd me unto bitterness and shame!" Eudora's bitterness soon deepens: "I'd pray to heaven for fifty live-long years / And travel through the world, to take his life! . . . Revenge in woman hath no limitations!"[13]

Just then, Eudora's childhood sweetheart, Conrad—who has been away in Mexico—returns, intent on courting her. Eudora turns him away, for she has "retir'd forever from the world." He finally gains an audience with her and pledges his devotion, but she will have no man's hand until Alonzo is dead: "Never will I marry mortal man, / till he turn priest, and wed him unto death!" Conrad swears, "Truly shall this earth receive his blood. . . . These hands shall wash thy name as white as snow." Determined to slay Alonzo "in the daylight, like a man," Conrad travels to Frankfort, finds Alonzo, and challenges him to a duel. "Oh! Conrad, do not kill me! Let me live!" Alonzo whines. Conrad throws him a dagger and demands, "Defend thyself." Yet Alonzo will not fight: "I owe thee no ill will! And will not strike. . . . I have wronged Eudora, and am sorry for't!" Conrad kicks him, shouting, "Go, dog! Go to thy vomit! Go foul hog!" As Alonzo slinks away, Conrad muses, "Tis hard to kill a coward!" [14]

Eudora is dismayed when she learns that Alonzo yet lives—"This hand shall ne'er be thine, / Until you wash my misery clean with blood!"—and accuses Conrad of weakness, exclaiming, "I would not have a coward in my sight— / I do detest such bipeds." She formulates a plan:

> Get you a mask! Go, dress yourself in black,
> and during the election, get him out—
> then, no one will suspect by whom he's kill'd!
> But all will say the rival party did it.

So back to Frankfort goes Conrad, who finds Alonzo's house and calls him to the door in the dead of night. "Look in my face, and call my name," Conrad hisses. And even as the sniveling villain begs for his life ("Conrad! Conrad! Do not kill me, have mercy!"), our hero plunges his knife into Alonzo's chest, exclaiming, "Drink the wormwood which Eudora drank."[15]

When Conrad returns to Eudora and tells her Alonzo has "gone to hell!" she blurts, "I am thine all!" Soon, however, the authorities arrive to take Conrad back to Frankfort, where public opinion rallies to him as word gets out that Alonzo seduced Eudora. "I would have done the same," one person exclaims, while another expounds, "He did what you, and I, and all had done!" In the public's eyes, Conrad becomes "a man amongst a thousand men." Yet Alonzo's family and political friends set about fabricating evidence and bribing witnesses. His widow, Angeline, falsely claims to have seen and heard Conrad ("I saw that bloody rebel! Heard his voice!"), while his brother, the Doctor, promises the district attorney a generous bribe should he procure a guilty verdict. Conrad, meanwhile, denies having killed Alonzo and even declares, "Poor Alonzo . . . all of us do mourn his sudden loss." Privately, he exults, "There is no evidence beneath yon sun, / Whereby they can convict me of this crime." The trial judge, after hearing the evidence, is forced to agree with Conrad, exclaiming, "I've heard no evidence can hang that man." Then an acquaintance of Conrad's turns over a document written by Conrad addressed to Eudora instructing her to suborn a witness. After the prosecutor reads it, he exclaims, "'Twill hang them both." Hearing the testimony and knowing his fate is sealed, Conrad impotently rages at the court: "If I die, I die by hands, most foul!"[16]

Found guilty and sentenced to death, Conrad is soon joined in prison by Eudora. They form a suicide pact, but when the poison they take fails to work, unintended hilarity ensues. Waking, Eudora asks, "Am I not in heaven? This can't be heaven! Else Conrad would be here!" Yet right beside her is Conrad, who also reviving, exclaims, "Eudora!—'tis too dark for heaven—'tis hell!" After an interminable discussion, they realize that they are still in the dungeon and still alive—so they stab themselves. Eudora dies, and the drama ends as Conrad is taken to the gallows.[17]

Chivers, understandably dissatisfied with this first attempt to dramatize the episode, almost immediately began to rewrite his play and completed a new version before 1839. Yet it was not until 1851 that the revised (and equally forgettable) version—*Leoni, or The Orphan of Venice*—was published in a Georgia newspaper. Chivers invested *Leoni* with Byzantine complexity, and the result, once again, is ludicrous, overwrought, and pretentious drivel, a play that, in the considered judgment of one critic, "abounds in rapid and illogical changes in attitude and emotions as well as unexplained circumstances and developments."[18]

This time around, Sharp is Count Alvar, Beauchamp is Alvino, and Anna is Leoni, the "orphan of Venice." When the play opens, the seduction has already taken place, thus sparing us the spectacle of Count Alvar begging Leoni to let him go where he has never been before. When Alvar abandons Leoni, she warns him, "revenge in woman hath no limitations." She continues,

> I swear that never shall my soul find rest,
> Until the purple mirror of his blood
> Reflect the deep damnation of his deed
> And make Seduction stare him in the face!

Here, Chivers further develops Anna's anger and bitterness: "The fiery blood leaps through my burning brain . . . foul murderous thoughts." Soon, Alvino, a "schoolboy friend" of Leoni's, hears of the seduction and vows to "pluck out the thorn that wounds Leoni's heart."[19]

From here, the play descends into a meaningless labyrinth of intrigue and murder plots, as superfluous and seemingly innumerable characters conspire to assassinate one another. In the end, however, Alvino and Leoni wind up in prison—where Chivers, inexplicably, keeps the atrocious "Am I in hell?" routine. As the pair resolve to commit suicide, Leoni announces, "I, who have been thy pathway to the tomb, / Will be thy partner through the shades of death." (Just as they expire, a friend shows up with a document that would have freed them both.) For our purposes, it is the figure of Leoni, newly invested with a stunning ferocity, that merits attention. "Revenge?" she asks, "The sweetest music to my soul." When Alvino murders Alvar, Leoni announces that her "woes are baptized in his blood," for now Alvar has "Gone down to hell, where all seducers go!" Alvino is overcome:

> Oh, blessed woman! Angel that thou art!
> Man says that thou art weaker than his sex;
> But what is lost in feebleness of limb,
> Is made up in the cunning of thy soul!

In *Leoni,* as Richard Beale Davis has noted, "the title character is at last worthy of her original."[20]

The most accomplished nineteenth-century author to try his hand at the Kentucky Tragedy was Edgar Allan Poe. Poe had long been enthralled by the story, proclaiming, "No more thrilling, no more romantic tragedy did ever the brain of a poet conceive." Drawing on the *Confession* and *The Letters of Ann Cook,* he produced his only attempt at verse drama, *Politian.* Although five scenes of the work were published in the *Southern Literary Messenger* in 1835 and later reprinted in *The Raven and Other Poems* (1845), *Politian* was never finished and went unperformed until the twentieth century. Having abandoned it in the mid-1830s, Poe himself never thought much of the work; the few scholars who have acknowledged the play's existence have tended to share his dim view.[21]

This flawed fragment of Poe's vision nonetheless occasionally achieves real poignancy. Politian is the Beauchamp character, while Sharp becomes Castiglione, a complex and conflicted man overwhelmed by guilt, and Anna is Lalage, named after the "sweetly-smiling, sweetly-speaking" heroine of Horace's odes (which, it must be admitted, is a fairly poor description of

Anna). Poe, almost alone among dramatists, never tried to disguise the fact that she was not a young naif. Lalage at one point looks into a mirror and sees a "ruined maid" with "sunken eyes, and wasted cheeks, and beauty long deceased."[22]

Poe transposes the scene of action to sixteenth-century Rome, where the young aristocrat Castiglione is a wastrel, but one of recent vintage. Not long before, as his servants tell us, he was "a very nobleman in heart and deed." But he seduced Lalage, and the defiler, wracked with guilt, has become the defiled. Now indulging in "low debaucheries" and "numerous vices," Castiglione in vain tries to forget "the sin [that] sits heavy on his soul and goads him to these courses." Such was Castiglione's transgression that his own servants have turned against him: "His conduct there has damned him in my eyes," one pronounces, while another exclaims that "the count's a rake."[23]

Castiglione's father, the Duke di Broglio, blames Lalage for his son's infirmity and "treats her with such marked severity as humbles her to dust." Brokenhearted, Lalage languishes "in her chamber with clasped hand," with only her books to console her. She soon loses herself in reading; after finishing one book in which the heroine dies, Lalage exclaims, "She died!—the maiden died! O still more happy maiden who couldst die!"[24]

At first glance Poe seems to have drained Anna of any spirit, confining her to her apartments, where she passively bewails her situation. Yet when Lalage finally unleashes her fury at having been abandoned, the result is the most arresting scene—in either prose or verse—ever inspired by the Kentucky Tragedy. A monk appears in Lalage's room as she is cursing Castiglione and bids her to "think of eternal things! Give up thy soul to penitence, and pray." She turns on him: "I *cannot* pray!—My soul is at war with God!" But the friar persists, and just when it seems he has won her over, she whispers that she wants to make a "sacred vow." The monk attempts to hand Lalage a crucifix, but she shudders, "Not that! Not that!—I tell thee, holy man, thy raiments and thy ebony cross affright me! Stand back! I have a crucifix myself,—*I* have a crucifix!" Lalage draws a cross-handled dagger and raises it: "Behold the cross wherewith a vow like mine is written in Heaven!" "Thy words are madness, daughter," the horrified monk croaks; "tempt not the wrath divine! . . . Swear not the oath—oh swear it not!"[25]

Castiglione, meanwhile, plunges ever deeper into despair and self-reproach: "Never in woman's breast enthroned sat a purer heart!" the guilt-stricken man laments. "If ever plighted vows most sacredly solemnly sworn perfidiously broken will damn a man, that damned villain am I!" His friend and fellow libertine, San Ozzo, eavesdrops on the anguished Castiglione and is not impressed: "Exceeding fine! I never heard a better speech in my life," he mocks his friend, adding, "I crave your patronage when you become a cardinal." After San Ozzo leaves, his servant arrives bearing two gifts from which Castiglione must choose: a case of wine or a sackcloth and ashes. Castiglione laughs; San Ozzo has made his point.[26]

Then a celebrated Englishman, Politian, Earl of Leicester, arrives at the duke's estate. He is a mercurial, capricious, and inscrutable young man: Some swear he is "a prodigy pre-eminent in arts and arms, and wealth, and high descent," an intellectual of unusual power. Yet others swear he is "gay, volatile, and giddy," that "he is a dreamer and a man shut out from common passions." When Politian appears, Castiglione finds him to be a man of unusual humor, wit, and whim, but on their second meeting, Politian has nothing to say and retires to his quarters.[27]

It is there that Politian hears Lalage's plaintive voice singing an English tune—"the sweetest that ear ever heard!" So beautiful is the sound that Politian falls in love with Lalage sight unseen. When the two find each other, he at once confesses his love: "Sweet Lalage, *I love thee—love thee—love thee.*" Learning of her seduction, Politian swears to revenge her and rushes to confront Castiglione, who does not understand the Englishman's hostility: "My lord, some strange, some singular mistake—misunderstanding—hath without doubt risen. . . . I am aware of nothing which might warrant thee in this thing." Without bothering to explain the cause of his anger, Politian commands, "Draw villain, and prate no more!" Only as they are about to engage does Politian shout, "Thus to the expiatory tomb, untimely sepulchre, I do devote thee in the name of Lalage." Finally understanding, Castiglione drops his sword: "Of Lalage! Hold off—thy sacred hand! . . . I will not fight thee." Although Politian taunts him as a coward, Castiglione can only kneel in front of his persecutor: "Oh let me die thus on my bended knee. It were most fitting that in this deep humiliation I perish." Castiglione bares his chest: "Strike home. I *will not* fight thee." Politian cannot kill him but vows that he should "prepare for public insult in the streets—before eyes of the citizens."[28]

The final scene of the unfinished play takes place in the Colosseum, where Lalage exhorts Politian to kill Castiglione. They speak of a suicide pact, but there the play abruptly ends. Poe, in a later review of two novels based on the Kentucky Tragedy, asserted that such works were doomed to failure because "the real events were more impressive than are the fictitious ones. . . .

Nothing was left to the novelist but the amplification of *character.*" Apparently this conviction froze Poe himself; he never completed the play.[29]

Charlotte Mary Sanford Barnes's dramatization of the Kentucky Tragedy, *Octavia Bragaldi, or The Confession,* was written in 1836 and first performed a year later at the National Theater in New York with Barnes herself performing the title role. Barnes's life revolved around the theater. Born in 1818 to British performers in New York City, she first appeared on the stage at age three, made her debut in a leading role at sixteen, and at twenty-nine married fellow actor Edmond S. Conner. Yet critics were never kind to her, consistently questioning both her ability and her stage presence. Noah M. Ludlow, for one, thought that what recognition she received was "on account of her parents . . . more than for her talent," adding that "her voice was unmusical and weak; she was near-sighted, and her eyes lacked expression." Another nineteenth-century critic, Joseph Ireland, thought that, "notwithstanding her unwearied application and unbounded ambition," Barnes "was too studied and artificial." As a playwright, however, Barnes garnered more respect—Ireland thought "her intellectual powers were of a high order, her perception was clear, her judgment excellent." *Octavia Bragaldi,* her best-known work, was generally well received by audiences and critics alike and enjoyed a successful run. Staged at least fifty times across the United States, the play was eventually taken to London and Liverpool and sporadically performed as late as 1854.[30]

Keeping with the fashion of her day, Barnes relocated the murder's setting to Renaissance Italy. She transformed Anna into Octavia Bragaldi, while Beauchamp became Francesco Bragaldi, and Sharp, Count di Castelli. As the play opens, Francesco and Octavia have been married for only a few months and Octavia is telling her story. She is an orphan who met and fell in love with Castelli when she was sixteen. The two eloped (she believed) and "a priest pronounced the words that made us one." When Octavia's father learned of the marriage, he, although upset, blessed the two just before "he fell upon the earth, before my eyes! He never rose again." Her distress exposed Castelli's fickleness: "At first Castelli tended and consoled me. But when, amid his soothing words, my heart refused all comfort, soon he spoke unkindly, and then declared I wearied him with grief." Later, after Castelli deserted Octavia, she was left "a friendless stranger, houseless, penniless," asking "no mercy but to die unknown."[31]

Such was how the noble Francesco, a childhood friend, found the abandoned and heartbroken Octavia. Only after years of "grief and prayer" and the news that Castelli had died on a faraway battlefield did she consent to marry Francesco. Soon, Octavia was completely devoted to her beloved, "for whose dear sake I live!" He is a true-hearted, hot-headed hero, "all dignity and truth," whose "word was ever sacred" and who gloried "in the unblemished honour of his name." Should anyone dare question his integrity, "calumny or censure undeserved would send angry blood into his cheeks, lend fire to every word, and prompt his arm to silence the accuser."[32]

One day Francesco tells Octavia that they have been invited to remove to the court of the Duke of Milan. "Wilt thou consent awhile to leave thy home?" he asks. "Ever with thee and ever as thou wilt," she simpers, "my only joy's to live on earth with thee—My earnest prayer, that we may die together." Once in the Duke's court, the Bragaldis learn of a "strange confession" of a certain prisoner: the man once admitted to taking a "heavy bribe" from Castelli to pose as a priest and "wed" him to Octavia. Francesco tells his wife, "Thou Octavia, . . . Castelli's widow, ne'er had been a wife." Once assured that Octavia had been unaware of the deception, he consoles her: "Here is thy shelter in a husband's arms. No tongue dare whisper 'gainst Bragaldi's wife."[33]

Then comes the news that Castelli is still alive. Wounded on the battlefield and left for dead, he had been held prisoner for five years. Francesco instantly vows to take his revenge, but Octavia begs him to relent: "In his hopeless, long captivity he hath received most ample retribution." Francesco submits: "Thy love can conquer all. I will be calm. No hate shall crush our peace." Castelli, meanwhile, marries a young woman named Vitellia and thereby acquires a substantial dowry. When told that Octavia is at court with a husband, Castelli exclaims, "Mighty heaven! I hoped e'er this a convent or the grave had shrouded her from every living eye. . . . Can she yet have learned she never was my wife?" Although Castelli dreads an impending conflict with Francesco, he resolves, "So let it be. Away regret! No tongue shall ever triumph over Count Castelli. One object—power! One feeling—vast ambition!" Like most dramatists of the Kentucky Tragedy, Barnes did not do nuance.[34]

Octavia begs Francesco to let them return home, and he consents to depart the next day. But at a banquet that evening, Vitellia, hearing that Castelli had falsely wed Octavia, threatens to return to her father. Castelli swears that it is all a lie and claims, "I ne'er did wed her—never loved her—no! I could not love a wanton. . . . Her name was even then a scorn and by-word 'mongst the peasantry." Octavia, nearby, overhears the slander and confronts Castelli: "You've crushed my heart, and worse, disgraced my fame. . . . Revoke the foul aspersion, and I pardon." When he refuses, she curses him: "May thy wife's fame unjustly be destroyed, and thou be scorned. . . . May ev'ry plague, save madness, haunt thee! Mayst thou pray, like me, for madness, as a blessing."[35]

Typical of Anna characters in these dramatizations, Octavia, her reputation blasted, becomes unhinged: "The very walls around me have a voice and cry—'revenge!'—But how? No means—but blood. . . . Life without it is one cheerless void." Fearing that "the world, whose pigmy souls do feed on slander, will repeat the tale with added taunts," she demands that Francesco assassinate Castelli under the cover of night. When Francesco hesitates, fearing to act "like a midnight murderer that slays for gold," she cries, "Bragaldi, think! If heaven should bless, or curse,—our union with a child . . . think of the foul plage-spot that will haunt him ever, his mother's infamy!" Further stroking his fury, Octavia appeals to his own considerable pride: "Behold thy honour as a husband lost, and thou held in the world a tool and dupe!" Now Octavia becomes the instigator—"Thou'lt madden me, Octavia!" Francesco groans—who drives him not only to kill the Sharp character but to do it by stealth. At last he relents: "This night, this very hour, Castelli dies." After Francesco's exit, madness descends on Octavia: "Voices whisper to me—and shadows move—Brain! Brain! Turn not with agony! I'll not stay here—I'll follow him, ere I go mad."[36]

Francesco finds Castelli in the courtyard. "What seek you here?" asks Castelli. "Your blood," answers Bragaldi, and he stabs him to death. As Octavia enters, the dying Castelli declares, "Octavia! Oh! Forgive my falsehood." Overwhelmed, she wishes for insanity: "Would heaven, in its mercy, drive me mad!" Later, after a jeweled cross belonging to Octavia is discovered at the murder scene and Francesco's cloak is found to be caked with blood, he is charged with the murder. Shortly, he admits to the killing, yet he will not divulge his motive. Octavia enters and exclaims, "'Twas I that murdered him—I say 'twas I. I urged my husband on—I swear 'twas I. If he is doomed, why I alike am guilty." Francesco, in a line lifted straight from the *Confession,* proclaims, "I've lived for thee alone, Octavia; for thy sake I'll gladly die." The pair retire to an inner apartment, where he stabs himself and she takes poison. Just before death, she, like a poor man's Lady Macbeth, hallucinates that she is drowning: "What flood rises around me? 'Tis dark and thick—'tis blood—blood—blood!"[37]

The closing scene underscores the anti-romantic moral of *Octavia Bragaldi:* revenge and unregulated passion in general are to be shunned. The Kentucky Tragedy itself, Barnes herself later wrote, "admirably illustrate[s] the futile and lamentable results of revenge, even under circumstances which in the world's opinion serve in some degree to palliate it." As Octavia early in the play exclaims (and later forgets), "wild passion, fierce, and e'en idolatrous, is but the desert whirlwind that scorches and destroys."[38]

Barnes, like Poe, delves into the psychological darkness of betrayal and madness and manages to create poignant characters forced by circumstance and personal weakness alike into nightmarish dilemmas. At the same time, Barnes softens some of the sharper edges of the episode itself. Most significant, the sexual morality of the Anna character is preserved by the introduction of a false marriage—a plot device copied by later dramatists. The illusion of marriage serves as a means of explaining the fall of the heroine without having her actually fall. She does not recklessly succumb to the blandishments of the villain—rather, she is tricked into believing she has every right to be intimate with her "husband."

If plays were the medium of choice for the earliest dramatists of the Kentucky Tragedy, prose narratives soon came to dominate the genre. As early as the mid-1830s, at least two short stories were published: "The Infidel" by Ann S. Stephens, in the *Portland Magazine* (1835), and "The Kentucky Tragedy" by Mary E. MacMichael, in *Burton's Gentlemen's Magazine* (1838).[39]

The infidel of Stephens's title is Caroline Pope, the Anna character, whose professed atheism—embraced after being allowed, years earlier, to attend a lecture by an atheist—is at the root of the tragedy. Young Caroline, although "so very beautiful and full of talent," understood "nothing of religion with all its beautiful consolations." Bereft of a moral compass, she took William Dayton as a lover, relying not on the marriage tie but "in the confidence of her heart, in the strength of his honor." Yet the relationship was poisoned by jealousy and distrust, and William soon threw "off his irksome shackles, whose very looseness [made] them galling." And thus Caroline was not seduced—at least not by the Sharp character—for the trysts in which the two indulged were the result not of deception but of a mutual conviction that marriage was unnecessary. Caroline's seduction had occurred long before she met William, when she "first drank of the poisonous cup of Atheism." But if William did not seduce Caroline, he certainly abandoned her, and as the child she bore lies dying, the sick boy has only one request: "Mother, dear, I am very sick; may I not see my father now?" Caroline summons William, who lives nearby, having since married another woman, but he refuses. The child dies, and Caroline despondently broods over the corpse of her dead child. He was not at peace; he was not in heaven; he was simply no more: "Eternity to her was chaos—a black seal placed on time—a season of decomposition and death in its darkest form."[40]

Caroline, her son dead and she abandoned by the father, is overcome with grief and rage. She resolves to murder William. Creeping into the house where William, his young wife, and their baby are lost in domestic bliss, she finds him alone, asleep. Caroline raises a dagger and is about to murder her erstwhile lover when she hears "a slight wail from the infant in the next chamber." Reminded that William was still a father, "a terrible burst of feeling rushed through her, her limbs shook as with a palsy, her hand relaxed its hold." She returns home.[41]

The next day, George Edmonds—the Beauchamp figure—visits Caroline. He is a young man whose overtures Caroline has previously rejected, yet she now promises herself to him if he will kill William. George joyfully agrees to the terms, but William refuses his challenge to a duel, so Caroline and George plan to kill William. As George sets out to assassinate William, Caroline dons her wedding dress, and upon George's return—he exclaims, "It is done! Let us away from the murder to the bridal"—the two depart on their honeymoon. Yet George, whether from ignorance or carelessness, "had taken no precaution to hide the crime he had committed, and consequently in a few days was tried and condemned. He had taken the whole weight of crime on himself; leaving his wife unsuspected as the instigator." On the day of the execution, George begs Caroline to read the Bible after his death, so that she will come to know she is mistaken in her atheism. "I cannot, indeed I cannot," she wails, for she has already taken poison. She dies, and George is taken to the gallows. The two are laid to rest in one casket, and "were so buried—the penitent murderer with his arm over the victim of an *infidel lecture.*"[42]

Ann Stephens, who was also the editor of the *Portland Magazine,* made clear that the Caroline Pope character was a "softened" depiction of Anna Beauchamp, who was "beautiful, talented, and an infidel." Stephens, like many other writers who worked with the Kentucky Tragedy, claimed to have "only copied a dark picture drawn and fearfully colored by the demon of atheism."[43]

MacMichael's "Kentucky Tragedy" appeared three years later. The tale opens with the angelic Geraldine Heathwood, whose eyes are "as deep and holy a blue as ever painted the heavens," communing with her beau, Claude de Wilton, the Sharp character: "tall and athletic in figure, with eyes flashing with animation" yet possessed of "reckless gayety." The young lovers are engaged, but Claude leaves to pursue his ambition. His letters grow shorter and further apart, and Geraldine hears that Claude is courting a rich woman. And then one day, he sends a letter releasing her from their engagement. Geraldine is crushed; soon she contracts tuberculosis and dies, but not before asking God to forgive Claude for his sins.[44]

A month later, de Wilton has found yet another woman he desires: Ianthe Willoughby, here the Anna character. She is possessed of a "haughty grace, a rich and breathing beauty in her very movement." Her fiancé, Frank Beauchamp—possessed of a "pale face, blue eye, and Herculean person"—sees Ianthe flirting with Claude and is enraged. They fight, and Beauchamp leaves town. Instantly regretting her actions, Ianthe rudely rejects Claude. Years later, Beauchamp returns, the young couple reunites, and "happiness seemed in store."[45]

But then, for some unexplained reason, de Wilton, who had married "and was in a prosperous condition," spreads the rumor that he had seduced Ianthe. Learning of the slander, she curses de Wilton, and "as she spoke, she pressed her hands until the blood oozed from beneath the nails." She vows that "blood—blood must atone for this," and when Beauchamp learns of Claude's slander, he instantly swears to avenge her. After they are married, Beauchamp goes to de Wilton's residence and shoots him in the chest: "Lie there, thou foul slave, and rot; thou hast died for thy crime, and I am comforted." Beauchamp declares, "I have been the minister of divine justice, which, existing before all law, strikes the criminal in his most trusting hour, and proudly vindicates Heaven, without the tardy formalities of man." Arrested, tried, and found guilty, Beauchamp is sentenced to hang. Ianthe joins him in prison, where they both commit suicide. "When the jailor entered the cell, he found the unhappy pair lying almost locked in each others' arms. . . . They left no kindred; but their history has been told in many a place, from the far south, even to the frozen north; there is scarcely a hearth that has not re-echoed 'THE KENTUCKY TRAGEDY.'" One student of the dramatizations of the episode well summarized the story as "extravagant nonsense without direction or purpose."[46]

The first full-length treatment of the episode—and the most successful of the American novels to dramatize the Kentucky Tragedy—was Charles Fenno Hoffman's *Greyslaer: A Romance of the Mohawk,* published in 1840. Hoffman was a native of New York City and the scion of two prominent families—

his father, Josiah Ogden Hoffman, was an associate of Alexander Hamilton, while his maternal grandfather was John Fenno, publisher of the Federalist Party organ *Gazette of the United States.* Though a child of privilege, Hoffman was early introduced to misfortune—while sitting on the Courtlandt Street dock, the eleven-year-old Charles's leg was crushed by a steamboat and had to be amputated.[47]

Hoffman attended classes at Columbia and later moved to Albany, where he studied law and was admitted to the bar in 1827. But Hoffman soon abandoned his legal career for his first love: literature. Gaining entrée to the burgeoning New York literary scene—the "Knickerbocker" set—Hoffman edited several influential magazines in the 1830s. By all accounts, Hoffman combined an exceptionally refined temper with an affable and generous personality—Edgar Allan Poe thought it "quite impossible" that such "a chivalric, frank, yet well-mannered" man could "have an enemy in the world." Evert Duyckinck corroborated Poe's judgment, believing Hoffman to be a "man of taste and scholarship, ingenious in speculation," who "unites the sentiment of the poet and the refinements of the thinker to a keen perception of the humors of the world in action."[48]

Yet Hoffman suffered from poor physical and, as it turned out, mental health. In an effort to restore both, he embarked in 1833 on a tour of the West, which resulted in his widely praised two-volume travelogue, *A Winter in the West* (1835). While staying in Frankfort, Hoffman became fascinated by the Kentucky Tragedy—"one of the deepest domestic tragedies of ancient or modern times." The entire episode, he thought, with its "exaggerated sentiment and romantic rashness," seemed "as belonging to a bygone age, or transpiring in a different planet." Although Hoffman doubtlessly spoke to some who had firsthand knowledge of the affair, most of his information was gleaned from the *Confession* itself. Hoffman, like so many before and after, was beguiled by the Beauchamps' tale, by "the story of their strange loves, of her cruel wrong and his dark revenge, of the savage retribution they exacted from the author of their misery and their crime, and the touching heroism of the death they shared at last together."[49]

On his return home, Hoffman began work on a novel that embedded the gist of the Kentucky Tragedy within the story of upstate New York during the Revolutionary War. The result was *Greyslaer,* the first novel based on the Kentucky Tragedy. At the center of the story are Max Greyslaer, the Beauchamp character, and Alida de Roos, the Anna character. Greyslaer, whose very name connotes a destroyer of old ways, is a young patriot firebrand, emblematic of the Revolution itself. He is a "dreaming enthusiast" and a well-educated law student whose eloquent denunciations of the mother country earn the displeasure of the local Loyalist officials. Far from an overeducated weakling, Greyslaer has been trained in the ways of the woods by Balt, a frontiersman who is James Fenimore Cooper's Natty Bumppo in everything but name. Time and again, Balt gives wise counsel, formulates the shrewd plan, and saves the day.[50]

Alida de Roos is a "dark lady," who, among all the fictional Annas, is easily the most erotic: "a dark-eyed, luxuriant beauty," as Hoffman describes her, with a mouth of "ripe and melting softness" and shoulders that are "white and exquisitely turned." A "mystic gleam" in her eyes bespeaks "the pride of rich resistless womanhood." Her regal bearing elicits comparisons to a "proud dame of princely courts." One Indian, on seeing Alida, recoils from her and exclaims, "That tall girl could wield the souls of a hundred rebels with her eyes!"[51]

Alida is obsessed with avenging her dishonor at the hands of Walter Bradshawe, here the evil Sharp character. Bradshawe is a consummate villain, "a low-browed, lank-haired, saturnine man, whose age might be somewhere about thirty." Years earlier, when Alida was "scarcely more than a child," Bradshawe and his chief henchman, Wolfert (Red) Valtmeyer, deceived her into believing they were married. After having his way, Bradshawe abandoned her, and Alida, bereft of anyone to avenge her dishonor—her father being feeble and her brother, Derrick, but an adolescent at the time—was left to obsess in impotent rage. So she chose a "pistol and rapier, instead of needle and distaff," and dreamed of the day she would kill Bradshawe.[52]

As the Revolutionary War escalates, a combined force of British and Indians attacks Hawksnest, the de Roos estate. Alida is abducted, and Greyslaer, madly in love with her, gives chase. The young man is wounded and taken captive. While recuperating at a "Squaw Camp," he finds Alida, who, alas, thinks of Max as a mere "stripling" whose "impracticable, feeble, or misapplied energies doomed him to mediocrity in life." After weeks of frustration, he finally arranges a late-night rendezvous in a clearing away from the camp to confess his true feelings. "You love me?" asks Alida. "To idolatry, to madness," he blurts, flinging himself before Alida, who proceeds to crush his fondest hopes: "This fancy will soon pass away." In the face of his continuing avowals of true love, Alida confesses all: she has a husband. Greyslaer instantly swears to avenge Alida's humiliation: "The destiny of my life is written; for good or evil, 'tis henceforth twined with yours." No, she replies, she will avenge herself, "if this poor brain hold out. And, pressing both hands to her temples, the unfortunate young woman looked so bewildered for a moment, that Greyslaer could hardly resist the conviction that her intellects were disordered." Just as he demands the name of the villain, Bradshawe's crony, Valtmeyer, springs out from his hiding spot and abducts Alida. Still suffering the effects of his gunshot wound, Max is unable to give pursuit.[53]

Valtmeyer takes Alida to the Cave of Waneonda, where assorted and dastardly Loyalists are holed up ("Never from Tartarus itself arose a wilder discord of horrid blasphemy, intermingled with drunken laughter"). There, Alida spends months in captivity, albeit aided by enough servants and furniture to make her stay comfortable. Bradshawe, of course, is behind all this, and when he pays her a visit, Alida bitterly reminds him of the "horrid nuptials [that] were forced upon me." When the villain avows his love and asks her to "be my Lady Bradshawe," Alida fairly snaps: "Thou wretched minion of power debauched and misapplied! Thou most fitting tool of drunken tyranny!" In time, Alida escapes the cave and, after wandering through the woods for days, is predictably rescued by Balt.[54]

Back at Hawksnest alone, Alida languishes. Greyslaer has never returned from his attempted rescue of her and is presumed dead. Actually, he has spent the winter in the hands of the Indians, and he has escaped with the help of an Indian woman and is found wandering through the woods by—who else?—Balt.

The trials of Max and Alida have changed them both—Max has become more rugged and less reckless; Alida is less assertive and gentler. In other words, by the lights of Hoffman's day, he has become a man and she a woman. Yet Max's attempts to court Alida are still met with polite indifference; believing herself to be married to Bradshawe, she can never return his love. And then a letter falls into the hands of Max proving that the "parson" who supposedly wed Bradshawe and Alida was no minister at all but merely another of Bradshawe's henchmen. Max gallops off to Hawksnest: "They deceived you Alida; the supposed ties which so manacled your soul have never yet had an existence; it was a false marriage." In a fit of passion, they declare their love for one another: "His lips met hers in one long kiss, as if each then drank in the other's soul for ever." And thereby Alida "yielded up all thought of seeking redress for her wrongs, save through him who was shortly to become the rightful guardian of her honor." Her Amazonian spirit "gradually melted"; her "strange" and "unfeminine dream of vengeance" evaporated.[55]

Before they can marry, however, Max is summoned to the war in the

South, and a year passes before he makes it back to Alida. Once at Hawksnest, he finds a "half-breed" four-year-old boy named Guise, a "wild off-shoot of her house," the son of Derrick de Roos, Alida's "wayward and reckless brother." Although the family resemblance is obvious, Derrick de Roos, before he can admit to fathering the child, is killed on the fields of Oriskany. Soon a "monstrous tale" begins to circulate: the Indian child who looked so much like a de Roos was Alida's. Her "woman's name" is now "blasted beyond all hope of retrieval." The rumor, of course, is the work of Bradshawe, whose "plotting brain and relentless hand of malignity" have been "fired with a burning lust of vengeance." Distraught beyond words, Alida soon loses the will to live, "and she spoke as one whose hopes were no longer of this world."[56]

As is usual in these tales, the Beauchamp character, once he is made aware of the racial component of the slander, loses all semblance of rationality and becomes a stone-cold killer: "The fierce lust of vengeance shot through his veins and agitated every fibre of his system; a horrid craving seized his heart—the craving for the blood of a human victim." Greyslaer heads to Albany, where Bradshawe has been convicted as a spy and is awaiting execution. Yet Max, his eyes "dull, cold, and glassy," wants to do the job himself. As it happens, Bradshawe's confederates are simultaneously plotting his rescue, and when Max bursts into Bradshawe's chamber, the rogue is truly startled. "Do you know me, Walter Bradshawe?" Max demands. "Your own heart must suggest the errand which brought me hither." For once, Bradshawe's unbounded arrogance fails him, as Greyslaer's "passionless, icy tone . . . seemed to unnerve even the iron heart of Bradshawe." Drawing his sword, Max approaches the "damned felon," but he is startled by the sudden appearance of one of Bradshawe's men. Bradshawe strikes Max with a chair and escapes through the window.[57]

Greyslaer, pursuing Bradshawe through the streets of Albany, comes upon Valtmeyer. After a desperate struggle, Max kills Valtmeyer, whose body falls in the Hudson River and is swept away by the current. With Bradshawe missing and the corpse gone, Greyslaer is arrested for the murder of Bradshawe. Witnesses saw him go up the stairs to Bradshawe's apartment, and all assumed that the body that fell into the river was Bradshawe's. Max is thrown into a dungeon and Alida comes to him, believing herself to blame for his predicament: "I—*I* was the one whose guilty dream of vengeance first quickened such intention into being. . . . Twas I . . . that taught you this impious lesson of murderous retribution." Her former spirit is completely wilted: "I am a woman, a poor weak woman. I am no heroine at the call of duty, as I thought myself. . . . I would nestle in thy bosom, I would share thy counsels, I would comfort, I would sustain thee. . . . Thou wert made for worship, for me to worship." Alida's spirit has been tamed, domesticated by love and gratitude and murder.[58]

At the trial, the prosecution portrays Greyslaer as "the luckless victim of an artful and most abandoned woman," a "wild enthusiast, who, in some besotted hour of passion, had betrothed himself to the abandoned outcast of an Indian profligate." Max, meanwhile, serves as his own counsel and tells his story with honesty and passion, but judge and jury remain unmoved. And so Max denounces the court, charging it with "judicial murder" and with "aiding and abetting in a conspiracy to take away my life."[59]

With both time and hope running out, Balt, of course, comes to the rescue. Dramatically, he enters the courtroom, bearing a document proving that the child was Dirk de Roos's, not Alida's. Now, with Alida's purity proven and the rumor revealed to be slander, murder suddenly becomes excusable, and Greyslaer is exonerated: "There was no man present but must feel that the prisoner had been driven to vengeance by temptation, such as the human heart could scarcely resist." The whole trial, it seems, and indeed Greyslaer's life, hinged on the racially pure virtue of Alida.[60]

That autumn Alida and Max are married, and they live happily ever after: "Thenceforward the current of their days was as calm as it had hitherto been clouded, and both Max and Alida, in realizing the bounteous mercies which brightened their after lives, as well as in remembering the dark trials they had passed through."[61]

Despite its implausibility (why would Whig Albany try to railroad a Revolutionary War hero for murdering a soon-to-be executed British spy?), its plot-driven and artless narrative, and a storyline that reads like the bastard offspring of Cooper's overworked melodramas and Beauchamp's fevered imagination, *Greyslaer* was, in the words of Perry Miller, "one of the most popular . . . exonerations of Romantic America." The novel went through three editions in its original incarnation, and Hoffman completed a revised version in 1849. Although some reviewers, notably Edgar Allan Poe, had their reservations about the book, the reviews were, by and large, positive: *Godey's Lady's Book* pronounced *Greyslaer* to be "an exciting, interesting, and vigorous production," while the *Southern Literary Messenger* thought the novel displayed "the powers of a master-painter of human passion. We regard the author of this book as one of the best writers in the country." The book was quickly adapted to the stage; on August 3, 1840, only a month after the novel appeared, the play *Greyslaer* was performed at the Bowery Theater. The *New York Evening Post* lauded the play's "soul-stirring incidents" and predicted "a long and profitable run."[62]

If Hoffman managed to inveigle a happy ending to the Kentucky Tragedy, his own story was much darker. By the time the revised version of *Greyslaer* was published, Hoffman had begun exhibiting signs of serious mental illness. He soon entered the state hospital at Harrisburg, Pennsylvania, where he stayed until his death in 1884.[63]

William Gilmore Simms's take on the Kentucky Tragedy, although it was the most influential in its day, was a disappointment to its author. A Charleston, South Carolina, native, William Gilmore Simms wrote three novels before his thirtieth birthday that were unqualified successes: *Guy Rivers* (1834), *The Yamassee* (1835), and *The Partisan* (1835). Yet Simms's subsequent work—including *Beauchampe,* a two-volume work published in 1842 and later lightly revised and split into *Charlemont* (1856) and *Beauchampe* (1856)—was not nearly so well received.[64]

Part of the problem may have been the furious pace at which Simms wrote *Beauchampe.* As he confided to his friend and literary agent, James Lawson, "I average from 15 to 20 pages per diem—write like steam, recklessly, perhaps thoughtlessly. . . . It is now while I write 2 P.M. and I have written 17 pages since breakfast." A month later, he was still "very busy on Beauchampe—writing myself half blind and not done yet. It will be the most voluminous of my books—exceeding in m. s. 700 pages already." Simms well understood that he was not crafting a masterpiece, confessing that his "goon like" pace was "not very favorable to a work of permanent merit."[65]

Yet, interestingly, the most common criticism of *Beauchampe* (and few then, or subsequently, were kind to the novel) was not its production or its slapdash style but its very subject. Poe, for one, questioned "the selection of his theme," a puzzling criticism, given that Poe had tried his hand at the tragedy only a few years earlier. William P. Trent, in his error-riddled 1892 biography of Simms, likewise berated Simms for using the Kentucky Tragedy as a basis for a book: *Charlemont* and *Beauchampe,* he claimed, were "repulsive and uncalled-for stories." In the 1920s Vernon Louis Parrington dismissed the volumes as "preposterous accounts" that "deserve no better fate than the rubbish heap. They are in no sense literature." Later critics disparaged the works on more aesthetic grounds. Carl van Doren asserted that the books were "amazingly sensational—bloody and tearful and barbarously ornate," and Robert Penn Warren thought them "nigh unreadable."[66]

Simms closely followed both *The Letters of Ann Cook*—which clearly informed his characterization of the Anna character—and Beauchamp's *Confession,* the "rude chronicle from which we have borrowed many of the materials for this sombre history." Simms kept the setting of his "melancholy narrative" in Kentucky, and although he likewise retained the names, or close variants, of the actual people, he insistently played on the theme of pseudonyms and the shock, horror, or ecstasy of discovering the person behind the alias. So, for example, the Sharp character, Warham Sharpe, seduces the novel's heroine under the alias of Alfred Stevens. The victim, Margaret Cooper, later takes the name Anna Cooke in an attempt to escape her shame. Another character in the book, William Hinkley—who has no counterpart in reality—assumes the name William Calvert after he and his father have a falling out. "J. Orville Beauchampe," the headstrong and artless protagonist, alone among the principals never adopts an alias.[67]

The village of Charlemont, nestled in a glen fifty miles west of Frankfort, was an idyllic settlement, home to "a dozen snug and smiling cottages [that] seem to have been dropped in this natural cup, as if by a spell of magic." Indeed, as described by Simms, Charlemont—a place where "speculation has not made it populous and prosperous, by destroying its repose, stifling its charities, and abridging the sedate habits and comforts of its people"—bears a very close resemblance to Oliver Goldsmith's "Sweet Auburn." Yet, as in the "Deserted Village," change is imminent; throughout the state, "speculation was beginning to chink his money-bags; three hundred new banks, as many railways, were about to be established; old things were about to flee and disappear; all things were becoming new."[68]

The very personification of this external and amoral threat to the Edenic Charlemont is a heartless seducer of young women, a "serpent" (to use Simms's term): Warham Sharpe. The young man, though "well-formed" and handsome, possessed "something sinister" in his countenance: "a curling contempt upon the lip, which seemed to denote a cynical and sarcastic turn of mind" as well as a "caprice of character, and a flexibility of moral." He is a monster, the very symbol of modernity, which had destroyed Goldsmith's Auburn generations earlier and now threatened not only female virtue but an entire way of life.[69]

Sharpe happens on Charlemont purely by chance while traveling with his uncle through the countryside. Preferring "the artificial existence of city life," Warham is contemptuous of all he sees until a young woman appears, "tall, erect, majestic—beautiful after no ordinary standard of beauty." Awestruck, Warham stares, even as the young woman "haughtily averted her head." "'A proud gipsy!' muttered the youth . . . 'just such a spirit as I should like to tame.'" It is Margaret Cooper, whose cold eyes mask "lurid fires of an intense, unmethodized ambition." Possessing a mind "of a masculine and commanding character," the nineteen-year-old Margaret is "ardent, commanding, and impatient," disliked by the young women of the village and feared by the young men. She is given to long, solitary walks in the woods and fields and, like Sharpe, despises Charlemont. She is also inordinately well read, having consumed the vast library of her deceased father. The works of the romantic poets—Byron and Shelley especially—"filled her thoughts"; indeed, they "made her thoughts." Under their influence, she craved "the vague, the unfathomable" and became "a creature of impulse only, not of reflection."[70]

Margaret's untutored reading has taught her to question the most sacred dictates of her society. She "lived without God," and "secretly laughed" at the itinerant ministers who happened through Charlemont, believing Christianity to be fit only for "babes and sucklings—people to be scared by shadows—the victims of their own miserable fears and superstitions." She bitterly rails against the gender limitations of her day: "What is expected of woman! These duties of the meanest slave! From her mind nothing is expected. . . . What can I be, in such a world? Nothing, nothing!" Her neighbors think her deranged, for "the indignation of a powerful mind denied—denied justice—baffled in its aims—conscious of the importance of all its struggles against binding and blinding circumstances—is akin to insanity."[71]

Warham, drawn by the imperious beauty of Margaret Cooper, returns to Charlemont under the unholy guise of a minister in training, a protégé of a bumpkin itinerant Methodist preacher he meets along the road. Taking the name "Alfred Stevens," Warham adopts the trappings of piety—"never did a saint wear the aspect of such supernatural devotion"—and the act thoroughly fools and charms the locals. Stevens lodges with "Brother Hinkley," the father of a disappointed suitor of Margaret's, and is "soon perfectly at home." And thus the serpent enters the garden.[72]

The cosmopolitan, experienced, and exquisitely corrupt Stevens initiates his seduction of the well-read but still provincial Margaret. So skilled is the seducer that in the midst of "their hourly increasing intimacy," the proud young woman has "no sort of apprehension that the spells of an enslaving passion were rapidly passing over her soul." Margaret is thrilled to find someone with whom she can confide her thoughts, someone who seems to sympathize with her dreams and hopes. Yet Stevens, "in his secret heart," laughs at her ambitions. He plays to her vanity, he "flattered and beguiled her," and promises that "he had power and influence in the outside world—that he could make her genius known." And so "evening after evening found them together," much to the delight of Margaret's foolish peasant mother, who encourages the match, believing that she will soon get a minister for a son-in-law. Finally, when "the arch-hypocrite" confesses his love for her, Margaret is "no longer the self-willed, imperious damsel, full of defiance"; she has been reduced to "a timid, trembling girl."[73]

The only inhabitants to suspect Stevens are William Hinkley, a young, gentle, and naive rustic smitten with Margaret despite her indifference; his neighbor and cousin Ned Hinkley, "a thoughtless, light-hearted son of the soil"; and Mr. Calvert, Hinkley's mentor and ex-schoolmaster, whose entire being exudes "the most unembarrassed benevolence and peace." Seeing the object of his affection wooed by another—one who is staying at his own house—William confesses his love for Margaret, but she unequivocally rejects him. When William tries to warn her about Stevens's intentions, she refuses to hear it and berates William for doubting the character of her newfound love. Now, as "darker feelings got possession of his mind," William thirsts for revenge. That night at the dinner table, William insults "Brother Stevens," and Hinkley's father, already angry at his son's surliness toward their guest, seizes a leather strap and whips his son. William tears the cowskin from his father. "That blow has lost you your son!" He then turns and strikes Stevens three times. "If there is any skin beneath the cloak of the parson, I trust I have reached it." A duel is secretly arranged, but as they are about to square off, William's father comes from behind and knocks his son on the head with a large club. Calvert takes William in and convinces him to leave Charlemont, giving him the money and recommendations needed to go off into the world. Overcome, William asks to use his name so that "I may be your son." And so William Hinkley becomes William Calvert. Disgraced and despondent, he leaves Charlemont forever.[74]

With William Hinkley out of the way, Stevens is free to resume his siege on Margaret's defenses. He promises marriage, and it is only a matter of time before—in a fit of "momentary madness"—Margaret allows her "virtue" to be "murdered." Shortly, "a sad change had come over her heart and all her features in the progress of a few days. . . . The intercourse of Margaret Cooper with her lover had had the most serious effect upon her manners and her looks." Pale and haggard, Margaret's "eye had a dilated, wild expression." Their trysts are regular, and soon Margaret is pregnant.[75]

Her suspicions raised by old man Calvert, Margaret meets Stevens at the spot of their trysts, prepared, it turns out, to kill herself. "Save me from this shame!" she implores, "Save me!" Falsely, he reassures her—"I regard you as sacredly my wife as if the rites of the church had so decreed it"—and promises to marry her the very next Sunday. The day before the wedding, Stevens rides to a nearby town, where he has his mail sent. There, he runs into an old crony named Ben, to whom he tells everything. Ben is particularly amused by Warham's ruse of being a preacher in training: "You pray?" "And preach!" "Ha! Ha! Ha!" And Margaret? "The game was a short one," Warham boasts; "she thought only of her poetry and her books." And now, she "is mine—soul and body—she is mine!" The evil Warham promises to let Ben have Margaret when he is done.[76]

Unknown to Warham, he has been followed by William's cousin, Ned Hinkley, who jumps out of his hiding spot, brandishing two pistols: "Don't let me interrupt. . . . I'd like to hear you out." Understanding that Stevens is a fraud but not quite comprehending what he has been describing, Ned challenges him to a duel, and although Sharpe agrees, he has no intentions of returning to Charlemont. He flees to Frankfort.[77]

When Ned returns to Charlemont with his story, no one believes it except old man Calvert and Margaret herself, who instantly knows it to be true: "Every word which he spoke went like some keen, death-giving instrument into her heart." When Stevens does not show for their wedding on Sunday, all doubts vanish, and she knows she has been abandoned. Margaret, robbed of her virginity, her one "treasure," "now envied the innocence of the very meanest of her companions." She tells her brainless mother everything: "He promised to marry me. . . . He held me panting to his breast. His mouth filled mine with kisses . . . and I was dishonored—made a woman before I was made a wife! Ruined, lost, abused, despised, abandoned! Ha! Ha! Ha! No marriage ceremony." She "fell to the floor as if stricken in the forehead. The blood gushed from her mouth and nostrils." For days she lies between life and death.[78]

Although she recovers, Margaret "bore within her an indelible witness of her shame." In utter despair, suicide "possessed all her mind. It became the one only thought." She secures a pistol, goes into the woods where she and Stevens had rendezvoused, kneels, and is about to pull the trigger when she feels the baby move. Now "there was yet another voice to be heard which was more potent than all. It was the mother's voice!" Yet months later, moments after the child is born, Margaret screams as she beholds her newborn son:

"Its features were those of Alfred Stevens." And thus "the milk which it drew from the mother's breast, was the milk of bitterness, and it did not thrive"; the child soon dies.[79]

Here, Simms undertakes a postmortem of Margaret's virtue. The root cause of the disaster was her refusal to "make an habitual reference to religion," which was itself the result of Margaret's intellectualism and her questioning of women's place: "The affections are not apt to be strong in a woman whose mind leads her out from her sex! . . . It is dangerous when the woman, through sheer confidence in her own strength, ventures upon the verge of the moral precipice. The very experiment, where the passions are concerned, proves her to be lost." Her native intelligence, Simms contends, was actually a curse, a weakness, for her "mere mind" could not make up for the lack of her finer female attributes. Ned, watching Margaret at the burial of her child, gives a folksy translation of Simms's warning: "A woman's never safe unless she's scary of herself, and mistrusts herself, and never lets her thoughts and fancies get from under a tight rein of prudence."[80]

Soon afterward, the wretched Margaret and her foolish mother leave Charlemont in shame and return to the farmstead seven miles away where Margaret was born. But it is not just a young woman Stevens has ruined; it is the whole village. Aware that they have all been taken in by "Brother Stevens," the community begins to unravel, and soon Charlemont, like Margaret, is abandoned, the village deserted.

Charlemont's sequel, *Beauchampe*, picks up the story five years later. Sequestered in her shame and "self-abasement," Margaret assumes an alias, "Anna Cooke," and lives only to exact revenge on Alfred Stevens. "If I am a woman, I can be an enemy—and such an enemy!" She undertakes target practice until she is a crack shot. Her very appearance undergoes a stark transformation: "Her beauty assumed a wilder aspect. Her eye shot forth a supernatural fire. She never smiled." But she does not know how or where to find "Stevens"—she does not even know her destroyer's real name.[81]

The serpent himself is in Frankfort, the state capital, where he has become a well-respected lawyer and a powerful new court politician married to a woman he does not love. He is, of course, still morally debased, as he enjoys nothing more than carousing with his fellow degenerates in a "lawyer's club," where they are currently celebrating a law student of Sharpe's having just passed the bar. J. Orville Beauchampe is "a young man, not more than twenty-one, tall, and of very handsome person. His eye was bright, and his whole face full of intelligence." Beauchampe possesses an "excitable constitution, passionate, and full of enthusiasm; and, when aroused," he is incapable of self-restraint and blind to "the strict course of propriety."[82]

After his initiation, Beauchampe returns home to his mother and loving sisters after an absence of two years. Hearing a pistol shot, he comes on a clearing in the woods and finds "a female, well-dressed, tall, and of a carriage unusually firm and majestic." It is, of course, "Anna," honing her marksmanship and dreaming of the day she will kill Stevens. "Here, in these woods," she later declares, "I pursue a sort of devotion, where Hate is the deity—Vengeance the officiating priest." Beauchampe is instantly beguiled by her "thunderstorm beauty . . . dark and dismal, with such keen flashes of lightning as to dazzle one's eyes and terrify one's heart!" Beauchampe's sisters later tell him that she avoids company entirely, never smiles, and is possessed of "such a deep look of sadness about her eyes."[83]

Determined to know her better, Beauchampe attempts to call on Anna, but she has her servants send him away, albeit with a borrowed book. After a number of failed attempts, he finally barges into her sanctuary. She tells him that although he may make use of her library, she has long since abandoned society: "The world can be nothing to me. I am nothing to it." Despite Anna's discouragement, Beauchampe continues to sally forth, and before long, "Anna Cooke gradually took pleasure in seeing him." Yet she persists in telling him that "an insuperable barrier" prevents their marriage. He confesses his love and demands to know what stands between them: "You have been wronged," he tells her; "you have an enemy. I will seek him. I will be your champion—die for you if need be—only tell me that you will be mine!" As Beauchampe presses his affections, Anna "felt the darker passions of her mind flickering like some sinking candle-flame," and her sanguinary dream of vengeance "grew nightly less vivid."[84]

Finally, she reveals her secret—she has been "dishonored." She tells him the story of Alfred Stevens—"no idle apologies for weakness offered—no excuses urged in behalf of sinful impulses"—and reveals to Beauchampe her real name: Margaret Cooper. Any man who would have her hand, she says, "must avenge my dishonor. . . . He must devote his life to the work of retribution." Beauchampe is more enthralled than ever. He takes from her the pistol and the responsibility of killing her tormentor: "It is *mine* now, remember, not yours."[85]

And they are married. Beauchampe, awash in marital bliss, "lost sight of the weeks and months" and completely forgets the turmoil of law and politics. Likewise, Anna's soul "poured forth strains of such sweet eloquence and song," and she comes to fear the fulfillment of the awful oath she has exacted from Beauchampe. Having recently learned to pray, she "implored that the trial might be spared him, to which, previously, her whole soul had entirely been surrendered." Once again, as during her seduction, the fiery Margaret/Anna is subdued by love, and is "now timid as a child." Simms's moral is obvious: a woman alone is dangerous; a woman in love is bridled.[86]

Back in Frankfort, Sharpe is running for the state assembly. He faces a political opponent of unexpected skill and popularity—a young, rising lawyer named William Calvert (né Hinkley). Sharpe sends word that he needs the help of his old law student. Beauchampe, although he has reservations about Sharpe's "loose principles," agrees to campaign for his mentor. The young man's debut on the hustings is a terrific success, and "the friends of Colonel Sharpe were in ecstasies."[87]

Meanwhile, at an inn during a campaign stop, Sharpe and Calvert meet. Introducing himself, Calvert suddenly recognizes Sharpe as his old nemesis. "Villain—a base, consummate villain. . . . Look at me, Alfred Stevens," he demands; "look at me, and behold one who is ready to avenge the dishonor of Margaret Cooper." Sharpe turns "deadly pale. His eyes wandered. He had been stunned by the suddenness of Calvert's revelations." But he quickly recovers and denies everything. Yet a duel must be fought, and Sharpe, who is a expert marksman, tells his crony Ben that he must kill Calvert, for "if he goes on to blab this business . . . he will play the devil with my chances." Alas, in the duel Sharpe only manages to wound Calvert in the hip.[88]

While Calvert recuperates, Sharpe wins the election and is shortly thereafter appointed the state's attorney general. Sharpe and yet another "arch-vassal," Barnabas, plan a visit to the Beauchampes to personally thank Orville for helping him win the election. And thus the serpent slithers into another Eden. To her "unmitigated horror," Anna, of course, recognizes Sharpe as Alfred Stevens. But fearing for her husband's safety, she resolves not to tell Orville. Sharpe, learning that Anna Beauchampe is Margaret Cooper, conspires, incredibly, to seduce Margaret all over again. While Beauchampe is out, he approaches Anna. "Come to me: let us renew those happy hours that we knew in Charlemont. . . . You were my first love—you shall be my last." She replies: "O man! O man! Blind and desperate, you know not how nearly you stand on the brink of the precipice." As he tries to kiss her hand, she slaps him and draws a pistol. "I told him the whole story of my folly and my shame. . . . I swore Beauchampe on the Holy Evangelists, ere he made my hand his own, to avenge my dishonor on my betrayer." Anna demands that he leave immediately and warns him, "A word from me, sir, brings down his vengeance upon your head!" When Sharpe refuses to leave, Anna tells Beauchampe, "Colonel Sharpe and Alfred Stevens are the same person!" and demands he avenge her. Beauchampe hears the news with "agony, the utter recoil and shrinking of soul," but he swears, "Before God, my wife, I renew my oath." Beauchampe tells Barnabas that Sharpe must leave his house, and "when we meet it is with the one purpose of taking his life or losing my own. There can be no half struggle between us. There can be no mercy. Blood, alone!"[89]

Even after he is forced to flee the Beauchampes, Sharpe does not think himself in any danger; he even muses on the possibility of seducing Margaret again: "I shall have her at my feet yet." But once Sharpe is back in Frankfort, a gentleman—John A. Covington—shows up at his "elegant mansion" and delivers Beauchampe's challenge. Sharpe, finally realizing the seriousness of the situation, can only stammer, "I will not fight Mr. Beauchampe!" Covington tells him that Beauchampe will post Sharpe "as a scoundrel and a coward" and that "the extent of the wrong which you have done to Beauchampe only makes your accountability the greater. Nobody will acquit you on this score." Horrified, Sharpe cooks up a scheme—he will spread the rumor that Margaret's child was black. "The dread of such a report would effectually discourage him from any prosecution of this business."[90]

A few nights later, there is a knock at Sharpe's door; it is Beauchampe, who barges inside, catches Sharpe by the arm, and forces him into a chair. "You dared to bring your lust into my dwelling." Sharpe whines, "Spare me Beauchampe! Oh! Spare my life. Do not murder me—for I can not fight you on account of that injured woman!" Unmoved, Beauchampe presents two dirks for them to fight with. Sharpe denies ever seducing Margaret, contends that the child was not his, and then whispers something into the ear of Beauchampe. Even as Sharpe hisses the lie, an overcome Beauchampe instantly stabs Sharpe: "The sharp edge of the dagger had answered the shocking secret—whatever might have been its character—and the terrible oath of the husband was redeemed! . . . The wrongs of Margaret Cooper were at last avenged!" Here Simms editorializes on the necessity of vigilante justice. Such honor killings are necessary, for reputation is "soul-blood"—the "life of all life": "Give us, say I, Kentucky practice, like that of Beauchampe, as a social law."[91]

When Beauchampe returns to Anna with the news, she can only weep, for "she no longer possessed those feelings which would have desired the performance of the deed. She no longer implored revenge." When suspicion falls on Beauchampe and he is imprisoned, Anna joins him in jail. She believes his acquittal is all but certain once he explains the circumstances: "The blow which your arm has struck, was a blow in behalf of every unprotected female, of every poor orphan—fatherless, brotherless, and undefended—who otherwise would be the prey of the ruffian and the betrayer." But Beauchampe resolves to deny the crime so that Anna's shame will not be made public.[92]

Told that William Calvert is the best defense attorney in Frankfort, Anna travels to his home to engage his services. On entering the house—"the very seat of elegance and art"—she sees his portrait and realizes that Calvert is none other than her youthful admirer, William Hinkley. Old Calvert, the schoolmaster who now lives with William, sees her and is stupefied: "You, Miss Cooper: can it be?" William, still recovering from the wound suffered in his duel with Sharpe, appears and beholds Margaret, for whom he still pines after all these years. Fighting back the tears, he asks, "Can I serve you, Margaret—is it for this you seek me?" "It is," she answers. He tells her that Beauchampe is in very real danger—that the murder has become politicized and Sharpe's very powerful friends will do anything to see Beauchampe hang. Anna/Margaret teeters on the edge of sanity: "These storms have shattered me, William—shattered me quite! I am no longer what I was—strong, proud, confident. I fear, sometimes, that my brain will go wild."[93]

At the trial, Calvert tries his best but is beaten by perjury—"there were witnesses to swear to his footsteps, to his voice, his face, his words, his knife and clothes." The guilty verdict was all but foreordained. Awaiting his execution, Anna resolves to share the fate of her husband, for "her nature was too magnanimous to think of surviving him." She says, "I am tired, very tired, of these walls of life—that keep us in bonds—put us at the mercy of the false and the cruel, the base and the malicious! Oh, my husband, we have tried them long enough!" They take poison, but it does not work. Anna stabs herself, and Beauchampe, determined to escape the indignity of hanging, follows suit.[94]

Simms's work was adapted for the stage by Irish-born New York writer John Savage. The play, *Sybil,* was first staged in September 1858 in St. Louis and was thereafter performed in dozens of cities—including Louisville, New Orleans, San Francisco, Chicago, Boston, New York City, Philadelphia, and even Melbourne, Australia. In most places, the play enjoyed "remarkable success" and was received with "great enthusiasm," but when it was brought north to New York City during the Civil War, in April 1862, *Sybil* was met with indifference. After only a few performances, production was shut down.[95]

Easily the most wretched and unintentionally funny novel based on the Kentucky Tragedy is Hannah Daviess Pittman's *The Heart of Kentucky* (1908). Here, Anna is coded as Marguerite Darrall, Beauchamp as her devoted and heroic husband Wallace, and Sharp as the preternaturally diabolical Colonel Steale. Though keeping the setting in Kentucky of the 1820s, Pittman transfers the initial scene of action to the Cumberland Plateau of eastern Kentucky, where there lived a beautiful woman the locals called "the Strange Lady," in whose "eyes was kindled a strange, disturbed light." This is Marguerite, whom Pittman drains of any intimation of strength or resilience: "I am only a woman," she repeats ad nauseam; "love has made of me only a poor weak woman." She comes from a proud and distinguished family, but she has been left "defenseless" after the death of her father. A man masquerading as a student of divinity and calling himself "Claude Montrose" pursues Marguerite "with false vows of love, with false promises." In time, he "lured this innocent, trusting child, who knew nothing of the world, to leave with him her home." A fellow miscreant—subtly named "Benedict"—impersonates a minister and "marries" them. Having then "ruined her life," Montrose abandons the pregnant Marguerite.[96]

Years later, Marguerite encounters our knight-errant, Wallace Darrall—"tall and sinewy and good to look upon" and forever blurting out such lines as "I must always perform my duty as I see it, without faltering." They meet after he hears gunshots in the woods and finds Marguerite, alone and now embittered, practicing marksmanship in a clearing, waiting for the day that she will kill Claude Montrose. Though unwilling at first to entertain the gallant young man's suit, she eventually relents and agrees to become his wife, but only if he swears to avenge her honor. Wallace enthusiastically agrees to the terms, and they embark on a life of domestic bliss.[97]

But politics intrudes on their idyll when the leaders of the anti-relief old court party recognize Wallace's heroic qualities and implore him to become their champion. When he declares his candidacy for the state senate, Marguerite is apprehensive, but soon it occurs to her that "it is only my poor, weak woman's heart that fears." Wallace wins the election, and thereafter he and Marguerite travel to the state capital, Frankfort, where, at a reception, Wallace introduces Marguerite to Colonel Steale, Wallace's mentor and friend, who has been elected to the state senate as a relief candidate. Marguerite is overcome, for Steale is none other than Claude Montrose. Although stunned to see her betrayer again, she tells Wallace nothing, for Marguerite's "thirst for justice, vengeance, is all gone," quenched by her newfound happiness.[98]

During the ensuing legislative session, all pretense of decorum disintegrates, and "the sword was soon drawn and the scabbard thrown away in the duel to the death between the two parties, not only in the legislative halls, but in the streets and in the privacy of homes, so great was the excitement." The political rivalry strains Wallace and Steale's relationship. Before long, the friendship is broken, and "hard things were often said."[99]

At session's close, the Darralls return home, but Wallace is soon called away. Knowing of his absence, Colonel Steale pays a visit. For Marguerite, Steale's appearance is a cruel irony, for "the time for which she had prayed for ten years has come at last, and finds her unprepared." Forcing his way into the house, he mewls that it was all a misunderstanding, that he "meant to come back." She is repulsed: "It were better if I had died." Yet he insists that he still loves her, and "to my grave I will carry no other love save that love for you." He reaches for her, but she recoils in horror: "You violate the sanctity of my home with your presence." He sputters, "You are a wife, my wife!" She cannot take it and draws a pistol, yet she hesitates to shoot him for the sake of her husband, the man who saved her from the bitterness of impotent and unrequited vengeance. She tells Steale that she has told Wallace her story. "He knows?" asks Steale. "He knows all—save the name of my betrayer. . . . I spare your life; but the price of it is silence." Now Steale perceives that "she had triumphed over him." "For you, Colonel Steale, there is but one word. Go!"[100]

When Wallace returns, Marguerite says nothing of Steale's visit, but Jefferson, their slave, unwittingly lets slip the secret: "I furgit to tell yer, Massa Darr'll, that Colonel Steale wuz here." As she begs Wallace not to ask too many questions, Wallace suddenly remembers "an old forgotten story of Steale's past—not unlike this. His blood rushes in a mad torrent to his brain. Putting her aside, he arises and as he walks, moans aloud with pain." Suddenly understanding all, Wallace is "maddened by love, shame, and jealous anger." Marguerite begs him to renounce his vow of vengeance, yet he is unmoved and speaks "as one bidding good-by to life." Inexplicably, Marguerite decides to throw fuel on the fire, and she tells him everything about Steale's visit, about the villain's lust and audacity. "This man—this man who has dared to seek you in my—your husband's—his friend's home,—to touch your hand? While he lives he overshadows my life." The next morning, Wallace learns that Steale will be in town for a celebration in his honor.[101]

The narrative skips to the next day, about noon, as Wallace is awakening to the news that Steale was assassinated the night before. The widespread assumption is that the murder was political: one particularly high-strung local exclaims to Wallace, "Party lines is wiped out and everybody is afeard that it is a conspiracy; that the whole administration from the Gov'nor down is in danger." Pittman elides the details of the murder, and when Wallace proclaims, "I am no midnight assassin," the reader cannot be completely sure whether he is telling the truth.[102]

Suspicion almost immediately falls on Wallace, and although he is taken into custody, he denies any involvement in the murder and is confident of acquittal. His friend Judge Randolph, however, worries that Wallace will be sacrificed to the political turmoil of the day: "If they can succeed in picturing Steale a martyr to his political views and efforts to bring relief to the people ground down to the earth and maddened with debt, they will be ready to turn and rend you." Before long, Wallace confesses the murder to Randolph and another friend named Sothern: "For the punishment of such transgression nature has implanted in the breast of every man an instinct, an Unwritten Law, which provides retribution for the crime. I followed him to Frankfort—and,—*I killed him!*" Wallace had gone to Steale's Frankfort house and challenged him to a duel. But even as Steale fell on his knees, "paralyzed . . . with fear, and begged me to spare his life," he grabbed the pistol from Wallace's hand and aimed it point-blank at him. "Seeing his murderous intention to take advantage of me, with the dagger left in my right hand I struck the fatal blow, as he fired." Randolph is overcome: "'Well done,' ejaculated the Judge." Sothern adds, "I only wish it could have happened in the sight of all men." Thus Pittman makes the murder wholly honorable—in defense not only of his wife's virtue but of his own life has "Beauchamp" killed "Sharp." Indeed, as Pittman presents it, moral order demanded Steale's murder, for the man was the equivalent of a distempered dog that needed to be put down. The killing of Steale—a man of such unmitigated venality that his "whole life [was] a living lie, and transgression of God's commands"—was Wallace's duty not just to his wife but "to the world."[103]

At the trial, however, Wallace is forced to dissimulate, to plead not guilty, such is the poisoned political atmosphere of Frankfort. Wallace, moreover, wants to spare Marguerite the shame of her story being made public. The trial itself is riddled with perjury and political corruption: "Many witnesses were brought in to testify to the ill-feeling existing between the two; either perjuring themselves for gain, or carried away by the political aspect given the trial." Yet Wallace took care not to leave behind any incriminating evidence, and the prosecution's case is weak. But just when it seems that Wallace will be found innocent, evil Benedict takes the stand and produces a note Wallace wrote challenging Steale to a duel.[104]

When the jury returns a guilty verdict, Wallace rises to his feet and proudly confesses the murder, detailing his attempts to fight honorably and Steale's dastardly attempt to kill him. Yet the judge is not moved: "Whatever the offense against his honor, the prisoner should have sought the redress afforded by the law. Taking the law into his own hands, he must abide by what the law provides." The judge denies a request for a new trial and sentences Wallace to hang.[105]

Days before his execution, Marguerite joins her husband in prison. When Sothern gives her a knife for Wallace to kill himself with, she is overcome: "I—I—am but a poor weak woman that shudders at the thought of blood!" The morning of his execution, Wallace hands Sothern a written confession, "the outpouring of the heart of a doomed man sitting in the shadow of the scaffold." Yet before they can take him to the gallows, Marguerite and Wallace stab themselves. In Pittman's maudlin description, "When the guard opens the door he finds them clasped in each other's arms, passing together through the Valley of the Shadow of Death, where the dear Lord walked with them."[106]

It is hard to imagine the critical legerdemain that could transform *The Heart of Kentucky* into a literary triumph. Certainly, this artless retelling of the Kentucky Tragedy is more a pastiche of borrowed plotlines than an original piece of work. Pittman lifts a number of plot devices from earlier dramatists. Like Barnes in *Octavia Bragaldi* and Hoffman in *Greyslaer,* she invents a sham marriage conducted by an accomplice impersonating a minister to provide the means of the Anna character's seduction, rather than a momentary lapse of judgment or an ill-judged lowering of her womanly defenses. But *The Heart of Kentucky* is more obviously a reworking of *Beauchampe,* given the vast number of similarities to Simms's work. Like Margaret, Marguerite is a mysterious woman whose desire for revenge is eventually tamed by a happy marriage, and the scene in which the seducer and victim confront one another years later is almost exactly the same. Steale, meanwhile, is a replica of Warham Sharpe: a serial seducer who preys on naive young country girls; a shameless rogue who actually tries to renew the relationship with a married "Anna"; an overconfident miscreant who fails to comprehend the deadly seriousness of "Beauchamp" until it is too late.

The sole original contribution of *The Heart of Kentucky* lies in its moral, which bears the unmistakable imprint of the turn-of-the-century South: the violation of (white) women equals death and, specifically, death by lynching, for which the book offers a thinly veiled defense. At one point, Judge Randolph pleads in vain to the governor, "Listen to the beating of the heart of Kentucky, if you would learn the temper of the men whom you represent. Hear their cries for release! Not pardon, mind you—but for a vindication of that higher law which alone safeguards the sanctity of our homes!" Three pages later, Pittman, apparently concerned that her point has not been sufficiently made, proclaims that, since the execution of Wallace Darrall, no court of justice in the state has "adjudged guilty a vindicator of the 'unwritten law.' In a clear, unmistaken tone 'THE HEART OF KENTUCKY HAD SPOKEN.'"[107]

The work that towers above all other attempts to engage the episode is Robert Penn Warren's *World Enough and Time.* Far and away the most illuminating and deeply researched fictionalization of the Kentucky Tragedy, Warren's novel succeeds to a large extent because only he, with the partial exception of Edgar Allan Poe, glimpsed the self-created, self-dramatizing, and self-justifying nature of Jereboam and Anna Beauchamp's bizarre story. The book was published in 1950, six years after another southern author of remarkable talent, Katherine Anne Porter, put a copy of Beauchamp's *Confession* into Warren's hands. The tale intrigued him, he later wrote, not only because "it had happened around my home section . . . and I had some sense of what that world had been like" but also because Warren "had known the story for years, or at least I had heard a garbled word-of-mouth version of it, for it had entered folklore and in my childhood still had a vague and fugitive existence in the memories of older people."[108]

Warren possessed the instincts of a historian—C. Vann Woodward thought him "the Southern novelist who comes nearest approaching an historical subject after the manner of an historian"—and he undertook extensive research into the primary sources. (One can find notes and memoranda of Warren's in the Franklin County circuit court trial records at the Kentucky Department of Libraries and Archives.) In particular, Warren took care to accurately portray the political context of the murder: Kentucky's infamous and still barely understood relief war. Warren's treatment of this tumultuous era—the years of combat over the necessity and constitutionality of debt relief legislation, the pro-relief majority's attempt to dissolve the state supreme court, the viciousness of the resultant court battle—is astute:

> The Old Court said: The Law exists, The Constitution exists. They exist by the sanction of Nature and Society. They are not Justice, for Justice is a spirit never seen, but only through them can Justice speak. Untune them and all is jangle. The New Court said: The Law exists. The Constitution exists. But they exist only by the decision of man and what man can make he can unmake. As for Justice, that is the name for the needs of man. Justice is man's Goddess but is also his slave. Let man seize her naked and make her speak.

Warren precisely traced the passion and violence unleashed by the relief war, a tumult that, "like a tide, washed into the farthest county seat or settlement tavern to release new violence to flood back on the big towns where the great men debated and the rich gave themselves airs and the banker totted up accounts and calculated interest and the fanatic or ambitious man called for justice and uttered the words that, printed on handbills or broadsides or in newspapers, or passed from mouth to mouth, spread over the land to bring blood." It is at once a testament to the brilliance of Warren and to the poverty of relief war historiography that these brief sketches buried within a fifty-nine-year-old novel stand as the greatest insights into the era's political conflagration.[109]

World Enough and Time, like much of Warren's substantial body of work, is preoccupied with the manner in which the past and present fold on one another and ensnare even those—particularly those—who believe themselves above history. Yet, of all his novels (including, notably, *All the King's Men*), *World Enough and Time* was the only one that Warren allowed to be labeled a "historical novel." The core characters are obviously and admittedly based on their real-life counterparts: Jeremiah Beaumont is Jereboam Beauchamp; Rachel Jordan is Anna Cooke; Cassius Fort is Solomon Sharp. Warren does, however, flip the political sensibilities of the primary characters: Beaumont becomes the very personification of the relief impulse—noble, well intentioned, visionary, naive, and hopelessly doomed in a cold-blooded world—while Fort is the wearied embodiment of the old court belief that "justice is a spirit never seen." With an artistry and expertise borne of exhaustive research, Warren weaves together the search for public justice that characterized Kentucky's new court party with Beaumont's private quest to avenge the honor of a woman who has supposedly been seduced. The two quests for justice rise and, in the end, fall together.[110]

Warren places the reader two steps removed from the action. There is, first, the historian-narrator, who, far from omniscient, struggles to understand the events. His principal source, the journal of Jeremiah Beaumont, composes the second layer of narration, a justification of events Beaumont wrote while awaiting his execution in a Frankfort dungeon. In the opening pages, Warren—with a sure understanding of the advantages and limitations of the historian—has the narrator muse over the remains of the episode: "I can show you what is left. After the pride, passion, agony, and bemused aspiration, what is left is in our hands." The historian-narrator can only muse over the remaining newspapers, diaries, and letters.[111]

Jeremiah Beaumont is squarely at the center of the story. It is he who initiates and drives the events, he who is ultimately responsible for the destruction of three lives. Beaumont is idealistic, and ultimately fooled, but never a fool. He is driven on a quixotic mission because he feels he has come of age in a barren time and place: the West in the first quarter of the nineteenth century, a time when the memory of the great and daring deeds of Kentucky's founding generation linger and yet their sons—noble and romantic and eager to prove themselves—have little so dramatic or meaningful to fight or die for: "He felt that life was empty and he would live for nothing."[112]

At seventeen, Jeremiah comes under the tutelage of Colonel Cassius Fort, a "son of old Kaintuck," born to "poor, feckless, unlettered parents, the kind who had lost hope back in Virginia and had drifted across the mountains in the old days by the Wilderness Road, toward a last promise." Orphaned young, Fort "had made his way in a hard world, and he stood steady on his legs and looked any man in the eye." But behind the bold stare of this middle-aged man of brilliance and political cunning is the pain of "a suffering animal that has no words for what it feels."[113]

For his part, Jeremiah drifts through adolescence and early manhood, vaguely and chronically dissatisfied, until his reckless and free-spirited friend, Wilkie Barron, relates to him the tragic tale of Rachel Jordan. She is a well-educated young woman who was born and raised in the highest circles of Virginia society, but the death of her father left the family in dire financial straits and forced a move to the backwoods of southwestern Kentucky. There, she met Cassius Fort. The two were a study of contrasts: "With nothing, the pauper boy of a stockade, he had seized and molded the world, while she, with everything, had let the world slip through her fingers like water." Fort, according to Wilkie's story, seduced and abandoned Rachel, who then gave birth to a stillborn baby. And now, Rachel, ruined and alone, "has no father and no brother, no one to defend her." Beaumont is at once horrified and thrilled. He has found his life's purpose—he will love this woman he has never met and avenge her dishonor. Immediately, he severs all ties with Fort and so turns his back on the fame and influence and fortune that Fort's patronage offer. But such means little to Beaumont compared to his idols of justice and selfless gallantry; he has at last found a means "to define himself, to create his world."[114]

So Beaumont pursues Rachel. He calls on her, but she has him turned away, albeit with a book: *Poems,* by Byron. Finally, he surprises her outside her house, and they meet for the first time. Yet, far from being swept off her feet, she is merely annoyed at his impertinence, flatly stating, "I wish nothing of the world. I have put it aside and I have no place for it as it has no place for me." Beaumont persists in his visits, desiring nothing more than Rachel's permission to avenge her, but she wants nothing of it. The affair with Fort, she says, was not a case of cruelty and deception; it "was just—it was just something that happened. To him. To me. Something that happened to me it was nobody's fault." But Beaumont insists, "There must be justice. You have suffered enough and there must be justice. And when there is justice you will not suffer." She replies, "You are a very foolish and fanciful young man, who reads too many books and knows nothing of the world." He continues to intrude on her solitude and, more important, to stoke resentment of Fort. Finally, Beaumont asks her to marry him, and she accepts, but only, she blurts out, if he does one thing: "Kill Fort!" "So she had said it," comments Warren's historian, "and had laid on him the obligation. Or we may say more accurately that he had at last succeeded in laying the obligation on her and thereby on himself, for the obligation sprang from the depth of his nature." The narrator muses, "We can only surmise that she could not resolve her own feelings, that she was torn by their contradictions, and that she passed the decision on to Jeremiah as you flip a coin or draw a card, passing on to him, or to fate, the responsibility." In Warren's hands, Anna becomes a strangely passive character who does not quite know what she wants, whose fate is sealed by the strong-willed, obsessive Beaumont.[115]

Beaumont rushes to Frankfort and challenges Fort to a duel. "I am your enemy!" he thunders; "I come from Miss Jordan." Fort, however, refuses to fight, even after Beaumont strikes him across the face: "I cannot fight you. I cannot fight any man on this point." When Beaumont tells Fort that Rachel has sent him, the older man loses any remaining inclination to resist. As Beaumont "seized his throat and raised the dirk," Fort whispers, "Do it—

do it—if she said . . ." It is nothing like the honorable and dramatic scene Beaumont envisioned—it is only ignoble and sad—and Jeremiah cannot kill him. When he returns, having failed in his self-appointed mission, Rachel is not disappointed; she never wanted revenge anyway. "I didn't hate him," she admits, "not before you came. But you came and your tortured me and you made me tell you." Nonetheless, they are married, and soon Rachel is again pregnant. Jeremiah sets about working on his fortunes and slowly learns to forget his vow of revenge.[116]

Warren alone among the dramatists of the Kentucky Tragedy, develops a complex, even dysfunctional relationship between the Jereboam and Anna characters. Neither the virtuous and outraged defender of an innocent woman's lost virtue nor the patsy of a demented shrew, Beaumont is an idealistic, even quixotic adventurer who pushes Rachel Jordan into asking for revenge. Most interesting, and in the most profound departure from other dramatizations, Rachel is neither aggrieved nor vengeful; her relationship with Fort was not even a seduction—just "something that happened." Wilkie Barron and the rest of Western society composed a sordid tale of seduction for their own purposes, and Beaumont in turn forced it upon her.

Beaumont's talents and resolve soon draw the attention of new court partisans—among them his old friend Wilkie and the éminence grise of the party, Percival Skrogg, the tubercular editor of the *Freeman's Advocate* who "smiled his smile which was not a smile but a tantalizing exposure of the white skull under the inadequate flesh." Thin, pale, and sickly, Skrogg—who is clearly modeled after Amos Kendall—has hired a couple of thugs, "ex-keelboat ruffians, brothers, Lilburn and One-eye Sam Jenkins," to serve as his henchmen. Although Beaumont is not particularly concerned with the intricacies of the relief war, he does generally sympathize with the relief–new court faction, and after Wilkie repeatedly urges him to run for office, Beaumont assents. During the campaign season, Cassius Fort defects to the old court and is quickly denounced as a heretic by his erstwhile new court allies, who now resurrect the old story of his "seduction" of Rachel. Beaumont eventually loses the election and gladly resigns himself to a quiet life with Rachel. But then a handbill is delivered to their house bearing the name Cassius Fort, an answer to the old charge of seduction. The baby Fort supposedly fathered with Rachel could not have been his, the handbill claims, for the child was black. On reading it, Rachel collapses and miscarries. Now, with his dreams of domestic happiness in ruins, Beaumont sees everything clearly, "like a man lost in the pitch dark in ground that should be familiar, who suddenly sees in a lightning flash the old way before him." He must renew his covenant and kill Fort.[117]

Pointedly, Rachel's bitterness even now is directed not toward Fort but toward Jeremiah for entering the political arena and thus exposing her to such slander—indeed, for pressing her to swear vengeance at all. She is indifferent toward Jeremiah's crusade and the fate of Fort himself: "You do not have to go," she says as he leaves for Frankfort to assassinate Fort. But he is inwardly thrilled to keep his word, to exact vengeance, to have justice. He has decided to murder Fort by stealth, for if he challenged Fort to a duel and were himself killed, no one would be left to see after Rachel. Moreover, Jeremiah plans to kill him the night before the legislature convenes, hoping the murder will be understood as a political assassination.[118]

Once in Frankfort, Beaumont finds Fort's house, and, spying through the window, he sees Mrs. Fort, a prematurely gray, haggard, and childless woman: "She doesn't love him, I can see from her face that she does not," he thinks; "Ah, poor ghost, I will revenge, you too." He taps on the window; as Fort opens the door, "Jeremiah shoved the door wide, stepped over the threshold, and seized Fort's right wrist with his own left hand. . . . 'Oh don't you know me, Colonel, sure enough?' Jeremiah demanded in an aggrieved voice. . . . 'Ah . . . Jerry!'" Fort gasps. "'Not Jerry to you, villain, but Beaumont!' The blade sank deep into Fort's chest above the heart, with shocking ease, like a blade driven into a ripe melon." With his dying breath, Fort exhales, "Ah, Jerry—so you had—to come."[119]

Jeremiah flees before he is seen and makes it back to Rachel undetected. "'It is done,' he said, and took her in his arms. . . . She was passive in his arms for a second, then her shoulders began to shake, and he knew she was weeping." The next morning, armed men show up to take Jeremiah back for questioning. When they produce the evidence against him—a dirk and handkerchief they claim to have been found near the crime scene—Jeremiah realizes he is being framed, for he distinctly remembers leaving the handkerchief on his bed. Moreover, Fort's political allies arrange for testimony to be given that Beaumont threatened Fort. Amid these conspiracies to convict him, "Jeremiah Beaumont was a chip on the tide of things, a tide shot through by sudden rips and twisted currents." What he had hoped would shield him from suspicion—the political chaos of the day—was instead ensuring his conviction. Knowing that "lies were everywhere, waiting to strike him," Jeremiah decides to counter with a lie of his own. He will suborn a witness named Marlowe, whose testimony will direct suspicion away from Beaumont. He prepares a script—a "speech for the drama he had contrived"—and sends it to Rachel for Marlowe to memorize.[120]

Although the trial is laced with perjury and political opportunism, Beaumont's skilled lawyers manage to shoot the prosecution's case full of holes, and the possibility of acquittal looks promising. Marlowe, however, double-crosses Beaumont and turns over the script. Rachel had fallen ill and, instead of coaching Marlowe, had given him the document and thereby "had undone Jeremiah." Wilkie Barron takes the stand as a witness for the prosecution and administers the coup de grâce, testifying that he heard Jeremiah vow to avenge Rachel. The inevitable guilty verdict is not nearly as devastating to Beaumont as the foul means by which it has been secured: "They had lied, they had snared him with lies, and it was not fair. It was not fair, for he acted in justice, and justice was all he wanted, it was not fair, to make him die for doing justice. . . . Now justice was the bright needle lost in the haystack of lies."[121]

Rachel comes to him in jail. Knowing that her carelessness led to his conviction, she is determined to die with him. For the first time, she professes her love for Jeremiah, yet in his dark disillusionment he can only vaguely remember having once loved her. Nonetheless, they cling to one another and lose themselves in "a kind of crazy, black honeymoon." And he writes his story—his confession—so everyone will know the foul means by which he was brought down. "Jeremiah and Rachel lived in the only way left to them," Warren's historian interjects, "acting out the noble drama in the dark hole, piling up the manuscript that was to 'justify' all, clutching and straining together in their last violence of life or the first of death." Toward the end, the pair attempt suicide so Beaumont will not have to "kick in the air for their sport." They take an overdose of laudanum, but it merely makes them ill, and thus, "after the fine speeches and the tragic stance, the grand exit was muffed. The actors trip on their ceremonial robes, even at the threshold of greatness, and come tumbling down in a smashing pratt-fall, amid hoots and howls from the house, and the house gets its money's worth."[122]

In his most dramatic and blatant departure from the historical record, Warren then has Jeremiah and Rachel broken out of jail by, of all people, Wilkie, who offers weak excuses for his testimony and claims he would never let Jerry hang. They then head westward with Lilburn Jenkins, to "a place nobody keers what yore name is or what you done." From there, in the last sixty pages of the novel, the story takes on a nightmarish cast as they travel to an island in the Tennessee River, a settlement of horror and despair where men have descended into abject savagery, ruled over by a great and ancient humpbacked monstrosity named Gran Boz, an ex–river pirate rendered obsolete by the steamboat. As Beaumont looks around, "a wild anguish swept over him: *was it all for this, was it all for this!*" Rachel soon loses her mind—she keeps stealing another woman's baby—while Jeremiah descends into debauchery and syphilitic drunkenness: "He could sit with the men of this place in their brutal silence and drink, drink from the jug that passed from hand to hand and mouth to mouth, that was smeared with the common spit, that was lipped by every mouth, that was their bond and communion."[123]

In time, Lilburn Jenkins's brother, One-eye, arrives at the fetid camp. The brothers had had a falling-out, and the truth had come along with it: The broadside that set Jeremiah on the road to Frankfort to kill Fort had been written by Skrogg and Wilkie. Jeremiah had been used to assassinate Fort to punish his defection to the old court. "It was all a lie! . . . Everything was a lie. They betrayed me. Everybody betrayed me. Even Wilkie, even Wilkie betrayed me. They used me, they betrayed me, Skrogg and Wilkie and Marlowe and all . . ." He turns on Rachel for letting the letter fall into the hands of Marlowe "when I had done all for you!" Softly, she returns, "'No. No. Not for me.' 'For you,' he said, 'and then you . . . ' 'Oh, for yourself!' She exclaimed suddenly. 'Not for me. For yourself. You came and you used me. You made me hate Fort and you used me. Oh, I didn't hate him, I loved him, and you used me, you used me to kill him, you used me, you ruined me, you used me, used . . .'" Amid her half-mad ravings, Rachel stabs herself and dies.[124]

At the end, stranded in a swamp surrounded by the most depraved of humanity, Jeremiah realizes that, amid all the lies and the manifold betrayals, he murdered the only good man he had ever known. Fort was "a great man. He was my friend and benefactor. He loved me like a father, and I killed him." Jeremiah realizes that Skrogg has done to him what he had done to Rachel: "Skrogg for his idea of justice had in the end, sent Fort to my knife, and me to the rope. So I, no better than Skrogg, and in the same error, had put the mask on my face and lurked by night in the dead lilacs." As he shambles back toward civilization, Jeremiah is ambushed by One-eye, who kills him for the reward money.[125]

Back in Frankfort, Beaumont's downfall is paralleled by that of the relief movement—a compound of "political chicanery, ambition, the despair of the debtor, the laziness of louts, the cunning of speculators, and, even, a crazy dream of justice." The summer elections are a disaster for the party, and thus "daylight came, the ghosts fled, and a mortgage was again worth more than the paper it was written on, laziness was no longer put at a premium, the laborer was worthy of his hire, and the rich man did not bury his talent but put it out at twelve, or fifteen, or even twenty per cent. For daylight, too, brought its own crazy dream of justice. For all men believe in justice. Otherwise they would not be men. But there is the world and there is the idea, there are the Old Court and the New."[126]

The reader is left with an inescapable sense of disgust and revulsion. The book is anti-romantic in the extreme, a work whose existential anguish is well summed up in the book's last words: "Was all for naught?" In A. B. Guthrie's wonderful phrase, *World Enough and Time* is "a book of immense and mature disillusion."[127]

Warren took a number of liberties with the historical record: Beauchamp was never a protégé of Sharp's, nor was he a supporter of the new court. Anna is bled of her spirit and becomes a passive observer of Jeremiah's fixation. The two never escaped jail, let alone lived in a western island swamp. But Warren perceived something that escaped all other dramatists of the episode: the principals were acting out their self-prescribed and self-assigned roles. As he wrote by way of introduction, "The drama which Jeremiah Beaumont prepared was to be grand, with noble gestures and swelling periods, serious as blood. It was to be a tragedy, like those in the books he read as a boy. . . . But the actors were not well trained. At times even he, the hero, forgot his lines." A quarter century after the publication of *World Enough and Time,* Warren laid bare the import of the novel: "It's a story about the young idealist who can't find an object for his idealism, you see, he creates a dream world in which he can play the hero. It's a story about the romantic temperament. That's what it is. . . . He wants to find a cause that will justify a violent and heroic act, as it were. . . . He wants to create a romance for himself to be in."[128]

In early 1827, Timothy Flint, on hearing that "tragedies and novels have grown, or are to grow out of these transactions," predicted that any such tales will "terminate in flat farce." He was not at all far from the mark. The dramatizations that followed closely hewed to the hackneyed plot and characters the Beauchamps themselves created in the *Confession.* Believing they were embroidering a true story, the authors were hamstrung by previous fabrication. Such is why the one true literary genius of the nineteenth century who worked with the material—Edgar Allan Poe—felt so frustrated, and such is a good explanation for his quitting the project. Several years after abandoning *Politian,* Poe concluded that the Kentucky Tragedy was a barren soil, for "too little has been left for invention." Poe was correct, but he failed to grasp why: the episode had already been fictionalized. The "actual circumstances" with which these dramatists worked were the creation of previous dramatists—Anna and Jereboam Beauchamp, who themselves, as we have already seen, based their story on romantic cliché. The Kentucky Tragedy was already secondhand by the time Chivers and Poe and Hoffman and Simms tried their hands at it—fictions based on a fiction itself based on fictions. No wonder it was all so stale.[129]

The Beauchamps themselves would have been pleased with the characters trotted out by the playwrights and novelists. The Jereboams of the dramatizations are—as Simms described his Beauchampe—heroes of a "high, manly bearing, and honorable purpose." Barnes's Bragaldi was "formed all dignity and truth. His word was ever sacred, and he gloried . . . in the unblemished honour of his name." Yet, in the end, with the partial and unrealized exception of the enigmatic Politian, the Jereboams of early fictions are bland, one-dimensional figures—the best example being the utter nullity of Wallace Darrall in *The Heart of Kentucky*—whose virtue is marred only by "enthusiasm" and, when aroused, by an incapacity to restrain themselves. Only Jeremiah Beaumont is a figure of any real complexity and depth, for only Warren attempted to probe the inner workings of the Jereboam character to understand his actions.[130]

Time and again, the simplistically virtuous Jereboam character is undone not by any mistake of his own but by politics—specifically by the relief party, which unleashes a horde of perjurers to secure his conviction. Even in *World Enough and Time*, the one work in which Beauchamp is portrayed as pro-relief, it is the relief party that frames him. And although politics enters most of the stories, only the anonymous author of *Beauchamp*, Hannah Pittman, and, of course, Robert Penn Warren bothered to learn much about the relief war that formed the backdrop of the assassination. All others merely copied the Beauchamps' own depiction of a morally debased party that rigged a murder trial.

Almost without exception, the Anna character is the most interesting figure in these dramatizations. In particular, Alida de Roos and Margaret Cooper are fascinating figures who, in their bold challenges to the gender constraints of their day, faintly echo the real Anna. Some early treatments of the episode present Anna as conventionally insipid. The anonymous 1833 play *Beauchamp* has Ann reading the Bible under a weeping willow as faithful slaves frolic about. Barnes portrays Octavia Bragaldi as a truly innocent young woman who is not seduced but deceived into believing she and Count di Castelli are married (a conceit repeated by Hoffman and Pittman). Yet dramatists soon realized the darker possibilities of Anna, injecting a spirit, ferocity, and eroticism into the character. Chivers's Leoni declares, after the murder, that her "woes are baptized in his blood," while Poe's Lalage commits blasphemy, declaring that she will worship a crosslike dagger. Even Octavia, once slandered by Castelli, becomes bloodthirsty, inciting Francesco to commit murder. Simms's Margaret Cooper is a dark beauty possessed of "lurid fires of . . . intense, unmethodized ambition."[131]

Yet however assertive and unruly these Anna characters are, they ultimately serve to demonstrate that the female temperament is too frail for prolonged hate—such a burden, in these tales, either warps or maddens a woman. Repeatedly, the Anna character teeters on the precipice of insanity as the weight of revenge rests on her shoulders. "Voices whisper to me," Octavia groans, "and shadows move—Brain! Brain! Turn not with agony!" Later, she deliriously imagines herself drowning in blood. Hoffman likewise presents the female constitution as unable to support the strain; Alida's dream of vengeance is "strange" and "unfeminine" and puts a terrific strain on her "poor brain." Yet once Greyslaer lifts the burden of exacting retribution from her, she undergoes a remarkable and instant transformation from an Amazon to a docile helpmeet. The moral is clear: feminine vengeance leads to madness. A woman needs a man to relieve her of this unnatural burden—thus the necessity of the impetuous and honor-bound Jereboam.[132]

Few of the dramatists were subtle in their portrayal of Solomon Sharp, assigning him names such as Steale and Wolfe. Although some of the Sharp characters have momentary regrets for their diabolical behavior—Alonzo cries, "Oh! Conscience! Why wert thou given to torture me," and Poe's Castiglione truly agonizes over his sins—the rule was to portray the seducer as utterly depraved and, often, a sniveling coward as well. Walter Bradshawe is "a low-browed, lank-haired, saturnine man." Warham Sharpe is a moral vacuum, possessed of "a curling contempt upon the lip, which seemed to denote a cynical and sarcastic turn of mind" as well as a "caprice of character, and a flexibility of moral." Barnes's Castelli, meanwhile, is prone to blurt out such lines as "One object—power! One feeling—vast ambition!" before slandering the woman he has victimized. (Again, as with the Jereboam character, only Warren infuses the Sharp character with complexity; Fort feels the pain of "a suffering animal that has no words for what it feels," and, as it turns out, is "a great man" who loves Beaumont like a son.)

The Sharp character is almost uniformly portrayed as an uncaring husband and Mrs. Sharp as either neglected and miserable or herself wanting integrity. In *Conrad and Eudora* she perjures herself; in *Octavia Bragaldi* she is spoiled and immature; in *Politian* she is an unbearable scold. Simms depicts her as pathetic, a "lady in whose meek, sad countenance might be read the history of an unloved, neglected, but uncomplaining wife." In *World Enough and Time,* Mrs. Fort is a "poor ghost," old before her time, and Beaumont, peering through the window moments before the murder, muses, "She doesn't love him, I can see from her face that she does not." No devastated, broken-hearted widows in these accounts. And certainly no small children whose shrieks, as Amos Kendall described the actual murder scene, "pervaded the stillness of the night and echoed throughout the dark and melancholy mansion."

In this way, the novelists lessened the enormity of a murder that was committed, as this literature is quick to admit, as revenge for Sharp's spreading the rumor that Anna slept with a black man. In fact, none of these dramatizations have a problem with this premise; to almost all of these authors, that a man would be driven to murder by charges of interracial sex was the most natural thing in the world. In *Greyslaer,* once it becomes known that Bradshawe spread the rumor that the father of Alida's child was not a white man, murder becomes not only excusable but advisable, and Max goes free. In *The Heart of Kentucky,* the entire plot hinges on the fact that killing a man for such a slander is necessary—that the execution of Wallace is a mistake that the Kentucky of 1908 knows better than to make.

The dramatists repeated the simplistic conventions the Beauchamps had used—the nobility of Jereboam, the virtue of Anna, and the villainy of Solomon Sharp—and then in turn imitated each other, repeating scenes concocted by earlier authors. With the exception of Warren, all of the dramatists were too credulous, too naive, too anxious to believe the Beauchamps' fable. Distortions followed distortions, and the tales were repeated until they were accepted as fact.

The word "tragedy" began to be bandied about almost immediately after the deaths of the Beauchamps; by August 1, 1826, the *New Hampshire Gazette* used the phrase "Kentucky Tragedy," and the label stuck. But was it a tragedy? If defined as "a play or other literary work of a serious or sorrowful character, with a fatal or disastrous conclusion," then the term fits well enough. But if the word "tragedy" has overtones of a story in which the characters are swept along by vaguely understood and impersonal forces, the name may not be appropriate. The Beauchamps understood the social imperatives that surrounded them; their mistake was miscalculating how easily such forces, even if comprehended, could be manipulated.[133]

And if "tragedy" connotes a story with an unhappy yet "morally significant" or "meaningful" outcome, then "Kentucky Tragedy" is surely a misnomer. Bracketing for a moment any significance we of the twenty-first century might attach to the episode, and taking it in and of itself—understood as it was lived by the victims and survivors—the Kentucky Tragedy had no moral significance. The Beauchamps' claims to nobility and honor and the defense of wronged womanhood are all hollow. Certainly for the survivors of the episode, there was little meaning—for Eliza Sharp and her children, for Thomas and Sally Beauchamp, for Leander Sharp and his siblings, for the dozens of Kentuckians whom the Beauchamps slandered. As best we can tell, the Kentucky Tragedy was nothing but a sad farce unleashed because an unstable and capricious couple were pushed off the deep end by a rumor that the wife had had sex with a black man. What meaning the politicians and the politically enraged citizenry tried to assign the murder was soon rendered moot by Beauchamp's exoneration of Darby and, more broadly, by the end of the relief war. And thus, after all the strutting and fretting, the Kentucky Tragedy was not a tragedy at all. Fittingly, it turns out that a great work of fiction arrived at this essential insight sixty years ago: "Was it all for naught?"[134]

Yet human nature tends to abhor a vacuum of significance, and thus the events were given meaning—or, rather, America lazily adopted the meaning assigned by the Beauchamps. Maybe that is the significance of the Kentucky Tragedy: Anna and Jereboam had a better story than the truth. That was what the people wanted to hear; that was how the Beauchamps, in the end, got away with murder; and that is how, for generations of Americans, madness was made beautiful.

Coda

He left a Corsair's name to other times,
Linked with one virtue, and a thousand crimes.

—Byron, *The Corsair*

In 1835, Samuel Q. Richardson, one of Beauchamp's three lawyers and himself known for his volatility, was shot dead at the age of forty-four by John U. Waring. The motive was unclear—either "family differences" (Richardson was related to Waring's wife) or resentment over Richardson's successfully arguing the state's case in *Commonwealth v. John U. Waring.*

Eleven years later, in March 1846, the psychopathic Waring was himself murdered, shot in the head in Versailles, Kentucky. One newspaper cheerfully relayed the gory details: "Upon examination it was found that the ball had entered the skull [of Waring] just above the left eye, which it cut out, passed down through the mouth cutting the root of his tongue, and buried itself in the lungs." His killer was never found; no one seems to have minded.[1]

Three years after Beauchamp's hanging, John Pope was appointed territorial governor of Arkansas. In 1835, he resumed the practice of law in Springfield, Kentucky; in 1837, he was elected to Congress as a Whig. After serving three terms, he was defeated for reelection in 1842. He died three years later, on July 12, 1845, at the age of seventy-five.

On July 29, 1826, *Niles' Register* reported that John F. Lowe had been shot and intimated that it was due to his refusal "to give the testimony desired." The account was completely false; Lowe lived to be sixty-eight years old, dying in 1854.

Patrick Henry Darby, having worn out his welcome in yet another town, moved from Frankfort to Brandenburg, the Ohio River town in which he falsely claimed to have met Beauchamp. There, in December 1829, he died. The *Kentucky Reporter* gave Darby a one-line obituary.[2]

Amos Kendall campaigned furiously for Andrew Jackson in the 1828 presidential election and was instrumental in winning Kentucky for Old Hickory. The new president rewarded Kendall with a position as fourth auditor of the Treasury and later as postmaster general. Yet it was as a member of the notorious Kitchen Cabinet that Kendall became both influential and famous. As a confidant of Jackson's, Kendall authored the famous bank veto message, the defining statement of Jacksonian antipathy toward the "monied aristocracy" that millions believed was undermining American republicanism. In 1845, after a number of lean years, Kendall had the good fortune to become Samuel F. B. Morse's agent just as the new telegraphic technology was becoming profitable. He died a millionaire in 1869.[3]

Like Kendall, Francis Blair became an ardent Jacksonian, and in part thanks to Kendall's influence in the Jackson administration, he was given the responsibility of establishing the organ of the Democratic Party, the *Washington Globe,* which he would edit for fifteen years. "Blar"—as Andrew Jackson referred to him—was also a member of the Kitchen Cabinet and was one of the primary architects of the modern Democratic Party. Improbably, twenty years later he became as well a founder of the Republican Party—he had tirelessly opposed the spread of slavery westward, and it was at his estate in Maryland that Charles Sumner recuperated from the beating he suffered at the hands of Preston Brooks on the floor of the Senate. Five years later still, it was Blair whom Abraham Lincoln delegated to offer Robert E. Lee the command of Union forces. After the war he became an advocate of both a lenient Reconstruction and of labor unions' struggle against what he saw as a resurrection of the moneyed aristocracy that Jackson battled. He died in 1876 at the age of eighty-five.

John J. Crittenden was reelected to the Kentucky House of Representatives from 1829 to 1832. (Although he had been nominated in 1828 by President John Quincy Adams as an associate justice of the U.S. Supreme Court, he had failed to win Senate confirmation.) In 1835 he was again elected to the U.S. Senate as a Whig and served until 1841, when he was made William Henry Harrison's attorney general. Resigning after Harrison's death, Crittenden returned to the Senate. In 1848, he was elected governor of Kentucky, a position he resigned two years later to become the U.S. attorney general once again, this time under President Millard Fillmore. Reelected to the U.S. Senate in 1854, Crittenden served until March 3, 1861. For all of his success, however, he is today most widely remembered for his failed efforts to avert the sectional crisis in early 1861. He died in Frankfort on July 26, 1863, and is buried in the Frankfort Cemetery, not far from Solomon Sharp.

Thomas Beauchamp was reappointed Simpson County justice of the peace in 1828 and in 1831 was elected sheriff. He lived into his eighties, dying just before the Civil War.

Eliza Sharp never remarried. In 1829, her brother-in-law, Leander Sharp, wrote that Eliza, "despairing of justice on earth, . . . expects it at the hand of her Redeemer and her God, at whose altar she has long been a pious, humble, and sincere worshipper." In November 1840, president-elect William Henry Harrison visited her, "the daughter of his old companion in arms." His wife being ill, Harrison asked Eliza if she would "preside" over the White House, but she "declined, preferring the quiet life of her home and the care of her family." Solomon had left her an ample estate, and she and her children lived in material comfort. When she died in 1844 at the age of forty-six, her will left to her youngest son, Solomon Leander Sharp, "the portrait of my dear, dear husband, to me the most valued article I have to bequeath."[4]

Solomon Sharp's daughter, Jane Maxwell Sharp, six years old at the time of her father's murder, became the wife of William D. Reed, a lawyer of note, and moved to Louisville. They had seven children, five boys and two girls. Jane was an opinionated and spirited woman; at her death sometime after 1898, her will left varying amounts of money to her grandchildren, more to the three granddaughters named after her. John M. Sharp, the Sharps' first son, built a substantial estate. In 1861, the thirty-eight-year-old father of four became a colonel on the staff of General Simon B. Buckner in the Confederate army. In May 1863, while returning from Europe, where he had been sent on a governmental mission for the Confederacy, he died in a shipwreck. John's younger brother, Solomon Leander Sharp, graduated Centre College in Kentucky in 1843 and, after studying law in New Orleans and practicing for a while in Chicago, became a prominent and influential citizen of Bardstown, Kentucky. He married Anna Grundy and had four children. Like his older brother, he established an estate outside Louisville. In 1859, he vainly protested the depiction of his father in William Savage's play *Sybil*, which was playing at the time in Louisville. Unlike those of so many Kentuckians, his fortunes survived the Civil War. He died in 1878.[5]

After the death of the Beauchamps, Dr. Leander Sharp devoted himself to the exoneration of his brother: writing the *Vindication*, discouraging authors from dramatizing the Kentucky Tragedy, protesting newspapers' depictions of his brother. As he explained in an 1829 letter printed in Duff Green's *U.S. Telegraph*, "Perhaps it is a hopeless task, to attempt to conquer the impression made on the minds of men, by the manner in which Mr. and Mrs. Beauchamp died, followed up by his confession; but in making the effort, I feel that I discharge a sacred duty." Thereafter, Leander quickly disappears from the historical record. Whatever taste for politics Dr. Sharp had died with his brother. Lewis Sanders Jr. wrote to Francis P. Blair in early 1831, "I have been thinking of D. Sharp [to run for the General Assembly]. He has money and he has a capacity for electioneering. I spoke to him on the subject, he seemed to decline it." Dr. Sharp continued to live with his brother's family and never married. He died at an advanced age in Frankfort, leaving everything to Solomon and Eliza's children and grandchildren. He is buried near his beloved brother.[6]

Anna and Jereboam's grave lies on a hill just off Taylorsville Road, about a quarter mile past downtown Bloomfield, Kentucky (population: 845). There is not much to see. The original tombstone has become all but illegible, although a more recent marker has been erected to help the reader discern their epitaph.

Solomon and Eliza lie in Frankfort Cemetery, where their children had their remains moved in the 1850s. Solomon's grave is inscribed "To father Solomon P. Sharp: was assassinated while extending the hand of hospitality on the morning of Nov. 7, 1825, in the 38th year of his age." And then: "What thou knowest not now, thou shall know hereafter."

Notes

INTRODUCTION

Epigraph: Beauchamp quoted in *Frankfort (KY) Commentator and Constitutional Advocate,* November 25, 1826.

1. For descriptions of Jereboam Beauchamp (pronounced "BEECH-um") that day and conditions along the road to Frankfort, see "Beauchamp's Trial" in Loren J. Kallsen, ed., *The Kentucky Tragedy: A Problem in Romantic Attitudes* (Indianapolis: Bobbs-Merrill, 1963), 208–9, 301, 308, 302. Vincent Nolte described meeting John James Audubon in 1811 in a Pennsylvania tavern: the naturalist was sitting by the fire, "a Madras handkerchief wound around his head, exactly in the style of the French mariners, or laborers, in a seaport town." *The Memoirs of Vincent Nolte: Reminiscences in the Period of Anthony Adverse, or Fifty Years in Both Hemispheres* (1854; repr., New York: Watt, 1934), 177.

2. Robert Penn Warren, *World Enough and Time: A Romantic Novel* (New York: Random House, 1950), 116, 3–4. Warren's book, the last and the greatest of the novels inspired by the Kentucky Tragedy, is discussed at length in chapter 10. The first book-length history of the episode, *The Beauchamp-Sharp Tragedy: An Episode of Kentucky History during the Middle 1820's* (Frankfort, KY: Roberts, 1950), is a short narrative by the amateur historian J. Winston Coleman Jr. J. W. Cooke (who is himself, incidentally, a descendant of Anna Cooke Beauchamp) brings to light a good deal of information concerning the episode in a series of articles: "'Pride and Depravity': A Preliminary Examination of the Beauchamp-Sharp Affair," *Border States* 6 (1987): 1–12; "Portrait of a Murderess: Anna Cook(e) Beauchamp," *Filson Club Historical Quarterly* 65 (1991): 209–30; and "The Life and Death of Colonel Solomon P. Sharp," pt. 1, "Uprightness and Inventions; Snares and Nets," *Filson Club Historical Quarterly* 72 (1998): 24–41, and pt. 2, "A Time to Weep and a Time to Mourn," *Filson Club Historical Quarterly* 72 (1998): 121–51. Dickson Bruce, in "Sentimentalism and Honor in the Early American Republic: Revisiting the Kentucky Tragedy," *Mississippi Quarterly* 55 (2002): 185–208, and "The Kentucky Tragedy and the Transformation of Politics in the Early American Republic," *American Transcendental Quarterly* 17 (2003): 181–95, explores the linkages between the murder and broader political and social currents of the era. His recently published *The Kentucky Tragedy: A Story of Conflict and Change in Antebellum America* (Baton Rouge: Loui-

siana State University Press, 2006) finds the primary significance not in the episode itself but in how the numerous dramatizations that appeared over the next thirty-five years reflected transformations in American society. The Kentucky Tragedy has also been briefly explored in several other works, including Bertram Wyatt-Brown, *Southern Honor: Ethics and Behavior in the Old South* (New York: Oxford University Press, 1982), 306–7, and Catherine Clinton, *The Plantation Mistress: Woman's World in the Old South* (New York: Pantheon, 1982), 119.

3. Dickson Bruce, who has done admirable work on the Kentucky Tragedy and its cultural implications, adopts an essentially agnostic stance when it comes to the events themselves: "No one can be exactly sure to what extent the murder was the result of a private vendetta involving mainly the Beauchamps and Sharp and to what extent it was an assassination organized by Sharp's political opponents, including, perhaps, Beauchamp." Bruce, "Sentimentalism and Honor," 188. Likewise, Nettie Henry Glenn asserts that "history will never really know where fiction leaves off and fact begins." Nettie Henry Glenn, *Early Frankfort, Kentucky, 1786–1861* (n.p.: Glenn, 1986), 129.

4. *The Confession of Jereboam O. Beauchamp, Who Was Executed at Frankfort, Ky on the 7th of July, 1826* (Bloomfield, KY: Holmes, 1826); Leander Sharp, *Vindication of the Character of the Late Col. Solomon P. Sharp* (Frankfort, KY: Kendall, 1827); Coleman, *Beauchamp-Sharp Tragedy,* 69n8; J. G. Dana and R. S. Thomas, *Beauchamp's Trial: A Report of the Trial of Jereboam O. Beauchamp before the Franklin Circuit Court in May 1826 upon an Indictment for the Murder of Col. Solomon P. Sharp* (Frankfort, KY: Hodges, 1826); *Frankfort (KY) Argus of Western America,* May 31, July 7, July 14, 1826. Also see *The Confession of Jereboam O. Beauchamp,* ed. Robert D. Bamberg (Philadelphia: University of Pennsylvania Press, 1966).

5. W. B. Gates, "William Gilmore Simms and the Kentucky Tragedy," *American Literature* 32 (1960): 162; Coleman, *Beauchamp-Sharp Tragedy,* 45. J. W. Cooke contends that "all sources of information concerning the tragedy are tainted." Cooke, "Portrait of a Murderess," 216. Dickson Bruce likewise asserts that "it is impossible to know who was telling the truth about the murder of Solomon Sharp. All conflict, all are self-serving, and none appears particularly reliable." Bruce, *Kentucky Tragedy,* 47. *The Letters of Ann Cook, Late Mrs. Beauchamp, to Her Friend in Maryland, Containing Short History of the Life of That Remarkable Woman* (Washington, DC: n.p., 1826) is, in fact, not a source document but an epistolary novel, as discussed at greater length in chapter 9. See Jack E. Surrency, "The Kentucky Tragedy and Its Primary Sources," in *No Fairer Land: Studies in Southern Literature before 1900,* ed. J. Lasley Dameron and James W. Mathews (Troy, NY: Whitston, 1986), 110–23, and Fred M. Johnson, "Letters of Ann Cooke: Fact or Factoid," *Border States* 6 (1987): 13–21.

6. Richard Wightman Fox, "These Hours of Backward Clearness," *Common-place* 1, no. 2 (2001), http://www.historycooperative.org/journals/cp/vol-01/no-02/author/index.shtml; Richard Wightman Fox, *Trials of Intimacy: Love and Loss in the Beecher-Tilton Scandal* (Chicago: University of Chicago Press, 1999), 5.

7. "Beauchamp's Confession" in Kallsen, *Kentucky Tragedy,* 3.

8. Sharp, *Vindication*, 140.

9. Arthur O. Lovejoy, "The Meaning of Romanticism for the Historian of Ideas," *Journal of the History of Ideas* 2 (1941): 259, 258, 261; Jacques Barzun, *From Dawn to Decadence: 1500 to Present; 500 Years of Western Cultural Life* (New York: HarperCollins, 2000), 466–67. More recently, Warren Breckman has written that "Romanticism itself is marked by an extreme pluralism that seems to defy all efforts to identify a specific set of essential Romantic elements" and that, in fact, "contradiction itself should be recognized as a defining feature of Romanticism." Warren Breckman, *European Romanticism: A Brief History with Documents* (Boston: Bedford/St. Martins, 2008), 2–3. One of the very few exceptions to historians' lack of interest in romanticism per se is Rollin G. Osterweis, *Romanticism and Nationalism in the Old South* (New Haven, CT: Yale University Press, 1949), the influence of which has not been substantial. The scholar of early America who has taken the romantic movement most seriously—at least as it pertains to the antebellum South—is Michael O'Brien. See his *Rethinking the South: Essays in Intellectual History* (Baltimore: Johns Hopkins University Press, 1988) and *Conjectures of Order: Intellectual Life and the American South, 1810–1860* (Chapel Hill: University of North Carolina Press, 2004). Andrew Burstein's *Sentimental Democracy: The Evolution of America's Romantic Self-Image* (New York: Hill and Wang, 1999), despite its subtitle, does not tell us much about the influence of romanticism in early America. David Reynolds's *Beneath the American Renaissance: The Subversive Imagination in the Age of Emerson and Melville* (New York: Knopf, 1988), although it is essentially a work of literary criticism, ably examines social and cultural currents of the mid-nineteenth century.

10. Henry F. May, "After the Enlightenment: A Prospectus," in *Divided Hearts: Essays on Protestantism and the Enlightenment in America* (New York: Oxford University Press, 1991), 195–96; Henry Clay to Josiah S. Johnston, August 2, 1826, in *The Papers of Henry Clay*, ed. James F. Hopkins and Mary W. M. Hargreaves (Lexington: University Press of Kentucky, 1959–1992), 5:586. See Sean Wilentz, *The Rise of American Democracy: Jefferson to Lincoln* (New York: Norton, 2005), and Daniel Walker Howe, *What Hath God Wrought: The Transformation of America, 1815–1848* (New York: Oxford University Press, 2007). Recent trends in Enlightenment historiography are summarized in Darren Staloff, "Secular Culture in Search of an Early American Enlightenment," in *A Companion to Colonial America*, ed. Daniel Vickers (Malden, MA: Blackwell, 2003), 389–407.

11. Isaiah Berlin, "The Apotheosis of the Romantic Will: The Revolt against the Myth of an Ideal World," in *The Proper Study of Mankind: An Anthology of Essays* (New York: Farrar, Straus and Giroux, 1998), 554–55, 565, 580; Isaiah Berlin, "The Counter-Enlightenment," in *Proper Study of Mankind*, 262; Breckman, *European Romanticism*, 38. Berlin sees romanticism as "a deep and radical revolt against the central tradition of Western thought"—the notions that "to all genuine questions there is one true answer and one only," that "the true answers to such questions are in principle knowable," and that "these true answers cannot clash with one another." Berlin, "Apotheosis of the Romantic Will," 563.

12. Lovejoy, "Meaning of Romanticism," 261. Henry May, in dissecting a similarly broad movement—the Enlightenment—diagrams successive, overlapping Enlightenments: the moderate, the skeptical, the revolutionary, and the didactic. Henry F. May, *The Enlightenment in America* (New York: Oxford University Press, 1976).

13. Breckman, *European Romanticism,* 8. For the subversive nature of early American seduction novels, see Cathy N. Davidson, *Revolution and the Word: The Rise of the Novel in America* (New York: Oxford University Press, 1986).

14. I do not mean to suggest that these tales, as hackneyed as many of them were, do not tell us much about antebellum America. For a number of trenchant insights, see Bruce, *Kentucky Tragedy.*

15. Alexis de Tocqueville, *Democracy in America* (New York: Vintage Books, 1990), 2:207. See also Victoria Bynum, *Unruly Women: The Politics of Social and Sexual Control in the Old South* (Chapel Hill: University of North Carolina Press, 1992).

16. "Republicanism in Old and New Contexts," *William and Mary Quarterly* 43 (1986): 20–34, esp. 28–29; "A Different Kind of Independence: The Postwar Restructuring of the Historical Study of Early America," *William and Mary Quarterly* 50 (1993): 261, 248.

17. Jill Lepore, "Historians Who Love Too Much: Reflections on Microhistory and Biography," *Journal of American History* 88 (2001): 142. In her study of a late-nineteenth-century murder in Lunenburg County, Virginia, Suzanne Lebsock discovers that "time and again . . . people acted bravely and against type": an illiterate young African American woman defends herself in a courtroom with astounding skill; a dozen white men risk life and limb to prevent a lynching of African Americans. Suzanne Lebsock, *A Murder in Virginia: Southern Justice on Trial* (New York: Norton, 2003), 18. Likewise, Melvin Patrick Ely finds antebellum Virginians deviating "from the path their social ideology prescribed" by tolerating the existence of a free black community. Melvin Patrick Ely, *Israel on the Appomattox: A Southern Experiment in Black Freedom from the 1790s through the Civil War* (New York: Knopf, 2004), 440. As Rhys Isaac has recently maintained, history "must stand tall to remind the others of the power of contingency in human life." Rhys Isaac, "History Made from Stories Found: Seeking a Microhistory That Matters," *Common-place* 6, no. 1 (2005), http://www.historycooperative.org/journals/cp/vol-06/no-01/author/. See also Suzanne Lebsock, "Snow Falling on Magnolias," in *Shapers of Southern History: Autobiographical Reflections,* ed. John Boles (Athens: University of Georgia Press, 2004), 307–8.

18. See James M. McPherson, *Battle Cry of Freedom: The Civil War Era* (New York: Oxford University Press, 1988), 857–62, and David Hackett Fischer, *Paul Revere's Ride* (New York: Oxford University Press, 1994), xiv–xv, 374, 423. For explicitly counterfactual studies, see Robert Cowley, ed., *What If? The World's Foremost Military Historians Imagine What Might Have Been* (New York: Putnam, 1999); Robert Cowley, ed., *What If? 2: Eminent Historians Imagine What Might Have Been*

(New York: Putnam, 2001); and Niall Ferguson, ed., *Virtual History: Alternatives and Counterfactuals* (New York: Basic Books, 1999). Other fascinating counterfactual studies include John Murrin, "No Awakening, No Revolution? More Counterfactual Speculations," *Reviews in American History* 11 (1983): 161–71; James Axtell, "Colonial America without the Indians: Counterfactual Reflections," *Journal of American History* 73 (1987): 981–96; and Gary Kornblith, "Rethinking the Coming of the Civil War: A Counterfactual Exercise," *Journal of American History* 90 (2003): 76–105.

19. Gordon S. Wood, *The Purpose of the Past: Reflections on the Uses of History* (New York: Penguin, 2008), 42–43.

20. Richard D. Brown, "Microhistory and the Post-modern Challenge," *Journal of the Early Republic* 23 (2003): 18–19; Wood, *Purpose of the Past,* 129; Edward Gray, "The Little Picture, or Who's Afraid of the Big Question?" *Common-place* 6, no. 4 (2006), http://www.historycooperative.org/journals/cp/vol-06/no-04/talk/; Lepore, "Historians Who Love Too Much," 131, 133; Robert Darnton, "It Happened One Night," review of *A Sentimental Murder: Love and Madness in the Eighteenth Century,* by John Brewer, *New York Review of Books,* June 24, 2004, 60–64.

21. As some readers will have doubtlessly perceived, I adhere to the old-fashioned notion that there is a "there" back there, that it can be approximated, and that all approximations are not created equal. For an extremely lucid and persuasive discussion of theoretical matters, one that suggests the increasingly obvious aridity of postmodern theory, see Thomas Haskell, *Objectivity Is Not Neutrality: Explanatory Schemes in History* (Baltimore: Johns Hopkins University Press, 1998), especially the title essay, which focuses on one example of the disjunction between professed postmodernist sensibilities and actual practice. Such disjunction—if Joyce Appleby, Lynn Hunt, Margaret Jacob, and Elizabeth Fox-Genovese, among others, are correct in arguing that postmodern history is an oxymoron—may well be unavoidable. See Joyce Appleby, Lynn Hunt, and Margaret Jacob, *Telling the Truth about History* (New York: Norton, 1994), 237, and Elizabeth Fox-Genovese, "History in a Postmodern World," in *Reconstructing History: The Emergence of a New Historical Society,* ed. Elizabeth Fox-Genovese and Elisabeth Lasch-Quinn (New York: Routledge, 1999), 40–55. Let me add that the purpose of this book is not to needlessly "complicate our understanding" of anything. Rather, it is to clarify a series of events already quite complex enough. For the argument that "complexity for its own sake is no virtue," see Russell Jacoby, "Not to Complicate Matters, but . . . ," *Chronicle of Higher Education,* February 29, 2008, B5.

1. THE ARCHITECT OF HIS OWN FORTUNES

1. Lewis Collins, *Historical Sketches of Kentucky* (1847; repr., New York: Arno Press, 1971), 311; John Rowan, John Adair, R. M. Johnson, and W. T. Barry to Eliza Sharp, n.d., reprinted in H. Levin, ed., *The Lawyers and Lawmakers of Kentucky* (1897; repr., Easley, SC: Southern Historical Press, 1982), 113. See also Gordon S. Wood, *Radicalism of the American Revolution* (New York: Knopf, 1992), and Joyce

Appleby, *Inheriting the Revolution: The First Generation of Americans* (Cambridge, MA: Harvard University Press, 2000).

2. Levin, *Lawyers and Lawmakers,* 110.

3. George D. Blakey, "Men I Have Known" (typescript, n.d.), 52, Kentucky Library, Department of Library Special Collections, Western Kentucky University, Bowling Green (hereafter cited as WKU). Although born in England, Thomas Sharp fought for American independence against both Loyalists and American Indians. He first saw action on July 20, 1776, at the Battle of Long Island Flats near Kingsport, Tennessee, in which the Virginia militia under Colonel William Russell defeated seven hundred Chickamauga Cherokees led by Dragging Canoe. Daughters of the American Revolution, *Lineage Book, National Society of the Daughters of the American Revolution* 12 (1896): 200. For the backcountry generally, see Richard Beeman, *The Evolution of the Southern Backcountry: A Case Study of Lunenburg County, Virginia, 1746–1832* (Philadelphia: University of Pennsylvania Press, 1984); Michael Puglisi, ed., *Diversity and Accommodation: Essays on the Cultural Composition of the Virginia Frontier* (Knoxville: University of Tennessee Press, 1997); and Gregory H. Nobles, "Breaking into the Backcountry: New Approaches to the Early American Frontier, 1750–1800," *William and Mary Quarterly* 46 (1989): 641–70.

4. "Memoranda Made by Thomas R. Joynes on a Journey to the States of Ohio and Kentucky, 1810," *William and Mary Quarterly,* 1st ser., 10 (1902): 222–23; Durrett codices 94, 40, Reuben T. Durrett Collection, University of Chicago Library, Chicago. See also Joan Cashin, *A Family Venture: Men and Women on the Southern Frontier* (New York: Oxford University Press, 1991), and Daniel Blake Smith, "'This Heaven in Idea': Image and Reality on the Kentucky Frontier," in *The Buzzel about Kentuck: Settling the Promised Land,* ed. Craig Thompson Friend (Lexington: University Press of Kentucky, 1999), 77–98. One of the most poignant accounts of the situation of a frontier wife and mother comes from *Democracy in America.* Although Tocqueville wrote of the Michigan frontier fifty years after the settlement of Kentucky, the woman he described would have been easily recognizable to pioneers of the late eighteenth century: "By the side of the hearth sits a woman with a baby on her lap; she nods to us without disturbing herself. . . . Her delicate limbs appear shrunken, her features are drawn in, her eye is mild and melancholy; her whole physiognomy bears marks of religious resignation, a deep quiet of all passions, and some sort of natural and tranquil firmness, ready to meet all the ills of life without fearing and without braving them." Tocqueville, *Democracy in America,* 2:364.

5. Gabriel Lewis to Peter [?], May 25, 1806, quoted in Stephen A. Aron, *How the West Was Lost: The Transformation of Kentucky from Daniel Boone to Henry Clay* (Baltimore: Johns Hopkins University Press, 1996), 156; Christopher Waldrep, "Opportunity on the Frontier South of the Green," in Friend, *Buzzel about Kentuck,* 153–72; Joan Wells Coward, *Kentucky in the New Republic: The Process of Constitution Making* (Lexington: University Press of Kentucky, 1979), 54; Fredrika Johanna Teute, "Land, Liberty, and Labor in the Post-Revolutionary Era: Kentucky as the Promised Land" (PhD diss., Johns Hopkins University, 1988), 215; Richard E. Ellis,

Jeffersonian Crisis: Courts and Politics in the Young Republic (New York: Oxford University Press, 1971), 149.

6. Aron, *How the West Was Lost,* 153–56.

7. Jacob Young, *Autobiography of a Pioneer* (Cincinnati: Cranston and Curts, 1857), 34; Daniel Drake, *Pioneer Life in Kentucky, 1785–1800* (New York: Schuman, 1948), 11; Harry Toulmin, *The Western Country in 1793: Reports on Kentucky and Virginia,* ed. Marion Tinling and Godfrey Davies (San Marino, CA: Huntington Library, 1948), 80; Chilton Allan, interview by John Shane, ca. 1840, 11CC53, Lyman Copeland Draper Manuscript Collection, Wisconsin Historical Society, Madison.

8. Blakey, "Men I Have Known," 52; tax lists, Logan County, KY, 1795–1805, microfilm, Kentucky Department for Libraries and Archives, Frankfort (hereafter cited as KDLA); Cooke, "Uprightness and Inventions," 27. In 1800, almost one-third of the households owned no land; another 21.3 percent owned 1–199 acres; and 32.7 percent owned 200–299 acres. Aron, *How the West Was Lost,* 205, table A-8. In 1800 in Logan County, 20.4 percent of households owned slaves. Most of them owned one to four slaves; no one owned more than twenty (although by 1810, thirteen households would). Coward, *Kentucky in the New Republic,* 63, table 6. See also Aron, *How the West Was Lost,* 206, table A-9.

9. Malcolm J. Rohrbough, *The Trans-Appalachian Frontier* (New York: Oxford University Press, 1978), 4; "Diary of Rev. David Barrow" (typescript, [1795]), 23, WKU; Daniel Blowe, *A Geographical, Historical, Commercial, and Agricultural View of the United States of America* (London: Edwards and Knibb, 1820), 593; Allan, interview, Draper Collection; Michel Chevalier, *Society, Manners, and Politics in the United States,* ed. John William Ward (1837; repr., Ithaca, NY: Cornell University Press, 1961), 207. For a very sharp analysis of the effects of the endemic violence that attended the settling of Kentucky, see the first chapter of Ellen Eslinger, *Citizens of Zion: The Social Origins of the Camp Meeting* (Knoxville: University of Tennessee Press, 2000), 3–27.

10. For the persistence of old world cultural habits, see Wyatt-Brown, *Southern Honor,* and David Hackett Fischer, *Albion's Seed: Four British Folkways in America* (New York: Oxford University Press, 1988).

11. *Autobiography of Peter Cartwright,* ed. Charles L. Wallis (New York: Abingdon, 1956), 30, 33; Elliot J. Gorn, "'Gouge and Bite, Pull Hair and Scratch': The Social Significance of Fighting in the Southern Backcountry," *American History Review* 90 (1985): 18–43.

12. Boynton Merrill Jr., *Jefferson's Nephews: A Frontier Tragedy,* 2nd ed. (Lexington: University Press of Kentucky, 1987), 226–27. The coroner's report in the case, reprinted in Robert Penn Warren, *Brother to Dragons: A Tale in Verse and Voices* (Baton Rouge: Louisiana State University Press, 1996), 134–35, underscores the sheer barbarity of the attack: "The said Jimmy received several wounds in his head some of which appeared to have been made by strokes of a Club or Clubs[;] in one place on his head the Scull seemed indented[;] one wound in his head was about five inches long another about three inches long at right angles from the other[;] those were

apparently made by two or more strokes beside which we found one considerable burned spot on his back[;] his nose was badly hurt[;] we find the deceased was badly kicked about his face by means of all which wounds the said Indian has lost his life."

13. Merrill, *Jefferson's Nephews,* 256–65; James Hall, *Letters from the West* (1828; repr., Gainesville, FL: Scholars' Facsimiles and Reprints, 1976), 269. For accounts of the Harpes' rampages, see Hall, *Letters from the West,* 265–82; Otto Rothert, *The Outlaws of Cave-In Rock: Historical Accounts of the Famous Highwaymen and River Pirates Who Operated in Pioneer Days upon the Ohio and Mississippi Rivers and over the Old Natchez Trace* (Cleveland: Clark, 1924), 55–157, 241–66; W. D. Snively Jr. and Louanna Furbee, *Satan's Ferryman: A True Tale of the Old Frontier* (New York: Ungar, 1968), 46–56; and *Westward into Kentucky: The Narrative of Daniel Trabue,* ed. Chester Young (Lexington: University Press of Kentucky, 1982), 146–51, 195–98. Trabue's twelve-year-old son was brutally murdered by the Harpes.

14. Breckinridge quoted in Ellis, *Jeffersonian Crisis,* 148; "Memoranda Made by Thomas R. Joynes," 223.

15. *Autobiography of Peter Cartwright,* 30; Christine Heyrman, *Southern Cross: The Beginnings of the Bible Belt* (New York: Knopf, 1997), 128; Reverend John Rankin quoted in Eslinger, *Citizens of Zion,* 193; T. Marshall Smith, *Legends of the War of Independence and Early Settlements,* quoted in Edward Coffman, *The Story of Logan County* (Nashville: Parthenon Press, 1962), 82; John Boles, *The Great Revival* (Lexington: University Press of Kentucky, 1972), 44, 18; McGready quoted in Eslinger, *Citizens of Zion,* 229.

16. *Journal of the House of Representatives of the Commonwealth of Kentucky,* 1818, 138, 216; James C. Klotter, "Two Centuries of the Lottery in Kentucky," *Register of the Kentucky Historical Society* 87 (1989): 405–25; Eslinger, *Citizens of Zion,* 231; Christopher Waldrep, "The Making of a Border State Society: James McGready, the Great Revival, and the Prosecution of Profanity in Kentucky," *American History Review* 99 (1994): 767–84; Mary P. Ryan, *Cradle of the Middle Class: The Family in Oneida County, New York, 1790–1865* (Cambridge: Cambridge University Press, 1981), 18–59. After the murder, two ministers—Silas M. Noel and Gideon Blackburn—testified that Solomon had expressed to them his belief in "the authenticity of the Holy Scripture" and his "profound veneration for the Christian religion as a system of practical truth." Sharp, *Vindication,* 10.

17. Henry Cogswell Knight [Arthur Singleton, pseud.], *Letters from the South and West* (Boston: Richardson and Lord, 1824), 96–97. For more general critiques of the evangelicals and their subculture, see Heyrman, *Southern Cross.*

18. Heyrman, *Southern Cross,* 65–66. For a sample of deist articles in Kentucky newspapers, see *Maysville (KY) Eagle,* November 8, 1816, and January 24, 1817. In 1795, the Reverend David Barrow wrote that deists were "much strengthened . . . by a late publication of Thomas Paine which has lately appeared among them." "Diary of Rev. David Barrow," 27, WKU. Christopher Grasso makes a convincing case that historians have underestimated both the extent and the subtle influence of religious doubt in the early republic in "Skepticism and American Faith: Infidels, Converts,

and Religious Doubt in the Early Nineteenth Century," *Journal of the Early Republic* 22 (2002): 465–508.

19. H. C. Northcott, *Biography of Rev. Benjamin Northcott* (Cincinnati: Western Methodist Book Concern, 1875), 19; Boles, *Great Revival,* 58; Merrill, *Jefferson's Nephews,* 198–99; Heyrman, *Southern Cross,* 3–27; F. A. Michaux, *Travels to the Westward of the Allegheny Mountains, in the States of the Ohio, Kentucky, and Tennessee, in the Year 1802* (London: Barnard and Sultzer, 1805), 196; *Memorandums of a Tour Made by Josiah Espy in the States of Ohio and Kentucky and Indiana Territory in 1805* (Cincinnati: Clarke, 1870), 24; James Gallaher, *The Western Sketch-Book* (Boston: Crocker and Brewster, 1850), 68; Stuart quoted in Robert Stuart Sanders, *The Reverend Robert Stuart, D.D., 1772–1856, a Pioneer in Kentucky Presbyterianism, and His Descendants* (Louisville, KY: Dunne Press, 1962), 57. In 1817, Joseph Cabell Breckinridge advised his little brother, Robert, "I have never known [revivals] to fail to operate infinite mischief to the cause of unfeigned and rational piety. Religion is neither fear, nor enthusiasm. It is not founded in despair—it cannot be support[ed] by terror. Wicked men may become alarmed from the recollection of their offenses, and weak minds may catch by sympathy the contagion of the passions. These are influences either corrupt, or transitory. To pray because it is the fashion—to importune heaven from a sudden dread of hell, is pitiful, is base. Shun all such silly and degenerate profaneness of God's mercy and grace. Either they don't understand religion, or they don't understand themselves." Joseph C. Breckinridge to Robert Jefferson Breckinridge, June 11, 1817, Breckinridge Family Papers, Manuscript Division, Library of Congress, Washington, DC.

20. Blakey, "Men I Have Known," 52.

21. Drake, *Pioneer Life in Kentucky,* 100.

22. William Savage, *Observation on Emigration to the United States of America* (London: Savage, 1819), 46; "Memoranda Made by Thomas R. Joynes," 222; Colonel Charles Lewis to Thomas Jefferson, September 17, 1810, quoted in Merrill, *Jefferson's Nephews,* 126; Knight, *Letters from the South and West,* 93.

23. Blakey, "Men I Have Known," 52; Drake, *Pioneer Life in Kentucky,* 240; Abraham Lincoln to Jesse Fell, December 20, 1859, in *Abraham Lincoln, Slavery, and the Civil War: Selected Writings and Speeches,* ed. Michael P. Johnson (Boston: Bedford/St. Martins, 2001), 15.

24. Cooke, "Uprightness and Inventions," 27; Sharp, *Vindication,* 4; *Frankfort (KY) Argus of Western America,* November 30, 1825; Solomon P. Sharp to Henry Clay, January 27, 1813, in *Papers of Henry Clay,* 1:777; *Frankfort (KY) Spirit of '76,* March 17, 1826; *Frankfort (KY) Harbinger,* August 10, 1825.

25. William Henry Perrin, ed., *County of Christian, Kentucky* (Chicago: Battey, 1884), 408; "Memoirs of Micah Taul," *Register of the Kentucky Historical Society* 27 (1929): 362; Robert Triplett, *Roland Trevor, or The Pilot of Human Life; Being an Autobiography of the Author* (Philadelphia: Lippincott, Grambo, 1853), 20.

26. Arthur K. Moore, *The Frontier Mind: A Cultural Analysis of the Kentucky Frontiersman* (Lexington: University of Kentucky Press, 1957), 58; George Huston,

Memories of the Eighty Years (Morganfield, KY: Sun Print, 1904), 142; Savage, *Observation on Emigration,* 24, 20.

27. Buchanan quoted in Lucius P. Little, *Ben Hardin: His Times and Contemporaries, with Selections from His Speeches* (Louisville, KY: Courier-Journal Job Printing, 1887), 352–53.

28. Sharp, *Vindication,* 8; *Russellville (KY) Mirror,* June 16, 1808. In all, there lived in Logan County, between 1800 and 1825, four governors of Kentucky, six governors of other states, six U.S. senators, and three men who would serve in a U.S. president's cabinet. According to tax lists, Sharp began living in Warren County in 1807. Tax lists, Warren County, KY, microfilm, KDLA.

29. "Memoirs of Micah Taul," 367; Sharp, *Vindication,* 4; Rowan et al. to Sharp, in Levin, *Lawyers and Lawmakers,* 113.

30. Little, *Ben Hardin,* 41; "Beauchamp's Confession" in Kallsen, *Kentucky Tragedy,* 18; Joseph Underwood to Edmund Rogers, March 15, 1812 (transcript), Underwood Collection, WKU; Levin, *Lawyers and Lawmakers,* 111; *Frankfort (KY) Commentator,* April 22, 1826; *Frankfort (KY) Argus of Western America,* November 30, 1825; Collins, *Historical Sketches of Kentucky,* 311–12; William B. Northcutt, diary, n.d., 148–51, microfilm, Kentucky Historical Society, Frankfort (hereafter cited as KHS). John Randolph, of all people, described Hardin thus: "Like a kitchen knife whetted on a brick, he cuts roughly but cuts deep." Randolph quoted in Little, *Ben Hardin,* 63.

31. *Frankfort (KY) Argus of Western America,* November 30, 1825; *Frankfort (KY) Spirit of '76,* March 17, 1826.

32. Rowan et al. to Sharp, in Levin, *Lawyers and Lawmakers,* 113; *Frankfort (KY) Spirit of '76,* March 17, 1826; *Frankfort (KY) Argus of Western America,* November 30, 1825.

33. *Frankfort (KY) Spirit of '76,* March 17, 1826; "Beauchamp's Trial" in Kallsen, *Kentucky Tragedy,* 193, 307; Sharp, *Vindication,* 4; "Beauchamp's Trial" in Kallsen, *Kentucky Tragedy,* 305.

34. Richard H. Collins, *History of Kentucky* (1882; repr., Frankfort: Kentucky Historical Society, 1966), 2:626–27; Randall Capps, *The Rowan Story: From Federal Hill to My Old Kentucky Home* (Bowling Green, KY: Homestead Press, 1976), 29; *Frankfort (KY) Argus of Western America,* December 7, 1825. Genealogist Sandra Gorin is the authority on the Hamilton trial. See Sandra Kaye Laughery Gorin, *Blood Runs in the Barrens: A Historical Look at the Murders of Barren County, Kentucky* (Glasgow, KY: Gorin Genealogical, 1993). Hamilton, it seems, was not guilty of the murder of Sanderson, although the evidence of his innocence was not discovered until fifty years later. R. H. Collins, *History of Kentucky,* 2:627.

35. Article 2, section 4 of the 1799 state constitution clearly mandates that "no person shall be a Representative who at the time of his election . . . hath not attained the age of twenty-four years."

36. Edward George Geoffrey Smith Stanley, Earl of Derby, *Journal of a Tour in America, 1824–1825* (London: n.p., 1930), 213, 218; *Kentucky Gazette,* April 16, 1811.

37. R. H. Collins, *History of Kentucky,* 2:27; Little, *Ben Hardin,* 41; *Journal of the House of Representatives of the Commonwealth of Kentucky,* 1818, 11. Although the remarks were issued by a committee, the piece was undoubtedly composed by Sharp, as he was not only the prime mover behind the bill but also the only committee member to have served when the bill was passed. For a brief description of taking the oath in March 1815, see *Autobiography of Amos Kendall,* ed. William Stickney (Boston: Lee and Shepard, 1872), 140.

38. *Kentucky Gazette,* September 15, 1812; Francis Wright, *Views of Society and Manners in America,* ed. Paul R. Baker (Cambridge, MA: Harvard University Press, 1963), 183; Collins, *Historical Sketches of Kentucky,* 68–69; *Journal of the House of Representatives of the Commonwealth of Kentucky,* 1811, 238; *Autobiography of Dr. J. J. Polk* (Louisville, KY: Morton, 1867), 15.

39. Levin, *Lawyers and Lawmakers,* 110. For an analysis of the early American militia as a proving ground for young men, as well as a forum in which embattled notions of manhood itself were clarified and strengthened, see Harry S. Laver, "Refuge of Manhood: Masculinity and the Militia Experience in Kentucky," in *Southern Manhood: Perspectives on Masculinity in the Old South,* ed. Craig Thompson Friend and Lorri Glover (Athens: University of Georgia Press, 2004), 1–21.

40. Elizabeth A. Perkins, *Border Life: Experience and Memory in the Revolutionary Ohio Valley* (Chapel Hill: University of North Carolina Press, 1998), esp. 132–41; Elias Pym Fordham, *Personal Narrative of Travels in Virginia, Maryland, Pennsylvania, Ohio, Indiana, Kentucky, and of a Residence in the Illinois Territory, 1817–1818,* ed. Frederic Austin Ogg (Cleveland: Clark, 1906), 177; Little, *Ben Hardin,* 20; Allan, interview, Draper Collection.

41. Samuel McKee quoted in *Annals of the Congress of the United States,* 13th Cong., 1st sess., 136; *Kentucky Gazette,* September 15, 1812; Robert Hamilton to Polly Hamilton, September 30, 1812, in "The Expeditions of Major-General Samuel Hopkins up the Wabash, 1812: The Letters of Captain Robert Hamilton," *Indiana Magazine of History* 43 (1947): 395.

42. Cooke, "Uprightness and Inventions," 30–32; James W. Hammack, *Kentucky and the Second American Revolution: The War of 1812* (Lexington: University Press of Kentucky, 1976), 44–46; C. Edward Skeen, *Citizen Soldiers in the War of 1812* (Lexington: University Press of Kentucky, 1999), 157–58; *Kentucky Gazette,* October 13, 1812, November 10, 1812. Hopkins himself would expend a good deal of energy attempting to restore his good name. In early 1813, he requested a court of inquiry to investigate accusations of incompetence that had been leveled at him. After convening in Frankfort, the court cleared Hopkins of all charges. *Kentucky Gazette,* February 16, 1813.

43. Perry M. Goldman and James S. Young, *The United States Congressional Directories, 1789–1840* (New York: Columbia University Press, 1973), 61–62, 70; John C. Calhoun to Martin Hardin, January 27, 1819, in *The Papers of John C. Calhoun,* ed. Robert L. Meriwether (Columbia: University of South Carolina Press, 1959–2003), 4:348–49. For the general importance of the boardinghouse fraternities, or "messes,"

which constituted the basic social and political units of the Capitol Hill community, see James S. Young, *The Washington Community, 1800–1828* (New York: Columbia University Press, 1966), esp. 98–109.

Although some historians are skeptical about claims of a close friendship between Calhoun and Sharp, they did in fact know one another well. At the inauguration of Kentucky governor John Adair in August 1820, Sharp gave a toast, exclaiming that "John C. Calhoun, if not the first is justly titled to be second, in the choice of the American people." The first, at least to Sharp's mind in 1820, was Henry Clay. Another version of Calhoun's compliment has him asserting that Sharp was "the ablest man of his age that had ever crossed the mountains." The comment may very well be apocryphal, but if by "age" Calhoun meant how old Sharp was (as opposed to the era in which they lived), then the remark's power is significantly reduced. How many men in their mid- to late twenties crossed the mountains to be members of Congress? One of the few, in fact, was Henry Clay. Although they shared a desire to go to war with Britain, Clay and Calhoun were also inordinately ambitious young men between whom some tensions existed. The remark, therefore, if authentic, could very well have been a subtle dig at Clay. Collins, *Historical Sketches of Kentucky,* 312.

44. *Annals of the Congress of the United States,* 13th Cong., 1st sess., 294; Young, *Washington Community,* 267; *Annals of the Congress of the United States,* 13th Cong., 1st sess., 295.

45. *Abridgement of the Debates of Congress,* 1857, 5:52; John Bowman to Stephen F. Austin, August 5, 1813, in *Annual Report of the American Historical Association for the Year 1919,* ed. Eugene C. Barker (Washington, DC: GPO, 1924), 227–28; *Annals of the Congress of the United States,* 13th Cong., 3rd sess., 746; *Annals of the Congress of the United States,* 14th Cong., 2nd sess., 734–35; *Annals of the Congress of the United States,* 13th Cong., 1st sess., 296; *Annals of the Congress of the United States,* 13th Cong., 3rd sess., 1166. The verses are apparently Sharp's own work, although J. W. Cooke speculates that Anna Cooke may have written the lines. For studies of early American militarism, see John Hope Franklin, *The Militant South, 1800–1861* (Cambridge, MA: Harvard University Press, 1956), and Marcus Cunliffe, *Soldiers and Civilians: The Martial Spirit in America, 1775–1865* (Boston: Little, Brown, 1968).

46. *Annals of the Congress of the United States,* 13th Cong., 3rd sess., 859; Donald Hickey, *The War of 1812: A Forgotten Conflict* (Urbana: University of Illinois Press, 1989), 266–67; Solomon P. Sharp, *Mr. Sharp's Motion, Relating to the Conduct of Martin Chittenden, Governor of Vermont* (Washington, DC: Way, 1814); *Annals of the Congress of the United States,* 13th Cong., 3rd sess., 735.

47. Artemus Ward and Morris S. Miller quoted in Henry Adams, *History of the United States of America during the Administrations of James Madison* (New York: Library of America, 1986), 2:1100–1101; *Annals of the Congress of the United States,* 13th Cong., 3rd sess., 713, 714; Solomon P. Sharp, *Fellow Citizens* (Washington, DC: Sharp, 1816), 3. For the transformative nature of the War of 1812, see Steven Watts, *The Republic Reborn: War and the Making of Liberal America, 1790–1820* (Baltimore: Johns Hopkins University Press, 1987).

48. "Memoirs of Micah Taul," 496. For an overview of the ambitions of the Fourteenth Congress, see Charles Sellers, *The Market Revolution: Jacksonian America, 1815–1846* (New York: Oxford University Press, 1991), 70–79. The best account of this remarkable assemblage, however, remains Adams, *History of the United States,* 2:1253–67.

49. Adams, *History of the United States,* 2:1263.

50. Sharp, *Fellow Citizens,* 2.

51. *Annals of the Congress of the United States,* 13th Cong., 3rd sess., 1202; Sharp, *Fellow Citizens,* 3.

52. *Annals of the Congress of the United States,* 14th Cong., 1st sess., 1395, 1208.

53. Sharp, *Fellow Citizens,* 1; *Annals of the Congress of the United States,* 14th Cong., 1st sess., 1396. Sharp had also voted for a national bank (13th Cong., 3rd sess.), which Madison vetoed.

54. Thomas Jefferson to John Adams, January 24, 1814, in *The Adams-Jefferson Letters: The Complete Correspondence between Thomas Jefferson and Abigail and John Adams* (Chapel Hill: University of North Carolina Press, 1959), 424; Adams, *History of the United States,* 2:1261; *Annals of the Congress of the United States,* 14th Cong., 1st sess., 1396, 1106–7. Sharp had earlier proposed that Congress impose a 10 percent tax on the notes of banks that continued to suspend payments after a specified day. Sharp, however, withdrew his motion after Clay expressed his opinion that the measure was drastic. *Papers of Henry Clay,* 2:195.

55. *Annals of the Congress of the United States,* 14th Cong., 1st sess., 1188.

56. "Early Political Papers of Governor James Turner Morehead," ed. Willard Rouse Jillson, *Register of the Kentucky Historical Society* 22 (1924): 283–84; "Beauchamp's Trial" in Kallsen, *Kentucky Tragedy,* 308.

57. Hardin quoted in C. Edward Skeen, "*Vox Populi, Vox Dei:* The Compensation Act of 1816 and the Rise of Popular Politics," *Journal of the Early Republic* 6 (1986): 265. For Clay's unexpectedly close 1816 contest with the previously unelectable John Pope, see George T. Blakey, "Rendezvous with Republicanism: John Pope vs. Henry Clay in 1816," *Indiana Magazine of History* 62 (1966): 233–50. At one point during the campaign, Clay encountered an old supporter of his, an Irish immigrant. Clay asked the man whether he planned to vote for him or Pope, who had lost an arm in a childhood accident. "Och, Misther Clay," the Irishman replied, "I have concluded to vote for the man who has but one arm to sthrust into the sthreasury." Blakey, "Rendezvous with Republicanism," 241. Like Hardin, Senator Isham Talbot, a boardinghouse mate of Sharp's in the Fourteenth Congress, also refused to apologize; when asked why he voted for the bill, Talbot explained that he had "a very good reason" for his vote: "I wanted the money, be gud." Triplett, *Roland Trevor,* 146–47. Joseph Desha, who had voted against the measure, was reelected. *Kentucky Reporter,* August 14, 1816.

58. *Autobiography of Amos Kendall,* 183; *Kentucky Reporter,* November 27, 1816, December 11, 1816.

59. *Kentucky Reporter,* December 10, 1817.

60. *Kentucky Reporter,* September 17, 1817; *Kentucky Gazette,* February 7, 1818.

61. *Kentucky Reporter,* January 8, 1817.

62. Dale M. Royalty, "Banking, Politics, and the Commonwealth: Kentucky, 1800–1825" (PhD diss., University of Kentucky, 1971), 35–37, 58, 166, 419, 420; charter of the Bank of Kentucky and "An Act to Establish a State Bank" reprinted in ibid., 348–52, 340; Basil Duke, *History of the Bank of Kentucky* (Louisville, KY: Morton, 1895), 14. For the Spanish conspiracy, see Lowell H. Harrison, *Kentucky's Road to Statehood* (Lexington: University Press of Kentucky, 1992), 48–72.

In addition to the common stipulations—setting the paper issue-to-specie ratio and interest rate, dictating the institution's capitalization, number of shares, and share prices—the Kentucky assembly reserved significant powers of oversight, including the conducting of annual audits, the ability to increase the number of directors, and most important, the right to elect half the directors and the president. Royalty points out that this tethering is strong evidence of a "commonwealth ideal," and he goes so far as to describe the state bank's enabling legislation as "based on the principle of mercantilism." Dale M. Royalty, "Banking and the Commonwealth Ideal in Kentucky, 1806–1822," *Register of the Kentucky Historical Society* 77 (1979): 91. This suspicion of the banks was typical of an agrarian people. Banking historian Bray Hammond almost fifty years ago put it as well as anyone: "The source of wealth was the earth, and the producers thereof were those who tilled it and mined it and fished in its waters. The wealth possessed by bankers and stock-jobbers must have been taken somehow from these toilers. Whence otherwise could it come?" Bray Hammond, *Banks and Politics in America from the Revolution to the Civil War* (Princeton, NJ: Princeton University Press, 1957), 38–39. One correspondent to the *Kentucky Reporter* asserted that "the commercial interest is at war with that of the people generally." *Kentucky Reporter,* February 28, 1816.

63. Henry Clay to William Jones, February 4, 1818, in *Papers of Henry Clay,* 2:435.

64. Royalty, "Banking, Politics, and the Commonwealth," 153–89; Thomas Barton, "Politics and Banking in Republican Kentucky, 1805–1824" (PhD diss., University of Wisconsin, 1968), 175–235; *Kentucky Reporter,* February 5, 1817, May 13, 1818.

65. One of the amendments Sharp helped kill stated that the charters could be repealed "whenever the public good shall require it." *Journal of the House of Representatives of the Commonwealth of Kentucky,* 1818, 164.

66. "An Old Republican," *Kentucky Gazette,* June 27, 1814; Royalty, "Banking, Politics, and the Commonwealth," 153, 154–89; *Kentucky Reporter,* November 15, 1815; Barton, "Politics and Banking in Republican Kentucky," 234; "An Act to Establish Independent Banks in This Commonwealth," *Journal of the House of Representatives of the Commonwealth of Kentucky,* 1817, 159–65; *Kentucky Reporter,* February 28, 1816; *Russellville (KY) Weekly Messenger,* April 18, 1818; William Murphy to Joseph Desha, February 16, 1818, Joseph and John R. Desha Papers, Manuscript

Division, Library of Congress, Washington, DC; William E. Connelley and E. M. Coulter, *History of Kentucky*, ed. Charles Kerr (Chicago: American Historical Society, 1922), 2:596.

67. *Kentucky Reporter*, January 27, 1819; *Kentucky Gazette*, January 10, 1818, February 7, 1818. The act established a five-thousand-dollar annual tax, or fifty cents on every one hundred dollars of capital (or twenty-five cents of every one hundred dollars of notes discounted), to be levied on each branch of the Bank of the United States. If the tax was not paid, then bank officials were to be fined ten thousand dollars. *Acts Passed at the First Session of the Twenty-sixth General Assembly for the Commonwealth of Kentucky*, 1818, 527–28.

68. *Kentucky Reporter*, January 27, 1819; *Acts Passed at the First Session of the Twenty-sixth General Assembly for the Commonwealth of Kentucky*, 1818, 637–39.

69. *Kentucky Reporter*, January 27, 1819; John C. Calhoun to Martin Davis Hardin, August 8, 1819, in *Papers of John C. Calhoun*, 4:217; *Russellville (KY) Weekly Messenger*, January 26, 1819; *Executive Journal*, 1825, 259, Joseph Desha Papers, KDLA.

70. *Kentucky Reporter*, March 3, 1819; *Russellville (KY) Weekly Messenger*, April 3, 1819.

71. *Frankfort (KY) Patriot*, April 17, 1826; Glenn Clift, *Remember the Raisin! Kentucky and Kentuckians in the Battles and Massacre at Frenchtown, Michigan Territory, in the War of 1812* (Frankfort: Kentucky Historical Society, 1961), 117–19.

72. *Journal of the House of Representatives of the Commonwealth of Kentucky*, 1818, 88; *Kentucky Gazette*, December 25, 1818.

73. Sharp, *Vindication*, 5, 13, 91; *Frankfort (KY) Commonwealth*, January 23, 1844; *Frankfort (KY) Patriot*, April 17, 1826; will book 2, Franklin County, KY, 148, KDLA; Eliza Sharp, "To the Public," *Frankfort (KY) Argus of Western America*, March 22, 1826.

74. Tax lists, Warren County, KY, 1819, microfilm, KDLA.

2. THE DIMINUTIVE FURY

1. *Vermont Gazette*, August 1, 1826; *Amherst (NH) Farmers' Cabinet*, July 29, 1826; Cooke, "Portrait of a Murderess," 218; Coleman, *Beauchamp-Sharp Tragedy*, viii. There were a number of variations in the spelling of her name, both during her life and after: Ann, Anne, and Anna; Cook and Cooke. In the few documents that she left behind, she signed her name "Anna." See, for example, Anna Cooke Beauchamp to a lady in Frankfort [Francis R. Hawkins?], July 5, 1826, reprinted in *Lexington (KY) Western Luminary*, August 9, 1826; Anna Cooke Beauchamp to John U. Waring, January 7, 1826, reprinted in Jack Edward Surrency, "The Kentucky Tragedy in American Literature: From Thomas Holley Chivers to Robert Penn Warren" (PhD diss., University of Tennessee, Knoxville, 1977), 176–78; and Anna's will in will book D, Warren County, KY, 119, WKU. In addition, Jereboam usually referred to his wife as "Anna" (see "Lines Written by J. O. Beauchamp, While in Jail, upon Being

Aroused from Sleep by a Vision of His Wife's Spirit," in Kallsen, *Kentucky Tragedy,* 91, 92), although the *Confession* does refer to her as "Ann" at one point, as does one piece of her poetry. A second piece immediately following, however, attributes a poem to "Mrs. Anna Beauchamp." "Cooke" was the spelling she and her family used. For a number of worthy insights concerning Anna, see Cooke, "Portrait of a Murderess."

2. For a discussion of the spuriousness of the document, see Johnson, "Letters of Ann Cooke," and chapter 9.

3. Warren, *World Enough and Time,* 45. This is Warren's description of his fictional character Rachel Jordan, the character closely based on Anna. Yet here, as throughout the novel, Warren was obviously drawing on his own extensive research on the Kentucky Tragedy.

4. There are only a few documents attributable to Anna, all of which date from the few months before her death: Beauchamp to Waring, in Surrency, "Kentucky Tragedy in American Literature," 176–78; Anna Cooke Beauchamp to William C. Bradburn, March 18, 1826, reprinted in *Frankfort (KY) Commentator,* July 15, 1826; Beauchamp to [Hawkins?], in *Lexington (KY) Western Luminary,* August 9, 1826; and four pieces of poetry, published in the *Confession* and reprinted in Kallsen, *Kentucky Tragedy,* 92–97. These poetry manuscripts, all from 1826, are housed at the Filson Historical Society, Louisville, KY (hereafter cited as FHS): "Verses Addressed by Mrs. Ann Beauchamp, to Her Husband—J. O. Beauchamp, a Few Days before Their Death," "Verses Addressed by Mrs. Anna Beauchamp to J. O. Beauchamp, a Few Hours before Their Death," "Lines Addressed to Mrs. Francis R. Hawkins, by Mrs. Beauchamp, in Jail, the Day Before the Death of Her and Her Husband," and "Epitaph: To Be Engraven on the Tomb-stone of Mr. and Mrs. Beauchamp."

5. Anna's birth date on her tombstone is February 6, 1786, but a family Bible lists the date as February 7, 1785. Given the births of a brother in 1783 and a sister in 1787, 1785 is the more probable year.

6. Dr. and Mrs. William Carter Stubbs, *Descendants of Mordecai Cooke, of "Mordecai's Mount," Gloucester Co., Va., 1650, and Thomas Booth, of Ware Neck, Gloucester Co., Va., 1685* (New Orleans: n.p., 1923), 102–11; Brooke Payne, *The Paynes of Virginia,* 2nd ed. (Harrisonburg, VA: Carrier, 1977), 244, 246. However, J. W. Cooke, in the most careful examination of Anna Cooke's early life, concludes that Giles Cooke "was a planter of the middling sort." Cooke, "Portrait of a Murderess," 218. The Cookes, according to tradition, were neighbors of the venerable Fitzhugh family estate, Ravensworth.

7. Patrick Darby, "To the Public," no. 3, *Frankfort (KY) Commentator,* April 29, 1826; Duke of La Rochefoucauld-Liancourt quoted in Adams, *History of the United States,* 2:92; Richard Beale Davis, *Intellectual Life in Jefferson's Virginia, 1790–1830* (Chapel Hill: University of North Carolina Press, 1964), 73–118; wills and inventories, Warren County, KY, 1813–1824, 2:280, 396, WKU; Stubbs, *Descendants of Mordecai Cooke,* 110. For private libraries of the early republic, see Davidson, *Revolution and the Word,* 24–27, and Mildred K. Abraham, "The Library of Lady Jean Skipwith:

A Book Collection from the Age of Jefferson," *Virginia Magazine of History and Biography* 91 (1981): 296–347.

8. Linda Kerber, *Women of the Republic: Intellect and Ideology in Revolutionary America* (Chapel Hill: University of North Carolina Press, 1980), 193, 185–231; Mary Beth Norton, *Liberty's Daughters: The Revolutionary Experience of American Women, 1750–1800* (Boston: Little, Brown, 1980), 257; Jan Lewis, *The Pursuit of Happiness: Family and Values in Jefferson's Virginia* (Cambridge: Cambridge University Press, 1983), 149–50; *Louisville (KY) Gazette*, May, 26, 1826.

9. Hannah Webster Foster, *The Coquette, or The History of Eliza Wharton*, new ed. (Boston: Fetridge, 1855), 140; Patrick Darby, "To the Public," no. 6, *Frankfort (KY) Commentator*, July 15, 1826; Clinton, *Plantation Mistress*, 61–62; Daniel Blake Smith, *Inside the Great House: Planter Family Life in Eighteenth-Century Chesapeake Society* (Ithaca, NY: Cornell University Press, 1980), 133; Martha Saxton, *Being Good: Women's Moral Values in Early America* (New York: Hill and Wang, 2003), 97–170, esp. 117; Ellen K. Rothman, *Hands and Hearts: A History of Courtship in America* (Cambridge, MA: Harvard University Press, 1987), 3–84.

10. Lewis, *Pursuit of Happiness*, esp. 1–39.

11. Tocqueville, *Democracy in America*, 2:192. For the late-eighteenth-century transformation of Virginia families, see Smith, *Inside the Great House*, and Lewis, *Pursuit of Happiness*. More broadly, see Lawrence Stone, *Family, Sex, and Marriage: England, 1500–1800* (New York: Harper and Row, 1977). For efforts to place such familial transformations within a broader context in which dependencies of all sorts—national and international, political and cultural—were brought into question in the Revolutionary era, see Jay Fliegelman, *Prodigals and Pilgrims: The American Revolution against Patriarchal Authority, 1750–1800* (Cambridge: Cambridge University Press, 1982), and Wood, *Radicalism of the American Revolution*.

12. Smith, *Inside the Great House*, 266; Lewis, *Pursuit of Happiness*, 170; Harry Toulmin, "Comments on America and Kentucky, 1793–1802," *Register of the Kentucky Historical Society* 47 (1949): 9. For relations between siblings, see Lorri Glover, *All Our Relations: Blood Ties and Emotional Bonds among the Early South Carolina Gentry* (Baltimore: Johns Hopkins University Press, 2000).

13. "Verses Addressed by Mrs. Ann Beauchamp, to Her Husband," in Kallsen, *Kentucky Tragedy*, 93.

14. Cooke, "Uprightness and Inventions," 36. For the Randolph family's flight from the "culture of decline," see Cynthia A. Kierner, "'The Dark and Dense Cloud Perpetually Lowering over Us': Gender and the Decline of the Gentry in Postrevolutionary Virginia," *Journal of the Early Republic* 20 (2000): 185–217, esp. 192–95. See also Rhys Isaac, *The Transformation of Virginia, 1740–1790* (Chapel Hill: University of North Carolina Press, 1982); Merrill, *Jefferson's Nephews*, esp. chap. 6; and David Hackett Fischer and James C. Kelly, *Bound Away: Virginia and the Westward Movement* (Charlottesville: University of Virginia Press, 2000).

15. Sharp, *Vindication*, 13; Stubbs, *Descendants of Mordecai Cooke*, 110; will books A and B, Warren County, KY, 77–78, 98–99, 121, 128, WKU. I have been

unable to find any evidence as to whether Cooke and Sharp ran against one another in 1817.

16. "Narrative of the Attempts Made by the Late J. O. Beauchamp to Procure a Pardon and of the Incidents Attending the Tragical Death of Himself and Wife, So Far as They Are Known to the Writer," *Frankfort (KY) Argus of Western America,* July 12, 1826; Sharp, *Vindication,* 12; Channing quoted in Boles, *Great Revival,* 18; Randolph quoted in Lewis, *Pursuit of Happiness,* 47. Anna's jailer, John McIntosh, confirmed Anna's skepticism: "Her husband told me that she did not believe in a future state of existence." McIntosh quoted in Sharp, *Vindication,* 132.

17. *Frankfort (KY) Commentator,* September 2, 1826; Sharp, *Vindication,* 12. Further into the *Vindication,* McIntosh describes her in suspiciously similar terms: "She was of slender form, and I think dark eyes and dark hair, fair skin, a middling, long slender nose, rather a large forehead, mouth rather large, with upper foreteeth all artificial, low chin, face tapering downward, inclined to be stoop shouldered, not much, if any, appearance of breasts, about ninety pounds weight, and was, to me, by no means a desirable looking woman." McIntosh quoted in Sharp, *Vindication,* 132. Another acquaintance of Anna's, John Jackman, confirmed that her "fore teeth were bad, or gone." Sharp, *Vindication,* 71.

18. Wyatt-Brown, *Southern Honor,* 229; Sharp, *Vindication,* 12; *Frankfort (KY) Commentator,* September 2, 1826; Cooke, "Portrait of a Murderess," 219. See also Lee Virginia Chambers-Schiller, *Liberty, a Better Husband: Single Women in America; The Generations of 1780–1840* (New Haven, CT: Yale University Press, 1984), and Christine Jacobson Carter, *Southern Single Blessedness: Unmarried Women in the Urban South, 1800–1865* (Urbana: University of Illinois Press, 2006).

19. Sharp, *Vindication,* 135; Tocqueville, *Democracy in America,* 2:201. See also Darby, "To the Public," no. 6.

20. Sharp, *Vindication,* 13; *Louisville (KY) Gazette,* May 26, 1826; Bynum, *Unruly Women;* William T. Barry to Susan Barry, May 21, 1826, quoted in Clinton, *Plantation Mistress,* 126.

21. Sharp, *Vindication,* 13; Jereboam Beauchamp to John J. Crittenden, November 25, 1825, in Bamberg, *Confession of Jereboam O. Beauchamp,* 139; Sharp, "To the Public"; Sharp, *Vindication,* 13, 16; *U.S. Telegraph,* March 21, 1829; Bynum, *Unruly Women,* 45. Leander also served as a witness for Anna's brother, Thomas, when his will was probated in January 1819, and as a witness to a land transaction involving John W. and Anna Cooke in September 1819. There was a lawsuit between the families—*Giles Cooke v. Solomon Sharp,* in September 1818, most likely a dispute over land—but the suit was shortly dismissed by mutual consent. Deed abstracts, Warren County, KY, 1812–1821, 182, WKU; order book E, Warren County, KY, 192, KDLA.

22. "Beauchamp's Confession" in Kallsen, *Kentucky Tragedy,* 10; Sharp, *Vindication,* 12; Kerber, *Women of the Republic,* 260–64; Richard Godbeer, *Sexual Revolution in Early America* (Baltimore: Johns Hopkins University Press, 2002), 266–67, 269; Rodney Hessinger, "'Insidious Murderers of Female Innocence': Representations of Masculinity in the Seduction Tales of the Late Eighteenth Century," in *Sex and Sexu-*

ality in Early America, ed. Merril D. Smith (New York: New York University Press, 1998), 262–82; Davidson, *Revolution and the Word*, 135.

23. Bynum, *Unruly Women*, 42; Sharp, *Vindication*, 14, 16, 18, 32; *Louisville (KY) Gazette*, May 26, 1826.

24. Godbeer, *Sexual Revolution in Early America*, 119–53, 121, 150; Woodmason quoted in Godbeer, *Sexual Revolution in Early America*, 120; John Mack Faragher, *Daniel Boone: The Life and Legend of an American Pioneer* (New York: Holt, 1992), 58–59; Fischer, *Albion's Seed*, 682; *Winding Down: The Revolutionary War Letters of Lieutenant Benjamin Gilbert of Massachusetts, 1780–1783*, ed. John Shy (Ann Arbor: University of Michigan Press, 1989), 47. Virtually nothing has been written about the sexual culture of the trans-Appalachian West.

25. Daniel Scott Smith and Michael Hindus, "Premarital Pregnancy in America, 1640–1971: An Overview and Interpretation," *Journal of Interdisciplinary History* 5 (1975): 556. For excellent summaries of these trends in late-eighteenth-century America, see Godbeer, *Sexual Revolution in Early America*, 227–98, and Fliegelman, *Prodigals and Pilgrims*. For a general survey of the breakdown of colonial social mores, see Wood, *Radicalism*, esp. 145. For a convincing argument that a large gulf separated prescriptive literature advocating repression of sexual urges and the actual behavior of nineteenth-century women, see Carl N. Degler, "What Ought to Be and What Was: Women's Sexuality in the Nineteenth Century," *American Historical Review* 79 (1974): 1467–90.

26. Sharp, *Vindication*, 13, 14.

27. Ibid., 7–10, 9, 13.

28. Ibid., 13, 15; Sharp, "To the Public."

29. Sharp, *Vindication*, 18, 14, 16–17, 22. Later, however, when Dr. Sharp composed his *Vindication*, he claimed that Anna herself had exonerated Solomon. Dr. Sharp claimed that Dr. Payne, a cousin of Anna's and executor of her brother John W. Cooke's estate, found a letter from Anna to her brother among Cooke's papers shortly after his death in 1821. M. Harrison—also a relation of Anna's—claimed to have read this letter, and he swore that it detailed "fully the circumstances of her seduction, nam[ed] the guilty person and entirely exonerat[ed] Col. S. P. Sharp." Richard Hallaway, who lived about a mile from Anna after she married Jereboam Beauchamp (and whom Beauchamp himself later described as a man of "honor" and "firmness"), testified, "I recollect distinctly to have heard [Anna] say, when speaking of Col. S. P. Sharp, that he had never injured her, and that she had no harm against him." Sharp, *Vindication*, 15, 16. Much less convincingly, Dr. Sharp related that "a man who is now dead, afterwards stated, that he had seen Ann Cook in the act [of] criminal intercourse with another individual, *on that very day*"—that is, the Sunday that Anna claimed to have had her assignation with Solomon. Sharp, *Vindication*, 14.

30. Darby, "To the Public," no. 6; Beauchamp to Bradburn, in *Frankfort (KY) Commentator*, July 15, 1826; Beauchamp to Waring, in Surrency, "Kentucky Tragedy in American Literature," 176–78.

31. Cooke, "Uprightness and Inventions," 39; John U. Waring quoted in Sharp,

Vindication, 21. One of the few other histories that pointed to Anna's family's inaction was S. Foster Damon, *Thomas Holley Chivers, a Friend of Poe, with Selections from His Poems: A Strange Chapter in American Literary History* (New York: Harper, 1930), 72. The *Confession* lets slip that after murdering Sharp, Beauchamp stopped by the house of Peyton Cooke, "who is a brother to my wife." "Beauchamp's Confession" in Kallsen, *Kentucky Tragedy,* 38.

32. Tocqueville, *Democracy in America,* 2:213; Wyatt-Brown, *Southern Honor,* 53, 54, 294; Robert M. Ireland, "Homicide in Nineteenth-Century Kentucky," *Register of the Kentucky Historical Society* 81 (1983): 134–53; Little, *Ben Hardin,* 42; Chevalier, *Society, Manners, and Politics,* 412; Robert M. Ireland, "The Libertine Must Die: Sexual Dishonor and the Unwritten Law in the Nineteenth-Century United States," *Journal of Social History* 23 (1989): 27–44, esp. 29–30. Ireland makes the mistake of taking Beauchamp's story at face value and thus interprets Beauchamp's failure to publicly kill Sharp as evidence that the "unwritten law" had not yet been embraced by the 1820s. Yet more than a few observers of the Kentucky Tragedy, including Leander J. Sharp, argued that if the seduction story were true, public murder—either by Anna's brothers or by Beauchamp—would have been justified.

33. Wyatt-Brown, *Southern Honor,* 53, 54, 294; Ireland, "Homicide in Nineteenth-Century Kentucky"; Sharp, *Vindication,* 14; Sharp, "To the Public."

34. Cooke, "Portrait of a Murderess," 227–28, 227n31; "Verses Addressed by Mrs. Ann Beauchamp, to Her Husband," in Kallsen, *Kentucky Tragedy,* 93.

35. Cooke, "Portrait of a Murderess," 227–28; Beauchamp to Waring, in Surrency, "Kentucky Tragedy in American Literature," 177.

36. *Jamestown (NY) Journal,* August 2, 1826.

37. D. C. Humphreys, interview by John Shane, 1854, 16CC294–95, Draper Collection; Sharp, *Vindication,* 13. Joseph Underwood wrote to Edmund Rogers on February 13, 1812, "We stepped into a book store where I met with Mr. Sharp of Warren." For another scenario that also suggests a sexual relationship, see Cooke, "Time to Weep."

38. William Buchan, *Advice to Mothers, on the Subject of Their Own Health, and of the Means of Promoting the Health, Strength, and Beauty of Their Offspring* (1809), in *The Physician and Child-Rearing: Two Guides, 1809–1894* (New York: Arno Press, 1972), 13; John D'Emilio and Estelle B. Freedman, *Intimate Matters: A History of Sexuality in America* (New York: Harper and Row, 1988), 95; Francis Grose, *1811 Dictionary of the Vulgar Tongue, or A Dictionary of Buckish Slang, University Wit, and Pickpocket Eloquence* (London: Chappel, 1811). Dr. Sharp related that Anna claimed that the tryst took place on "the Sabbath before the birth of Mrs. Sharp's first child." Sharp, *Vindication,* 14. Daniel Defoe, in *Conjugal Lewdness, or Matrimonial Whoredom* (1727; repr., Gainesville, FL: Scholars' Facsimiles and Reprints, 1967), 297-99, categorized sex between a husband and his pregnant wife as one of the "abuses of the marital bed."

39. "Lines Addressed to Mrs. Francis R. Hawkins, by Mrs. Beauchamp," in Kallsen, *Kentucky Tragedy,* 95.

40. *Kentucky Reporter,* February 23, 1820.

41. *Niles' Register,* May 11, 1820, quoted in William M. Gouge, *A Short History of Paper Money and Banking in the United States* (1833; repr., New York: Kelley, 1968), 2:123.

42. *Lexington (KY) Western Monitor,* April 18, 1818; *Kentucky Reporter,* February 5, 1819.

43. *Frankfort (KY) Argus of Western America,* April, 4, 1819; *Kentucky Reporter,* January 15, 1819, June 2, 1819; *Kentucky Gazette,* April 16, 1819, April 9, 1819, April 30, 1819.

44. *Kentucky Reporter,* August, 18, 1819; *Kentucky Gazette,* August 13, 1819. The vote was Cornelius Turner, 843; James Thomas, 719; Sharp, 677; Thomas Middleton, 619.

45. *Frankfort (KY) Argus of Western America,* November 5, 1819; *Kentucky Reporter,* August 4, 1819; William T. Barry to Catherine Barry, October 3, 1819, William Taylor Barry Papers, FHS; *Kentucky Reporter,* January 26, 1820; Barton, "Politics and Banking in Republican Kentucky," 277, 283–84; *Frankfort (KY) Argus of Western America,* November 5, 1819; *Kentucky Gazette,* December 10, 1819.

46. *Kentucky Reporter,* December 8, 1819. For overviews of debt relief legislation in early America, see Murray N. Rothbard, *The Panic of 1819: Reactions and Policies* (New York: Columbia University Press, 1962), 32–111, 196–97; Peter Coleman, *Debtors and Creditors in America: Insolvency, Imprisonment for Debt, and Bankruptcy, 1607–1900* (Madison: State Historical Society of Wisconsin, 1974); Bruce Mann, *Republic of Debtors: Bankruptcy in the Age of American Independence* (Cambridge, MA: Harvard University Press, 2002); and Edward J. Balleisen, *Navigating Failure: Bankruptcy and Commercial Society in Antebellum America* (Chapel Hill: University of North Carolina Press, 2001). In 1821, Kentucky became the first state to outlaw imprisonment for debt. See Emmet V. Mittlebeeler, "The Decline of Imprisonment for Debt in Kentucky," *Filson Club Historical Quarterly* 49 (1975): 169–89.

47. *Executive Journal,* 1825, 255, Josepha Desha Papers. For an excellent account of relief legislation in the early republic, and for further confirmation that such laws were not novel, see Steven Boyd, "The Contract Clause and the Evolution of American Federalism, 1789–1815," *William and Mary Quarterly* 44 (1987): 529–48.

48. *Danville (KY) Olive Branch,* June 16, 1820; M. Lyon, "A Review," *Kentucky Reporter,* May 24, 1820; Lynn Marshall, "The Early Career of Amos Kendall: The Making of a Jacksonian" (PhD diss., University of California, Berkeley, 1962), 224. According to the *Kentucky Reporter,* January 19, 1820, "There is but little doubt of the passage of a property law (so-called) and in all human probability, a long replevin law connected with it." See also Aleine Austin, *Matthew Lyon: "New Man" of the Democratic Revolution, 1749–1822* (University Park: Pennsylvania State University Press, 1981).

49. *Journal of the House of Representatives of the Commonwealth of Kentucky,* 1819, 9; Sandra Francis VanBurkleo, "'That Our Pure Republican Principles Might

Not Wither': Kentucky's Relief Crisis and the Pursuit of 'Moral Justice,' 1818–1826" (PhD diss., University of Minnesota, 1988), 74–76; John Speed Smith to Green Clay, February 26, 1820, Green Clay Papers, Special Collections Library, University of Kentucky, Lexington; Lyon, "Review"; *Russellville (KY) Weekly Messenger,* May 30, 1820; *Danville (KY) Olive Branch,* June 16, 1820; *Lexington (KY) Public Advertiser,* February 12, 1820; John Brown to Orlando Brown, March 4, 1820, Orlando Brown Papers, FHS. Additionally, the legislators, in a concession to reality, admitted that the independent bank experiment was not working—at least as a relief measure—and repealed the charters of those independent banks that had survived the early days of the financial crisis. *Lexington (KY) Public Advertiser,* February 12, 1820.

50. *Kentucky Reporter,* February, 16, 1820, February 23, 1820; *Kentucky Gazette,* May 29, 1819; Henry Clay to Nicholas Biddle, November 28, 1829, in *Papers of Henry Clay,* 8:129; Connelley and Coutler, *History of Kentucky,* 2:613; Paul Gates, "Tenants of the Log Cabin," *Mississippi Valley Historical Review* 49 (1962): 8; *Lexington (KY) Public Advertiser,* July 5, 1820. See also Thomas D. Clark, *History of Kentucky,* 142–43.

51. John Adair, governor's message, *Journal of the Senate of the Commonwealth of Kentucky,* 1820, 7; "An Act to Establish the Bank of the Commonwealth of Kentucky," reprinted in Royalty, "Banking, Politics, and the Commonwealth," 369–78; Naomi R. Lamoreaux, *Insider Lending: Banks, Personal Connections, and Economic Development in Industrial New England* (Cambridge: Cambridge University Press, 1994). See also *Kentucky Gazette,* May 10, 1821, July 12, 1821; *Frankfort (KY) Patriot,* March 6, 1826, March 27, 1826, April 10, 1826; Joseph C. Breckinridge to Robert J. Breckinridge, December 19, 1820, Breckinridge Family Papers; and *Lexington (KY) Public Advertiser,* November 18, 1820.

52. Triplett, *Roland Trevor,* 105–6; *Kentucky Reporter,* January 13, 1819; VanBurkleo, "'That Our Pure Republican Principles,'" 76–81, 116; *Lexington (KY) Public Advertiser,* January 5, 1820, April 12, 1820, April 26, 1820; Albert D. Kirwan, *John J. Crittenden: The Struggle for the Union* (Lexington: University of Kentucky Press, 1962), 50. Not all Kentuckians, before the passage of the property law, passively accepted the loss of their property. Englishman William Faux, visiting Lexington in October 1819, reported, "I saw an execution defeated lately by that boasted spirit, which they call liberty, or independence. The property, under execution, was put up to sale, when the eldest son appeared with a huge, Herculean club, and said, 'Gentlemen, you may bid for and buy these bricks and things, which were my father's, but, by God, no man living shall come on to this ground with horse and cart to fetch them away. The land is mine, and if the buyer takes any thing away, it shall be on his back.' The father had transferred the land, and all on it, to the son, in order to cheat the law. Nobody was, therefore, found to bid or buy." William Faux, *Memorable Days in America: Being a Journal of a Tour to the United States* (1823; repr., New York: AMS Press, 1969), 192.

53. Richard Hofstadter, *The American Political Tradition and the Men Who Made*

It (New York: Vintage Press, 1948), 243; *Frankfort (KY) Argus of Western America,* December 10, 1819; *Kentucky Reporter,* May 24, 1820.

54. General Assembly, "Report on the Currency," *Kentucky Reporter,* November 18, 1822; Gouge, *Short History of Paper Money,* 2:126; William G. Sumner, *Andrew Jackson as a Public Man* (Boston: Houghton, Mifflin, 1882), 162; Thomas Senior Berry, *Western Prices before 1861: A Study of the Cincinnati Market* (Cambridge, MA: Harvard University Press, 1943), 402. Gouge added, "An obligation to pay 10,000 dollars entered into in 1816 or 1818, when the current dollar was in some parts of the country worth perhaps but 50 cents in silver, was enforced according to the strictness of the letter, in 1819 or 1820, when the current dollar was of equal value with the legal dollar, and worth one hundred cents in silver." Gouge, *Short History of Paper Money,* 2:126.

55. Arndt Stickles, *The Critical Court Struggle in Kentucky, 1819–1829* (Bloomington: Indiana University Press, 1929), 25; *Frankfort (KY) Argus of Western America,* May 10, 1821; John Adair, governor's message, *Journal of the House of Representatives of the Commonwealth of Kentucky,* 1821, 12; *Kentucky Reporter,* July 23, 1821.

56. *Russellville (KY) Weekly Messenger,* June 13, 1820; Lance Banning, "Republican Ideology and the Triumph of the Constitution, 1789–1793," *William and Mary Quarterly* 31 (1974): 167–88; *Frankfort (KY) Argus of Western America,* April 13, 1820; *Kentucky Gazette,* December 31, 1819; *Russellville (KY) Weekly Messenger,* June 13, 1820; *Kentucky Reporter,* May 14, 1821; Gordon Wood, *Creation of the American Republic, 1776–1787* (Chapel Hill: University of North Carolina Press, 1969), 393–425. For James Madison's perceptions of the parallels between the events of the 1820s and those of the confederation era, see Drew McCoy, *The Last of the Founding Fathers: James Madison and the Republican Legacy* (Cambridge: Cambridge University Press, 1989), 39–83.

57. *Lexington (KY) Western Monitor,* June 13, 1820; *Kentucky Reporter,* July 23, 1821; "One of the People to the People of Fayette" (broadside no. 50, August 1, 1822), John M. McCalla Papers, West Virginia University Library, Morgantown (hereafter cited as WVU); Wood, *Creation of the American Republic,* 393–425; *Frankfort (KY) Argus of Western America,* March 22, 1821, through May 3, 1821; *Kentucky Reporter,* May 7, 1821; *Russellville (KY) Weekly Messenger,* June 13, 1820; *Frankfort (KY) Argus of Western America,* April 13, 1820; *Kentucky Gazette,* December 31, 1819; *Russellville (KY) Weekly Messenger,* June 13, 1820; *Kentucky Reporter,* May 14, 1821; *Russellville (KY) Weekly Messenger,* December 28, 1819, June 13, 1820; *Frankfort (KY) Argus of Western America,* April 13, 1820; *Russellville (KY) Weekly Messenger,* July 25, 1823; "Lee to the Voters of Fayette County" (broadside no. 47, 1822), McCalla Papers; George Robertson, *Scrapbook on Law and Politics, Men, and Times* (Lexington, KY: Elder, 1855), 127; "Protest . . . against the Act to Repeal the Law Organizing the Court of Appeals," *Kentucky Reporter,* January 24, 1825; Ben Hardin, speech, October 20, 1824, in Little, *Ben Hardin,* 133; *Letter from Robert Wickliffe to His Constituents* (Frankfort, KY: n.p., 1825), 9. See also "The Importance of the Present Election" (broadside no. 88, July 1825), McCalla Papers.

58. *Kentucky Reporter,* August 9, 1821.

59. *Kentucky Gazette,* November 9, 1820; John Adair, governor's message, special session, *Journal of the Senate of the Commonwealth of Kentucky,* 1821, 5; VanBurkleo, "'That Our Pure Republican Principles,'" 457–87; John Adair, governor's message, special session, *Journal of the Senate of the Commonwealth of Kentucky,* 1822, 5; Henry Clay to Benjamin Leigh, October 29, 1822, in *Papers of Henry Clay,* 3:304–5; *Kentucky Gazette,* November 4, 1823; *Kentucky Reporter,* November 8, 1824; General Assembly, "Report on the Currency." Other leaders of the relief movement, including Amos Kendall and legislator Jesse Bledsoe, were careful to distinguish between delaying repayment of debt and avoiding repayment altogether. "One of the first principles of morality seems to be," Bledsoe maintained, "that every one should pay his debts, if he is able." *The Speech of Jesse Bledsoe, Esq. on the Resolutions Proposed by Him, Concerning Banks* (Lexington, KY: Norvell, 1819), 13. Kendall expounded that "the people must pay their own debts at last." *Frankfort (KY) Argus of Western America,* July 5, 1821.

60. Levin, *Lawyers and Lawmakers,* 113; Thomas S. Hinde, diary, n.d., 29Y196, Draper Collection; Sharp, *Vindication,* 5; *Journal of the Senate of the Commonwealth of Kentucky,* 1821, 76; *An Outline of the Life of George Robertson, Written by Himself* (Lexington, KY: Transylvania, 1876), 57.

61. Sharp, "To the Public." For the timing of the move, see Sharp, *Vindication,* 6, 23. Dr. Sharp was a Warren County representative to the General Assembly in 1822, and he later wrote, "I remained in Bowlinggreen some time after Col. Sharp's family left that country." Sharp, *Vindication,* 24.

62. Rowan et al. to Sharp, in Levin, *Lawyers and Lawmakers,* 110; Sharp, *Vindication,* 4; tax lists, Franklin County, KY, 1813, 1821, microfilm, KDLA.

63. Sharp, *Vindication,* 18; *Kentucky Reporter,* October 29, 1821.

64. Huston, *Memories of the Eighty Years,* 77; *Louisville (KY) Courier-Journal,* January 3, 1937; Sharp, *Vindication,* 3, 18; "Recollections of Henry Fox, Aged 86" (typescript, 1898), 7, WKU; *Frankfort (KY) Commonwealth,* March 31, 1846, quoted in Lewis Franklin Johnson, *History of the Franklin County Bar, 1786–1931* (Frankfort, KY: Kavanaugh, 1932), 36; Coleman, *Beauchamp-Sharp Tragedy,* 66.

65. Sharp, "To the Public"; Sharp, *Vindication,* 22. The middle name of Waring's father, who was from Essex County, Virginia, was Payne. It is possible, therefore, that Anna and John were distantly related. She, however, in a letter to Waring, made no mention of a family tie. A likelier and simpler explanation for Waring's involvement was his sociopathic delight in conflict.

66. The handbill was reprinted in Sharp, *Vindication,* 21–22. For comments on the senate investigation, see Young Ewing's testimony in ibid., 7.

67. Christopher L. Doyle, "The Randolph Scandal in Early National Virginia, 1792–1815: New Voices in the 'Court of Honor,'" *Journal of Southern History* 69 (2003): 283–318; Cynthia A. Kierner, *Scandal at Bizarre: Rumor and Reputation in Jefferson's America* (New York: Palgrave Macmillan, 2004), 37–61, 71–80.

68. Sharp, *Vindication,* 5.

3. ROMANCE AND DELUSION

1. John McIntosh, deposition, January 30, 1827, Circuit Court of Franklin County, KY, file 442, KDLA.

2. Jereboam Beauchamp to Governor Joseph Desha, June 5, 1826, reprinted in *Frankfort (KY) Commentator,* November 25, 1826. In contemporary documents, Beauchamp's name was alternately spelled "Jereboam" and "Jeroboam"; he himself spelled his name "Jereboam."

3. Michaux, *Travels to the Westward,* 64; Thomas Ashe, *Travels in America Performed in 1806* (London: Blunt, 1808), 171; Louis-Philippe, *Diary of My Travels in America,* trans. Stephen Becker (New York: Delacorte Press, 1977), 110–11; Anne Royall, *Letters from Alabama, 1817–1822,* ed. Lucille Griffith (Tuscaloosa: University of Alabama, 1969), 86–87.

4. "Beauchamp's Confession" in Kallsen, *Kentucky Tragedy,* 5; tax lists, Simpson County, KY, 1820, microfilm, KDLA; deed abstracts, Warren County, KY, deed book H-8, 1816–1818, Simpson County Archives, Franklin, KY; Cooke, "Time to Weep," 126; Eslinger, *Citizens of Zion,* 225–35; W. M. Vertrees, "Ann Cook's Revenge: Account of the Sharp-Beauchamp Tragedy, Which Occurred Many Years Ago in Kentucky; a Singular and Pathetic Story of Love and Crimes," *Nashville Banner,* September 8, 1894. Although a number of accounts depicted Thomas Beauchamp as "old Beauchamp" during the trial (see, for example, Sharp, *Vindication,* 120), he was only forty-nine years old in 1826. Interestingly, it was Solomon Sharp who introduced the enabling legislation that created Simpson County.

5. "Beauchamp's Trial" in Kallsen, *Kentucky Tragedy,* 289–90; Darby, "To the Public," no. 6; "Beauchamp's Confession" in Kallsen, *Kentucky Tragedy,* 85, 5; "Questions and Answers," *Franklin (KY) Favorite,* April 10, 1902.

6. "Beauchamp's Confession" in Kallsen, *Kentucky Tragedy,* 5, 6. See also Sanford Duncan's testimony in "Beauchamp's Trial" in Kallsen, *Kentucky Tragedy,* 292. One study of Barren County schools contains no reference to an academy run by Benjamin Thurston, although it does point out that "there were doubtless many schools taught in Barren County before the establishment of the common school system [in 1838], of which there is no record." Richard Alsup Palmore, "History of Education of Barren County, Kentucky" (master's thesis, University of Kentucky, 1931), 9.

7. Two physical descriptions come from "Questions and Answers" and Vertrees, "Ann Cook's Revenge." The former is an interview in a Simpson County newspaper of "a gentleman of this place who is looked upon generally as a walking encyclopedia on all affairs pertaining to local history." Although the interview took place seventy-six years after the death of Beauchamp, the account is surprisingly accurate—especially given the great amount of misinformation about the Kentucky Tragedy that was circulating by then. "Questions and Answers" does contain some inaccuracies—for example, that Beauchamp's arrest took place a month after his return from Frankfort—but on the whole, it is a useful source. Vertrees's "Ann Cook's Revenge," on the

other hand, is riddled with inaccuracies, and it is used here only where it agrees with "Questions and Answers." For Beauchamp's self-description, see "Beauchamp's Confession" in Kallsen, *Kentucky Tragedy,* 29. For the timbre of Beauchamp's voice, see "Beauchamp's Trial" in Kallsen, *Kentucky Tragedy,* 285. However, a friend of Beauchamp's, George Work, testified that Beauchamp's voice was neither shrill nor peculiar. "Beauchamp's Trial" in Kallsen, *Kentucky Tragedy,* 305.

8. "Beauchamp's Confession" in Kallsen, *Kentucky Tragedy,* 5, 103; Sharp, *Vindication,* 23, 31, 29. For southern child-rearing practices, see Wyatt-Brown, *Southern Honor,* esp. 134–48, and Lorri Glover, *Southern Sons: Becoming Men in the New Nation* (Baltimore: Johns Hopkins University Press, 2007), 17–22.

9. "Beauchamp's Trial" in Kallsen, *Kentucky Tragedy,* 194; Sharp, *Vindication,* 32; "Beauchamp's Confession" in Kallsen, *Kentucky Tragedy,* 41. On July 14, 1823, a suit against Beauchamp "upon a recognizance to keep the peace" was dismissed. *Simpson County, Kentucky, 1819–1825, Circuit Court Orders,* comp. Dorothy Donnell Steers (Franklin, KY: Printers, 1985). It should be noted that it was not at all unusual to be heavily armed in early Kentucky; as English traveler E. S. Abdy observed, "nearly all the Kentuckians, of whatever rank and condition, carried pistols or dirks, and sometimes both, with them." Edward S. Abdy, *Journal of a Residence and Tour in the United States of North America from April, 1833, to October, 1834* (1835; repr., New York: Negro Universities Press, 1969), 2:343. Another Englishman noted that "a pistol, and a dirk, are as familiar, as a watch, and a penknife." Knight, *Letters from the South and West,* 94. What seems to be unusual about Beauchamp, however, is the sheer extent and variety of his personal armory.

10. *Frankfort (KY) Spirit of '76,* July 14, 1826; "Beauchamp's Trial" in Kallsen, *Kentucky Tragedy,* 304; "Questions and Answers"; *Simpson County, Kentucky, 1819–1825 Circuit Court Orders,* 99. Despite a number of accounts to the contrary, Beauchamp was never a law student of Solomon Sharp's. In the *Confession,* Beauchamp maintains that he planned to study law with Colonel Sharp and that Sharp proposed that Beauchamp read law with him. The claim is suspicious; although Beauchamp professed to be "somewhat intimately" acquainted with Sharp and had exchanged "cordial salutations of friendship," Leander Sharp later denied that there was "any intercourse of friendship or business" between them. "Beauchamp's Confession" in Kallsen, *Kentucky Tragedy,* 7; Sharp, *Vindication,* 24. While living in Bowling Green, Beauchamp roomed with a "Dr. Beauchamp," most likely a relative. A Bowling Green physician named "Beachamp" is mentioned in "Recollections of Henry Fox," 8.

11. Timothy Flint, review of *The Confession of Jereboam O. Beauchamp, Western Magazine and Review* 1 (1827): 57; "Beauchamp's Trial" in Kallsen, *Kentucky Tragedy,* 186, 287, 193, 192; "Beauchamp's Confession" in Kallsen, *Kentucky Tragedy,* 6, 7; Sharp, *Vindication,* 31–32; "Beauchamp's Trial" in Kallsen, *Kentucky Tragedy,* 176. The *Confession* relates, "I had studdied the law, but living in the country . . . I had not gone to the practice." "Beauchamp's Confession" in Kallsen, *Kentucky Tragedy,* 33.

12. "Beauchamp's Confession" in Kallsen, *Kentucky Tragedy,* 6–8.

13. Ibid., 6, 8–12.

14. Sharp, *Vindication*, 108; *Frankfort (KY) Commentator*, September 2, 1826; Sharp, "To the Public."

15. Clay to Johnston in *Papers of Henry Clay*, 5:586; tax lists, Simpson County, KY, 1825, microfilm, KDLA; Sharp, *Vindication*, 28–29; *Louisville (KY) Gazette*, May, 26, 1826; Flint, review, 57.

16. "Beauchamp's Trial" in Kallsen, *Kentucky Tragedy*, 319, 316.

17. "Beauchamp's Confession" in Kallsen, *Kentucky Tragedy*, 7, 11; "Verses Addressed by Mrs. Ann Beauchamp, to Her Husband" in Kallsen, *Kentucky Tragedy*, 92; "Epitaph" in Kallsen, *Kentucky Tragedy*, 97; "Verses Addressed by Mrs. Anna Beauchamp to J. O. Beauchamp" in Kallsen, *Kentucky Tragedy*, 94.

18. "Beauchamp's Confession" in Kallsen, *Kentucky Tragedy*, 9. The full quotation indicates that they "continued all the evening in my selecting and reading some books of philosophy which she had pointed out, as favorites of hers, and in the conversation to which this led." However, a number of Anna's acquaintances, as we shall see, gave evidence that her favorite books, the ones she loved to discuss, were not works of philosophy but novels.

19. *North American Review* 25 (July 1827): 183; Thomas Jefferson to Nathaniel Burwell, March 14, 1818, in Thomas Jefferson, *Writings*, ed. Merrill D. Peterson (New York: Library of America, 1984), 1411; Kemp Plummer Battle, *History of the University of North Carolina* (Raleigh, NC: Edwards and Broughton, 1907–1912), 1:285; Davidson, *Revolution and the Word*, 42, 39, 44, 69.

20. Leonard Tennenhouse, "Libertine America," *Differences: A Journal of Feminist Cultural Studies* 11 (1999–2000): 6, 1; Donna R. Bontatibus, *The Seduction Novel of the Early Nation: A Call for Socio-political Reform* (East Lansing: Michigan State University Press, 1999), 3. See Jan Lewis, "The Republican Wife: Virtue and Seduction in the Early Republic," *William and Mary Quarterly* 44 (1987): 689–721; Hessinger, "'Insidious Murderers of Female Innocence'"; and Rodney Hessinger, *Seduced, Abandoned, and Reborn: Visions of Youth in Middle-Class America, 1780–1850* (Philadelphia: University of Pennsylvania Press, 2005). Overwhelmed by the rising cult of domesticity, the fallen sentimental heroine, Davidson claims, all but disappeared after 1818 or so. But Davidson's account of the death of the seduction tale's heroine is greatly exaggerated; as she herself points out, editions of *The Coquette* were very popular in the 1820s and "remained steadily in print until 1874." Davidson, *Revolution and the Word*, 135, 149. As we will see, dramatizations of the Kentucky Tragedy were widespread until the eve of the Civil War. More broadly, Elizabeth Hardwick's study of seduction and betrayal in the novels of Nathaniel Hawthorne, George Eliot, Leo Tolstoy, Edith Wharton, and Thomas Hardy makes clear the continuing ubiquity of the theme throughout the nineteenth century. It seems that the headstrong and seduced heroine coexisted, or at least substantially overlapped, with the pure, pious, and domestic feminine ideal of the mid-nineteenth century. Elizabeth Hardwick, *Seduction and Betrayal: Women and Literature* (New York: Vintage Books, 1975), esp. 185–218.

21. Davidson, *Revolution and the Word,* viii, 149.

22. Abraham, "Library of Lady Jean Skipwith"; Catherine Kerrison, "The Novel as Teacher: Learning to Be Female in the Early American South," *Journal of Southern History* 69 (2003): 516–19, 546–48. Although the bulk of those who consumed the novels were women, readership cut across boundaries of class and gender. Kerber, *Women of the Republic,* 243.

23. Boston Gleaning Circle quoted in Kerber, *Women of the Republic,* 241; Cathy N. Davidson, "The Life and Times of *Charlotte Temple:* The Biography of a Book," in *Reading in America: Literature and Social History,* ed. Cathy N. Davidson (Baltimore: Johns Hopkins University Press, 1989), 157–79. For the tendency to blend society, politics, economics, and literature in early America, see Joseph J. Ellis, *After the Revolution: Profiles of Early American Culture* (New York: Norton, 1979), xiv, 24–25; Wood, *Radicalism of the American Revolution,* 5; and Jane Tompkins, *Sensational Designs: The Cultural Work of American Fiction, 1790–1860* (New York: Oxford University Press, 1985), xi.

24. Robert Darnton, *The Great Cat Massacre and Other Episodes in French Cultural History* (New York: Basic Books, 1984), 242, 243, 248, 251, 227.

25. Davidson, *Revolution and the Word,* 73, 262; Davidson, "Life and Times," 168; Julia Stern, *The Plight of Feeling: Sympathy and Dissent in the Early American Novel* (Chicago: University of Chicago Press, 1997), 11. Note, however, that the grave may—we cannot be certain—contain the remains of Charlotte Stanley, a young woman supposedly lured from her home in England and seduced by British army engineer John Montresor. Carl van Doren, *The American Novel* (New York: Macmillan, 1921), 8.

26. Doyle, "Randolph Scandal in Early National Virginia," 304–5; Darnton, *Great Cat Massacre,* 252.

27. Hall quoted in Kerrison, "Novel as Teacher," 526; Davidson, *Revolution and the Word,* 258, 262, 14; Eve Kornfeld, "Culture and Counterculture in Post-Revolutionary America," *Journal of American Culture* 12 (1989): 71–77, 72, 73, 74. Kornfeld builds on the earlier work of Linda Kerber and Cathy Davidson, among others.

28. Sharp, *Vindication,* 12, 132; *U.S. Telegraph,* March 21, 1829; Flint, review, 59. On the influence of novels on southern women generally, see Kerrison, "Novel as Teacher," 513–48.

29. Jefferson to Burwell, in Jefferson, *Writings,* 1412; Washington Irving, "Sketch Book of Geoffrey Crayon, Gent.," in *History, Tales, and Sketches* (New York: Library of America, 1983), 990.

30. Peter X. Accardo, "Byron in America to 1830," *Harvard Library Bulletin* 9, no. 2 (1998): 33; William H. Prescott, "Kenyon's Poems," *North American Review* 48 (April 1839): 405. The indispensable works are Accardo, "Byron in America to 1830," 1–60, and Peter X. Accardo, "American Editions of Byron, 1811 to 1830," *Papers of the Bibliographical Society of America* 93, no. 4 (1999): 484–93. The standard (albeit substandard) work on Byron's influence in America is still William Ellery Leonard, *Byron and Byronism in America* (1907; repr., New York: Gordian Press, 1965).

31. Accardo, "Byron in America to 1830," 8; George Gordon, Lord Byron, *Childe Harold's Pilgrimage,* canto 1, sts. 5, 2; Joseph Addison, *Cato,* act 1, scene 2; George Gordon, Lord Byron, *Don Juan,* canto 13, st. 18.

32. Samuel Griswold Goodrich, *Recollections of a Lifetime* (New York: Miller, Orton and Mulligan, 1856), 104, 105.

33. Henry Wadsworth Longfellow, "Defence of Poetry," *North American Review* 34 (January 1832): 76; Greenwood quoted in H. L. Kleinfield, "Infidel on Parnassus: Lord Byron and the *North American Review,*" *New England Quarterly* 33 (1960): 176; W. G. Hunt, "Don Juan," *Western Review and Miscellaneous Magazine* 2 (1820): 7, 3, 14, 3, 6, 7, 8; Goodrich, *Recollections of a Lifetime,* 106.

34. Andrews Norton, "Lord Byron's Character and Writings," *North American Review* 21 (October 1825): 359, 306, 327, 328, 359, 342.

35. Presbyter Anglicanus, "Lord Byron's Faults," *Blackwood's Magazine,* reprinted in *Southern Literary Messenger* 4 (1838): 269, 271; J. E. Snodgrass, "Lord Byron," *Southern Literary Messenger,* reprinted in *Ladies Repository* 1 (May 1841): 155.

36. Hunt, "Don Juan," 8, 3, 6. As a number of scholars argue, the transatlantic "Byronism" of the early nineteenth century was a larger social phenomenon than Byron himself, who "was simply the first, or the most successful among the first, to dramatize the attitudes of the new man, the unknown who risks life for glory. . . . The traits he singled out were not of inventions of his own." Jacques Barzun, "Byron and the Byronic," *Atlantic Monthly,* August 1953, 47–52. The same point is made by Peter Thorslev in *The Byronic Hero: Types and Prototypes* (Minneapolis: University of Minnesota Press, 1962) and by several contributors to Frances Wilson, ed., *Byromania: Portraits of the Artist in Nineteenth- and Twentieth-Century Culture* (New York: St. Martin's Press, 1999). But it was Byron's poetry that gave the figure its most lasting personifications.

37. *Lord Byron: The Major Works,* ed. Jerome J. McGann (New York: Oxford University Press, 1986), 1036; Byron, *Don Juan,* canto 2, sts. 189, 194, 188; John Clubbe, *Byron's Natural Man: Daniel Boone and Kentucky* (Lexington, KY: King Library Press, 1980), 18.

38. George Gordon, Lord Byron, *Manfred,* act 2, scene 2, lines 50–51; George Gordon, Lord Byron, *The Corsair,* line 11; Norton, "Lord Byron's Character and Writings," 306, 352.

39. Norton, "Lord Byron's Character and Writings," 329; Prescott, "Kenyon's Poems," 406; Byron, *Manfred,* act 1, scene 2, line 67; Norton, "Lord Byron's Character and Writings," 359.

40. Hunt, "Don Juan," 3; Norton, "Lord Byron's Character and Writings," 328, 351.

41. Byron quoted in *Lord Byron: The Major Works,* 1043; Norton, "Lord Byron's Character and Writings," 306; Goodrich, *Recollections of a Lifetime,* 105.

42. *Baltimore Emerald* quoted in Osterweis, *Romanticism and Nationalism,* 28; Norton, "Lord Byron's Character and Writings," 358–59; Prescott, "Kenyon's Poems," 405–6; Kleinfield, "Infidel on Parnassus," 184; James Pemberton Grund, "Bismarck

and Motley," *North American Review* 167 (1898): 370; Wilson, *Byromania,* 5; Longfellow, "Defence of Poetry," 75–76; Thorslev, *Byronic Hero,* 12.

43. Patricia Cohen, *The Murder of Helen Jewett: The Life and Death of a Prostitute in Nineteenth-Century New York* (New York: Knopf, 1998), 359, 337, 245, 341.

44. Catherine Claire Geoghegan, "Thomas W. Farrar: Major General, Worshipful Grandmaster and Jefferson County Pioneer" (unpublished paper, Samford University, 2004), 11.

45. Evert A. Duyckinck, *Cyclopædia of American Literature* (New York: Scribner, 1856), 2:43; Byron, *Don Juan,* canto 18, st. 5; *Baltimore Gazette,* April 21, 1835; T. Allston Brown, *A History of the New York Stage from the First Performance in 1732 to 1901* (New York: Dodd, Mead, 1903), 1:22; Hugh Murray, *The United States of America: Their History from the Earliest Period; Their Industry, Commerce, Banking Transactions, and National Works; Their Institutions and Character, Political, Social, and Literary* (Edinburgh: Oliver and Boyd, 1844), 170; James Grant Wilson, *The Life and Letters of Fitz-Greene Halleck* (New York: Appleton, 1869), 235; Rufus Wilmot Griswold, *The Poets and Poetry of America* (Philadelphia: Carey and Hart, 1843), 188; Byron, *Don Juan,* canto 18, st. 105; Brown, *History of the New York Stage,* 1:22. For the story of yet another melodramatic, manipulative, and deceptive killer—a young man who had a "lifelong passion for verse," who memorized Byron's *Giaour,* and whose biographer depicts him as a "Byronic hero, the tyrant-slayer of the past, resisting the advent of a new uncertain time"—see Michael W. Kauffman, *American Brutus: John Wilkes Booth and the Lincoln Conspiracies* (New York: Random House, 2004) , 87, 307, 394.

46. *Frankfort (KY) Spirit of '76,* July 14, 1826; "Beauchamp's Confession" in Kallsen, *Kentucky Tragedy,* 5, 7–8; Dennis Duffy, "John Richardson's Kentucky Tragedies," *Canadian Review of American Studies* 22 (1991): 3.

47. "Beauchamp's Trial" in Kallsen, *Kentucky Tragedy,* 251; Sharp, *Vindication,* 99; Darby, "To the Public," no. 6; Flint, review, 57.

48. Sharp, *Vindication,* 32; Clubbe, *Byron's Natural Man,* 18.

49. Kleinfield, "Infidel on Parnassus," 164–85, 164; George Bancroft, "On the Progress of Civilization," in *The Transcendentalists: An Anthology,* ed. Perry Miller (Cambridge, MA: Harvard University Press, 1967), 426; Prescott, "Kenyon's Poems," 405. For the general popularity of the romantic rebels, see Russel Nye, *Society and Culture in America, 1830–1860* (New York: Harper and Row, 1974), 115. For a number of suggestive comments in this vein, see May, "After the Enlightenment," 179–96.

50. Wood, *Radicalism of the American Revolution,* 232; Appleby, *Inheriting the Revolution,* 4; Daniel Feller, *The Jacksonian Promise: America, 1815 to 1840* (Baltimore: Johns Hopkins University Press, 1995), 13.

51. If, as Gordon Wood has convincingly argued, the American Revolution was "as radical and revolutionary as any in history," if there indeed occurred such a "momentous upheaval that . . . fundamentally altered the character of American society," then it would have been extraordinary if there had not been some sort of

reaction. Wood, *Radicalism of the American Revolution*, 5. It is this that explains the Federalist persuasion and the more general and longer-lived worry that the Revolution would precipitate a self-perpetuating upheaval that would overturn all in its path, a cultural chain reaction of sorts. The persistence well into the Jacksonian era of uneasiness with the democratization of America, of a surprisingly widespread sense that society was becoming unhinged, was well delineated by Francis J. Grund in *Aristocracy in America: From the Sketchbook of a German Nobleman* (1839; repr., New York: Harper and Row, 1959). This also fits well with the "counterrevolutionary" tendency in early America, well described if not well explained by Larry E. Tise in *The American Counterrevolution: A Retreat from Liberty, 1783–1800* (New York: Stackpole Books, 1998).

52. Henry James, *Hawthorne* (New York: Harper, 1879), 42–43; James Freeman Clarke to Margaret Fuller, December 15, 1834, in *The Letters of James Freeman Clarke to Margaret Fuller*, ed. John Wesley Thomas (Hamburg: Cram, de Gruyter, 1957), 86–87; Robert Baird, *View of the Valley of the Mississippi, or The Emigrant's and Traveller's Guide to the West* (Philadelphia: Tanner, 1832), 90; Faux, *Memorable Days in America*, 194; Harriet Martineau, *Retrospect of Western Travel*, ed. Daniel Feller (London: Sharpe, 2000), 46. This early American institutional vacuum is one of the central insights of Stanley Elkins's *Slavery: A Problem in American Institutional and Intellectual Life*, 3rd ed. (Chicago: University of Chicago Press, 1976), one that has, unfortunately, been almost completely lost in the furor over the "Sambo thesis."

53. Flint, review, 56. In a nation founded by "self-fashioned performers in the theater of life"—to use Gordon S. Wood's phrase—what Beauchamp and his romantic cohort represent, in this instance as in so many others, is democratization. Gordon S. Wood, *Revolutionary Characters: What Made the Founders Different* (New York: Penguin Press, 2006), 23–26. Yet, too, there was substantial alteration, for this generation had lost contact with the notion of virtue. Lewis Perry sees the same dynamic at work in Andrew Jackson: Capable of profound dissimulation and able to play a variety of roles with equal skill—"planter gentleman, political protector of liberty, tender husband, great soul brought to God." In this sense, Jackson truly was a "symbol of his age," though in ways early generations of historians never intended. Lewis Perry, *Boats against the Current: American Culture between Revolutionary and Modernity, 1820–1860* (New York: Oxford University Press, 1993), 25–38.

54. David Brion Davis, *Homicide in American Fiction, 1798–1860* (Ithaca, NY: Cornell University Press, 1957), 155, 13, 48–49, 35. Here, I use "antinomian" in the conventional sense of "one who rejects a socially established morality." Although Charles Sellers has used the term to describe certain tendencies in the early republic, I do not find his use of "antinomian" or "Arminian" especially useful. See Daniel Walker Howe, "The Market Revolution and the Shaping of Identity in Whig-Jacksonian America," in *The Market Revolution in America: Social, Political, and Religious Expressions, 1800–1880*, ed. Stephen Conway and Melvin Stokes (Charlottesville: University Press of Virginia, 1996), 259–81.

55. "Beauchamp's Confession" in Kallsen, *Kentucky Tragedy,* 12, 13–14.

56. Surrency, "Kentucky Tragedy and Its Primary Sources," 113; Faux, *Memorable Days in America,* 187; Eslinger, *Citizens of Zion,* 111–14; Ewing quoted in Sharp, *Vindication,* 6; Cravens quoted in Sharp, *Vindication,* 9. Elizabeth Perkins asserts that "social authority in early Kentucky . . . became concentrated in the hands of male leaders known for their physical courage and military prowess." Perkins, *Border Life,* 140. Dennis Duffy writes that Beauchamp's "smug assertion that the self-made frontiersman Sharp dissolved into tears at Beauchamp's challenge to a duel, attests to his powers as a storyteller." Duffy, "John Richardson's Kentucky Tragedies," 4. Dickson Bruce finds that this supposed confrontation has very close parallels with both Virginia novelist Samuel Relf's *Infidelity, or The Victims of Sentiment* (1797) and Kentucky novelist Jesse Lynch Holman's *The Prisoners of Niagara, or Errors of Education* (1810). Bruce, *Kentucky Tragedy,* 54.

57. Henry K. Brooke, *Tragedies on the Land, Containing an Authentic Account of the Most Awful Murders That Have Been Committed in This Country* (Philadelphia: Perry, 1840), 55. Dickson Bruce also perceives the centrality of the account: "For Beauchamp's *Confession,* the account of Sharp's refusal to fight was what counted. Beauchamp had tried, the account indicated, to face up to Sharp as a true man of honor, and Sharp had let him down in a way contrary to honor's demands." Bruce, "Sentimentalism and Honor," 193.

58. "Beauchamp's Confession" in Kallsen, *Kentucky Tragedy,* 15–18.

59. Ibid., 15, 16, 17, 19. The Zebulon X. Yantis letter can be verified; Sharp found the document, dated June 27, 1825, among his brother's papers and reprinted it in Sharp, *Vindication,* 55–56.

60. Sharp, *Vindication,* 109, 24–25, 52–53, 26; "Beauchamp's Trial" in Kallsen, *Kentucky Tragedy,* 176; Sharp, "To the Public." The Simpson County circuit court records were destroyed in a late-nineteenth-century courthouse fire.

61. "Beauchamp's Confession" in Kallsen, *Kentucky Tragedy,* 15, 18, 17; Sharp, *Vindication,* 27, 28; Sharp, "To the Public." Dr. Sharp went so far as to accuse Beauchamp of threatening his father with a gun if he did not consent. Given the relationship of father and son, as examined earlier, such does not seem probable.

4. POLITICS

1. *Kentucky Reporter Extra,* May 1822. Clark cited article 1, section 10 of the U.S. Constitution and article 10, section 18 of Kentucky's 1799 constitution, both of which prohibited the passage of ex post facto laws and of laws impairing the obligation of contract.

2. Although Clark flatly refused to appear before the assembly, he did travel to Frankfort, and on Friday, May 24, he submitted a written defense of his decision. See "Response of Judge James Clark, to the Charges Exhibited against Him in the House of Representatives," *Kentucky Reporter,* June 17, 1822.

3. *Kentucky Reporter,* June 24, 1822, July 1, 1822; *Frankfort (KY) Argus of West-*

ern America, April, 6, 1825. Shannon's speech was later published as *Speech of George Shannon on the Resolution for the Removal of Judge Clark from Office on Account of His Decision in the Bourbon Circuit Court against the Constitutionality of the Endorsement and Replevin Laws* (Frankfort, KY: Kendall and Russell, 1822[?]).

4. *Kentucky Reporter,* May 29, 1822, June 3, 1822. Legislative address was an action that harkened back to English practice in which kings, with the consent of Parliament, dismissed recalcitrant judges. Article 4, section 3 of Kentucky's constitution provided that "the Governor shall remove any of [the judges] on the address of two-thirds of each House of the General Assembly" in cases in which there was not "sufficient ground of impeachment." Address thus gave the legislature the power to remove judges without having to prove misconduct; indeed, it allowed legislators to remove judges for almost any reason—provided, of course, they could muster a supermajority. See American Judicature Society, "Methods of Removing State Judges," http://www.ajs.org/ethics/eth_impeachement.asp.

The blowup over *Williams v. Blair* notwithstanding, the judicial assault on the relief program continued apace. In the June term of the Montgomery County circuit court, Judge William W. Blair handed down his decision in *Rogers v. Mason,* which not only reaffirmed but extended Clark's ruling. Judge Blair, in addition to declaring the 1820 replevin law unconstitutional, proclaimed that obligation of a contract was impaired "when the law withdraws any part of the defendant's property from absolute subjection to the plaintiff's demand," thus challenging a number of minor relief laws that put certain classes of property—clothing, bedding, furniture, eating utensils, and tools of trade—beyond the reach of creditors. Kentucky had first passed such a law in 1815 and added to its provisions in 1820. "Opinion of Judge William W. Blair" 1822, 17, reprinted in *Frankfort (KY) Argus of Western America,* July 4, 1822, July 11, 1822.

5. Robertson, *Scrapbook on Law and Politics,* 49; Karl Bernhard, Duke of Saxe-Weimar-Eisenach, *Travels through North America, during the Years 1825 and 1826* (Philadelphia: Carey, Lea and Carey, 1828), 130. For the decisions of *Blair v. Williams* and *Lapsley v. Brashear,* see William Littell, *Reports of the Cases at Common Law and in Chancery* (Frankfort, KY: Kendall, 1824), 4:34–117. For the background of *Lapsley v. Brashear,* see *Kentucky Reporter,* August 1, 1825.

6. Robertson, *Scrapbook on Law and Politics,* 273; *Frankfort (KY) Patriot,* July 24, 1826. See also Mary K. Bonsteel Tachau, *Federal Courts in the Early Republic: Kentucky, 1789–1816* (Princeton, NJ: Princeton University Press, 1978), 167–90; Ellis, *Jeffersonian Crisis;* and Teute, "Land, Liberty, and Labor." For judicial review during the relief war, see Theodore W. Ruger, "'A Question Which Convulses a Nation': The Early Republic's Greatest Debate about the Judicial Power," *Harvard Law Review* 117 (2004): 826–97. For broader studies that stress the transformation of conceptions of judicial review in the early republic, see Gordon S. Wood, "The Origins of Judicial Review," *Suffolk University Law Review* 22 (1988): 1293–1307; Gordon S. Wood, "The Origins of Judicial Review Revisited, or How the Marshall Court Made More out of Less," *Washington and Lee Law Review* 56 (1999): 787–809; and Larry D. Kramer, *The*

People Themselves: Popular Constitutionalism and Judicial Review (New York: Oxford University Press, 2004).

Furthermore, it was not just the state but the federal judiciary that Kentuckians resented. The federal circuit court in Frankfort had been notorious for its consistent decisions in favor of creditors (which led many creditors to take extraordinary measures to get their cases heard there) and its mandate that all debts be repaid in specie. And when, in *Green v. Biddle* (1821 and 1823), the Marshall Court disallowed Kentucky's occupying claimant laws, a great number of Kentuckians became convinced that the Court was in the process of undermining states' rights and democracy itself. Charles Warren, *The Supreme Court in United States History* (Boston: Little, Brown, 1922), 646.

7. *Richmond (VA) Republican*, February 4, 1825; Earl Gregg Swem, ed., *Letters on the Condition of Kentucky in 1825* (New York: Heartman, 1916), 26; William Butler, interview by John Shane, 1858, 15CC64, Draper Collection; Stephen W. Fackler, "John Rowan and the Demise of Jeffersonian Republicanism in Kentucky, 1819–1831," *Register of the Kentucky Historical Society* 78 (1980): 1–26.

8. *Report of John Rowan, Esq. in Relation to the Late Decision of the Court of Appeals* (Frankfort, KY: Holeman, 1823), 15, 13; *Speech of Samuel Daveiss, Esq., One of the Representatives from the County of Mercer, on the Preamble and Resolutions Protesting against the Decision of the Supreme Court of the United States, Relative to the Occupying Claimant Laws, and the Decision of the Court of Appeals of Kentucky, Relative to the Endorsement and Replevin Laws* (n.p., 1823), 26. Rowan's report was reissued verbatim as Kentucky General Assembly, *Preamble and Resolutions of the Legislature of Kentucky: In Relation to the Late Decision of the Court of Appeals on the Replevin and Endorsement laws, and of the Supreme Court of the United States on the Occupying Claimant Laws of Said State* (Frankfort, KY: n.p., 1823).

9. Kentucky General Assembly, *Report of the Committee Appointed to Enquire into the Official Conduct of the Judges of the Court of Appeals, November 19, 1824* (n.p., 1824), 2, 3–4, 10, 2, 4, 5, 4. Rowan's revised preamble and resolutions were adopted by the General Assembly and published in this report.

10. Ibid., 2–3.

11. Paul E. Doutrich III, "A Pivotal Decision: The 1824 Gubernatorial Election in Kentucky," *Filson Club Historical Quarterly* 56 (1982): 14–29.

12. Bennett H. Young, *History and Texts of the Three Constitutions of Kentucky* (Louisville, KY: Courier-Journal Job Printing, 1890), pt. 2, art. 3, sec. 1, p. 45; *An Abstract of the Speech of John Rowan upon the Bill to Reorganize the Court of Appeals* (Louisville, KY: Tanner, 1825), 7; Stickles, *Critical Court Struggle in Kentucky*, 63; Connelley and Coulter, *History of Kentucky*, 2:631.

13. *Frankfort (KY) Argus of Western America*, December 29, 1824.

14. Andrew Hughes to John Payne, December 23, 1824, John Payne Papers, Manuscript Division, Library of Congress, Washington, DC; Robertson, *Scrapbook on Law and Politics*, 127; *Danville (KY) Olive Branch*, July 14, 1826; *Frankfort (KY)*

Spirit of '76, August 4, 1826; *Kentucky Reporter,* February 28, 1825; *Frankfort (KY) Spirit of '76,* August 4, 1826.

15. Amos Kendall to Henry Clay, March 23, 1825, in *Papers of Henry Clay,* 4:134. In a more playful mood, Francis Blair, still on good terms with Henry Clay, wrote, "Your friends are well except the judges." Francis P. Blair to Henry Clay, January 24, 1825, in *Papers of Henry Clay,* 4:41.

16. *Frankfort (KY) Argus of Western America,* December 29, 1824; Sharp, *Vindication,* 41; *Frankfort (KY) Argus of Western America,* September 20, 1826; *Louisville (KY) Public Advertiser,* January 1, 1825; Solomon P. Sharp to Ninian Edwards, February 11, 1824, in *The Edwards Papers: Being a Portion of the Collection of the Letters, Papers, and Manuscripts of Ninian Edwards* (Chicago: Fergus, 1884), 217.

17. According to the *Kentucky Gazette,* February 3, 1825, the three judges "were seen issuing from their chambers in the Mansion House, and moving slowly towards the Old Bank of Kentucky, followed by a procession of Court Party lawyers and other partisans, together with many others who joined them from mere curiosity." As it had since the burning of the state capitol, the old court met in the building that housed the Bank of Kentucky.

18. *Frankfort (KY) Argus of Western America,* February 9, 1825.

19. Ibid.; Achilles Sneed, *Address to the People of Kentucky* (Frankfort, KY: Holeman, 1825), 7; Sharp, *Vindication,* 42.

20. Sneed, *Address to the People,* 10–11, 9; tax lists, Franklin County, KY, 1825, KDLA.

21. Sneed, *Address to the People,* 22.

22. *Kentucky Reporter,* March 2, 1825; *Maysville (KY) Eagle,* March 16, 1825.

23. "Beauchamp's Confession" in Kallsen, *Kentucky Tragedy,* 21; *The Spirit of '76, to the People of Kentucky, or A History of the Bank-rupt Court* (n.p., [1825?]), 11–12; *Frankfort (KY) Commentator,* September 16, 1826.

24. *Frankfort (KY) Argus of Western America,* February 9, 1826, July 6, 1825; Sharp, *Vindication,* 45, 43.

25. *Bluegrass Craftsman: Being the Reminiscences of Ebenezer Hiram Stedman, Papermaker, 1808–1885,* ed. Francis L. S. Dugan and Jacqueline P. Bull (Lexington: University of Kentucky Press, 1959), 74, 75; Fred Somkin, *The Unquiet Eagle: Memory and Desire in the Idea of American Freedom, 1815–1860* (Ithaca, NY: Cornell University Press, 1967), 131–74; *Kentucky Reporter,* May 2, 1825. Sharp was appointed by Governor Desha as a member of the committee of arrangements, along with ex-governor John Adair, Lieutenant Governor Robert McAfee, William T. Barry, Jesse Bledsoe, John J. Crittenden, and George M. Bibb.

26. Levin, *Lawyers and Lawmakers,* 111; Edgar Erskine Hume, ed., "LaFayette in Kentucky," *Register of the Kentucky Historical Society* 33 (1935): 247; *Louisville (KY) Morning Post,* July 7, 1825. Sharp was not originally scheduled to speak, but "in the absence of the gentleman delegated to deliver the address at Louisville, [Sharp] was called upon to fill his place and made extemporaneously a most eloquent and touching address." In addition, at the public dinner, Sharp rose and toasted Lafayette in

typical new court fashion: "The People: Liberty will always be safe in their holy keeping." Hume, "LaFayette in Kentucky," 294.

27. George Robertson to John J. Crittenden, May 25, 1825, John Jordan Crittenden Papers, microfilm, FHS. Crittenden, like Beauchamp's father and Solomon Sharp, had participated in General Hopkins's expedition during the War of 1812.

28. Swem, *Letters on the Condition of Kentucky,* 37; *The Life of John J. Crittenden, with Selections from His Correspondence and Speeches,* ed. Mrs. [Ann Mary] Chapman Coleman (Philadelphia: Lippincott, 1873), 1:43.

29. "Joseph Underwood's Fragmentary Journal on the New and Old Court Contest in Kentucky," ed. Arendt M. Stickles, *Filson Club Historical Quarterly* 13 (1939): 207; Kirwan, *John J. Crittenden,* 43. For Jefferson's dinner parties, see Catherine Allgor's brilliant *Parlor Politics: In Which the Ladies of Washington Help Build a City and Government* (Charlottesville: University of Virginia Press, 2000), 4–48.

30. Swem, *Letters on the Condition of Kentucky,* 37–38; Francis P. Blair to Henry Clay, January 30, 1826, in *Papers of Henry Clay,* 5:70; "Letter from Francis P. Blair to the Workingmen," August 14, 1869, microfilm, KHS; *Frankfort (KY) Argus of Western America,* June 29, 1825; "Joseph Underwood's Fragmentary Journal," 205; Thomas Green, diary, December 24, 1826, WVU. Some new court supporters had difficulty accepting that Crittenden had embraced the old court; one essayist, "Franklin," wrote, "I firmly believe he has been grossly deluded." *Frankfort (KY) Argus of Western America,* June 29, 1825. Crittenden had substantial personal relationships with members of the new court faction; he was a schoolmate of Blair's, had studied law under George M. Bibb, and had served as an aide to Isaac Shelby during the War of 1812, along with future pro-relief governor John Adair and future chief justice of the new court, William T. Barry. Kirwan, *John J. Crittenden,* 21.

31. *Frankfort (KY) Argus of Western America,* February 22, 1826; *Louisville (KY) Morning Post,* July 7, 1825; "Beauchamp's Trial" in Kallsen, *Kentucky Tragedy,* 199.

32. Sharp, *Vindication,* 46; Sharp, "To the Public."

33. Sharp, *Vindication,* 49, 77 (Dr. Sharp believed that this handbill was sent to Beauchamp and helped provoke the murder of Colonel Sharp); *U.S. Telegraph,* March 21, 1829; Patrick Darby, "To the Public," no. 1, *Frankfort (KY) Commentator,* April 1, 1826; Sharp, "To the Public."

34. *Spirit of '76, to the People of Kentucky,* 11–12; *Autobiography of Amos Kendall,* 189; *Frankfort (KY) Harbinger* quoted in Sharp, *Vindication,* 44, 46–47. Incidentally, Marshall's taunting of Sharp as Catiline, a Roman aristocrat who won popular favor in part because of his proposals for the cancellation of debt, was, as it turned out, eerily apt: after being acquitted of charges of fornication with a vestal virgin, Catiline, who held the judicial office of praetor, met a violent death after an attempted coup d'état.

35. *Kentucky Gazette,* August, 3, 1821, June 2, 1820; Robert J. Breckinridge to A. S. Breckinridge, July 15, 1825, Breckinridge Family Papers.

36. *Kentucky Reporter,* March 29, 1826; John A. Clark, *Gleanings by the Way* (Philadelphia: Simon, 1842), 70; Stanley, *Journal of a Tour in America,* 227.

37. Prentice quoted in Clement Eaton, *The Leaven of Democracy: The Growth of the Democratic Spirit in the Time of Jackson* (New York: Braziller, 1963), 56–57.

38. *Life of John J. Crittenden,* 1:46; Triplett, *Roland Trevor,* 109–10.

39. *Frankfort (KY) Argus of Western America,* August 10, 1825. According to the *Frankfort (KY) Harbinger,* August 10, 1825, with affiliations (new court, NC, or old court, OC) from the *Frankfort (KY) Argus of Western America,* August 10, 1825, the final vote was as follows:

	Sharp (NC)	Sanders (NC)	Downing (NC)	Crittenden (OC)
Frankfort	503	451	573	701
Lawrenceburg	397	376	66	130
Total	*900*	*827*	*639*	*831*

This breakdown of the voting shows that Sharp's popularity was not centered in Frankfort, where he came in third place. It was in the outlying regions of the county that Sharp's support was the strongest. Had Anderson County—which was formed two years later out of the part of Franklin County that included Lawrenceburg—existed, Sharp would not have been elected.

Upon his election, Sharp officially resigned the position of Kentucky attorney general and was replaced by Frederick W. S. Grayson of Louisville. See *Frankfort (KY) Argus of Western America,* August 10, 1825. By next May's trial, however, J. W. Denny was attorney general.

40. William T. Barry to daughter, August 22, 1825, Barry Papers; Francis P. Blair to Henry Clay, August 30, 1825, in *Papers of Henry Clay,* 4:603; *Frankfort (KY) Patriot,* March 27, 1826; *Kentucky Reporter,* August 8, 1825.

41. "Beauchamp's Confession" in Kallsen, *Kentucky Tragedy,* 18; Sharp, *Vindication,* 49; *Letter from Robert Wickliffe to His Constituents,* 3; *Frankfort (KY) Spirit of '76,* July 14, 1826; Merrill, *Jefferson's Nephews,* 181; John Pope, deposition, January 30, 1827, Circuit Court of Franklin County, KY, file 442, KDLA; "One Face to the Voters of Washington County" (broadside, [1825–1826]), FHS; "Beauchamp's Confession" in Kallsen, *Kentucky Tragedy,* 84. The practice of "treating" went well back to colonial Virginia; see Charles Sydnor, *Gentlemen Freeholders: Political Practices in Washington's Virginia* (Chapel Hill: University of North Carolina Press, 1952).

42. *Frankfort (KY) Patriot,* May 22, 1826; "Beauchamp's Confession" in Kallsen, *Kentucky Tragedy,* 3, 18, 19. Tompkins, in the early part of the century, lived about two and a half miles outside Glasgow, near Boyd's Creek.

43. Darby, "To the Public," no. 1; Sharp, *Vindication,* 130; "Narrative of the Attempts Made"; "Beauchamp's Confession" in Kallsen, *Kentucky Tragedy,* 20, 81–82. Two of the Beauchamps' neighbors, Mary Prescott and Martha Dowell, later deposed that they had seen, on separate occasions, letters written to Beauchamp from Frankfort claiming that Sharp was spreading the rumor that Anna's child was black. According to Prescott, the night Beauchamp returned home after killing Sharp, Anna "took down a little bag of dried fruit, ripped open one corner of it and

took out a bundle of rags which appeared to be carefully wrapped up and fastened. On unrolling them, she took out a letter and handed it to her husband, and asked him if it ought not to be burned. He opened and read it, and then put it in the fire and burnt it." Dowell deposed that after Beauchamp was taken into custody, she saw Anna "go to a bed and rip open one corner of it, and take out some letters that had been secreted there, and burn them." Sharp, *Vindication,* 50–52; "Narrative of the Attempts Made."

44. Bynum, *Unruly Women,* 45; Charles Fenno Hoffman, *A Winter in the West* (New York: Harper, 1835), 2:327; *Providence (RI) Literary Cadet,* April 14, 1827; Darby, "To the Public," no. 3. Three scholars—Martha Hodes, in *White Women, Black Men: Illicit Sex in the Nineteenth-Century South* (New Haven, CT: Yale University Press, 1997); Joshua D. Rothman, in *Notorious in the Neighborhood: Sex and Families across the Color Line in Virginia, 1787–1861* (Chapel Hill: University of North Carolina Press, 2003); and Diane Miller Sommerville, in "The Rape Myth in the Old South Reconsidered," *Journal of Southern History* 61 (1995): 481–518—argue that sex "across the color line," involving white women and black men, although never accepted, was "tolerated" in the sense that the black man was not immediately subject to violent death, as was the case after the Civil War.

45. *Frankfort (KY) Patriot,* April 3, 1826; John M. Bass, deposition, February 15, 1828, Circuit Court of Woodford County, KY, file 442, KDLA; Sharp, *Vindication,* 76, 80. Old court partisans later countered with a number of witnesses who said that they had heard friends of Colonel Sharp say that if the Cooke story came up, Sharp had a certificate to prove the child a mulatto. John and George Gayle, Charles Miles, and William Turner all testified that they had, in George Gayle's words, "heard it frequently stated by the political friends of Col. Sharp, that . . . he had obtained a certificate from the midwife, proving the child to be a mulatto." *Frankfort (KY) Commentator,* July 15, 1826. Yet Dr. Sharp claimed to have actually visited each of these men, demanding the name of any new court partisan who retailed the story of the midwife's certificate: "Not one of them could name a single individual!! All was vague and indefinite." Dr. Sharp charitably surmised that they must have "unconsciously thrust back conversations heard after my brother's death." Another purported witness who claimed to have heard the charge, Solomon Snow, testified that in July 1825, Colonel Sharp, along with a man named Stafford Pemberton, came to Snow's house and stated that he could prove that Anna's child was black. Yet Dr. Sharp later produced a document signed by Pemberton, who swore that "no such subject as Snow speaks of was mentioned to me by the Colonel, in my hearing, during our ride, either before or after we were at Snow's; nor did I ever hear a word of the bastard child alluded to, having been coloured, during the whole canvassing, nor until after Col. Sharp was murdered. I was his friend, and actively engaged in his support, and mixed much with the people on the south side of the river." Sharp, *Vindication,* 76–79.

46. Sharp, *Vindication,* 81, 82; *Frankfort (KY) Commentator,* September 9, 1826; *Frankfort (KY) Argus of Western America,* July 19, 1826. For the supposition that the

child was "cyanotic, or what we would call a 'blue baby,'" see Cooke, "Portrait of a Murderess," 221.

47. "Beauchamp's Confession" in Kallsen, *Kentucky Tragedy,* 20; "Narrative of the Attempts Made."

48. "Beauchamp's Confession" in Kallsen, *Kentucky Tragedy,* 20, 49.

49. "Narrative of the Attempts Made"; Sharp, *Vindication,* 49, 77, 92; Darby, "To the Public," no. 1; Sharp, "To the Public"; "Beauchamp's Confession" in Kallsen, *Kentucky Tragedy,* 20; "Narrative of the Attempts Made." See also John McIntosh's statement in Sharp, *Vindication,* 130.

When John F. Lowe arrived in Frankfort for Beauchamp's trial, he cryptically told Eliza and Dr. Sharp that he knew of information that would make their "hair stand on end." Lowe eventually divulged to Joel Scott and General Elijah Covington that "a particular individual, deeply involved in the politics of the country, had been the chief agent in stimulating Beauchamp to the murder." Kendall thereafter reported that Lowe's statement "pointed so directly at an individual in Frankfort as an accomplice of Beauchamp, that he could not be mistaken." *Frankfort (KY) Argus of Western America,* June 14, 1826. In *Vindication,* Dr. Sharp wrote, "I know the name of the individual alluded to; but neither do I feel it necessary or prudent to disclose it. . . . He was one of the chief agents in instigating Beauchamp, nothing but the consideration that it can now do no good, prevents my writing his name in full. It was not Darby." Sharp, *Vindication,* 92.

50. Sharp, *Vindication,* 129–30; Francis P. Blair to John Payne, July 10, 1826, Payne Papers; *Frankfort (KY) Patriot,* July 17, 1826.

51. *Frankfort (KY) Patriot,* July 17, 1826; Sharp, *Vindication,* 50, 87, 140, 51, 49, 52–53.

52. "Beauchamp's Confession" in Kallsen, *Kentucky Tragedy,* 20.

53. Ibid., 22, 23, 21; "Beauchamp's Trial" in Kallsen, *Kentucky Tragedy,* 317, 318; "Narrative of the Attempts Made."

54. "Beauchamp's Confession" in Kallsen, *Kentucky Tragedy,* 23–24; "Beauchamp's Trial" in Kallsen, *Kentucky Tragedy,* 296.

55. "Beauchamp's Confession" in Kallsen, *Kentucky Tragedy,* 24–25; Sharp, *Vindication,* 29–30. Thomas Hail, the Simpson County constable and justice of the peace who attempted to serve the bastardy warrant on Beauchamp, also deposed that, in his opinion, Beauchamp did not issue the warrant, for when Hail arrived at the Beauchamps' with the complaint, Anna told him that Jereboam had heard of the warrant and had sworn that he would "kill before he will be taken." Sharp, *Vindication,* 30. See also Fred Johnson, "New Light on Beauchamp's Confession?" *Border States* 9 (1993): 5. The expunged section continues, "[Ruth Reed] has had the justice several times to declare I was not [the father of her child]. But far be it from me to say anything which might add in the slightest degree to her misfortune. She has repeatedly however declared to the neighborhood that he did not doubt at all but that it was the child of another man." Johnson remarks, "Somehow, given his own scenario as an avenging redeemer of wronged women, one doubts that it would involve a charge

of fathering a child out of wedlock!" Johnson, "New Light on Beauchamp's Confession," 5.

5. MURDER

1. Stanley, *Journal of a Tour in America,* 217; Hoffman, *Winter in the West,* 1:155.

2. Carl E. Kramer, *Capital on the Kentucky: A Two Hundred Year History of Frankfort and Franklin County* (Frankfort, KY: Historic Frankfort, 1986), 18, 39–40; Carl Kramer, "Frankfort," in *Kentucky Encyclopedia,* ed. John E. Kleber (Lexington: University Press of Kentucky, 1992), 352–54; Randolph quoted in Paul David Nelson, "James Wilkinson," *American National Biography* (New York: Oxford University Press, 1999), 23:400–402.

3. Victor Collot, *A Journey in North America, Containing a Survey of the Countries Watered by the Mississippi, Ohio, Missouri, and Other Affluing Rivers* (Paris: Bertrand, 1826), 105.

4. *Daily Kentucky Yeoman,* March 13, 1876, WKU; Louis Marshall, interview by John Shane, 1854, 16CC241, Draper Collection; Mary Breckinridge to Robert Jefferson Breckinridge, January 18, 1826, Breckinridge Family Papers; T. L. Crittenden to John Coyle, April 12, 1860, Crittenden Papers; Agness Templin to Joshua Lacy Wilson, July 18, 1799, September 7, 1799, in *The First American West: The Ohio River Valley, 1750–1820,* http://memory.loc.gov/cgi-bin/query/d?fawbib:0:./temp/~ammem_8gVa:.

5. Triplett, *Roland Trevor,* 95.

6. Horace Waring to Henry Waring, December 23, 1828, miscellaneous manuscripts, FHS; "Joseph Underwood's Fragmentary Journal," 206; Swem, *Letters on the Condition of Kentucky,* 20.

7. Blowe, *Geographical, Historical, Commercial,* 588; "Beauchamp's Trial" in Kallsen, *Kentucky Tragedy,* 167; Mary Willis Woodson, "My Recollections of Frankfort," *Register of the Kentucky Historical Society* 61 (1963): 203; "Beauchamp's Confession" in Kallsen, *Kentucky Tragedy,* 21. The Mansion House "was always the Democratic headquarters. [Most new court partisans became Democrats when the party formed.] . . . Every year on the 8th of January, the anniversary of the battle of New Orleans, a grand ball was given at this house, where assembled the beauty, fashion and chivalry of the town and surrounding country." *Frankfort (KY) Capital,* October 1886, vertical files, KHS.

8. "Beauchamp's Trial" in Kallsen, *Kentucky Tragedy,* 209, 210.

9. Ibid., 211, 183; "Beauchamp's Confession" in Kallsen, *Kentucky Tragedy,* 31; L. F. Johnson, *History of Franklin County, Kentucky* (Frankfort, KY: Roberts, 1912), 78–79; William C. Sneed, *A Report on the History and Mode of Management of the Kentucky Penitentiary, from Its Origin, in 1798, to March 1, 1860* (Frankfort, KY: Major, 1860), 204, 217. Beauchamp wrote that Joel Scott was a relative of Eliza Scott Sharp, and later commentators, such as Henry St. Clair, in *The United States Criminal Calendar, or An Awful Warning to the Youth of America* (Boston: Gaylord, 1835),

284–310, repeated the claim. The two, in fact, were not related, at least not closely. Eliza Scott's father, John Mitchell Scott, was born in Pennsylvania and later settled in Franklin County; Joel Scott's father, also named John Scott, was born in Culpepper County, Virginia, and later settled in Scott County. See Eliza's father's obituary in *Kentucky Gazette,* December 29, 1812, and Thomas D. Clark, *Footloose in Jacksonian America* (Frankfort: Kentucky Historical Society, 1989), 108.

10. "Beauchamp's Trial" in Kallsen, *Kentucky Tragedy,* 211–12.

11. *U.S. Telegraph,* March 21, 1829. According to Levin, *Lawyers and Lawmakers,* 109, "Mr. Sharp was regarded as one of the most active and powerful of the advocates of the Relief party and its candidate for speaker of the house, for which high office he had received the caucus nomination on the night of his death." Joseph R. Underwood, an old court stalwart from Warren County who was nonetheless staying at the Mansion House, recorded in his journal, "Col. Sharp visited me & proposed that I should become a candidate for the office of speaker of the house of representatives & promised if I would that he would with pleasure support me & told me that my prospects of being elected were very good if not very sure." Although the two were old acquaintances, Underwood knew that it was Sharp himself who many thought would become speaker—according to one source, Sharp had that very evening attended a new court party caucus, which had nominated him as their candidate for speaker. And thus Underwood, with good reason, suspected his old friend's intentions and supposed that Sharp wished to run against him rather than against George Robertson, another old court supporter of substantial influence and power who many thought would be the old court's nominee. "Joseph Underwood's Fragmentary Journal," 206. According to Leander Sharp, Solomon actually had a plan to compromise "our judicial troubles," but if he did, he apparently neglected to share his ideas with anyone else. Sharp, *Vindication,* 62.

12. "Beauchamp's Confession" in Kallsen, *Kentucky Tragedy,* 26, 29. George Bibb later testified that "it was light enough to walk the streets without the aid of a lanthern." "Beauchamp's Trial" in Kallsen, *Kentucky Tragedy,* 286.

13. "Beauchamp's Confession" in Kallsen, *Kentucky Tragedy,* 26–28.

14. Sharp, *Vindication,* 63; "Beauchamp's Trial" in Kallsen, *Kentucky Tragedy,* 211–12, 214, 215. Beauchamp dismissed the testimony of Crane and Downing as that of "street walkers, going in the character of a patrole," contending, "I was on that street that night, but it was before 11 o'clock, and I had on no cloak," although he admitted to wearing "an old ragged surtout coat" like the one worn by the man described by Crane and Downing. Downing did acknowledge that although his "impression" was that it was Beauchamp, "I may be mistaken; I can't be positive." A third night watchman, Asahel Carl, was not allowed to testify because he was a member of the group that apprehended Beauchamp and was thus eligible for a portion of the reward money should Beauchamp be found guilty. "Beauchamp's Confession" in Kallsen, *Kentucky Tragedy,* 65, 26; "Beauchamp's Trial" in Kallsen, *Kentucky Tragedy,* 235, 242.

15. Beauchamp to Crittenden, November 25, 1825, in Bamberg, *Confession of Jereboam O. Beauchamp,* 145; Sharp, *Vindication,* 63.

16. Sharp, *Vindication,* 65.

17. "Beauchamp's Confession" in Kallsen, *Kentucky Tragedy,* 26–27; Coleman, *Beauchamp-Sharp Tragedy,* 7. After the crime, Anna told a neighbor that Jereboam, under the pretense of wanting "to get a black girl of Col. Sharp's," had given a dollar to a black man to show him where Sharp slept. Dr. Sharp, clinging to the conspiracy thesis, rejected this story and later went to "considerable pains" trying to "discover the negro who was said to have shown the murderer where Col. Sharp slept; but all inquiries proved fruitless." If this slave-informant did exist, it would have been surprising indeed for him to be willing to confess his complicity, even if unintentional, in the most explosive murder in the history of the state. "Beauchamp's Trial" in Kallsen, *Kentucky Tragedy,* 317; Sharp, *Vindication,* 95.

18. *Lexington (KY) Western Luminary,* June 28, 1826; "Narrative of the Attempts Made."

19. Coleman, *Beauchamp-Sharp Tragedy,* 7; Sharp, *Vindication,* 119; *Frankfort (KY) Argus of Western America,* May 31, 1826; "Beauchamp's Confession" in Kallsen, *Kentucky Tragedy,* 28.

20. *Frankfort (KY) Argus of Western America* reprinted in *Danville (KY) Advertiser,* June 8, 1826; "Beauchamp's Confession" in Kallsen, *Kentucky Tragedy,* 27–28; *Frankfort (KY) Commentator,* November 12, 1825; "Beauchamp's Trial" in Kallsen, *Kentucky Tragedy,* 180, 285.

21. "Beauchamp's Confession" in Kallsen, *Kentucky Tragedy,* 29–30.

22. J. O. Beauchamp, "The Death Scene," in Kallsen, *Kentucky Tragedy,* 95–96.

23. "Beauchamp's Trial" in Kallsen, *Kentucky Tragedy,* 180. During the trial, Harvie, the president of the Bank of Kentucky and one of the first to arrive at the murder scene, testified that Eliza's "several statements were uniformly the same" in describing the murder. Ibid., 272.

24. Ibid., 221; Bass, deposition.

25. "Beauchamp's Trial" in Kallsen, *Kentucky Tragedy,* 173–74; Bass, deposition; Sharp, *Vindication,* 66. Dr. Sharp testified that "the wound was closed up by the inner coat of the stomach," and George Bibb testified that "there was but little blood from the wound; it was checked by some intestines which prevented it from issuing—that on the night shirt, appeared pale and rather thin." "Beauchamp's Trial" in Kallsen, *Kentucky Tragedy,* 310, 309, 279.

According to Beauchamp, who did not immediately leave the murder scene, when Dr. Sharp arrived, "he exclaimed, 'Great God, Beauchamp has done this! I always expected it!'" Two eyewitnesses, Austin Cox and Richard Taylor, also claimed that Dr. Sharp "immediately said that Beauchamp was the murderer." In addition, one old court newspaper editor, Patrick Henry Darby, later said that Dr. Sharp had admitted to him that he had immediately accused Beauchamp of the crime. Yet Dr. Sharp strongly denied ever saying anything to that effect, asserting that he "did not know, that my brother had a personal enemy on earth, that was base enough to seek his life." The law student Bass, who was present all along, was "certain that he did not" hear "either Dr. Sharp or Mrs. Sharp at that time say 'that Beauchamp had done it' or 'that Beauchamp was the man' nor did either of them then . . . at that time suspect any known person." The point may seem trivial, but if the Sharps did immediately suspect Beauchamp, it would suggest, as Beauchamp and the old court partisans claimed, that Solomon had wronged the Beauchamps and that the Sharps were well aware of it. "Beauchamp's Confession" in Kallsen, *Kentucky Tragedy,* 30; Darby, "To the Public," no. 1; Sharp, "To the Public"; Bass, deposition. See also Sharp, *Vindication,* 119.

26. "Beauchamp's Trial" in Kallsen, *Kentucky Tragedy,* 278; Sharp, *Vindication,* 66; *Frankfort (KY) Argus of Western America,* December 7, 1825; *Frankfort (KY) Commentator,* November 12, 1825.

27. "Beauchamp's Trial" in Kallsen, *Kentucky Tragedy,* 181, 281, 273; "Beauchamp's Confession" in Kallsen, *Kentucky Tragedy,* 30.

28. Sharp, "To the Public"; *Frankfort (KY) Argus of Western America,* November 30, 1825; "Beauchamp's Trial" in Kallsen, *Kentucky Tragedy,* 271. The *Frankfort (KY) Patriot,* April 17, 1826, called the event "the dreadful catastrophe which happened on her BIRTHDAY, and which closed with her 27th year, the happiness of a life so intimately connected with that of her husband."

29. "Beauchamp's Confession" in Kallsen, *Kentucky Tragedy,* 31.

6. THE POLITICS OF MURDER

1. Sharp, *Vindication,* 66; *Frankfort (KY) Argus of Western America,* November 9, 1825; Robert J. Breckinridge to A. S. Breckinridge, November 7, 1826, Breckinridge Family Papers; *Frankfort (KY) Argus of Western America,* November 30, 1825, November, 9, 1825; Caroline Breckinridge to Robert J. Breckinridge, December 7, 1826, Breckinridge Family Papers; Lewis, "Republican Wife," 706; Theodore W. Clay to Henry Clay, November 11, 1825, in *Papers of Henry Clay,* 4:817; Andrew Jackson to Arthur Lee Campbell, June 12, 1826, Arthur Lee Campbell Papers, FHS. According to an early resident, Andrew Jackson regularly traveled to Bowling Green to race his horses. "Recollections of Henry Fox." See also Robert V. Remini, *Andrew Jackson and the Course of American Empire, 1767–1821* (New York: Harper and Row, 1977), 134.

2. "Joseph Underwood's Fragmentary Journal," 207.

3. *Frankfort (KY) Argus of Western America,* November 16, 1825, November 9, 1825; "Beauchamp's Trial" in Kallsen, *Kentucky Tragedy,* 310. Still another thousand dollars was to be raised by private subscription, but "on enquiry it was found, nothing had been raised by private subscription." The legislature also moved to create a county named after Sharp, but nothing came of it. Frank Mathias, "Solomon P. Sharp," in Kleber, *Kentucky Encyclopedia.*

4. "Joseph Underwood's Fragmentary Journal," 208; Sharp, *Vindication,* 67; Coleman, *Beauchamp-Sharp Tragedy,* 14–17; *Frankfort (KY) Argus of Western America,* November 16, 1825; *Louisville (KY) Gazette,* November 18, 1825. Sharp's grave was removed to the new Frankfort cemetery after it was opened in 1846.

5. Robert J. Breckinridge to A. S. Breckinridge, November 7, 1826, Breckinridge Family Papers; Sharp, *Vindication,* 23; *Frankfort (KY) Argus of Western America,* December 7, 1825. For good measure, an affidavit was appended to the statement asserting that Hamilton was in Barren County the night of the murder.

6. "Beauchamp's Trial" in Kallsen, *Kentucky Tragedy,* 212, 213, 221, 217, 275; "Beauchamp's Confession" in Kallsen, *Kentucky Tragedy,* 31, 32.

7. "Beauchamp's Trial" in Kallsen, *Kentucky Tragedy,* 220, 213; "Beauchamp's Confession" in Kallsen, *Kentucky Tragedy,* 32–33, 34, 36, 39.

8. *Frankfort (KY) Argus of Western America,* November 9, 1825; Sharp, *Vindication,* 67–68; Little, *Ben Hardin,* 140; *Frankfort (KY) Commentator,* November 12, 1825; "Beauchamp's Trial" in Kallsen, *Kentucky Tragedy,* 311.

9. "Beauchamp's Confession" in Kallsen, *Kentucky Tragedy,* 39–40.

10. "Beauchamp's Trial" in Kallsen, *Kentucky Tragedy,* 188, 226, 246; "Beauchamp's Confession" in Kallsen, *Kentucky Tragedy,* 72.

11. "Beauchamp's Confession" in Kallsen, *Kentucky Tragedy,* 40, 41, 44. The four men were William Jackson, a Franklin County constable whom Beauchamp described as "one of the more frank and sensible of the men"; Asahel Carl, one of the night watchmen who had seen Beauchamp out on the streets the night of the murder; a man named Kelly whom Beauchamp dismissed as "a poor worthless coward"; and another man named Carroll. According to Beauchamp, he had resolved to shoot Dr. Sharp if he were among the guard. He also claimed to have toyed with the idea of killing anyone who came for him, and then fleeing the country, but "I had calmly come to the resolution that I would rather die than fly my country. And as they had no shadow of proof against me, I resolved to go quite quietly and cheerfully forward and submit to an investigation, should any one come for me." Two other men rode with the group back to Frankfort—Isaac and John W. Covington, of the same Covington family of which Beauchamp claimed to be a member when he knocked at Sharp's door—but did not come up to Beauchamp's house. Beauchamp claimed the brothers were "famous for their cowardice." Ibid., 40–42, 45; "Beauchamp's Trial" in Kallsen, *Kentucky Tragedy,* 257, 266.

12. *Frankfort (KY) Commentator,* November 12, 1825; "Beauchamp's Confession" in Kallsen, *Kentucky Tragedy,* 42–43.

13. "Beauchamp's Trial" in Kallsen, *Kentucky Tragedy,* 223, 273, 221, 240.

14. "Beauchamp's Confession" in Kallsen, *Kentucky Tragedy,* 40, 41, 44, 45; "Beauchamp's Trial" in Kallsen, *Kentucky Tragedy,* 240–41; "Beauchamp's Confession" in Kallsen, *Kentucky Tragedy,* 44–45.

15. "Beauchamp's Confession" in Kallsen, *Kentucky Tragedy,* 46.

16. Ibid., 46–47, 53; Sharp, *Vindication,* 53; "Beauchamp's Confession" in Kallsen, *Kentucky Tragedy,* 53–54; *Danville (KY) Advertiser,* November 24, 1825; *Kentucky Reporter,* November 21, 1825; Coleman, *Beauchamp-Sharp Tragedy,* 22.

17. *Frankfort (KY) Argus of Western America,* November 9, 1825; *Louisville (KY) Public Advertiser,* November 19, 1825; *Kentucky Reporter,* November 14, 1825; *Lexington (KY) Whig* reprinted in *Frankfort (KY) Commentator,* January 28, 1826;

Frankfort (KY) Commentator quoted in Sharp, *Vindication,* 74; *Kentucky Reporter,* November 14, 1825; *Frankfort (KY) Commentator,* January 28, 1826.

18. Lunsford Pitts Yandell to Wilson Yandell, November 7, 1825, Yandell Family Papers, FHS; *Biographical Encyclopedia of Kentucky* (1878; repr., Easley, SC: Southern Historical Press, 1980), 35; Sharp, *Vindication,* 73–74; *Frankfort (KY) Commentator,* January 28, 1826; *Frankfort (KY) Argus of Western America,* November 18, 1825. See also *Speech of Robert Wickliffe, Esq., Delivered at Athens, (Late Cross Plains,) Saturday, June 17th 1826 on the Subject of the Proposed Compromise of the Judicial Department of the Government, in Which the Cause and Means That Led to Our Present Judicial Troubles Are Fully Discussed* (n.p., 1826), 13.

19. Levin, *Lawyers and Lawmakers,* 112, 114; F. P. Blair, "For the Argus," *Frankfort (KY) Argus of Western America,* February 22, 1826; *Frankfort (KY) Argus of Western America,* November 30, 1825.

20. Beauchamp to Crittenden, November 25, 1825, in Bamberg, *Confession of Jereboam O. Beauchamp,* 138. According to the *Frankfort (KY) Argus of Western America,* November 9, 1825, "It is evident that he must have known the house and the room where his victim was sleeping, for had he knocked at any other door he would probably have been met by some other person." See also Sharp, *Vindication,* 63.

21. Jereboam Beauchamp to George Bibb, November 21, 1825, in Kallsen, *Kentucky Tragedy,* 98; Beauchamp to Crittenden, November 25, 1825, in Bamberg, *Confession of Jereboam O. Beauchamp,* 145, 144.

22. Beauchamp to Crittenden, November 25, 1825, in Bamberg, *Confession of Jereboam O. Beauchamp,* 141–42, 143, 140, 145. Beauchamp had considered killing Sharp back in August, "on the second night of the election," an act which, Beauchamp knew, "would have raised a prodigious commotion in my favor throughout the state, amongst the new court faction." "Beauchamp's Confession" in Kallsen, *Kentucky Tragedy,* 23.

23. "Beauchamp's Confession" in Kallsen, *Kentucky Tragedy,* 47, 48; *Frankfort (KY) Argus of Western America,* February 22, 1826, February 8, 1826. See also *Frankfort (KY) Argus of Western America,* January, 25, 1826, and Sharp, *Vindication,* 63.

24. Joseph Underwood, diary, December 12, 1825 (transcript), 7, Underwood Collection; Sharp, "To the Public"; Richard Ivy Easter to Andrew Jackson, May 20, 1821, in *The Papers of Andrew Jackson* (Knoxville: University of Tennessee Press, 1996), 5:40; "Beauchamp's Trial" in Kallsen, *Kentucky Tragedy,* 204; John McNairy, Felix Grundy, William Hadley, Allan D. Campbell, and Hardy McCryer, depositions, July 26, 1826, August 7, 1826, *Patrick Henry Darby v. Jereboam Beauchamp,* file 440, Circuit Court of Franklin County, Franklin, KY; "Beauchamp's Confession" in Kallsen, *Kentucky Tragedy,* 49. Historians have generally concurred with such assessments. Thomas Abernethy depicted Darby as "a shyster of the worst type"; Joseph Parks labeled him a "land pirate." Thomas Perkins Abernethy, *From Frontier to Plantation in Tennessee: A Study in Frontier Democracy* (Chapel Hill: University of North Carolina Press, 1932), 266; Joseph Howard Parks, *Felix Grundy: Champion of Democracy* (Baton Rouge: Louisiana State University Press, 1940), 158.

25. Sharp, *Vindication,* 34; Abernethy, *From Frontier to Plantation in Tennessee,* 265, 266; *History of Tennessee from the Earliest Time to the Present* (Nashville: Goodspeed, 1886), 848; Sharp, *Vindication,* 35, 39–40, 34.

26. Jackson to Campbell, Campbell Papers; *Frankfort (KY) Argus of Western America,* December 7, 1825. See also William Butler, interview by John Shane, 1858, 15CC55, Draper Collection. William Darby was on Jackson's topographical staff in the campaign of 1814–1815, which may well have facilitated Patrick Darby's relationship with Jackson. See J. Gerald Kennedy, *The Astonished Traveler: William Darby, Frontier Geographer and Man of Letters* (Baton Rouge: Louisiana State University Press, 1981).

27. Sharp, *Vindication,* 38; Johnson, *History of Franklin County,* 72; *Paris (KY) Western Citizen,* September 3, 1825; Underwood, diary, December 12, 1825, 7, Underwood Collection.

28. "Beauchamp's Confession" in Kallsen, *Kentucky Tragedy,* 49–50; Sharp, "To the Public"; *Frankfort (KY) Argus of Western America,* May 3, 1826. Both the lawyer, John Jackman, and his wife later swore that Darby had never set foot in their house. Sharp, *Vindication,* 71–72.

29. "Beauchamp's Confession" in Kallsen, *Kentucky Tragedy,* 51.

30. Sharp, "To the Public"; Sharp, *Vindication,* 126–27.

31. Sharp, "To the Public." Dr. Sharp later confirmed the story: "During Mr. Darby's visit, I was in Mr. Bass' room and distinctly heard his voice through the partition." He added, "Colonel Sharp told him, and supposing that he wanted to see Mr. Bass, offered to conduct him to the room. Mr. Darby declined, and took his leave." Such was Colonel Sharp's poor opinion of Darby that he further surmised that Darby "would take the liberty to examine his papers, if he should chance to call when no person was in the office." Sharp, *Vindication,* 62.

32. Sharp, "To the Public." See also Sharp, *Vindication,* 67.

33. Sharp, "To the Public."

34. *Frankfort (KY) Commentator,* March 25, 1826; Darby, "To the Public," no. 1; "Beauchamp's Trial" in Kallsen, *Kentucky Tragedy,* 184; Pope, deposition; McIntosh, deposition; Amos Kendall, deposition, January 30, 1827, Circuit Court of Franklin County, KY, file 442, KDLA; James Davidson, deposition, January 30, 1827, Circuit Court of Franklin County, KY, file 442, KDLA; Bass, deposition.

35. Darby, "To the Public," no. 1; *Frankfort (KY) Patriot,* April 17, 1826; *Frankfort (KY) Argus of Western America,* March 29, 1826, February 22, 1826.

36. *Life of John J. Crittenden,* 1:21; Beauchamp to Crittenden, November 25, 1825, in Bamberg, *Confession of Jereboam O. Beauchamp,* 144; Jereboam Beauchamp to John J. Crittenden, November 18, 1825, in Bamberg, *Confession of Jereboam O. Beauchamp,* 137–38; Sharp, *Vindication,* 69; *Frankfort (KY) Commentator and Constitutional Advocate,* May 6, 1826.

37. Little, *Ben Hardin,* 14. Dr. James Priestley was the brother of Joseph Priestley, scientist and English expatriate.

38. Thomas Hinde, diary, n.d., 29Y208, Draper Collection; John Pope to Ninian Edwards, November 9, 1808, in *Edwards Papers,* 38; *Kentucky Gazette,* October 27,

1812; *Kentucky Reporter*, November 27, 1816; Bowman to Austin, in Barker, *Annual Report of the American Historical Association*, 227–28.

39. Pope to Edwards, in *Edwards Papers*, 34; Orval W. Baylor, *John Pope, Kentuckian: His Life and Times, 1770–1845* (Cynthiana, KY: Hobson Press, 1943), 64.

40. Ferris Essing, Worsley Papers, 6CC50, Draper Collection; Johnson, *History of the Franklin County Bar*, 35.

41. *Frankfort (KY) Commentator*, April 1, 1826; "Beauchamp's Trial" in Kallsen, *Kentucky Tragedy*, 167; *Frankfort (KY) Commentator*, March 25, 1826.

7. THE TRIAL

1. "Beauchamp's Confession" in Kallsen, *Kentucky Tragedy*, 79, 40, 33, 35; "Lines Written by J. O. Beauchamp" in Kallsen, *Kentucky Tragedy*, 91–92; "Lines Addressed to Mrs. Francis R. Hawkins, by Mrs. Beauchamp" in Kallsen, *Kentucky Tragedy*, 95; "Verses Addressed by Mrs. Anna Beauchamp to J. O. Beauchamp" in Kallsen, *Kentucky Tragedy*, 94. The *Confession* is littered with such statements.

2. Robert D. Bamberg, introduction to Bamberg, *Confession of Jereboam O. Beauchamp*, 12; Coleman, *Beauchamp-Sharp Tragedy*, ix.

3. *Frankfort (KY) Spirit of '76*, July 14, 1826; "Beauchamp's Trial" in Kallsen, *Kentucky Tragedy*, 318; Darby, "To the Public," no. 6; "Beauchamp's Confession" in Kallsen, *Kentucky Tragedy*, 63, 65, 67.

4. *Life of John J. Crittenden*, 1:21; *Frankfort (KY) Patriot*, May 22, 1826. For other descriptions of the courthouse, see Fortescue Cuming, *Sketches of a Tour to the Western Country* (Pittsburgh: Cramer, Spear, and Eichbaum, 1810), 192, and Woodson, "My Recollections of Frankfort," 200.

5. *Sixty Years in a School-Room: An Autobiography of Mrs. Julia A. Tevis* (Cincinnati: Western Methodist Book Concern, 1878), 353; Harrison D. Taylor, *Ohio County, Kentucky, in the Olden Days* (Louisville, KY: Morton, 1926), 80. See *Kentucky Reporter*, February 16, 1820. Henry Davidge should not be confused with Rezin Davidge, a justice of the new court of appeals.

6. Francis P. Blair to John Payne, April 7, 1826, Payne Papers; "Beauchamp's Trial" in Kallsen, *Kentucky Tragedy*, 186.

7. *Frankfort (KY) Commentator*, January 28, 1826; "Beauchamp's Confession" in Kallsen, *Kentucky Tragedy*, 79–80. Mayes, who had been an old court supporter from Christian County in the 1825–1826 Kentucky House of Representatives and who enjoyed a reputation as an outstanding lawyer, was "cold, distant, and somewhat exclusive in his associations, rarely mingling with his neighbors. He would pass from his residence to his office and from his office to his residence and never look to the right or to the left, or speak to any one unless first spoken to. But he was a man of undoubted intellect and ability, though not a politician or party schemer. As regarded political intrigue he was as innocent as a child." Perrin, *County of Christian, Kentucky*, 105–6. Later a professor of law at Transylvania University, Mayes moved to Mississippi in 1838, where he died two years later.

8. "Beauchamp's Trial" in Kallsen, *Kentucky Tragedy,* 230, 206.

9. *Frankfort (KY) Argus of Western America,* June 14, 1826. See also Sharp, *Vindication,* 92–93.

10. *Frankfort (KY) Patriot,* May 15, 1826; Darby, "To the Public," no. 3.

11. "Beauchamp's Trial" in Kallsen, *Kentucky Tragedy,* 168, 169; *Frankfort (KY) Patriot,* May 15, 1826. Although Davidge would not issue an attachment, believing that the court had no power at this special term to institute original proceedings of this character, he did speculate that a charge of contempt might be warranted. Bibb promised that, in his capacity as a commonwealth's attorney, he would "prosecute the motion, not only against the Editors named, but against all the publishers of papers in the county." "Beauchamp's Trial" in Kallsen, *Kentucky Tragedy,* 168. In his next editorial, Darby dismissed the complaint as a "tirade" full of "harsh epithets," asserting that Pope "neither produced or specified" how the papers had prejudiced the public against his clients. *Frankfort (KY) Commentator,* May 13, 1826. A similar problem appeared in the celebrated Helen Jewett murder case in New York City in 1836: "The penny papers inserted themselves between the crime and the audience. . . . Unprecedented, extensive pretrial publicity forced newspaper editors for the first time to consider the possibility that what they printed might have an effect on impending judicial proceedings. . . . What was to prevent editors from simply making up material to entertain or to win a competitive edge over other papers? Should editors declare their opinions on the guilt or innocence of the accused?" Cohen, *Murder of Helen Jewett,* 26.

12. "Beauchamp's Trial" in Kallsen, *Kentucky Tragedy,* 171–72; *Frankfort (KY) Patriot,* May 15, 1826. Ten of the twelve jurors can be located in the Franklin County tax lists. Although one contemporary, D. C. Humphreys, claimed that "every man on the jury was a New Court man," such was unlikely, given the closely contested nature of the court struggle in Frankfort. Humphreys, interview, Draper Collection.

13. Suzanne Lebsock, "Truth or Dare: On History and Fiction," *Common-place* 5, no. 1 (2004), http://www.common-place.org/vol-05/no-01/author/; Karen Halttunen, *Murder Most Foul: The Killer and the American Gothic Imagination* (Cambridge, MA: Harvard University Press, 1998), 99.

14. "Beauchamp's Trial" in Kallsen, *Kentucky Tragedy,* 186, 193, 195.

15. Ibid., 179; *Frankfort (KY) Patriot,* April 17, 1826.

16. "Beauchamp's Trial" in Kallsen, *Kentucky Tragedy,* 285, 185, 237; "Beauchamp's Confession" in Kallsen, *Kentucky Tragedy,* 56; "Beauchamp's Trial" in Kallsen, *Kentucky Tragedy,* 238, 181.

17. "Beauchamp's Trial" in Kallsen, *Kentucky Tragedy,* 228–29.

18. Ibid., 304, 291; "Beauchamp's Confession" in Kallsen, *Kentucky Tragedy,* 59, 60; "Beauchamp's Trial" in Kallsen, *Kentucky Tragedy,* 265.

19. *Frankfort (KY) Argus of Western America,* June 7, 1826; "Beauchamp's Trial" in Kallsen, *Kentucky Tragedy,* 220, 235–36.

20. "Beauchamp's Trial" in Kallsen, *Kentucky Tragedy,* 230, 298, 297.

21. "Beauchamp's Confession" in Kallsen, *Kentucky Tragedy,* 72; "Beauchamp's

Trial" in Kallsen, *Kentucky Tragedy,* 186, 188, 226, 246, 319, 267; *Lexington (KY) Western Luminary,* June 28, 1826.

22. "Beauchamp's Trial" in Kallsen, *Kentucky Tragedy,* 223, 221, 240, 273, 280; "Beauchamp's Confession" in Kallsen, *Kentucky Tragedy,* 63. Charles Murphy—an uncle of Beauchamp's who lived on the road to Frankfort and with whom Beauchamp stayed on the way there—testified, "I recollect his using a handkerchief in the house, and I think he put it on his head when he started." Colonel Absalom Stratton, a neighbor of Beauchamp's, said that "a little yellow boy" belonging to Beauchamp had been to his house twice, carrying a handkerchief belonging to Beauchamp that was similar to the one found at the murder scene. "Beauchamp's Trial" in Kallsen, *Kentucky Tragedy,* 301, 227. The *Confession* claims that the handkerchief was merely an old rag Beauchamp had left at the residence of Joel Scott, who thereafter smeared it with blood, cut off the corner ("to cast the insinuation," Beauchamp wrote, that "my name was on it!"), and planted the "evidence" at the crime scene. The accusation was ludicrous; it would have been impossible for Scott to sneak into Beauchamp's room, steal the handkerchief, stain and mutilate it, walk to Sharp's residence, and lay the handkerchief in the alley—all before first light. "Beauchamp's Confession" in Kallsen, *Kentucky Tragedy,* 34, 64, 68; Sharp, *Vindication,* 112.

23. "Beauchamp's Confession" in Kallsen, *Kentucky Tragedy,* 64; "Beauchamp's Trial" in Kallsen, *Kentucky Tragedy,* 280, 284, 272, 274, 280, 307.

24. "Beauchamp's Confession" in Kallsen, *Kentucky Tragedy,* 61–62; Sharp, *Vindication,* 136. For an account that confirms Edrington's, see that of Beauchamp's jailer, John McIntosh, in Sharp, *Vindication,* 130, who deposed that "Beauchamp often told me, the handkerchief found at Col. Sharp's door, had been tied around the cuff of his coat, covering his hand, with the knife pierced through it to prevent the blood from flying on his hand or sleeve; that he had dropped it, he knew not how, in the room or at the door." Although Harvie declared, "No doubt we were the first persons who examined the alley," he admitted under cross-examination that others may have examined the alley before him without his knowledge. "Beauchamp's Trial" in Kallsen, *Kentucky Tragedy,* 274.

25. "Beauchamp's Trial" in Kallsen, *Kentucky Tragedy,* 273, 281. Because of drought conditions, the soil was too hard to leave tracks, and only the recently tilled garden was soft enough to produce footprints. Ibid., 285.

26. Ibid., 277, 275.

27. Ibid., 247–49; "Beauchamp's Confession" in Kallsen, *Kentucky Tragedy,* 66.

28. "Beauchamp's Trial" in Kallsen, *Kentucky Tragedy,* 194, 195, 203, 201. Although Darby claimed that no one else witnessed the meeting at the well, former U.S. senator John Brown maintained that "a reputable man in Warren near Bowling Green has written to Mr. Mayes that a Mr. Searcy of undoubted credit living near Duncan's Well will if required swear that he saw Darby and J. O. Beauchamp conversing together at the well." John Brown to Orlando Brown, August 22, 1826, Brown Papers. Beauchamp, in the *Confession,* denied meeting Darby at Duncan's Well or, indeed, having ever met Darby before his arrest: "How did I chance to bawl out to a

perfect stranger, upon the highway, that I intended to kill Col Sharp[?]" Beauchamp, moreover, indignantly denied Darby's story about land and slaves being used to buy off the Beauchamps: "As though she had deigned to accept an offer of pecuniary compensation for an injury of that sort!" "Beauchamp's Confession" in Kallsen, *Kentucky Tragedy,* 52–53.

29. "Beauchamp's Trial" in Kallsen, *Kentucky Tragedy,* 194–208; Sharp, *Vindication,* 70, 89.

30. "Beauchamp's Trial" in Kallsen, *Kentucky Tragedy,* 190–91, 234–35; Colonel Beauchamp quoted in Davidson, deposition. Had they noticed, the first sign of trouble for the defense would have been that Lowe, when he arrived in town for the trial, "was invited to Mrs. Sharp's house, where he remained during his continuance in town." Sharp, *Vindication,* 91.

31. "Beauchamp's Confession" in Kallsen, *Kentucky Tragedy,* 71; "Beauchamp's Trial" in Kallsen, *Kentucky Tragedy,* 251–52; Sharp, *Vindication,* 28. Contrary to some accounts, Lowe was not killed shortly after the trial; he lived until 1854.

32. "Beauchamp's Trial" in Kallsen, *Kentucky Tragedy,* 251–52. The letter, apparently, was unknowingly delivered to Anna by Jereboam's father. John McIntosh, the Frankfort jailer, attested that Beauchamp "said he had sent the piece produced on the trial by Lowe, out of the jail in some socks, wrapped up in an old coat, to his wife, by his father; he said his father had no knowledge of what he was taking out." Sharp, *Vindication,* 131.

33. "Beauchamp's Trial" in Kallsen, *Kentucky Tragedy,* 266, 317; *Lexington (KY) Western Luminary,* June 28, 1826. Lowe testified that he "did not want to take the paper, but she insisted upon it." D. C. Humphreys, an inveterate gossiper, claimed that Anna was a "paramour" of Lowe's and that Beauchamp had directed her to "use her influence with him to get him to swear to these questions, so as to clear B[eauchamp]." Humphreys, interview, Draper Collection. See also Sharp, *Vindication,* 32.

34. "Beauchamp's Trial" in Kallsen, *Kentucky Tragedy,* 257, 256.

35. Ibid., 254–55.

36. Ibid., 265.

37. *Niles' Register,* July 29, 1826; *Frankfort (KY) Spirit of '76,* July 14, 1826. In the *Confession,* Beauchamp matter-of-factly writes, "I . . . added . . . many facts for Lowe to swear to, against Darby, which did not take place between them making out in the whole, a deep laid scheme to palm the murder on Darby." "Beauchamp's Confession" in Kallsen, *Kentucky Tragedy,* 76. If the attempt to suborn Lowe was ridiculous, it must be admitted that Beauchamp knew his law; Lowe was a witness for the prosecution, and Beauchamp knew that "being the Commonwealth's own witness, [Lowe] may tell his own story, and they can't contradict a word he says . . . nor can they even cross examine him a single word, but must admit all he says for true. They can't even prove what he has stated at other times, nor ask him what he has stated." Meanwhile, Beauchamp's counsel would have been free to call attention to the portions of Lowe's testimony that would help exonerate Beauchamp. "Beauchamp's Trial" in Kallsen, *Kentucky Tragedy,* 259.

38. *Kentucky Reporter,* May 22, 1826; "Beauchamp's Trial" in Kallsen, *Kentucky Tragedy,* 266–67.

39. *Niles' Register,* July 29, 1826; *Kentucky Reporter,* May 22, 1826; *Paris (KY) Western Citizen* quoted in *Vermont Journal,* June 10, 1826. Likewise, Dr. Sharp maintained that the attempt to get Lowe to perjure himself "doubtless had much effect in satisfying the jury of Beauchamp's guilt." Sharp, *Vindication,* 90.

40. "Beauchamp's Confession" in Kallsen, *Kentucky Tragedy,* 71–72, 77–78, 74, 76; "Confession of Jereboam O. Beauchamp," 65, FHS (the only source of the "corrupt heart" quotation); *John F. Lowe v. Gervis Hammond,* filed July 20, 1827, file 381, Simpson County Archives (see chap. 9).

41. "Beauchamp's Confession" in Kallsen, *Kentucky Tragedy,* 23; "Beauchamp's Trial" in Kallsen, *Kentucky Tragedy,* 314; *Frankfort (KY) Argus of Western America,* May 24, 1826. J. G. Dana and R. S. Thomas, the publishers of the trial transcript, pleaded that "a full report of the arguments of the counsel" would have swollen an already large publication "to a volume of such size, that few persons would be willing either to purchase or read it." "Beauchamp's Trial" in Kallsen, *Kentucky Tragedy,* 314.

42. *Frankfort (KY) Argus of Western America,* May 24, 1826; "Beauchamp's Trial" in Kallsen, *Kentucky Tragedy,* 314; *Autobiography of Amos Kendall,* 140; Adair quoted in Little, *Ben Hardin,* 251.

43. "Beauchamp's Confession" in Kallsen, *Kentucky Tragedy,* 80.

44. *Frankfort (KY) Argus of Western America,* May 24, 1826; "Beauchamp's Trial" in Kallsen, *Kentucky Tragedy,* 314; "Beauchamp's Confession" in Kallsen, *Kentucky Tragedy,* 79–80.

45. *Frankfort (KY) Argus of Western America,* May 24, 1826; "Beauchamp's Trial" in Kallsen, *Kentucky Tragedy,* 318–19; "Beauchamp's Confession" in Kallsen, *Kentucky Tragedy,* 80; "Beauchamp's Trial" in Kallsen, *Kentucky Tragedy,* 314. See also *Frankfort (KY) Commentator,* May 27, 1826.

46. *Frankfort (KY) Commentator,* May 20, 1826; "Beauchamp's Trial" in Kallsen, *Kentucky Tragedy,* 315.

47. "Beauchamp's Trial" in Kallsen, *Kentucky Tragedy,* 315–19; *Lexington (KY) Western Luminary,* June 28, 1826.

48. "Beauchamp's Trial" in Kallsen, *Kentucky Tragedy,* 320; *Louisville (KY) Gazette,* May 26, 1826; Sharp, *Vindication,* 93. Dr. Sharp thought that the whole of Anna's examination was illegal and that she should have been examined in Simpson County. Jereboam, incidentally, freely admitted that Anna "was strictly guilty, and liable as an accessory, before the fact," adding, "but there was no sort of evidence, whatever, of that truth." "Beauchamp's Confession" in Kallsen, *Kentucky Tragedy,* 81.

49. *Frankfort (KY) Argus of Western America,* May 24, 1826; "Beauchamp's Confession" in Kallsen, *Kentucky Tragedy,* 90; "Beauchamp's Trial" in Kallsen, *Kentucky Tragedy,* 315–19; Clinton, *Plantation Mistress,* 119–20; *Lexington (KY) Western Luminary,* June 28, 1826; "Beauchamp's Trial" in Kallsen, *Kentucky Tragedy,* 320; *Louisville (KY) Gazette,* May 26, 1826; Sharp, *Vindication,* 119–20.

50. "Beauchamp's Trial" in Kallsen, *Kentucky Tragedy,* 318; *Frankfort (KY) Spirit of '76,* May 26, 1826.

8. PRISON AND EXECUTION

1. *Frankfort (KY) Argus of Western America,* May 24, 1826, July 12, 1826.

2. Jereboam Beauchamp to Sally Beauchamp, May 21, 1826, in Kallsen, *Kentucky Tragedy,* 101; "Beauchamp's Trial" in Kallsen, *Kentucky Tragedy,* 317, 319; *Frankfort (KY) Patriot,* June 19, 1826. The 1796 act had taken away from the court of appeals appellate jurisdiction in criminal cases.

3. *Frankfort (KY) Patriot,* June 19, 1826.

4. Sharp, *Vindication,* 105; "Beauchamp's Confession" in Kallsen, *Kentucky Tragedy,* 18, 19.

5. Jereboam Beauchamp to Amos Kendall, May 22, 1826, reprinted in *Frankfort (KY) Argus of Western America,* July 12, 1826.

6. Beauchamp to Desha, June 5, 1826, in *Frankfort (KY) Argus of Western America,* July 12, 1826.

7. Davidson, *Revolution and the Word,* 141; Ann Fabian, *The Unvarnished Truth: Personal Narratives in Nineteenth-Century America* (Berkeley: University of California Press, 2000), 55.

8. Lewis, "Republican Wife," 689–90; Sharp, *Vindication,* 12; "Beauchamp's Confession" in Kallsen, *Kentucky Tragedy,* 22, 3–4. The marked decline in the literary quality of the *Confession*'s midsection—a captious, bitter, and self-pitying rant condemning the putative unfairness of Beauchamp's trial—gives further proof of Anna's contribution in the other parts. That the portion is noticeably less dramatic and less readable is very likely the result of Anna's diminished input—she was not present for most of the proceedings.

9. "Narrative of the Attempts Made"; Hardwick, *Seduction and Betrayal,* 175–84.

10. Byron quoted in *Lord Byron: The Major Works,* 1043; Goodrich, *Recollections of a Lifetime,* 105; Byron, *Don Juan,* canto 1, st. 20.

11. Flint, review, 60. Cathy N. Davidson writes, "People then as now read themselves into their fictions and their fictions into their lives." Davidson, *Revolution and the Word,* 73.

12. Coleman, *Beauchamp-Sharp Tragedy,* vii–viii, 41, 44; Duffy, "John Richardson's Kentucky Tragedies," 4, 3; Leslie A. Fiedler and Arthur Zeiger, eds., *O Brave New World: American Literature from 1600–1840* (New York: Dell, 1968), 627; Bruce, *Kentucky Tragedy,* 53. Bruce elaborates that "the language of such literature was part of the environment in which they lived and part of the framework in which they hoped their words would have appeal. Much in Beauchamp's *Confession* would have seemed familiar to readers of sentimental novels or, for that matter, fans of popular melodrama." Bruce, *Kentucky Tragedy,* 55. Catherine Clinton writes, "Beauchamp and his wife . . . were both aware of the melodramatic aspects of the tragedy, and

composed prose and poetry describing their emotions and motives—even planning their own epitaphs." Clinton, *Plantation Mistress,* 119.

13. "Beauchamp's Confession" in Kallsen, *Kentucky Tragedy,* 3–4.

14. Ibid., 81–82, 4, 8.

15. Ibid., 82, 10, 11, 12, 14, 76, 26, 50, 35, 26, 43; van Doren, *American Novel,* 8. Incidentally, the supposed "secret method of writing, known only to ourselves," like so much else claimed by the Beauchamps, turns out to be a ruse: the document that Beauchamp claims to have been written by a "secret method" is preserved in the Kentucky Department of Libraries and Archives, and it is not written in code. Perry Miller points out that early American readers readily distinguished between two forms of long fictional narrative: the novel, depicting the more mundane aspects of life—perhaps best typified by the works of Jane Austen—and the romance, which turned "upon marvellous and uncommon incidents," as Sir Walter Scott, himself the master of the romance genre, put it. Perry Miller, "Romance and the Novel," in *Nature's Nation* (Cambridge, MA: Harvard University Press, 1967), 243–45. On the influence of novels on southern women generally, see Kerrison, "Novel as Teacher."

16. "Beauchamp's Confession" in Kallsen, *Kentucky Tragedy,* 4, 3; "Verses Addressed by Mrs. Anna Beauchamp to J. O. Beauchamp" in Kallsen, *Kentucky Tragedy,* 94; "Verses Addressed by Mrs. Ann Beauchamp, to Her Husband" in Kallsen, *Kentucky Tragedy,* 93.

17. Stern, *Plight of Feeling,* 1, 9–10; Hessinger, *Seduced, Abandoned, and Reborn,* 38; "Beauchamp's Confession" in Kallsen, *Kentucky Tragedy,* 3, 7; "Lines Written by J. O. Beauchamp" in Kallsen, *Kentucky Tragedy,* 91, 92; "Epitaph" in Kallsen, *Kentucky Tragedy,* 97.

18. Kornfeld, "Culture and Counterculture," 73–74.

19. "Beauchamp's Confession" in Kallsen, *Kentucky Tragedy,* 22.

20. *Frankfort (KY) Argus of Western America,* August 24, 1825.

21. Susanna Rowson, *Charlotte Temple and Lucy Temple,* ed. Ann Douglas (New York: Penguin Books, 1991), 25–26; William Hill Brown, *The Power of Sympathy,* ed. Carla Mulford (New York: Penguin Books, 1996), 85.

22. "Verses Addressed by Mrs. Ann Beauchamp, to Her Husband" in Kallsen, *Kentucky Tragedy,* 92; "Verses Addressed by Mrs. Anna Beauchamp to J. O. Beauchamp" in Kallsen, *Kentucky Tragedy,* 94; "Epitaph" in Kallsen, *Kentucky Tragedy,* 97; Beauchamp to [Hawkins?], in *Lexington (KY) Western Luminary,* August 9, 1826; "Lines Written by J. O. Beauchamp" in Kallsen, *Kentucky Tragedy,* 91–92. David Brion Davis points out that throughout antebellum fiction "there was a constant monotonous repetition of the theme that seduction meant homicide." Davis, *Homicide in American Fiction,* 156. Such indeed was the case, but not necessarily before the 1820s. Although it may be too much to say that the Beauchamps introduced this factor into the day's literature, they were among the first to do so, and the enormous popularity of the Kentucky Tragedy helped fix the association between murder and sex in early America.

23. James Soderholm, "Byronic Confession," in Wilson, *Byromania,* 184; Davis,

Homicide in American Fiction, 123; Norton, "Lord Byron's Character and Writings," 350.

24. "Beauchamp's Confession" in Kallsen, *Kentucky Tragedy,* 5, 10, 9, 12, 80, 33.

25. Ibid., 22, 80, 3, 80, 27.

26. Ibid., 44, 34, 63.

27. Ibid., 5, 75, 48; "Verses Addressed by Mrs. Ann Beauchamp, to Her Husband" in Kallsen, *Kentucky Tragedy,* 92. For Byron's own obsession with Napoleon, see John Clubbe, "Between Emperor and Exile: Byron and Napoleon, 1814–1816," *Napoleonic Scholarship* 1, no. 1 (1997), http://www.napoleon-series.org/ins/scholarship97/c_byron.html.

28. "Beauchamp's Confession" in Kallsen, *Kentucky Tragedy,* 22, 23, 18, 23, 39, 48, 13.

29. Ibid., 20. For discussions of Byron's use of "island paradises," see *Lord Byron: The Major Works,* 1036, and Clubbe, *Byron's Natural Man,* 16–18.

30. "Beauchamp's Confession" in Kallsen, *Kentucky Tragedy,* 22. For examples of Retirement's social life, see "Beauchamp's Trial" in Kallsen, *Kentucky Tragedy,* 245–46, 257–58, 316, and Mary Prescott's deposition in Sharp, *Vindication,* 50–52.

31. "Beauchamp's Confession" in Kallsen, *Kentucky Tragedy,* 40, 85; "Narrative of the Attempts Made"; Miller, "Romance and the Novel," 251; Wilson, introduction to Wilson, *Byromania,* 12.

32. "Beauchamp's Confession" in Kallsen, *Kentucky Tragedy,* 3, 7–8, 4, 41, 54; "Beauchamp's Trial" in Kallsen, *Kentucky Tragedy,* 252; Beauchamp to Crittenden, November 18, 1825, in Bamberg, *Confession of Jereboam O. Beauchamp,* 138.

33. Cooke, "Time to Weep," 147; Bruce, "Transformation of Politics," 182. Elsewhere, Bruce writes more skeptically that "Beauchamp's *Confession* . . . was in large part an effort to frame Sharp's murder in terms of honor's demands" and that "there was much in Beauchamp's behavior that violated such honorable imperatives, including not only the clandestine killing but also Beauchamp's plea of innocence. Given standards of self-possession and courageous display, trying to escape the consequences of an honor killing was particularly inappropriate." Bruce, *Kentucky Tragedy,* 90, 102. Jack Surrency writes that the Kentucky Tragedy "was an actual application of the celebrated southern code of honor." Surrency, "Kentucky Tragedy in American Literature," 162. See also Steven Paul Beck, "The Southern Code of Honor in the Kentucky Tragedy" (master's thesis, East Carolina University, 1967). According to Bertram Wyatt-Brown, "Beauchamp's sentiments did not merely express the romance of nineteenth-century love, but reflected a much more ancient, primordial code of male possessiveness that was still very much alive." Wyatt-Brown, *Southern Honor,* 307. Catherine Clinton asserts that the deaths of Jereboam and Anna were the "pathetic and gruesome consequences of 'an affair of honor.'" Clinton, *Plantation Mistress,* 119.

34. Flint, review, 57; Darby, "To the Public," no. 3.

35. Flint, review, 57; Kenneth Greenberg, *Honor and Slavery: Lies, Duels, Noses, Masks, Dressing as a Woman, Gifts, Strangers, Humanitarianism, Death, Slave Rebel-*

lions, the Proslavery Argument, Baseball, Hunting, and Gambling in the Old South (Princeton, NJ: Princeton University Press, 1996), 19. James C. Klotter points out that Kentucky courts in the late nineteenth century found murder by ambush justifiable—and, by implication, within the bounds of the code of honor—if the attacker sincerely believed himself to be in imminent danger from his victim. James C. Klotter, *Kentucky Justice, Southern Honor, and American Manhood: Understanding the Life and Death of Richard Reid* (Baton Rouge: Louisiana State University Press, 2003), 78.

36. Wyatt-Brown, *Southern Honor,* 22, 25; Edmund Morgan, "The Price of Honor," *New York Review of Books,* May 31, 2001, 36–38.

37. In some respects, the precepts of honor and Byronic romanticism did overlap. Both honorable men and radical romantics, for example, professed a cavalier attitude toward death. According to Kenneth Greenberg, "The central virtue of a man of honor" was that he "did not fear death"; romantics, at least in their more melancholy moods, thought they looked forward to it. Greenberg, *Honor and Slavery,* 74. This is a key reason that the Kentucky Tragedy has been misunderstood; violence and early death were just as closely intertwined with radical romanticism as with honor.

38. Greenberg, *Honor and Slavery,* 3–23; *Mary Chesnut's Civil War,* ed. C. Vann Woodward (New Haven, CT: Yale University Press, 1981), 380. Chesnut added, "Takes a woman to talk wildly." Honor dictated proper appearances and made the South, as Greenberg puts it, a "masquerade culture." Greenberg, *Honor and Slavery,* 25.

39. "Epitaph" in Kallsen, *Kentucky Tragedy,* 96–97; The Power of Sympathy *by William Hill Brown and* The Coquette *by Hannah Webster Foster* (New York: Penguin, 1996), 102–3, 242. Dickson Bruce writes, "The Beauchamps appear to have gone out of their way to ensure that they would be remembered in sentimental terms. . . . Ann Beauchamp composed a lengthy verse epitaph calling to mind the verses William Hill Brown placed over the companion graves of his star-crossed lovers in the Power of Sympathy. . . . The Beauchamps thus orchestrated their legacy along lines defined by sentimental traditions." Bruce, "Sentimentalism and Honor," 199, 200.

40. *Frankfort (KY) Spirit of '76,* July 14, 1826; Darby, "To the Public," no. 6. The epitaph was etched on the Beauchamps' tombstone sometime after.

41. Jereboam Beauchamp to Lucy McCrearey and Phebe McCrearey, June 13, 1826, reprinted in *Frankfort (KY) Commentator,* December 16, 1826.

42. Green, diary, 1825–1827, WVU; Sharp, *Vindication,* 103–4, 102.

43. Sharp, *Vindication,* 99; Bruce, *Kentucky Tragedy,* 85.

44. Sharp, *Vindication,* 101; Pope, deposition; McIntosh, deposition.

45. Beauchamp to McCrearey and McCrearey, in *Frankfort (KY) Commentator,* December 16, 1826; *Frankfort (KY) Commentator,* December 16, 1826; *Frankfort (KY) Argus of Western America,* May 31, 1826; *Frankfort (KY) Commentator,* June 10, 1826; "Beauchamp's Confession" in Kallsen, *Kentucky Tragedy,* 83–84. Beauchamp continued that he and Darby had "agreed if I should be arrested to affect entire ignorance of each other, on seeing each other. We done so. Since that time, the villian has turned traitor against me, and procured my conviction. I wish now to shew the

world before I leave it, the guilt of this man as well as myself. I think it a duty I owe to my country and to my God." Beauchamp to McCrearey and McCrearey, in *Frankfort (KY) Commentator,* December 16, 1826.

46. McIntosh, deposition; Sharp, *Vindication,* 100.

47. Jereboam Beauchamp to Governor Joseph Desha, July 4, 1826, reprinted in *Frankfort (KY) Argus of Western America,* July 12, 1826; "Narrative of the Attempts Made."

48. *Frankfort (KY) Commentator,* June 10, 1826; "Narrative of the Attempts Made"; Sharp, *Vindication,* 102; "Beauchamp's Confession: Post Script" in Kallsen, *Kentucky Tragedy,* 87–88. See also "Tragical Scenes," *Lexington (KY) Western Luminary,* July 12, 1826, and Jereboam Beauchamp to Sally Beauchamp, July 4, 1826, in Kallsen, *Kentucky Tragedy,* 105.

49. "Narrative of the Attempts Made"; "Beauchamp's Confession" in Kallsen, *Kentucky Tragedy,* 89.

50. "Lines Addressed to Mrs. Francis R. Hawkins" in Kallsen, *Kentucky Tragedy,* 94–95; Beauchamp to [Hawkins?], in *Lexington (KY) Western Luminary,* August 9, 1826; will book D, Warren County, KY, 119, WKU; Cooke, "Portrait of a Murderess," 227–28.

51. "Beauchamp's Confession" in Kallsen, *Kentucky Tragedy,* 86; "Verses Addressed by Mrs. Anna Beauchamp to J. O. Beauchamp" in Kallsen, *Kentucky Tragedy,* 93–95. Flint scoffed at the Beauchamps' last-minute conversion to Christianity: "These two people, already guilty of murder, and not repenting of their deed, and in the very act of committing suicide, are persuaded, that they shall wake up among the blessed!" Flint, review, 58–60.

52. "Beauchamp's Confession: Post Script" in Kallsen, *Kentucky Tragedy,* 88; "Narrative of the Attempts Made"; "Directions for Our Burial" in Kallsen, *Kentucky Tragedy,* 90.

53. "Narrative of the Attempts Made"; *Frankfort (KY) Spirit of '76,* July 14, 1826.

54. "Beauchamp's Confession" in Kallsen, *Kentucky Tragedy,* 89. For the appearance of the handwriting, see "Confession of Jereboam O. Beauchamp," FHS.

55. "Narrative of the Attempts Made"; "Beauchamp's Confession" in Kallsen, *Kentucky Tragedy,* 89.

56. "Narrative of the Attempts Made"; *Frankfort (KY) Spirit of '76,* July 14, 1826.

57. J. H. Spencer, *A History of Kentucky Baptists: From 1769 to 1885* (1885; repr., Gallatin, TN: Church History Research and Archives, 1984), 1:316–19; George Waller, "Old Father Waller—a Word to His Brethren," *Christian Repository,* April 1858, 45–47; "Narrative of the Attempts Made."

58. Sharp, *Vindication,* 132; "Narrative of the Attempts Made"; Darby, "To the Public," no. 6.

59. "Narrative of the Attempts Made."

60. Ibid.

61. Ibid.; "Beauchamp's Confession" in Kallsen, *Kentucky Tragedy,* 86; Blair to Payne, July 10, 1826, Payne Papers.

62. "Narrative of the Attempts Made"; Darby, "To the Public," no. 6; "Beauchamp's Confession" in Kallsen, *Kentucky Tragedy,* 91.

63. "Narrative of the Attempts Made." According to Darby, "Beauchamp exclaimed, 'I wish Doctor Sharp was here to witness this scene! I wish he was here to behold this spectacle!'" Darby, "To the Public," no. 6.

64. Coleman, *Beauchamp-Sharp Tragedy,* 70; "Narrative of the Attempts Made." The gallows were "erected off Glenn's Creek Road, a spot now inhabited, ironically, by the state Cabinet for Families and Children." *Lexington (KY) Herald-Leader,* February 14, 2001.

65. See Louis P. Masur, *Rites of Execution: Capital Punishment and the Transformation of American Culture, 1776–1865* (New York: Oxford University Press, 1989), 25–49. The public execution of Beauchamp took place just as Americans were becoming more uneasy about public executions. Kentucky, however, would continue the practice until 1936, when Rainey Bethea, in the last true public execution in America, was killed in front of twenty thousand people in the western Kentucky town of Owensboro. Keith Lawrence, "1936 Hanging Remains Last Public Execution," *Owensboro (KY) Messenger Inquirer,* September 21, 2004.

66. Knight, *Letters from the South and West,* 103–4.

67. Such was not common: "Evidence of criminals refusing to act as they were expected to act is rare. And even when they did, the prisoner's dissent did not disrupt the proceedings." Masur, *Rites of Execution,* 43. Some accounts of the Kentucky Tragedy mistakenly maintain that Beauchamp was the first man to be executed in Kentucky.

68. "Narrative of the Attempts Made."

69. Darby, "To the Public," no. 6;"Narrative of the Attempts Made."

70. Sharp, *Vindication,* 121; "Narrative of the Attempts Made"; *Frankfort (KY) Argus of Western America,* July 19, 1826. Kendall did, however, always believe that it was Darby who had sent the information to Beauchamp that Sharp claimed the child was interracial. Sharp, *Vindication,* 121–23. "I never placed reliance on your nephew's declarations, in relation to Darby and waited for the last scenes to fix my opinion." Amos Kendall to Col. Beauchamp, July 10, 1826, reprinted in *Louisville (KY) Focus,* April 8, 1828.

71. "Account of His Execution" in Kallsen, *Kentucky Tragedy,* 108; "Narrative of the Attempts Made"; "Tragical Scenes."

72. "Beauchamp's Confession" in Kallsen, *Kentucky Tragedy,* 90; "Narrative of the Attempts Made."

73. "Narrative of the Attempts Made"; "Beauchamp's Confession" in Kallsen, *Kentucky Tragedy,* 89.

74. *Frankfort (KY) Spirit of '76,* July 14, 1826; Darby, "To the Public," no. 6; *Baltimore Patriot,* July 21, 1826.

75. Duffy, "John Richardson's Kentucky Tragedies," 18; *Frankfort (KY) Spirit of*

'76, July 14, 1826; "Beauchamp's Confession" in Kallsen, *Kentucky Tragedy,* 48.

76. "Narrative of the Attempts Made."

77. "Tragical Scenes"; "Narrative of the Attempts Made"; *Frankfort (KY) Spirit of '76,* July 14, 1826.

9. MEMORY AND THE INVENTION OF A TRAGEDY

1. *Portland (ME) Advertiser,* March 30, 1827; *Rhode Island Republican,* July 27, 1826; *New York Spectator,* August 1, 1826.

2. *Amherst (NH) Farmers' Cabinet,* July 29, 1826; *New Hampshire Gazette,* August, 1, 1826; *Philadelphia National Gazette and Literary Register,* July 21, 1826, quoted in *Albany (NY) Argus and City Gazette,* July 24, 1826; *Baltimore Patriot,* July 28, 1826; *Vermont Gazette,* August 1, 1826; *Worcester (MA) National Aegis,* August 9, 1826. Scholars studying the reception of nineteenth-century literature have long noted this tendency to cram reality's refractory chaos into a recognizable order provided by romantic literature. Cathy Davidson suggests that early American readers "were well versed in the process whereby the complexities of a disordered life could be reduced to a simply ordered moral allegory"—to such an extent that, for some at least, "fiction came to have a paramount reality of its own." Davidson, *Revolution and the Word,* 262, 141. Jane Tompkins likewise submits that the novels of the antebellum years provided "men and women with a means of ordering the world they inhabited." Tompkins, *Sensational Designs,* xiii.

3. *Philadelphia Democratic Press* reprinted in *Baltimore Patriot,* August 4, 1826; *Baltimore Patriot,* July 28, 1826.

4. *Baltimore Patriot,* July 21, 1826; *Philadelphia Democratic Press* reprinted in *Baltimore Patriot,* August 4, 1826.

5. *Philadelphia Democratic Press* reprinted in *Baltimore Patriot,* August 4, 1826; *Georgetown Metropolitan* reprinted in *Baltimore Patriot,* September 13, 1826.

6. Dickson Bruce also sees a bifurcated depiction of the Anna character in the later plays and novels: in one, she is "presented as just a woman" who is "no match to the seducer's appeals to her desires for love," and in the other, she is portrayed as one "whose very haughtiness and vanity were the means of her undoing." Bruce, *Kentucky Tragedy,* 80. The difference, as I see it, is not between sweetness and pride but between innocence and malevolence—and relates not to the explicit dramatizations but to the putative reportage of distant newspapers.

7. *National Advertiser* quoted in *New Hampshire Gazette,* August 1, 1826; Clay to Johnston in *Papers of Henry Clay,* 5:586; George Lillo, *The London Merchant, or The History of George Barnwell* (1731), in *Eighteenth Century Plays,* ed. Richard Quintana (New York: Random House, 1952), 287–341; James L. Steffensen, "George Lillo," *Oxford Dictionary of National Biography.*

8. Lillo, *London Merchant,* 313, 297, 301–2, 300.

9. Ibid., 318, 324, 325.

10. Ibid., 328–29.

11. Ibid., 330, 338.

12. Ibid., 315.

13. *Middlesex (CT) Gazette,* June 21, 1826; *Portland (ME) Eastern Argus,* July 28, 1826; *Philadelphia National Gazette and Literary Register* reprinted in *Amherst (NH) Farmers' Cabinet,* July 29, 1826; *Baltimore Patriot,* August 1, 1826. For further examples along these lines, see *Jamestown (NY) Journal,* August 2, 1826; *Rhode Island Republican,* July 25, 1826; and *New York Spectator,* July 25, 1826.

14. *Alexandria (VA) Herald* reprinted in *Newport (RI) Mercury,* August 12, 1826; *Baltimore Patriot,* September 13, 1826, August 4, 1826; *National Advertiser* quoted in *New Hampshire Gazette,* August 1, 1826; *Pittsburgh Statesman* reprinted in *Newport (RI) Mercury,* August 26, 1826.

15. Davis, *Homicide in American Fiction,* 85; *National Advertiser* quoted in *New Hampshire Gazette,* August 1, 1826; *Georgetown Metropolitan* reprinted in *Baltimore Patriot,* September 13, 1826.

16. *Philadelphia Democratic Press* reprinted in *Baltimore Patriot,* August 4, 1826; *Pittsburgh Statesman* quoted in *Newport (RI) Mercury,* August 26, 1826; *National Advertiser* quoted in *New Hampshire Gazette,* August 1, 1826.

17. *Washington (DC) National Journal* reprinted in *Portland (ME) Eastern Argus,* December 29, 1826, January 2, 1827; Coleman, *Beauchamp-Sharp Tragedy,* viii; Thomas Ollive Mabbott, introduction to *Politian: A Tragedy,* in *Collected Works of Edgar Allan Poe,* vol. 1, *Poems,* ed. Thomas Ollive Mabbott (Cambridge, MA: Harvard University Press, 1969), 244. For other examples of uncritical acceptance of *The Letters of Ann Cook,* see Leonard Casper, *Robert Penn Warren: The Dark and Bloody Ground* (Seattle: University of Washington Press, 1960), 144; Steven T. Ryan, "*World Enough and Time:* A Refutation of Poe's History as Tragedy," *Southern Quarterly* 31 (1993): 86–94; and James H. Justus, "Warren's *World Enough and Time* and Beauchamp's *Confession,*" *American Literature* 33 (1962): 503. For an advertisement of the *Letters,* see *Washington (DC) Daily National Journal,* January 10, 1827. For an example of a newspaper reprinting a portion of the *Letters,* see *Portland (ME) Eastern Argus,* January 2, 1827.

18. Johnson, "Letters of Ann Cooke." See also Duffy, "John Richardson's Kentucky Tragedies," 1–21, which flatly labels the letters a "hoax." According to Cathy Davidson, of the approximately one hundred novels written in America between 1789 and 1820, "almost one third . . . were epistolary." Davidson, *Revolution and the Word,* viii, 14.

19. "The Letters of Ann Cook" in Kallsen, *Kentucky Tragedy,* 113 (the editor's name appears as "W——R——n"), 119, 118, 122, 129, 119–20.

20. Ibid., 115–16, 124–28, 129.

21. Ibid., 137–39.

22. Ibid., 155, 154, 121.

23. Ibid., 143–44, 146, 147, 148.

24. Ibid., 149, 148.

25. Ibid., 146, 150, 145.

26. Ibid., 148, 150–52, 153, 156.

27. Ibid., 157–59.

28. Ibid., 159–60, 162, 161.

29. Ibid., 115, 133, 153–54, 157.

30. Ibid., 163, 113–14.

31. Ibid., 114.

32. Flint, review, 56; Bamberg, introduction, 15. The *Confession* was not published by Hammond and was not published on August 11 (although a copyright for the *Confession* was secured in August 1826; see *Frankfort (KY) Commentator,* September 2, 1826). Both mistakes seem to have originated with J. Winston Coleman, and they have been repeated by virtually every other student of the event. As late as November 25, 1826, Darby wrote in his paper that the *Confession* "is *about to* issue to the world" (emphasis mine). More to the point, the *Confession* itself contains an addendum written by Will H. Holmes dated November 28, 1826. See Kallsen, *Kentucky Tragedy,* 105. Advertisements for the *Confession* do not appear in newspapers until January 1827. Gervis Hammond was married to Beauchamp's sister, who had died August 30, 1825. For other publishing work by William H. Holmes, see, for example, John Taylor, *A History of Ten Baptist Churches* (Bloomfield, KY: Holmes, 1827). Holmes lent a hand in the creation of the Kentucky Tragedy myth by altering the manuscript, not so much to make it more readable but, as he himself admitted, to soften "some hard expressions against individuals" (Kallsen, *Kentucky Tragedy,* 105)—to expunge remarks that would have undercut Beauchamp's gallantry. So, for example, he deleted all mention of Ruth Reed's bastardy warrant, knowing that even the most credulous reader would not believe that Beauchamp chose to have such an action sworn on him as he was about to avenge a sexual transgression. Likewise, Holmes eliminated a diatribe Beauchamp launched against Eliza Sharp, one in which the murderer denounced the woman he made a widow as "a very weak minded female" who possessed a "licentious tongue" and "was not altogether guiltless of her husband's blood." "Confession of Jereboam O. Beauchamp," 67, FHS. As one scholar has duly noted, "Holmes actually did Beauchamp's image a good turn here, inasmuch as he had been at pains to present himself as woman's avenger and a chivalric idealist." Johnson, "New Light on Beauchamp's Confession," 4.

33. *Middlesex (CT) Gazette,* March 14, 1827; *Nashville National Banner* reprinted in *Portland (ME) Eastern Argus,* February 27, 1827.

34. *New York Commercial Advertiser* reprinted in *South Carolina State Gazette,* April 21, 1827; *Baltimore Gazette,* February 21, 1827. Newspapers across the country reprinted the *Nashville Banner* summary of the *Confession* in early 1827, including the *Baltimore Gazette,* February 21–22, 1827; *Salem (MA) Gazette,* February 23, 1827; *Rhode-Island American and Providence Gazette,* February 23, 1827; *Salem (MA) Essex Register,* February 26, 1827; *Portland (ME) Eastern Argus Semi-weekly,* February 27, 1827; *Amherst (NH) Farmers' Cabinet,* March 3, 1827; *Hagerstown (MD) Torch Light and Public Advertiser,* March 1, 1827; *Pittsfield (MA) Berkshire Star,* March 1, 1827; *Rochester (NY) Telegraph,* March 6, 1827; *Easton (MD) Repub-*

lican Star and General Advertiser, March 27, 1827; *Charleston (SC) City Gazette and Commercial Daily Advertiser,* April 12, 1827; and *South Carolina State Gazette,* May 5, 1827.

35. "Questions and Answers"; *Frankfort (KY) Commentator,* September 2, 1826; Flint, review, 56; Bamberg, introduction, 15. Standalone editions include *The Life of Jeroboam O. Beauchamp Who Was Hung at Frankfort, Kentucky, for the Murder of Col. Solomon P. Sharp* (Frankfort, KY: D'Unger, 1850); *The Avenger's Doom, or The Singular, Thrilling, and Exciting History and Lamentable Fate of J. O. Beauchamp and Miss Ann Cooke* (Louisville, KY: Barclay, Orton, 1851); *The Beauchamp Tragedy in Kentucky: As Detailed in the Confession of Jereboam O. Beauchamp* (New York: Dinsmore, 1859); and *The Kentucky Tragedy: A Full and Particular Account of the Lives and Tragical Deaths, of Jeroboam O. Beauchamp and Ann, His Wife, the Murderers of Colonel Sharp* (Philadelphia: Town, n.d.). Digests and brief accounts appear in St. Clair, *United States Criminal Calendar;* P. R. Hamblin, *United States Criminal History: Being a True Account of the Most Horrid Murders, Piracies, High-Way Robberies, etc* (Fayetteville, NY: Mason and De Puy, 1836); George N. Thomson, *Confessions, Trials, and Biographical Sketches of the Most Cold Blooded Murderers, Who Have Been Executed in This Country* (Hartford: Andrus, 1837); and Brooke, *Tragedies on the Land.*

36. "Diary for the Month of October," *London Magazine,* November 1826, 365–68.

37. *Album, and Ladies' Weekly Gazette,* August 30, 1826, quoted in Bruce, "Sentimentalism and Honor," 200; *Philadelphia National Gazette and Literary Register* reprinted in *Frankfort (KY) Commentator,* August 26, 1826; *Albany (NY) Argus and City Gazette,* August 10, 1826; *Boston Daily Advertiser* reprinted in *Middlesex (CT) Gazette,* August 2, 1826.

38. Sharp, *Vindication,* 10; *Frankfort (KY) Commentator,* September 2, 1826; *Rhode Island American,* January 5, 1827; *Providence (RI) Literary Cadet,* January 6, 1827.

39. Flint, review, 56–60.

40. Sharp, *Vindication,* 120, 112; Patrick Darby, "To the Public," no. 8, *Frankfort (KY) Commentator,* November 25, 1826; Levin, *Lawyers and Lawmakers,* 111.

41. *William C. Bradburn v. G. S. Hammond,* filed July 20, 1827, file 346, Simpson County Archives; *Lowe v. Hammond;* "Questions and Answers." According to Dr. Sharp, Hammond submitted the Beauchamps' manuscript "to at least two lawyers, who were zealous Old Court partisans, in the Green river country. Finding that it contained matter which might operate injuriously to their opponents in politics, although they knew most of it to be false, they advised its publication." Very likely, on seeing that Beauchamp's *Confession* exonerated the old court party while painting a devastating portrait of a new court martyr, the lawyers allowed their political calculations to overwhelm their scruples as well as their legal common sense. Sharp, *Vindication,* 120. Lowe and Bradburn also sued Sanford Duncan, the proprietor of an inn in Simpson County, for being "instrumental in the circulation" of the *Con-*

fession and "by giving out the libelous manuscript to be printed and by advancing money or pay or security of some sort for the same and by receiving the profits arising from the sale of said libelous production or the copyright thereof." See *William C. Bradburn v. Sanford Duncan,* filed July 20, 1827, file 2171, Simpson County Archives, and *John F. Lowe v. Thomas Beauchamp and Sanford Duncan,* filed July 20, 1827, file 2252, Simpson County Archives.

42. Stephen F. Miller, *Recollections of New Bern Fifty Years Ago* (Raleigh, NC: Pool, 1874), 338; *Baltimore Patriot,* October 28, 1826, August 30, 1826; "What Is Truth?" *Niles' Register,* August 26, 1826; Sharp, *Vindication,* 89. Notice of Hutton's plan to dramatize the events arrived in Kentucky by mid-September: "The *Newbern Sentinel* states that Mr. Joseph Hutton, of that place, is engaged in writing a tragedy, founded on the murder of Col. Sharp, the execution of Beauchamp &c." *Frankfort (KY) Commentator* September 16, 1826. This play is very likely the "new tragedy" announced in the *New York Mirror* that summer. See Charles Henry Watts, *Thomas Holley Chivers: His Literary Career and His Poetry* (Athens: University of Georgia Press, 1956), 14. Watts adds, "The play, if indeed it were written and produced, has never been found."

43. Sharp, *Vindication,* 89; Sharp, "To the Public"; Coleman, *Beauchamp-Sharp Tragedy,* 69; *U.S. Telegraph,* March 21, 1829.

44. *Nashville Daily Union and American,* January 20, 1859. The night the play was resumed, according to one witness, "there was a dead silence until Sybil presented a pistol at Col. Sharpe, her seducer, when there arose a yell of 'kill him!' 'Shoot him!' and from thenceforth there was no sympathy for Sharpe." Ever since, "the play . . . has filled the house night after night." *Montgomery (AL) Daily Confederation,* October 23, 1858. A New Orleans paper even reported—incredibly—that the play was eventually staged with the "approbation" of Sharp's son. *New Orleans Daily True Delta,* January 6, 1859.

45. *Portland (ME) Advertiser,* March 30, 1827; Fabian, *Unvarnished Truth,* 66; Cooke, "Portrait of a Murderess," 216–17. Daniel Cohen writes that "the last statements of dying men and women were believed to be both truthful and insightful." Daniel A. Cohen, *Pillars of Salt, Monuments of Grace: New England Crime Literature and the Origins of American Popular Culture, 1674–1860* (New York: Oxford University Press, 1993) 10, 249–50. See also Hiller B. Zobel, *Boston Massacre* (New York: Norton, 1970), 286: "Dying declarations are by definition unsworn; their admissibility depends not upon the sanction of the oath, but rather upon the premise, elegantly phrased by a later English judge [1881], that no man 'who is immediately going into the presence of his Maker, will do so with a lie on his lips.'"

46. One example of our continuing tendency to mistake story for reality is the "ticking time bomb" plot, a recurring plot device of the television show *24* and others, which, despite its utterly fictitious premise, has so saturated our collective psyche that politicians and pundits have repeatedly used it to defend our nation's malignant acceptance of torture. U.S. Army officials, including a brigadier general, met with the producers of *24* to ask them to tone it down, for young soldiers "watch the shows, and

then walk into the interrogation booths and do the same things they've just seen." Jane Mayer, "Whatever It Takes: The Politics of the Man behind '24,'" *New Yorker,* February 19, 2007; "Making Them Talk," *New Yorker,* February 19, 2007, http://www.newyorker.com/online/video/2007/02/19/070219_Mayer.

10. THE KENTUCKY TRAGEDY

1. C. Vann Woodward, *The Future of the Past* (New York: Oxford University Press, 1989), 233; *Lexington (KY) Herald-Leader,* February 14, 2001.

2. See Coleman, *Beauchamp-Sharp Tragedy*; Kallsen, *Kentucky Tragedy*; Jules Zanger, ed., *A Casebook on the Beauchamp Tragedy* (Philadelphia: Lippincott, 1963); and *Confession of Jereboam O. Beauchamp.* Richard Beale Davis claims that the Kentucky Tragedy was "one of the three great historical events, matters, or themes which American writers have drawn upon in creating fiction, poetry, and drama. Only Pocahontas and Merry mount rival it." Richard Beale Davis, "Thomas Holley Chivers and the Kentucky Tragedy," *Texas Studies in Literature and Language* 1 (1959): 281.

3. The list of dramatizations could be expanded to include Julia Ward Howe's play *Leonora, or The World's Own* (1857), the text of which makes it obvious that Howe was familiar with the Kentucky Tragedy plot and in particular had read Simms's novels (a number of scenes are very similar to episodes in *Charlemont*). Although the story clearly begins and develops as a variant of the Kentucky Tragedy, however, the denouement differs markedly. See also Alfred W. Arrington's *The Rangers and Regulators of the Tanaha* (1856), which contains a "Byronic character" who falls in love with a dishonored woman who urges her paramour to murder her seducer. Muted echoes of the episode also turn up in other works of the era; David Brion Davis claims that the basic theme of the Kentucky Tragedy is "faintly suggested by Hawthorne in *The Marble Faun.*" Davis, *Homicide in American Fiction,* 230. Dickson Bruce notes that Poe accused Henry Wadsworth Longfellow of plagiarizing *Politian* in his 1842 play *The Spanish Student.* Bruce, *Kentucky Tragedy,* 73.

In addition, several non-American treatments of the Kentucky Tragedy exist. In his preface to *Grace Darling, or The Heroine of the Fern Islands: A Tale Founded on Recent Facts* (London: Henderson, 1839), George William MacArthur Reynolds asserts that the story "is founded, in reference to its main incident, upon the 'Confession' of Jereboam O. Beauchamp, who was executed at Frankfort, Ky, (in the United States) on the 7th of July, 1826, for the murder of Colonel Solomon P. Sharp, Attorney General of Ky. Colonel Sharp had seduced, under aggravated circumstances of villany, Miss Ann Cook, whom Beauchamp subsequently married, and whose wrongs he avenged upon the head of the seducer" (viii). Canadian author John Richardson published *The Canadian Brothers* in 1840 and revised the work eleven years later as *Matilda Montgomerie* (1851). See also the works of two impossibly prolific English authors, George Payne Rainsford James, *Beauchamp, or The Error: a Novel* (1856), and Gabrielle Margaret Vere Campbell [Joseph Shearing, pseud.], *To Bed at Noon* (1951). Interestingly, these non-American works shift the moral blame from the Sharp character to the Anna character, depicting her as uniquely bloodthirsty and manipulative.

4. A Resident near the Scene of Action and Acquainted with All the Parties, *Beauchamp, or The Murder of Col. Sharp: A Drama, in Five Acts, Founded upon the Real Tragic Events and Facts, Which Transpired in Kentucky, Some Seven Years Since* (n.p., 1833); William Gilmore Simms, *Charlemont, or Pride of the Village: A Tale of Kentucky* (1856; repr., New York: AMS Press, 1970), 7; *Charleston (SC) Mercury* quoted in John Caldwell Guilds, *Simms: A Literary Life* (Fayetteville: University of Arkansas Press, 1992), 222; *United States Democratic Review* 37 (April 1856): 343–44; William P. Trent, *William Gilmore Simms* (Boston: Houghton, Mifflin, 1892), 117. See also William Gilmore Simms, *Beauchampe, or The Kentucky Tragedy: A Tale of Passion* (Philadelphia: Lea and Blanchard, 1842), vi. Trent's claim for Simms's "relentless accuracy" is seriously undermined by his exceedingly limited grasp of the Kentucky Tragedy itself. In a jaw-dropping series of misstatements, Trent maintains that the murder took place in 1828 and that it was committed by "Colonel Beauchamp," who killed Sharp as soon as he learned of the seduction and whose wife joined him in the jail the night before the execution. Trent, *William Gilmore Simms,* 117. Although W. B. Gates maintained that Simms's claims of veracity were "tongue-in-cheek," I can find absolutely no evidence to support this claim. Gates, "William Gilmore Simms," 162.

5. Poe quoted in Mabbott, introduction, 241.

6. Edgar Allan Poe, *Essays and Reviews* (New York: Library of America, 1984), 1208–9. Dickson Bruce writes, "As the events themselves became more distant, purportedly factual renditions of the Kentucky Tragedy came to comprise a tradition of their own." Bruce, *Kentucky Tragedy,* 59. I do not intend to condemn the novelists and playwrights for departing from the historical record. The duties of dramatists are not those of historians, despite facile arguments to the contrary.

7. Clay to Johnston in *Papers of Henry Clay,* 5:586; Oscar Wegelin, *Early American Plays, 1714–1830,* 2nd ed. (New York: Literary Collector Press, 1905), 50–51; *Delaware Gazette,* February 6, 1827; Duyckinck, *Cyclopædia of American Literature,* 2:43. According to the *London Magazine* of December 1826, Hutton "is at present somewhere in North Carolina, writing a tragedy upon the shocking murder of Colonel Sharp, which lately took place in Kentucky." "American Dramatists," *London Magazine,* December 1, 1826, 468.

8. Resident near the Scene of Action, *Beauchamp,* 11, 22, 25. Richard Beale Davis mistakenly writes, "Chivers seems to have been the first to appreciate the literary potentialities of the Beauchamp-Sharp affair." Davis, "Thomas Holley Chivers," 282. S. Foster Damon maintains that "Chivers was the very first to appreciate the literary possibilities of the Sharp-Beauchamp murder." Damon, *Thomas Holley Chivers,* 80. See Arthur Hobson Quinn, *A History of the American Drama: From the Beginning to the Civil War* (New York: Crofts, 1943), 260, and Jeffrey D. Groves, "Thomas Holley Chivers," in *American National Biography,* http://www.anb.org/articles/16/16-00294.html.

9. Resident near the Scene of Action, *Beauchamp,* 22, 35, 22, 34; Bruce, *Kentucky Tragedy,* 60.

10. Thomas Holley Chivers, *Conrad and Eudora, or The Death of Alonzo: A Tragedy in Five Acts, Founded on the Murder of Sharpe, by Beauchamp, in Kentucky* (1834), reprinted in *Conrad and Eudora and Birth-day Song of Liberty* (Delmar, NY: Scholars' Facsimiles and Reprints, 1978), 16, 21, 23, 24; Poe quoted in Groves, "Thomas Holley Chivers." For further confirmation of Chivers's limitations as an author, see Davis, "Thomas Holley Chivers," 285; Damon, *Thomas Holley Chivers,* 77, 79; and Duffy, "John Richardson's Kentucky Tragedies," 8.

11. See Watts, *Thomas Holley Chivers,* and Charles M. Lombard, *Thomas Holley Chivers* (Boston: Twayne, 1979). Regarding the publication of *Conrad and Eudora,* S. Foster Damon writes, "There is no publisher's name on the title-page; evidently he was paying . . . for the printing." Damon, *Thomas Holley Chivers,* 81.

12. Chivers quoted in *Georgia Citizen,* May 17, 1851. For assertions that Chivers was privy to information unknown to other dramatists, see, for example, Davis, "Thomas Holley Chivers," 283, and Lombard, *Thomas Holley Chivers,* vi. Also, Charles Lombard states that Chivers had access to "a defense of Colonel Sharpe's reputation by his brother," but "ostensibly Chivers was displeased by the tract the colonel's brother wrote in defense of Sharpe" Lombard, *Thomas Holley Chivers,* viii. Again, there is no evidence in the play for this statement, and Chivers himself never mentioned reading Dr. Sharp's *Vindication.* Another unlikely theory is that one of Beauchamp's lawyers, Thomas J. Lacey, was Chivers's tutor while he lived in Georgia. Chivers, according to his biographer Charles Henry Watts, was taught, sometime in the late 1810s and early 1820s, by a "Thomas Lacey, who was, in all probability, the 'Th. J. Lacey' who served with two others as Beauchamp's counsel during the trial." This acquaintance, Watts continues, "may have led him to provide the reader with the occasional glimpses into Anne Cook's true character which we find in 'Conrad' and 'Eudora.' . . . Lacey may have suggested her underlying qualities of passion and sensuality to Chivers." Richard Beale Davis and Charles Lombard repeat the assertion. However, the Thomas Lacey who was Chivers's tutor in Washington, Georgia, and the Thomas Lacey who helped defend Beauchamp were in all likelihood not the same person. Beauchamp, in his *Confession,* refers to Lacey as "quite young," and it is possible but not very likely that Lacey had lived in Georgia, spent time tutoring children there, and then moved back to Kentucky in time to read law and serve as Beauchamp's cocounsel. Moreover, if it were true, one would think that Chivers at some point would mention this connection to lend his drama a greater veracity—as when he explained how he came across the story when he was a student at Transylvania. Watts, *Thomas Holley Chivers,* 13, 15; "Beauchamp's Confession" in Kallsen, *Kentucky Tragedy,* 80. Jack Surrency confirms that "Chivers did not know the Thomas J. Lacy [*sic*] who served as one of Beauchamp's attorneys. Chivers wrote 'An Elegy on the Death of my friend, Mr. Thomas Lacey,' which appeared in *Path of Sorrow* in 1832. The Thomas Lacy who acted as Beauchamp's attorney did not die in 1832." Surrency, "Kentucky Tragedy in American Literature," 105.

13. Chivers, *Conrad and Eudora,* 44, 45, 6, 19, 9, 10, 24, 26.

14. Ibid., 32, 35, 36, 39, 44, 47.

15. Ibid., 51, 56.

16. Ibid., 61, 59, 60, 65, 68, 69, 72, 75, 76.

17. Ibid., 80, 81.

18. Charles M. Lombard, introduction to *The Unpublished Plays of Thomas Holley Chivers,* ed. Charles M. Lombard (Delmar, NY: Scholars' Facsimiles and Reprints, 1980), xxvii; Davis, "Thomas Holley Chivers," 281–88. The newspaper was the *Georgia Citizen.*

19. Thomas Holley Chivers, *Leoni, or The Orphan of Venice,* in *Unpublished Plays,* 8, 14, 10, 27.

20. Ibid., 97, 34, 55, 58–59; Davis, "Thomas Holley Chivers," 286–87.

21. Poe quoted in Duffy, "John Richardson's Kentucky Tragedies," 5; William J. Kimball, "Poe's Politian and the Beauchamp-Sharp Tragedy," *Poe Studies* 4 (1971): 24–27. Some scholars have questioned whether the play was based on the Kentucky Tragedy at all, but Kimball writes, "Despite the foreign locale and foreign names, Poe clearly based these characters and others in no small measure on the romantic figures of the Kentucky tragedy." Kimball, "Poe's Politian," 25. Since 1933, *Politian* has been staged several times. For the low critical appraisal of the play, see, for example, Duffy, "John Richardson's Kentucky Tragedies," 8, which concludes that *Politian* is "a deservedly obscure piece."

22. Poe, *Politian,* 262.

23. Ibid., 249–50.

24. Ibid., 249, 260.

25. Ibid., 263–64.

26. Ibid., 254–55.

27. Ibid., 259.

28. Ibid., 269, 272, 280–81, 282.

29. Poe, *Essays and Reviews,* 1208–9.

30. Noah M. Ludlow, *Dramatic Life as I Found It* (1880; repr., New York: Blom), 541–42; Joseph Norton Ireland, *Records of the New York Stage from 1750 to 1860* (1866–1867; repr., New York: Franklin, 1968), 2:79–80; Delmer Davis, "Charlotte Mary Sanford Barnes," *American National Biography,* http://www.anb.org/articles/18/18-00058.html; Charlotte Mary Sanford Barnes, preface to *Octavia Bragaldi, or The Confession: A Tragedy Founded on Facts,* in *Plays, Prose, and Poetry* (Philadelphia: Butler, 1848), iii, iv. Quinn, *History of the American Drama,* 260–61, suggests that "Miss Barnes evidently had read Poe's scenes, for the similarity of Castiglione, the name of Poe's villain, to Castelli is evident."

31. Barnes, *Octavia Bragaldi,* 20, 21, 22. Dickson Bruce notes that "Renaissance Italy . . . called up an environment Americans had learned to associate with the free play of passion and impulse." Bruce, *Kentucky Tragedy,* 114.

32. Barnes, *Octavia Bragaldi,* 25, 37.

33. Ibid., 29, 31, 36, 43, 45.

34. Ibid., 49, 55, 56.

35. Ibid., 72, 74, 76–77.

36. Ibid., 82–83, 86, 84–85, 85, 86, 87, 88.

37. Ibid., 94, 99, 110, 111, 118.

38. Ibid., 40; Barnes, preface, iv.

39. Ann S. Stephens, "The Infidel," *Portland Magazine,* October 1835; Mary E. MacMichael, "The Kentucky Tragedy: A Tale—Founded on Facts of Actual Occurrence," *Burton's Gentleman's Magazine,* April 1838, 265–71.

40. Stephens, "Infidel," 3–11, 3, 2, 3.

41. Ibid., 6.

42. Ibid., 9, 10, 11.

43. *Portland Magazine,* November 1835, 64.

44. MacMichael, "Kentucky Tragedy," 265.

45. Ibid., 268, 270, 269.

46. Ibid., 269, 270, 271; Surrency, "Kentucky Tragedy in American Literature," 92.

47. Charles Fenno Hoffman, *Greyslaer: A Romance of the Mohawk* (1840; repr., Albany, NY: NCUP Press, 1990); Duyckinck, *Cyclopædia of American Literature,* 2:476. Homer Barnes, in his 1930 biography of Hoffman, mistakenly asserts that Hoffman "did not actually make significant use of [the Kentucky] tragedy. . . . Indeed about the only important point of similarity between the Beauchamp-Sharp case and Greyslaer is in the kidnaping of the heroine." Homer Francis Barnes, *Charles Fenno Hoffman* (New York: Columbia University Press, 1930), 124–25. Of course, there was no kidnapping associated with the Kentucky Tragedy.

48. Edgar Allan Poe, *The Literati: Some Honest Opinions about Autorial Merits and Demerits, with Occasional Words of Personality* (1850), http://www.eapoe.org/works/misc/litratd6.htm#E:Hoffman,%20C; Duyckinck, *Cyclopædia of American Literature,* 2:477.

49. Hoffman, *Winter in the West,* 2:157. Hoffman quoted Beauchamp: "Merely because there was a feeling in the breast of every man which told him (he) ought to have killed Colonel Sharp. The plain, candid, common-sense sort of people thought me guilty, although they had no sort of proof even to raise a suspicion, only looking to the motive, and justification, or cause, which I had to kill him." Ibid. Hoffman, despite his generous nature, could not help but feel an intellectual superiority toward the Kentuckians. His description of his hosts—"There is an off-handedness—if I may use the term—a fearless ardour, a frankness and self-possession about them that engages your goodwill at once; while you are both interested and amused at the exaggerated tone of sentiment, half-romantic, half-vain-glorious, which their ideas and expressions betray"—reminds one of Robert Penn Warren's quip that "any pleasure we take in folksiness is a pleasure of snobbish superiority or neurotic yearning." Ibid., 135; Warren, *Brother to Dragons,* 31.

50. Hoffman, *Greyslaer,* 80; Miller, "Romance and the Novel," 249.

51. Hoffman, *Greyslaer,* 58, 50, 59.

52. Ibid., 27, 123.
53. Ibid., 115, 120, 123.
54. Ibid., 161, 169, 172, 173.
55. Ibid., 254, 259, 260, 290, 291.
56. Ibid., 288, 329, 340, 306, 329.
57. Ibid., 332, 336, 351.
58. Ibid., 361, 363, 360.
59. Ibid., 381, 383.
60. Ibid., 387. Note the parallel between this fictional account and Colonel Sharp's actual refutation of the charges that he seduced Anna Cooke, a defense that hinged not on the validity of the charge but on the virtue of Anna.
61. Ibid., 396.
62. Miller, "Romance and the Novel," 252; *Godey's Lady's Book* quoted in Barnes, *Charles Fenno Hoffman,* 130; *Southern Literary Messenger* quoted in Samuel Austin Allibone, *A Critical Dictionary of English Literature and British and American Authors* (Philadelphia: Lippincott, 1900): 858–59; Trent, *William Gilmore Simms,* 119; Ireland, *Records of the New York Stage,* 2:320; Barnes, *Charles Fenno Hoffman,* 132; *New York Evening Post* quoted in Barnes, *Charles Fenno Hoffman,* 133.
63. Herman Melville thought "poor Hoffman" was "just the man to go mad—imaginative, voluptuously inclined, poor, unemployed, in the race of life distanced by his inferiors, unmarried, without a port or haven in the universe to make." Herman Melville to Evert Duyckinck, April 5, 1849, quoted in Daniel A. Wells, introduction to Hoffman, *Greyslaer,* viii–ix.
64. I draw on the 1856 volumes. W. B. Gates has noted that, "with two important exceptions, the 1856 text differs from that of 1842 only in comparatively minor details. The exceptions are the addition of descriptive chapter titles and the inclusion of the oath of vengeance sworn by the heroine against her betrayer," which "effectively unifies the two parts of the story." Gates, "William Gilmore Simms," 158. John Caldwell Guilds, however, argues that "the two-novel sequence represents a significant improvement over the 1842 two-volume novel: Simms concentrated upon developing more fully his already powerful portrayal of Margaret Cooper, whose proud defiance and almost savage vindictiveness is gradually softened if never replaced by her growing realization that her love for her husband has outgrown her lust for revenge." Guilds, *Simms,* 221. Initially, Simms's authorship of *Beauchampe* was, as he himself put it, "a quasi secret, which, at present, I am not anxious to make generally known." William Gilmore Simms to Benjamin Franklin Perry, July 14, 1842, in *Letters of William Gilmore Simms,* ed. Mary C. Simms Oliphant, Alfred Taylor Odell, and T. C. Duncan Eaves (Columbia: University of South Carolina Press, 1952), 1:315–16.
65. William Gilmore Simms to James Lawson, September 10, 1841, October 13, 1841, in *Letters of William Gilmore Simms,* 1:278, 282; William Gilmore Simms to Benjamin Franklin Perry, July 14, 1842, in *Letters of William Gilmore Simms,* 1:316.
66. Poe quoted in Guilds, *Simms,* 165; Trent, *William Gilmore Simms,* 117, 123; Vernon Louis Parrington, *Main Currents in American Thought: The Romantic Revo-*

lution in America (New York: Harcourt, Brace, 1927), 2:130; van Doren quoted in Gates, "William Gilmore Simms," 159; Robert Penn Warren, "A Confession," *Wings: The Literary Guild Review,* July 1950, 5. See also John McCardell, "Trent's Simms: The Making of a Biography," in *A Master's Due: Essays in Honor of David Herbert Donald,* ed. William J. Cooper Jr. (Baton Rouge: Louisiana State University Press, 1986), 179–203. For another negative review of *Beauchampe,* see Duffy, "John Richardson's Kentucky Tragedies," 9, which characterizes the work as "little more than a bulky novelization of the case." Some critics, it should be noted, have been kinder. W. B. Gates, for one, argues that "*Charlemont* and *Beauchampe* are not slavish and inartistic transcriptions of the Kentucky story. With suggestions from Elizabethan drama and from 'Paradise Lost,' Simms handled the material freely and imaginatively. . . . *Charlemont* and *Beauchampe* are certainly not masterpieces, but they are no mere transcriptions of the 'Kentucky Tragedy'; they are in no way salacious; and they are not entirely lacking in art." Gates, "William Gilmore Simms," 258, 162, 166.

67. Simms, *Charlemont,* 445, 16.

68. Ibid., 18, 95.

69. Ibid., 21. If Simms uses the "Deserted Village" motif to romanticize the "world we have lost," he was not himself unconflicted about the joys of premodern rural life. He at one point writes of the "rusting and mind-destroying life of a country village," and he later has one character declare that "an old locality is liable to suffer from the worse evil of moral stagnation" and regret that the "habitual torpor" of village life is liable to render one an "imbecile." Ibid., 278; Simms, *Beauchampe,* 19, 21.

70. Simms, *Charlemont,* 32, 28, 29, 383, 37, 38, 125, 401.

71. Ibid., 383, 298, 168, 177. The power of Margaret Cooper's denunciations of women's place in the antebellum world might lead one to think Simms was sympathetic toward the nascent feminist movement: "If I weep," Simms has Margaret protest, "he smiles at my weakness. If I stifle my tears, he denounces my unnatural hardihood. If I am cold and unyielding, I am masculine and neglected—if I am gentle and pliant, my confidence is abused and my person dishonored." Ibid., 421. John Caldwell Guilds asserts, mistakenly in my opinion, that in the character of Margaret Cooper, Simms ventured a "bold statement of women's rights" and was himself "surprisingly progressive in his view toward women." Guilds, *Simms,* 221. Yet Margaret's dismal fate should have dispelled any suspicion that Simms was a closet feminist. Indeed, he asserted that his characterization of Margaret would "illustrate most of the mistakes which are made by that ambitious class, among the gentler sex, who are now seeking so earnestly to pass out from that province of humiliation to which the sex has been circumscribed from the first moment of recorded history." Thus in Simms's mind, Margaret—and Anna—demonstrated the mortal peril of a woman "goaded by an insane ambition, in the extreme development of her mere intellect" to "pass the guardian boundaries which hedge in her sex." Simms, *Charlemont,* 11, 12.

72. Simms, *Charlemont,* 78, 65.

73. Ibid., 297, 298, 300, 327, 307, 327, 308.

74. Ibid., 69, 139, 237, 243, 282.

75. Ibid., 333, 316, 322.
76. Ibid., 335, 336, 356–57.
77. Ibid., 362.
78. Ibid., 394, 385, 397–98.
79. Ibid., 405, 407, 422, 432, 433.
80. Ibid., 402, 403, 442.
81. Simms, *Beauchampe,* 26; Simms, *Charlemont,* 429, 431.
82. Simms, *Beauchampe,* 168, 67, 79.
83. Ibid., 83, 139, 104, 87.
84. Ibid., 320, 116, 122, 125.
85. Ibid., 144, 149.
86. Ibid., 163, 164, 159, 221.
87. Ibid., 169, 177.
88. Ibid., 196–97, 198, 206.
89. Ibid., 233, 276, 261, 267, 242, 289, 291, 293, 298.
90. Ibid., 301, 308, 310, 309, 315.
91. Ibid., 329, 333, 343, 342.
92. Ibid., 339, 346.
93. Ibid., 357, 372, 374, 376.
94. Ibid., 378, 379, 395.

95. John Savage, introduction to *Sybil: A Tragedy in Five Acts* (New York: Kirker, 1865), 6; George C. D. Odell, *Annals of the New York Stage* (New York: Columbia University Press, 1931), 7:393. For biographical information on Savage, see Duyckinck, *Cyclopædia of American Literature,* 2:823–24, and Stanley J. Kunitz and Howard Haycraft, eds., *American Authors, 1600–1900* (New York: Wilson, 1938), 672. In Savage's adaptation, Charlemont becomes Eaglemont; Beauchampe becomes Eustace Clifden; Margaret/Anna becomes Sybil Hardy; and Sharpe becomes Rufus Wolfe. Although the play hews close to the novels, Savage does make a few interesting departures from Simms's tale, most notably softening the play's heroine, Sybil. At one point Savage describes her as "frightened creature"—a far cry from Margaret Cooper. Wolfe, of course, is still "a base, consummate villain," a "wretch," and an "arch-fiend," and Clifden is still daring and noble. The moral remains the same: the wild justice of Clifden's actions was honorable, and according to Sybil, "The wives, the mothers, daughters of the State, are all your debtors for the deed." Savage uses Sybil to warn antebellum Americans of the dangers of waning masculinity. While awaiting the verdict, a frantic Sybil looks at the severe faces of the jury and declares, "Old man, beware! Your heartlessness makes way for such as dragged me down. Go, to! You have a sister, sir; protect the man who protected her! You smile to think she needs protection;—Fool! All women do. . . . Look at . . . my husband: think you he committed murder—ha! ha! He? No! . . . What a world of men, fathers, brothers, husbands—all gone." Savage, *Sybil,* 23, 38, 43, 85, 97–98.

96. Hannah Daviess Pittman, *The Heart of Kentucky* (New York: Neale, 1908), 23, 16–17, 34, 199, 200. Pittman's attempt at regional dialect is a clinic in bad writ-

ing. A slave, after hearing Wallace speak at a barbecue, exclaims, "I nebber befo' in my life hear a man talk like Marser Dar'al talk–'ceptin de yudder one; he sho' wuz a good talker, too. . . . An de people! You jis orter seed de people. Dey hollered an' hollered when Marser Dar'al wuz done, till I thought dey wuz gwinter fetch him home on deir shoulders." Ibid., 67. For biographical information on Pittman, see Joseph DeSpain, "Hannah Daviess Pittman: Neglected Kentucky Author," *Filson Club Historical Quarterly* 70 (1996): 186–95.

97. Pittman, *Heart of Kentucky,* 18, 52.

98. Ibid., 63, 89.

99. Ibid., 93, 98.

100. Ibid., 101, 110, 111, 112, 114, 118, 120, 122.

101. Ibid., 129, 134, 135, 137.

102. Ibid., 157, 178.

103. Ibid., 177, 211, 216, 234, 217, 211.

104. Ibid., 220–21.

105. Ibid., 235.

106. Ibid., 254, 261, 266–67.

107. Ibid., 264, 267. See George C. Wright, *Racial Violence in Kentucky, 1865–1940: Lynchings, Mob Rule, and "Legal Lynchings"* (Baton Rouge: Louisiana State University Press, 1990), esp. chap. 2. For another literary defense of lynching, see Hallie Erminie Rives, *Smoking Flax* (New York: Neely, 1897).

108. Warren, "Confession," 5; *Talking with Robert Penn Warren,* ed. Floyd C. Watkins, John T. Hiers, and Mary Louise Weaks (Athens: University of Georgia Press, 1990), 70.

109. C. Vann Woodward, *The Burden of Southern History,* rev. ed. (Baton Rouge: Louisiana State University Press, 1968), 34; Warren, *World Enough and Time,* 283–84, 157.

110. Woodward, *Future of the Past,* 225.

111. Warren, *World Enough and Time,* 3. Some critics have objected to this narrative mode. A. B. Guthrie complained that Warren "keeps reminding us that at this distance from the scene we cannot be sure of this point or that one. And by reminding us he keeps pulling us a century and more away from his story. . . . We see his characters dusty across the long field of time." A. B. Guthrie, review of *World Enough and Time,* by Robert Penn Warren, *Saturday Review,* June 24, 1950, 11–12. Such, it would seem to me, is exactly the effect Warren was trying to achieve.

112. Warren, *World Enough and Time,* 8.

113. Ibid., 35, 34, 35, 36.

114. Ibid., 58, 56, 116.

115. Ibid., 68, 112, 113, 73, 114, 115, 137.

116. Ibid., 127, 128, 129, 130, 186.

117. Ibid., 76, 83, 205.

118. Ibid., 217.

119. Ibid., 234, 235, 237.

120. Ibid., 247, 283, 287, 308.

121. Ibid., 349, 361.

122. Ibid., 377, 380, 395, 401–2.

123. Ibid., 416, 435, 441.

123. Ibid., 452.

125. Ibid., 457, 459.

126. Ibid., 463.

127. Ibid., 465; Guthrie, review, 11–12.

128. Warren, *World Enough and Time,* 5; *Talking with Robert Penn Warren,* 261, 187.

129. Flint, review, 60; Poe quoted in Guild, *Simms,* 165.

130. Simms, *Beauchampe,* 79; Barnes, *Octavia Bragaldi,* 37.

131. Interestingly, twentieth-century dramatists denuded Anna. Pittman's is weak, and Warren's, although given far more depth than Pittman's, is more an object than a subject.

132. David Brion Davis identifies this theme as one of the most popular in antebellum fiction: usually "a sympathetic character, preferably a young woman, was pictured as suffering from a mania or dementia after a traumatic experience." Such "demented heroines" had been paragons of virtue—often headstrong, but always innocent—until some intolerable trauma transformed them into dark and mysterious avengers. Davis, *Homicide in American Fiction,* 85, 116. Similarly, Barbara Welter writes, for a woman to fall by whatever means, as depicted in the era's literature, "brought madness or death." In women's magazines, madness very often followed the fall: "The frequency with which derangement follows loss of virtue suggests the exquisite sensibility of woman, and the possibility that, in the women's magazines at least, her intellect was geared to her hymen, not her brain." Barbara Welter, "The Cult of True Womanhood, 1820–1860," *American Quarterly* 18 (1966): 155–56.

133. *Oxford English Dictionary,* 2nd ed., s.v. "Tragedy."

134. *American Heritage Dictionary,* 4th ed., s.v. "Tragedy"; Warren, *World Enough and Time,* 465.

CODA

1. *Lexington (KY) Observer and Reporter,* March 11, 1846, quoted in Coleman, *Beauchamp-Sharp Tragedy,* 66–67.

2. Willard Rouse Jillson, *The Newspapers and Periodicals of Frankfort, Kentucky, 1795–1945* (Frankfort: Kentucky State Historical Society, 1945), 11; *Kentucky Reporter,* December 30, 1829.

3. See Donald B. Cole, *A Jackson Man: Amos Kendall and the Rise of American Democracy* (Baton Rouge: Louisiana State University Press, 2004).

4. *U.S. Telegraph,* March 21, 1829; Levin, *Lawyers and Lawmakers,* 111; Lewis Collins, *History of Kentucky* (Covington, KY: Collins, 1874), 45. A number of broader studies make no mention of Harrison's offer—Freeman Cleaves, *Old Tippecanoe: Wil-*

liam Henry Harrison and His Time (New York: Scribner, 1939); Robert Gray Gunderson, *The Log-Cabin Campaign* (Lexington: University of Kentucky Press, 1957); and Norma Lois Peterson, *The Presidencies of William Henry Harrison and John Tyler* (Lawrence: University Press of Kansas, 1989)—but they do establish that Harrison made a visit to Frankfort in December 1840. We also know that William Henry Harrison and John M. Scott, Eliza's father, were very close friends, each of them naming a son after the other.

5. *Nashville Daily Union and American,* January, 23, 1859.

6. *U.S. Telegraph,* March 21, 1829; Lewis Sanders Jr. to Francis P. Blair, January 30, 1831, Blair and Lee Families Papers, Princeton University Library, Princeton, NJ.

Index

CPSIA information can be obtained at www.ICGtesting.com
Printed in the USA
LVOW101312080113

314864LV00002B/3/P

9 780813 133874